Web Page Wizardry:

Wiring Your Site for Sound and Action

Dick Oliver

with

John J. Kottler	Brian K. Murphy
Janice Norton	Kit Gainer
Tod Foley	Kelly Murdock

sams
net

201 West 103rd Street
Indianapolis, Indiana 46290

Kit Gainer *would like to dedicate this book to Mildred Rhoads.*

Janice Norton *would like to dedicate this book to Rosemary Brumley, Jeff Norton, Jack Norton, and Rod Brumley.*

Kelly Murdock *would like to dedicate this book to the Web community, responsible for pushing the envelope of interactive Web pages.*

Copyright © 1996 by Sams.net Publishing

International Standard Book Number: 1-57521-092-4

Library of Congress Catalog Card Number: 96-67210

99   98   97   96   4   3   2   1

Interpretation of the printing code: the rightmost double-digit number is the year of the book's printing; the rightmost single-digit, the number of the book's printing. For example, a printing code of 96-1 shows that the first printing of the book occurred in 1996.

Composed in Frutiger and MCPdigital by Macmillan Computer Publishing

Printed in the United States of America

President, Sams Publishing: *Richard K. Swadley*

Publishing Manager *Mark Taber*

Managing Editor: *Cindy Morrow*

Marketing Manager: *John Pierce*

Assistant Marketing Manager: *Kristina Perry*

Acquisitions Editor
Beverly M. Eppink

Development Editor
Kelly Murdock

Software Development Specialist
Merle Newlon

Production Editor
Marla Reece

Copy Editor
Marilyn J. Stone

Technical Reviewers
John W. Nelsen
Alfonso Hermida

Editorial Coordinator
Bill Whitmer

Technical Edit Coordinator
Lynette Quinn

Resource Coordinator
Deborah Frisby

Formatter
Frank Sinclair

Editorial Assistants
Carol Ackerman
Andi Richter
Rhonda Tinch-Mize

Book Designer
Alyssa Yesh

Copy Writer
Peter Fuller

Production Team Supervisor
Brad Chinn

Production
Stephen Adams, Georgiana Briggs, Mona Brown, Jeanne Clark, Bruce Clingaman, Cheryl Dietsch, Mike Dietsch, Tim Griffin, Jason Hand, Ayanna Lacey, Clint Lahnen, Paula Lowell, Steph Mineart, Ryan Oldfather, Laura Robbins, Dana Rhodes, Bobbi Satterfield, Andrew Stone, Colleen Williams, Jeff Yesh

Overview

Contents

Acknowledgments

Janice Norton and Kit Gainer

With special gratitude to Rosemary Brumley and Mildred Rhoads, both instrumental in this and all endeavors. Also, we wish to thank Jeannine Parker and Bob Rice for their tremendous support, encouragement, and good humor, both presently and in the "early days," as well as Sharon and Michael Leventhal for intrepid navigational skills, determination, and humor, Stu and Charlotte Miller for inspiration, vision and faith, and Elaine Spooner, Peter Siegel, and Georgia Scott for their foresight and sense of adventure in the journey. Much appreciation to Allan and Suzanne Ream, Mark Matsuno, Jerry Witt, and Tod Foley. Many thanks to Victoria Dawson, Webmaster at Macromedia, Kathy Kozel, the amazing and inventive Lingoist and friend, and to the Intel tech support team. A special thank you to Marty Allen, Ivan Moffat, Brenda Holman, Leo and Diane Dillion, Ray Bradbury, Steven Barnes, and Steve Arbuss, who started it all, and to Marty Allen, Kit, and Sherrie at the Electronic Cafe, Chaz Austin, Steve Bradley, Joel Block, Elaine Palmer, Robin Barclay, Anne Mullen, Stu Coleman, Jeff Levin, Dick Glass, Sharyn Keller, Donny Neumann, Linda and Lucy Lane, Willette Klausner, Elizabeth and Bozena Kohler-Hotz, Michael Terpin, Will Russell, Tony Lewis, James Pollak, Marsha Hunt, Peter Duke, James Davenport, Dee Richter, Bill and Madelon Ficks, Tom and Debra O'Dell, Ted and Dottie Marche, Fred and Ann Luntsford, and Jack Sher.

Kelly Murdock

I would like to acknowledge the incredible team at Sams: Mark Taber for his quiet, effective leadership; Beverly Eppink for her tireless enthusiasm; Fran Hatton for her zany attitude that keeps us all in check; and for Merle Newlon who compiles our CDs out of thin air. And to the rest of the staff members who do daily miracles in producing high quality products. I would also like to acknowledge my wife and sons without whose support I would be nothing. I love you.

About the Authors

Lead author:

Dick Oliver

Dick Oliver has authored and co-authored several graphics programs, articles, and books, including *Netscape 2 Unleashed, Internet Graphics Gallery, Tricks of the Graphics Gurus*, and *FractalVision: Put Fractals to Work for You.* Dick is president of Cedar Software of Wolcott, Vermont, which specializes in new approaches to advanced graphics and 3D modeling. He also publishes the *Nonlinear Nonsense* netletter, an online Web site and paper newsletter covering creative computer graphics. You can contact Dick at `dicko@netletter.com`.

Contributing authors:

John J. Kottler

Jay Kottler has been programming for 14 years and has spent the past six years developing applications for the Windows platform. In addition to Windows development, Jay has been programming multimedia applications for over two years and has spent this past year developing for the Web. His knowledge includes C/C++, Visual Basic, Lotus Notes, PowerBuilder, messaging-enabled applications, multimedia and digital video production, and Internet Web page development. In the past, he has published numerous articles in a computer magazine, written original programs, and instructed developers on programming techniques. Jay has also recently been published in Sams.net's *Web Publishing Unleashed* and *Netscape 2 Unleashed,* and Sams Publishing's *Programming Windows 95 Unleashed*. He was also a co-developer of the shareware application Virtual Monitors. A graduate of Rutgers University with a degree in computer science, he enjoys inline skating, cycling, or playing digital music in his spare time. Jay may currently be reached at the following e-mail addresses: `73157.335@compuserve.com`, `jkottler@aol.com`, or `jay_kottler@msn.com`.

Brian K. Murphy

Brian Murphy (`bkmurph@mcs.net`) holds a law degree from the Ohio State University College of Law and a degree in film from Columbia College in Chicago. He is responsible for establishing the first Web home page for an inmate on death row, Girvies L. Davis. The Web page was one of the 1,001 best Internet sites, according to *PC Computing* magazine. Brian was a contributing author for Sams.net Publishing's *Netscape 2 Unleashed*. He has discussed the impact and power of the Internet through television and radio interviews with ABC, CBS, NBC, CNN, BBC, CBC, and NPR. He has also appeared in *People Magazine* and has been quoted on Internet issues by the *New York Times*, *Washington Post*, *The Economist*, *NetGuide* magazine, and the Associated Press. Brian makes his home in Naperville, Illinois with his wife Cheryl and their two children, Mallory and Jack. He is a practicing attorney with the law firm of Jenner and Block in Chicago.

Janice Norton
Kit Gainer

Janice Norton and **Kit Gainer** created **Hands of Time Animation & Design** in 1989, an interactive advertising agency and design partnership. Norton and Gainer are front-runners in the world of interactive advertising for the entertainment industry, with award-winning CD, floppy, Internet, and online-based promotions for the motion pictures of Martin Scorsese, Robert Altman, Mike Nichols, Jonathan Demme, Walt Disney, and Stephen King, and the television shows of Brandon Tartikoff, Sam Raimi, and the BBC. The design duo are also featured Shockwave developers in the Macromedia Developer's Gallery, and their work has received 14 national design and technology awards in the past two years, all in new media categories, including a Silver CINDY for technical excellence for "getting more on a floppy than had ever been done before," and an Interactive Academy Award.

Janice Norton has been nationally recognized for her work in advertising and graphic design. A native of Portland, Oregon, she performed as on-camera and voice talent from an early age, subsequently obtaining her BA degree in stage and screen dynamics/film design from Lewis and Clark College, while attending there as a national merit scholar. After relocating to Los Angeles, she completed a program in interactive multimedia at UCLA and joined forces with Kit Gainer. Kit hails from Washington, D.C. and holds a BA in world literature and fine arts. His professional specialties include cel animation, computer programming, and sound engineering.

Tod Foley

Tod Foley (asif@well.com) is an award-winning game designer, writer, and creator of interactive environments for all media. His wide body of work includes CD-ROM games, such as Ocean Voyager (Times Mirror Magazines); role-playing games, such as CyberSpace (Iron Crown Enterprises); live interactive theater games, such as Ghosts in the Machine (CyberArts International); and online environments, such as The Electronic Cafe International's ECI Palace (http://www.ecafe.com/palaceinfo.html).

Kelly Murdock

Kelly Murdock is a displaced engineer, currently enjoying his work as a development editor at Sams Publishing. He graduated with a degree in mechanical engineering with an emphasis in computer graphics and software development. After a number of years working as an engineer, he realized that working with computers and graphics is a lot more fun. He especially enjoys working with 3D graphics. He is founder of Tulip Multimedia, a producer of children's educational CD-ROMs. He can be reached at kmurdock@sams.mcp.com.

Introduction

In the fast-moving world of the Internet, plain old text and pictures are no longer enough. To attract and retain the attention of today's Web surfers and to differentiate your pages from the millions of others on the Web, you need something more. You need *action* and *interaction* to make your site a multisensory experience that people will want to visit again and again.

The step from a static "home page" to an animated multimedia presentation may seem like a giant one—both to your audience and to you as the person who has to make it happen. But this book will show you how to make that leap more easily and gracefully than you ever dared to think you could. It will step you through real-world, hands-on examples of how to create cutting-edge multimedia pages that work great with today's technology—even for people who access your site through ordinary modems.

Most importantly, these paper pages will be your guide through the complete sample pages and media files on the CD-ROM included with the book. These high-powered but easy-to-imitate sites were designed and selected specifically by our team of seven expert Web developers to get you up to speed as quickly as possible. With these examples and the friendly, plain-English tutorials in every chapter, you'll be adding animation and audio-visual excitement to your pages the very first day you open this book.

How far will you go? Here's a sneak preview of what lies in store for your Web pages:

+ Support all the new features for users of Microsoft Internet Explorer version 3.0 and Netscape Navigator version 3.0.
+ Add animation and sound to your pages without the need for plug-ins or programming.
+ Integrate audio, video, and interactive media into your Web pages as easily as old-fashioned graphics.
+ Create three-dimensional "virtual reality" worlds and objects that visitors to your site can interactively explore.
+ Use prewritten programs and scripts to add "live" functions and special effects without doing any programming yourself.
+ Put the latest Internet technologies to work for you, including Microsoft ActiveX, Netscape LiveMedia, and the new HTML 3.0.
+ Build sophisticated interactive sites with Shockwave and other cutting-edge Web multimedia authoring packages.
+ Use multiple fonts, sophisticated layouts, graphics stunts, and speed-up tricks to add zest to the static parts of your pages.

Though even experienced Webmasters will find plenty to keep them on their toes, you don't need to be an expert to put all this to use immediately. However, you will need to understand the basics of the *Hypertext Markup Language* (HTML), which is used for creating pages on the World Wide Web. Quick learners who've never used HTML may find everything they need to know about it in Appendix A, "HTML in a Nutshell" and Appendix B, "HTML Quick-Reference." For those who are totally new to the Web and want more hand-holding to get started, we recommend Laura Lemay's *Teach Yourself Web Publishing with HTML* books. This book picks up where she leaves off, giving you a complete introduction to the latest extensions and additions to HTML, along with the new techniques and technologies to take you far beyond HTML itself into the next level of media-rich Web publishing.

For a complete listing of the Web pages, software, plug-ins, objects, worlds, sounds, graphics, video clips, and complete site examples on the *Web Page Wizardry* CD-ROM, turn to Appendix D—or simply pop in the CD-ROM itself and open the home.htm document with your Web browser. The best way to use this book is to explore those examples on the CD-ROM, and turn straight to the chapters that show you how the ones you like the best were done. Of course, we've used abundant illustrations throughout every chapter, so you can easily follow the explanations in the book, even if you don't have the CD-ROM up on your screen.

Many of the examples in the book have also been placed online for you to see how they work on the real, live Internet instead of a CD-ROM. A directory of the best "Online Resources and Cutting-Edge Web Sites" is also included, both in Appendix C and as a hotlist on the CD-ROM.

Whether your Web site is for fun or profit, you can now have more of both with the latest interactive media. So on with the show! *Lights, cameras....*

The Wow! Factor: Gonzo Graphics Stunts

part **I**

Bigger, Faster, Better Graphics

This book will help you launch your site into the fast-moving world of interactive action and multisensory excitement. But no matter how many way-cool animations and epic soundtracks you add, you're still likely to need some images and text, too! The feeling and function of your Web pages will depend as much on the look of those unmoving graphics and words as on the more cutting-edge elements. And, of course, text and pictures are especially important for the many visitors to your site who don't yet have the technology or bandwidth to receive multimedia files.

In this chapter and the next, I show you the latest techniques to make the static elements on your pages look great and display quickly. Many of the skills and design issues covered here also apply in the action-oriented media discussed in other chapters. I will assume you are already familiar with HTML, though I do explain the syntax for implementing several advanced HTML tricks. (If you need some help with basic HTML, see Appendix A, "HTML in a Nutshell.")

You don't have to be an artist to put high-impact graphics and creative type on your Web site. You don't need to spend hundreds or thousands of dollars on software, either. This chapter and the enclosed CD-ROM will provide everything you need to design graphic pages and find or create the images you need to make them real.

chapter 1

by Dick Oliver

Don't Forget the Basics

The best place to begin gathering inspiration and raw materials for your new improved Web pages is the World Wide Web itself. When you see a fun or impressive graphic site, imagine what it would look like without the graphics, and think about how its creators made the images and coded any fancy text formatting.

Figure 1.1 is the kind of site many wizards-to-be lust after: lots of highly polished graphics, an animated masthead that pieces itself together, and a professional announcer's voice that automatically welcomes you to the site if you have a sound card.

Figure 1.2 is pretty nifty, too—but far less polished and more than a little hokey. At least that might be what you think when you see these two pages next to one another in a book. But the actual experience when you log on to these sites with a typical 28.8Kbps modem is another story; sixty seconds after you log on to the Modern Ferrets home page, you will have read intriguing descriptions of the magazine, seen several photos of cute ferrets, and probably moved on to enjoy an illustrated ferret fairy tale or tips on keeping your fur-slinky well groomed. But after sixty looooooong seconds at the "impressive" site, you will still be drumming your fingers waiting for the oh-so-prettily-rendered word "Talk" to slowly pour onto the screen and wondering what the name of the site might be as you watch all those oh-so-neato puzzle tiles at the top of the screen move around.

To their credit, the professional Web development team who got paid big bucks for designing the Entertainment Radio Network site in Figure 1.1 knew that part of their job was to get rid of people who didn't have the bandwidth (or patience) to handle long audio downloads. So a snazzy but slow site was the perfect choice for them.

Figure 1.1. This site was designed for high-bandwidth users—it's pretty, but deathly slow to display over a modem.

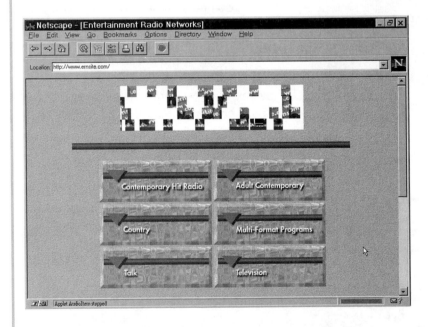

On the other hand, the two young self-publishers who put together the Modern Ferret home page in Figure 1.2 knew they didn't have—or need—to spend big money or long hours on building their home page. And they knew that most of their readers were probably low-budget modem users, so speed was key. The result may not be cutting-edge multimedia, but it does illustrate some important points that apply to all good graphic sites:

✦ The graphics convey the theme and mood of the topic effectively but are simple enough for a not-too-artsy person to create in an afternoon.

✦ The image looks big but is designed to compress efficiently and load quickly, even over a slow modem connection.

✦ Elements of the page could be reused on other pages (perhaps even your own, if you ask permission).

As you explore the far reaches of new media on the Web, you'll do well to keep in mind the principles that make this good old-fashioned site serve its purpose well: Simplicity, speed, and reusability become even more important as you invest more time and energy into ferreting out a modern Web site.

True "Web Page Wizardry" means knowing the needs of your intended audience and carefully balancing coolness with quickness. In this chapter, I show you how to squeeze much of the flavor of a high-end site out of as little bandwidth and development time as possible. And throughout this book, we'll emphasize not only the gee-whiz, techie stuff you need to know, but also the short-cuts and cheats that can save you (and your site's visitors) valuable time and resources.

Figure 1.2. Though not as polished as the site in Figure 1.1, this page displays much more quickly and conveys its message just as effectively.

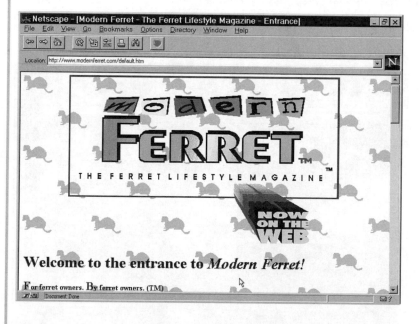

Finding Images and Media Files

One of the best ways to save time creating the graphics and media files is, of course, to avoid creating them altogether. With the entire World Wide Web at your fingertips, you have access to thousands upon thousands of images, sound clips, and animations. A rapidly growing number of video clips and interactive media can be found on the Net, too.

Any graphic or media clip you see on any site is instantly reusable, as soon as the copyright holder grants (or sells) you the right to copy it. Because almost all Web pages include the e-mail address of their creators, it's usually quick and easy to ask permission to download and adopt a piece of artwork.

The familiar Web search engines and directories such as Yahoo! (`http://`
`www.yahoo.com/`), Lycos (`http://` `lycos.cs.cmu.edu`), and InfoSeek (`http://` `www.infoseek.com/`) can become a gold mine of graphics images, just by leading you to sites related to your own theme. They can also help you discover the oodles of sites specifically dedicated to providing free and cheap access to reusable media collections.

A Lycos search for "background textures" turned up, among many other sites, the Texture and Background Wonderland pictured in Figure 1.3. This is one of my favorite hotlists, with links to consistently high-quality sites for finding great background tiles and graphic accents for Web pages.

On the CD-ROM that comes with this book, you'll find live links to many other graphics and multimedia hotlists and hot sites. To access these links, open the `home.htm` page with your Web browser and then click `Pages and Listings`. (Links to all the major search engines are on there, too, just in case you don't already have them all on your own bookmark list.)

Figure 1.3. Gini Schmitz's Textures and Backgrounds Wonderland is one of the best places to find lively graphics for your own Web pages.

Grabbing the Graphics You Find

As you probably know, grabbing a graphic from a Web page is as simple as clicking it with the right mouse button, then picking Save this image as... in Netscape Navigator or Save Picture as... in Microsoft Explorer (see Figure 1.3).

With Microsoft Explorer, extracting a background image from a page is just as easy: Right-click it and pick Save Background As. However, the procedure for grabbing a background tile isn't quite so obvious in Netscape Navigator and most other Web browsers:

1. View the source code (select View¦Document Source in Netscape; see Figure 1.4).

2. Select the filename in the BACK-GROUND= attribute in the BODY tag, and copy it to the Clipboard.

(In Windows, hold down the Control key and press the Insert key.)

3. Close the source window.

4. Paste the filename by clicking the location and pressing Shift-Insert, and then press Enter to go to that address.

5. The background file should appear, as shown in Figure 1.5. You can now use Save this image as... or the right-click menu to save the file.

Archie and Veronica Go to the Pictures

If you're looking for something so specific that you can guess part of the filename or title, you can use two Internet indexing systems called Archie and Veronica to find graphics files that may not be accessible through the World Wide Web.

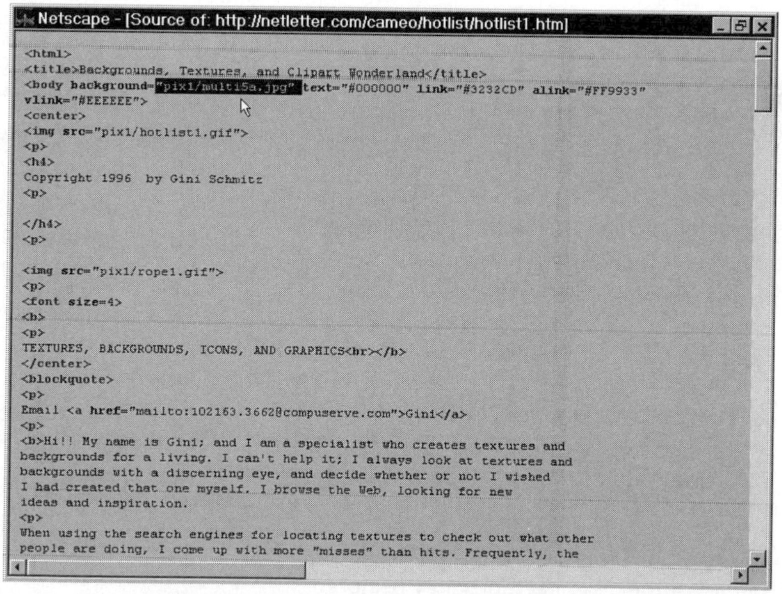

Figure 1.4. To find out the address of a background graphic in Netscape Navigator, view the source code for the HTML file.

Figure 1.5.
When you load
the background
tile by itself, you
can save it as you
would any other
image.

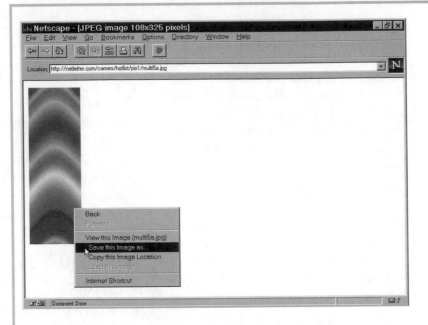

Even some experienced Webmasters have never used Archie and Veronica, so I'll explain the basics of using them to find graphics. I'll also let you in on the secret codes that enable you to limit your search to only graphics files.

Note: In the old days, you had to have special programs to access Archie and Veronica, but nowadays you can access them easily through the same browser program you use for the World Wide Web. Some advanced users still prefer the old-style search programs, but I'll explain how to do it without them.

Archie

Archie is a comprehensive, freely accessible, and automatically searchable index of every file accessible through public File Transfer Protocol (ftp). The bad news is that Archie knows only the names of the files and the names of the disk directories they're stored in. They don't have any text description attached, so a picture of five elephants juggling on bicycles might be called `ejob5.jpg` You could search Archie for the text "elephant," "juggle," and "bicycle" all day and not find the picture.

The good news is that people are generally nice and they often give files descriptive names. There very well might be a picture file named `elephants-juggling.gif` stored right next to `ejob5.jpg`. And the even better news is that many images have such specific content that you can easily guess what somebody would name the image file. If you were looking for an image of *The Three Stooges* TV show, an Archie search for the word "stooges" would be a pretty good bet. Archie indexes directory names, too—so you may discover a whole directory folder full of files related to your search topic.

To search Archie, start by pointing your browser to the list of all Archie servers at

```
http://pubweb.nexor.co.uk/public/archie/
     servers.html
```

Choose the Archie server nearest you, or one located in a time zone where it is night and few local people will be using it.

To run a search, click the What would you like to search for? box and type the letters you want to find. For the search type, you'll almost always want Case Insensitive Substring Match unless you know the exact name of the file you're looking for. Click the Submit button, and in a few seconds (sometimes longer at busy times), you will have a list of clickable links to every publicly archived filename in the world containing the letters you searched for.

Veronica

The image files that Archie finds are almost always hiding in a long list of other types of files with similar names. Of course, you can tell Archie to look for images containing the letters GIF or JPG if you want to increase the chances of hitting a graphics file. But wouldn't it be nice if you could just say, "Just find me image files, nothing else"? And while we're making out a wish list, it would also be handy if the files had short descriptions attached to them so we could search the descriptions for key words, too.

Veronica is another master searchable index of public files. Like Archie, all Veronica needs from you is a few letters or words to search for, and away she goes to fetch every file she can find that matches your query. Most of the files Archie has access to are also accessible through Veronica.

Often, however, Veronica has access to longer descriptions of the files than Archie does. And more importantly, Veronica knows what type of file she's looking at and tells you by displaying the appropriate icon on the search result menu; so you can go straight to the graphics and ignore the rest.

Tip: You may notice that the search list Veronica comes up with is titled Gopher menu. The file system that Veronica indexes is called Gopher, or sometimes GopherSpace. Gopher itself has been largely superseded by the World Wide Web, so you probably won't have much reason to access Gopher menus directly unless you're doing a Veronica search.

"Straight to the graphics and ignore the rest," I say. But the rest may still be a heck of a lot of files! Veronica searches often turn up thousands upon thousands of matching files, only 200 or so of which are shown unless you request to see more. Even with handy icons to guide you, weeding through 200 files or more for the desired graphics images is no fun.

But not to worry. You can tell Veronica to find just graphics files and ignore everything else: Simply enter -tIg (that's hyphen, small t, capital I, small g) as one of the words to search for. This will command Veronica to show you only graphics.

Let's walk through a Veronica search so you can get an idea of how it works. First, pick a Veronica server from the list at

```
http://www.scs.unr.edu/veronica.html
```

The Veronica search form (Figure 1.6) is pretty basic: Just type the keywords and hit the enter key. Along with the words to search for (which can be entered in any order), you can also give special commands to Veronica. For more information on the command language, choose the How to Compose Veronica Queries link from the Veronica server list page.

As mentioned previously, if you enter -tIg as if it were one of your search words, Veronica will return only graphics images and ignore all other file types. You may also include menus and Web pages with the command -tIgh1 (a dash followed by the letters tIgh and the number 1) instead of just -tIg.

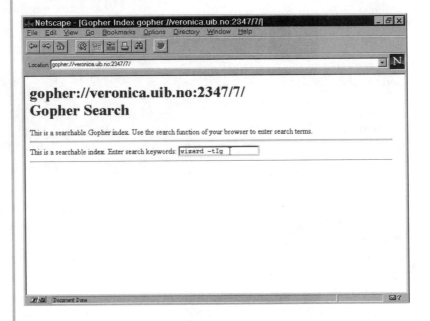

Figure 1.6. Veronica offers an express lane down the yellow brick road.

Figure 1.6 shows a Veronica query for graphics images whose names or descriptions include the letters "wizard." Veronica responds by building the Gopher menu shown in Figure 1.7, which leads to several images along the lines of Figure 1.8.

Figure 1.7.
In a flash of
shimmering light,
24 wizards
appear. Clicking
each menu item
will display or
download the
associated
image.

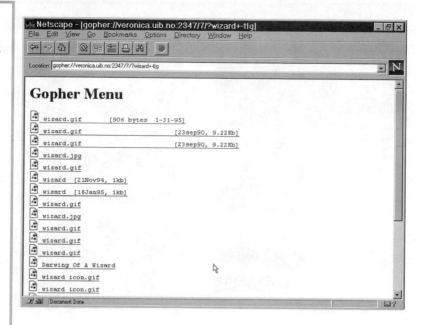

Searches often turn up several duplicates of the same image. The 24 links Veronica found (in Figure 1.7) led to less than a dozen unique images, and only the five shown in Figure 1.9 were interesting enough to be potentially useful.

Figure 1.8.
This image could
be really handy
if, for example,
you want to
illustrate
searching in a
document called
"Web Page
Wizardry."

*Figure 1.9.
The best wizards
Veronica could
find, viewed in
Paint Shop Pro.*

How to Make 90% of the Web Page Graphics You'll Ever Need

I now explain some tricks that savvy Webmasters like you can use to maximize the impact and speed of the graphics on your pages. These techniques are illustrated with Paint Shop Pro, a shareware Windows graphics editor that comes on the CD-ROM with this book.

If you haven't already installed Paint Shop Pro, you might want to do it now—before reading the rest of this chapter—so you can play with the techniques as you go along.

There are so many ways to produce images with Paint Shop Pro, I can't even begin to explain them all. I do offer a quick overview of some not-so-obvious techniques that are particularly well-suited for Web page graphics, but they barely scratch the surface of

Note: The Paint Shop Pro software on the CD-ROM is a fully functional shareware evaluation copy. If you agree with me that it's essential for working with Web page images, please be prompt about sending the $69 registration fee to the program's creators at JASC Software. (The address is in the online help in the software.) I'm confident that you're not going to find any other graphics software even close to the power and usability of Paint Shop Pro for anywhere near $69. (In fact, I have all the leading super-expensive commercial graphics programs from Photoshop on down, and Paint Shop Pro is the best by far for day-to-day work with Web graphics.)

what you can do. You'll have to explore the rest on your own.

Just be sure not to miss the Deformation browser and Filter browser on the Image menu. These give you access to a wide range of cool effects such as the embossing, warping, and smearing in Figure 1.10 and subsequent images in this chapter. And of course you should make good use of the text tool, which can use any TrueType or Postscript font on your system to make fancy graphic headings for your Web pages.

Transparency

By setting a color in your GIF image to be transparent, you can make nonrectangular graphics look good over any background color or background image tile.

To create a transparent GIF in Paint Shop Pro follow these steps:

1. Choose the eyedropper tool.

2. Right-click the color you want to make transparent.

3. Select File¦Save As...

4. Choose the GIF file format and Version 89a-Noninterlaced subformat (interlaced transparent GIFs are possible, but often don't display correctly).

5. Click on the Options button.

6. Choose Set the Transparency Value to the Background Color as shown in Figure 1.10 and click OK.

7. Enter a name for the file, then click OK to save it.

Figure 1.10. Paint Shop Pro's GIF Transparency Options dialog box lets you choose which palette color will become transparent.

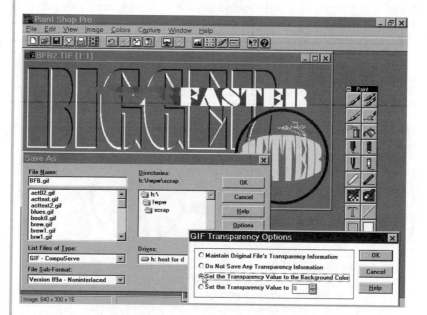

Backgrounds and Text Colors

Background tiling started as another unofficial extension to HTML but has quickly gained near-universal support. This powerful feature enables you to specify an image file to be used as a wallpaper tile behind all text and images in a document. It is implemented as an attribute in the <BODY> tag like this:

```
<BODY BACKGROUND="blues.gif">

(document text goes here)

</BODY>
```

As Figure 1.11 shows, background tiling can be combined with transparent images to add flair to your pages. Be warned, however, that some browsers don't always handle backgrounds and transparent images correctly. Background tiling also can significantly increase the time it takes for a page to download and display if you're not careful to keep your background image files reasonably small.

A faster way to wield some control over the background in Netscape is to use the body color extensions. These enable you to specify a color for the background, text, and hotlinks. No extra images must be loaded or processed, so images still download and display at maximum speed.

*Figure 1.11.
A good background can add color and interest to transparent graphics.*

You can specify colors by name or number. The basic colors can be specified using the English words "blue," "green," "purple," and so forth. To make the background blue, the text white, and the links yellow, you would use the following:

```
<BODY BGCOLOR="blue" TEXT="white"
  LINK="yellow">
```

You can also specify a color for links that have already been visited with ALINK= and a color for links to blink when they're activated with VLINK=.

Tip: A neat trick to try: Set VLINK and BGCOLOR to the same color on a home page or hotlist, and every link the visitor has already been to seems to disappear!

You can mix your own custom colors in the format #rrggbb, where rr, gg, and bb are a two-digit hexadecimal values for the red, green, and blue components of the color. If you're not familiar with hexadecimal numbers, don't sweat it: Just remember that FF is the maximum, 00 is the minimum, and 88 is in the middle. To make the background white, the text black, and the links blue, you would write

```
<BODY BGCOLOR="#FFFFFF" TEXT="#000000"
  LINK="#0000FF">
```

Use custom colors with caution, however, because they can make many computers display distracting dithered patterns behind text. You should generally stick to the basic named colors that almost every computer will show without any dithering: black, white, red, green, blue, yellow, magenta, and cyan.

Aqua, fuchsia, lime, maroon, navy, olive, gray, silver, and teal are also valid color names, but are not as reliable as the pure colors.

Note: You can change the text colors at any point during the document with the FONT COLOR= attribute. For example, to make the word "CAUTION" appear red, you could write

```
<FONT COLOR="red">CAUTION:</FONT> this
page is HOT!
```

You'll find out much more about the FONT tag in Chapter 2, "Wild Type, Far-Out Layouts, and Cheap HTML Tricks."

Note that if a user has selected Always use my colors, overriding document on Netscape's Options ¦ General Preferences ¦ Colors page, your background and text color specifications will be ignored. Any text colors set with the FONT COLOR= attribute *will* still work, however.

Fast Display Over Slow Modems

Two forces are always at odds when you post graphic on the Web: your eyes want graphic images to be as detailed and accurate as possible, but your clock and wallet want images to be as small as possible. Intricate, colorful graphics usually mean big (and we're talking BIG) file sizes, which can take a long time to transfer, even over a fast connection. So visual quality sometimes has to take a back seat to file size—especially now that most people on the Net are using 28.8Kbps modems and not high-speed university trunk lines.

So how do you maximize the quality of your images while minimizing file size? To make these choices, you need to understand what your options are and how color depth and resolution work together to create a subjective sense of quality. So read the next few paragraphs carefully—especially if you're fairly new at all this. They contain a concise summary of what you need to know about color and resolution.

Resolution and Color Depth

The vertical and horizontal resolution are the height and width of the image, measured in pixels (the individual dots that make up a digital image).

Color depth is the number of bits of information used to describe each pixel. Each bit can have two values, so two bits can have four unique values (2×2), four bits can have 16 unique values (2×2×2×2), and so on. For most images you'll put on the Net, a color look-up table, or palette, is included in the image file to specify which actual color corresponds to each value.

If you use enough bits per pixel, however, you can describe the color itself in terms of its red, green, and blue color components and you don't need a color look-up table. Most often, these true-color images use 24 bits per pixel, which provides more colors than the human eye can distinguish. When a visitor to your pages views a true-color image without a true-color graphics card, his or her browser will approximate the colors as closely as possible with 16 or 256 standard palette colors, but the graphics files themselves will still include all 24 bits of color information.

All these factors together determine the overall size of the image file. In Table 1.1, I show all the common color depths and resolutions and the resulting theoretical size of the image, including the color look-up table.

One of the most effective ways to reduce the download time for an image is to reduce the number of colors. In Paint Shop Pro, you can do this by selecting Colors¦Reduce Color Depth. (Most other graphics programs have a similar option.) The software will automatically find the best palette of 16 or 256 colors for approximating the full range of colors in the image.

When you reduce the number of colors in an image, you will see a dialog box with several choices (Figure 1.12). For Web page images, you will almost always want to choose an Optimized, Weighted palette, and Nearest Color instead of Error Diffusion or any form of dithering.

Table 1.1. How color depth and resolution affect the theoretical (uncompressed) file size (1KB = 1,024 bytes = 8,192 bits).

Resolution (pixels)	Bits per pixel (Number of colors) KB:				
	1(2)	4(16)	8(256)	15(32,768)	24(16,777,216)
160×120	3	10	20	35	58
320×200	8	31	64	117	188
640×480	37	150	300	563	900
800×600	59	234	469	879	1,406
1024×768	96	384	769	1,440	2,304

Figure 1.12. Reducing the color depth of an image can dramatically reduce file sizes without changing the appearance of the image too much.

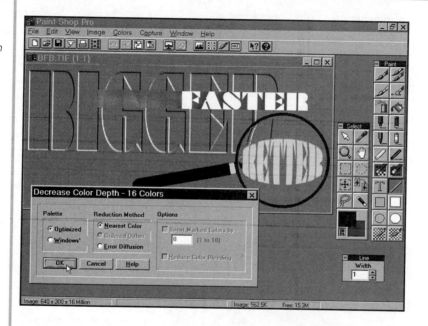

Tip: *Dithering* (called *error diffusion* in Paint Shop Pro) means using random dots or patterns to intermix palette colors. This can make images look better in some cases, but should usually be avoided for Web page graphics. Why? Because it substantially increases the information complexity of an image, and that almost always results in much larger file sizes and slower downloads. So, listen to your Great Uncle Oliver and "don't dither!"

Putting the Squeeze on Image Files

Most images will actually take much less space on your hard drive than Table 1.1 indicates, because they are stored in a compressed format. How much an image can be compressed depends on the image itself: A truly random sea of static image wouldn't compress at all, and a solid color image would compress to well under 1KB no matter what its resolution. Generally, the GIF images most often found on the Web achieve somewhere around 4:1 compression (meaning that a file typically would take up a quarter of the space listed in Table 1.1).

Lossy JPEG compression, however, can squeeze images even smaller. They'll usually start showing noticeable degradation at compression ratios greater than 4:1, but photographic images with fairly smooth transitions between colors will often tolerate JPEG compression as tight as 10:1 without too much uglification.

Tip: Combining colorful but blurry JPEG background tiles with sharp but simple 2- or 16-color transparent GIF images can give your pages the best of everything: lots of color, lots of precise detail, and teeny tiny file sizes.

Table 1.2 shows some typical file sizes from various compression settings for a photo scanned at 320×200 resolution. Keep in mind, however, that these results can vary quite a bit depending on the distribution of color and contrast levels in a particular image. (The percentages in the table refer to the compression level setting in Paint Shop Pro's Save As ¦ Options dialog box. Other graphics software may use slightly different numbers to signify the same compression settings.)

To estimate how long it will typically take for your images to download, you can assume that a standard 28.8Kbps modem with a good connection to a Net site can pull about two kilobytes (that is, 2KB) per second on average.

Remember, though, that many people are still accessing the Net through 14.4Kbps or slower modems. As a general rule, any Web page that includes more than 50KB worth of graphics should be accessed only from another, less graphics-intensive page. Links to the graphics-intensive page should warn the readers so they can turn off their Web browsers' automatic graphics downloading if they are using a slow dial-up modem connection.

Progressive Display and Interlacing

After you've compressed your files as tightly as possible, what more can you do to make them download and display faster? A lot! There are three ways to make a rough draft of an image appear well before the entire image is finished downloading. This can have a dramatic psychological effect, making the images seem to come up almost instantly, even though they may take quite a while to completely finish downloading.

Interlaced GIFs

The most popular way to get an illusion of speed is to use a special kind of GIF file called an *interlaced GIF*.

Table 1.2. Relative file sizes of a typical 320×200 photo, and approximate transfer time over a 28.8Kbps modem connection.

Color Depth (bits)	Actual File Format	File Size (in KB, approx.)	Compression (approx.)	Transfer Time (secs)
24	Uncompressed TGA	190.5	1:1	95
8	Compressed GIF	51.4	4:1	26
24	"Near perfect" JPEG	54.3	4:1	27
24	5% JPEG compression	32.5	6:1	16
24	25% JPEG compression	11.3	17:1	6
24	50% JPEG compression	7.3	26:1	4
24	75% JPEG compression	4.6	40:1	2

In a noninterlaced image file, the top line of pixels is stored first, then the next line down, then the next line after that, and so on. In an interlaced file, only every other line is saved, and then the missing lines are filled in at the end of the file. Most Web browsers display interlaced GIFs as they are being read, so a rough draft of the image appears quickly, and then the details are filled in as the download finishes.

Most graphics programs that can handle GIF files enable you to choose whether to save them interlaced or noninterlaced. In Paint Shop Pro, for example, you can choose the "Version 89a—Interlaced" File sub-format on the Save As... dialog box just before you save a GIF file (see Figure 1.13).

Progressive JPEGs

The JPEG format has its own corollary to interlaced GIF, called *progressive JPEG*. The mathematics are a bit more complex than interlacing, but the effect is essentially the same: a blurry version of the picture appears first and is replaced by a more precise rendition as the image finishes downloading.

Unfortunately, at this writing, the progressive JPEG standard is quite new and isn't supported by any of the major graphics programs or Web browsers except Netscape Navigator 2 and Microsoft Internet Explorer 3. This should change over the next year or so, at which point progressive JPEGs will undoubtedly become quite popular.

Note: Browsers that don't support progressive JPEG will *not* display the file as if it were just a regular JPEG—they will display nothing at all or a message saying the file isn't recognizable. So don't put progressive JPEGs on your pages unless you're sure that all your intended audience will be using a browser that supports them!

(Interlaced GIFs, on the other hand, will appear correctly even in older browsers that don't support two-stage display.)

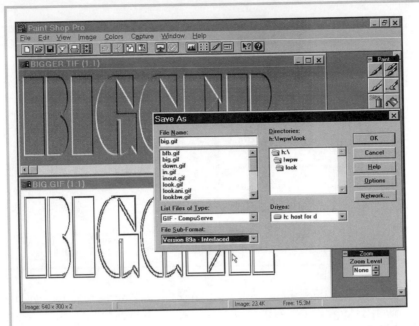

Figure 1.13. Paint Shop Pro lets you save interlaced GIF images, which appear to display faster when loading.

HTML Extensions for Speedy Display

The third way to appear faster than you really are is to use the LOWSRC, WIDTH, and HEIGHT attributes, which are HTML extensions to the IMG tag. These are currently supported only by Netscape Navigator, but other browsers will just ignore these tags. So you can use them safely even if some visitors to your site may not be using Netscape.

The LOWSRC attribute specifies an image to be loaded and displayed before the image specified in the SRC attribute. The idea behind this is to enable you to load a quick two-color GIF or *lossy* JPEG image first, then immediately replace it with a more colorful or detailed version of the same image. Basically, LOWSRC enables you to simulate the effect of an interlaced GIF or progressive JPEG, using two separate images.

But the two images don't *have to* look similar. By using two different images altogether, you can create a clever little two-frame animation or overlay effect. Keep in mind, however, that the LOWSRC image is not displayed at all if Netscape can find the SRC image in its memory or disk cache from a recent download. So if viewers return to your page more than once in a session, they usually won't see your nifty LOWSRC animation effect.

The WIDTH and HEIGHT attributes specify the size (in pixels) to make an image. Normally, these are the actual width and height of the image and are used by Netscape to lay out the page quickly and display any text that follows an image without having to load the image first. But they can also be used to stretch an image to fit a larger (or smaller) space. For example, if big.gif is a 200×200 pixel image, you could make a 100×100 pixel version called small.gif and use the following HTML command on your Web page:

```
<IMG SRC="big.gif" LOWSRC="small.gif"
   WIDTH=200 HEIGHT=200>
```

The smaller version would load first, and Netscape would automatically enlarge it to 200×200 pixels. Then the full-size version would overlay it as soon as it loaded.

Doing It All at Once

By using transparency, interlaced GIFs, and LOWSRC all at once, you can actually make the image display in several separate stages, with each stage appearing more detailed.

Even the slowest modem users get something to look at quickly and an interesting progression of layers to keep them entertained while the final image loads.

Figures 1.14 through 1.17 show the four stages that appear when you load the sample document designed earlier in this chapter. (To see this for yourself, open the /look/ bfb.htm file on the CD-ROM with Netscape Navigator.)

Figure 1.14. The first thing you see is a blocky image. This is the first pass of the interlaced LOWSRC image loading.

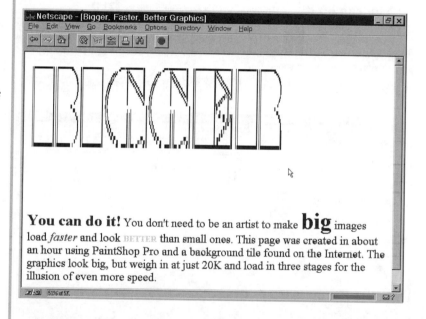

Figure 1.15.
Next, the more
detailed second
pass loads.

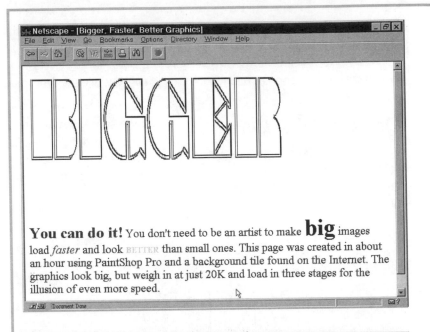

Figure 1.16.
As soon as
Netscape is
finished loading
the background
tile image, it is
displayed under
whatever is on
the screen at that
moment.

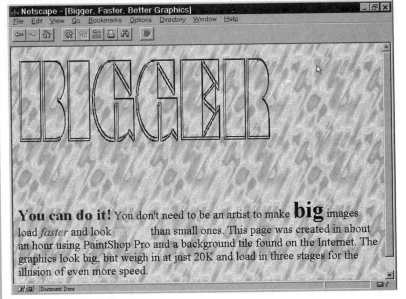

Figure 1.17.
Finally, the
LOWSRC image is
gradually
replaced by the
SRC image as it
downloads. (To
see the final
appearance of
this page, refer
to Figure 1.11.)

What's Next?

This LOWSRC business can be a cheap and easy way to do super-simple animation without the need for you or your viewing audience to mess with extra plug-ins, helper apps, or Java applets. But there are much better—and almost as cheap—ways to get animation without the fuss. In the next chapter, I show you how and explore some sneaky ways to get creative with graphics layout and type formatting, too.

Wild Type, Far-Out Layouts, and Cheap HTML Tricks

chapter 2

by Dick Oliver

Every time you sit down to design a Web page today, you're faced with an agonizing decision: Do you use the latest hot multimedia technology for maximum impact, or do you stick to basic HTML commands that every browser everywhere will display? In this chapter, I show you how to get the best of both worlds by pushing HTML to its creative limits. With the techniques you'll discover here, you can achieve creative layouts, special effects, and even full-blown animation without any special plug-ins, scripts, or add-on programs.

Some of the fancier stuff currently shows up only in Netscape Navigator 2.0 (or later), and Microsoft Internet Explorer 3.0. But because everything is in HTML, the same pages will still look great in most other popular browsers.

Dare to be Different

Let's face it, after a few hours of surfing, most of the pages on the Web all start to look the same. The logo, the heading, the too-wide single column of text with cute little iconic images to the left every once in a while. And then there are those all-one-big-graphic pages that take forever to download and contain only six words for you to read before you click yet another all-one-big-graphic page that takes forever to download…. It's enough to put you to sleep, even after that fifth cup of coffee.

But just when you're nodding off, you come across a page like the one in Figure 2.1 (which you can view online at `http://www.iterated.com/`). Most of the text is real text, so it pops up fast. But then those snappy little title graphics appear one by one, each in just the right place next to the text it refers to. And the whole thing is laid out in a distinctive and attractive way that just oozes cool without reeking of some artist's overripe ego.

Now, you may prefer a different aesthetic than what this page displays. But the tricks that its designer used to make it unique can be adapted to make your pages unique in a totally different direction. In any case, these are the key elements to notice:

✦ Most graphics that substitute for text are small, so they load and display first. The larger graphics are less essential for reading the page, so it's okay that they'll appear more slowly.

✦ Some of the graphics are used more than once (the Info and Demo buttons, for instance). This speeds display because they only need to be loaded once.

✦ The background image is quite small (just a thin horizontal strip, tiled down the page), but it creates a large and visually striking design element on the page.

✦ Multicolumn text and a unique layout make this page (and the others at this site) stand out from the crowd of "me-too" pages on the Internet.

✦ Almost all the actual text content of the page is "real text," not graphics, so visitors can use their browser's Find command to search it for keywords. And more importantly, Internet search indexes will index this page according to its text content so potential visitors can find it easily.

In this chapter, you'll learn how to make highly expressive pages that meet all these criteria and more; plus you'll go a giant step further and find out how to add simple animation to plain old HTML pages.

Note: If you aren't familiar with the other standard HTML font and formatting commands, you might want to flip through Appendix A, "HTML in a Nutshell," and Appendix B, "HTML Quick-Reference." Even old HTML pros should take note that the new HTML 3.0 `<DIV ALIGN="right">` tag finally allows you to right-justify text and replaces the old `<CENTER>` tag with `<DIV ALIGN="center">`. The `DIV` tag currently works only in Netscape, but most browsers do now support the once-Netscape-only `<IMG ALIGN="left">` and `<IMG ALIGN="right">` options, which enable you to wrap text around images.

Both Netscape Navigator and Microsoft Internet Explorer also support tables and frames, which are used in a number of the examples in this chapter and throughout the book to add variety to layouts.

Figure 2.1.
This site manages
a unique,
distinctive layout
and look without
giant, band-
width-hogging
graphics files.

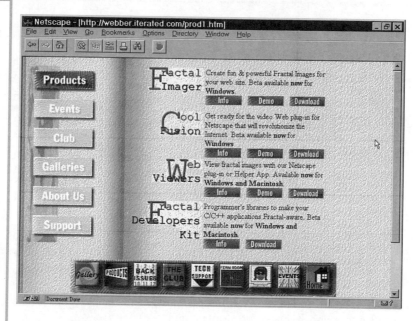

Font Manipulation and Text Formatting

You'll notice the FONT tag often in the examples throughout this chapter. Using this tag to set the size and color of text is pretty much a no-brainer: the SIZE attribute can take any value from 1 (tiny) to 7 (fairly big), and the COLOR attribute can take the standard English color names (black, white, red, green, blue, yellow, magenta, cyan, aqua, fuchsia, gray, lime, maroon, navy, olive, silver, and teal). The actual size and exact color of the fonts depend on the user's screen resolution and preference settings, but you can be assured that SIZE=6 will be a lot bigger than SIZE=2, and that COLOR="red" will certainly show its fire. Both Netscape Navigator and Microsoft Explorer now support FONT SIZE and COLOR, and most other browsers will soon support this tag, too.

Another font trick you should know about is the <TT> tag, which changes from the user's normal, proportionally spaced font to a monospaced "typewriter type" font. Theoretically, each user can choose any font he or she wants when configuring the browser, and the monospaced font may not even be monospaced for some crazy users. But the vast majority of people just stick with the standard fonts that the browser comes set up with, so you should design and test your pages with those default fonts, too. (The standard proportional font is usually Times New Roman, and the standard monospaced font is almost always Courier or Courier New.)

Putting a New Face on Your Page

With Internet Explorer version 3.0, Microsoft has added another extremely powerful form of font control: the FONT FACE attribute. This allows you to specify the actual typeface that should be used to display text—and has been the source of much rejoicing among Webmasters who are *awfully* sick of Times and Courier!

The site in Figure 2.2 uses these font controls (and another new Microsoft Explorer feature, borderless frames) to present a warmly welcoming homestyle site.

The code to set the font used in Figure 2.2 (in the file `/maple/main.htm` on the CD-ROM) is:

```
<FONT FACE="Lucida Handwriting, Brush
  Script, Brush Script MT" SIZE=5
  COLOR="#800000">
```

If Explorer can find a font named Lucida Handwriting on a user's system, that font is used. Otherwise, it checks for a font named Brush Script or Brush Script MT and uses whichever of those it can find. If the user doesn't have any of those fonts installed, the default font set up for Explorer is used (this is usually Times New Roman).

Tip: Note that both TrueType and Postscript fonts installed on the user's system can be used in Web pages. TrueType fonts are more common, but it's always a good idea to include the name of a similar Postscript font (if you know one), because some people don't use TrueType at all.

In this example, Brush Script is the customary name for the Postscript version of the font, but Brush Script MT is the most common name of the TrueType version of the same font. I included both names just to be on the safe side.

Browsers other than Microsoft Explorer also use the default fonts they always use. Figure 2.3 shows the same page as in Figure 2.2, displayed with Netscape Navigator 2.0.

Figure 2.2. If you have Lucida Handwriting or Brush Script installed on your computer, the text of this page appears in a handwritten style (/maple/ syrup.htm).

1 • The Wow! Factor: Gonzo Graphics Stunts

Currently, only fonts that each user happens to have on his or her system will show up, and you have no control over which fonts are installed. Furthermore, the exact spelling of the font names is important, and many common fonts go by several slightly different names. Extensions to HTML will soon support a new, highly compact font format that can be automatically downloaded along with your pages to solve these problems. But for now, you just have to stick to the most common fonts and make sure your pages still look acceptable in Times New Roman.

Figure 2.4 shows the most common TrueType fonts, many of which are also available in Postscript format. Microsoft offers a number of these fonts available for free download from this site:

`http://www.microsoft.com/truetype/`

Microsoft has also included these fonts (and variations on them) in Windows and other popular software packages. If you want to use a font on your Web page that isn't on this list, don't be afraid to do so! The user will never see an error message if the font can't be found—the worst thing that could happen is that the user won't see your special font, but will still see the text in the next best font that can be found. If one of the fonts in Figure 2.4 has a similar feel to the one you want, include it as a "second choice" as I did with Brush Script in the preceding example.

Figure 2.3. Netscape Navigator 2.0 doesn't recognize the FONT FACE attribute, so it displays the page in Figure 2.2 with plain old Times New Roman.

Figure 2.4.
The most
popular
TrueType fonts
are good bets
for inclusion in
your Web pages.
Arial is especially
reliable since
almost all
computers now
come with it
installed (/bfb/
fonts.htm).

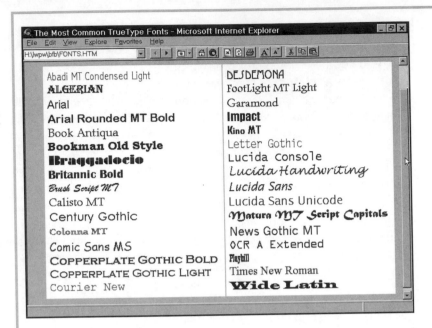

Type That Isn't Type (and Other Illusions)

In situations where you want to be sure that all viewers see a special font, you can substitute graphics images for a few key words in the text of your pages. Figures 2.5 and 2.6 show two very simple but visually powerful examples of real text mixed with graphics images of text in a fancy font.

These two-color graphics are quite large, but they compress tightly and load quickly because they're so simple.

Note that the image in Figure 2.6 does not use transparency but appears to because the background color in the graphic matches the background color of the page. (See Chapter 1, "Bigger, Faster, Better Graphics," for details on how to set the text and background colors and which colors can be relied on to match a graphic on most computers.)

The page in Figure 2.7 is a little trickier: Here, the text appears to "bleed" off the top of the page because it is actually a background tile. You can use background graphics for nonrepeating elements as long as you make the image wider than about 1000 pixels and taller than 750 pixels, and put little enough text on the page so that it will usually fit on a single screen without scrolling. (Very few people surf the Internet at screen resolutions greater than 1024×768.)

Figure 2.5.
Powerful visual
effects don't
have to be
complex.

Figure 2.6.
Nontransparent
images can look
transparent if
you match the
background color
of the page.

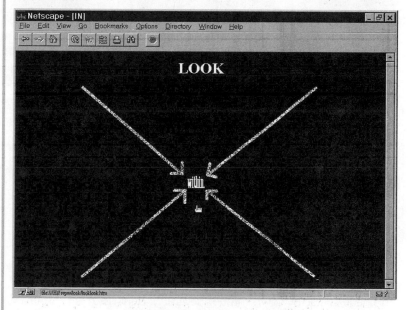

Figure 2.7.
You can make
graphics bleed
right up to the
edge of the
viewing window
by using them as
backgrounds.

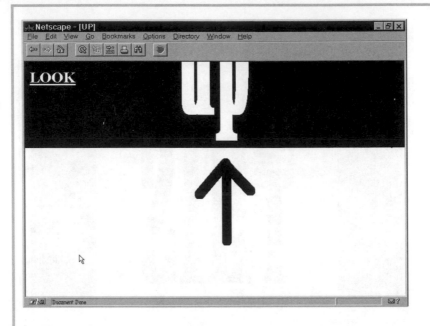

Tip: You might think that a 1000×750-pixel image would be too big to be practical as a background, but the black-and-white background graphic in Figure 2.7 is actually only 4KB, and loads in less than 2 seconds over a 28.8Kbps modem. Because GIF and JPEG files are compressed efficiently, the size of the image always depends more on its visual complexity than on the actual resolution.

In fact, blank space *of any size* will take up almost no space in the graphics file when compressed. So you could even use a 1000×3000-pixel image with 2500 pixels worth of blank space at the bottom for your text to scroll over and still keep the file size under 5KB.

The moral of the story: When you want to grab visitors' attention fast, don't be afraid to think *big* as long as you also think *simple*.

Figure 2.8 illustrates yet another background-as-graphic-as-text stunt. Visitors to this page can scroll down through several copies of the background image even though no text or foreground images appear on most of the page.

There are three ways to achieve this effect: the most common is to include a long, totally transparent GIF image as a "spacer" to fill the empty region on the page where

you want just the background to show. The other, which is even faster and more efficient, is to set the text color to match the background color and insert some "invisible" text down the page. The HTML code for Figure 2.8 appears in Listing 2.1. The third technique for achieving the same result would be to insert several blank lines between `<PRE>` and `</PRE>` tags, which specify preformatted text, including line breaks.

Figure 2.8.
Invisible text
enables the user
to scroll down
several times
without seeing
anything but the
repeating
background.

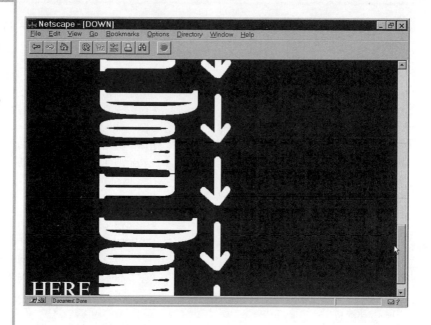

Listing 2.1. Inserting invisible text.

```
<HTML>
<HEAD><TITLE>DOWN</TITLE></HEAD>
<BODY BACKGROUND="down.gif" BGCOLOR="black"
  TEXT="black" VLINK="white" ALINK="white" LINK="white">
<H1><A HREF="looklook.htm">LOOK</A>
i<P>
n<P>
v<P>
i<P>
s<P>
i<P>
b<P>
l<P>
e<P>
-<P>
t<P>
e<P>
x<P>
t<P>
!<P>
<A HREF="looklook.htm">HERE.</A></H1>
</BODY>
</HTML>
```

Notice that no FONT COLOR commands need to be used because all the letters that I wanted
to be visible are within links, and the link color is set to white in the BODY tag.

Far-Out Layouts

The simplified demonstration pages in Figures 2.5 through 2.8 are just a warm-up to get you thinking about ways to do things differently while staying within the "letter of the law" of HTML. Now it's time to stop fooling around and create a seriously wild page or two.

Because the point here is to show you how to get noticed, I'll create an imaginary site called "LOOK," which uses a very nontraditional layout, thematic artwork, and everything else we can pull out of the bag to be eye-catching and distinctive. Your real-world site will probably be a bit more tame than the pages in this chapter—but of course, some of you will start getting even crazier ideas....

Making a Seamless Background Tile

If eye-catching is what we're after, what better way to start than by catching an eye? Figure 2.9 is my two-year old daughter's left eye, scanned with a cheap hand scanner from a snapshot and color corrected a bit within Paint Shop Pro. (See Chapter 1 for help installing Paint Shop Pro from the CD-ROM in this book.)

The eye is pretty effective as an attention-getting background—but wouldn't it be slick if the tiles all fit together seamlessly? It may not be at all obvious how to turn this into a seamless background tile, so I'll explain it, step by step. Follow these steps to turn almost any interesting pattern or image into a repeating tile.

The following instructions are specifically for Paint Shop Pro, but you can do the same thing in any good graphics editing program.

Figure 2.9.
The edges of this scanned photo don't fit together very well when tiled as a background.

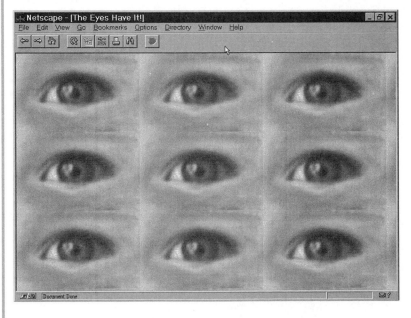

1. Open the graphics file you want to start with, and resize or crop it to suit the layout you have in mind. In this case, I chose a size that would tile nicely in a 640×480, 800×600, or 1024×768 window without the eye being cut in half on the right edge. (The image is 255×161 pixels.)

2. Select Image¦Enlarge Canvas and double both the vertical and horizontal size of the canvas. This will leave room to arrange four copies of the image next to one another.

3. Using the rectangle selection tool, select the original image (in this case, the rectangle from 0,0 to 254,160). Paint Shop Pro displays the current location of the cursor at the bottom of the screen to help you get exactly the region you want.

4. Using the move selection tool (the one with two people in dotted boxes on the toolbar), move a copy of the selection down as shown in Figure 2.10.

5. Using the smudge brush and/or the copy brush (the top right two brushes on the paint palette), smooth the transition at the edge between the two copies of the image.

6. Select the top part of the bottom image (here, the rectangle from 162,0 to about 350,255), and move it up to replace the top part of the top image. Now the top image will tile seamlessly in the vertical direction.

7. Repeat steps 3 through 6 for the horizontal direction; that is, move a copy of the top image to the right of it, smooth the edge between them, and copy the leftmost half

Figure 2.10. To make a seamless tile, start by copying the image and smoothing the top and bottom edges together.

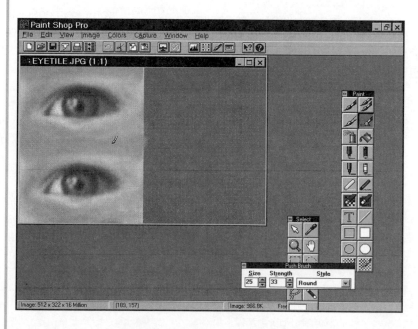

Figure 2.11.
Then smooth the
left and right
edges together,
being careful not
to change the
corners too
much.

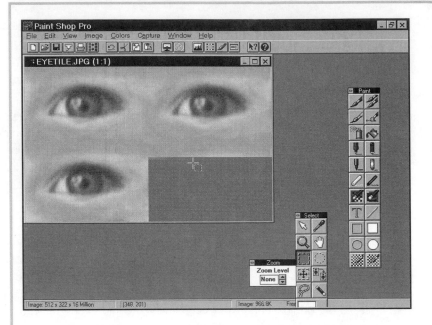

back onto the original image (see Figure 2.11).

8. There still may be some abrupt color changes right at the corners of the image. To check for and correct these, copy the top left image down into the empty region at the bottom right. Use the smudge or copy brushes to smooth the corner at the center of the four images, then copy that corner carefully back up into the upper left.

9. Copy the top left image onto the clipboard, paste it into a new image file, and save it in the JPEG or GIF format.

10. Create a quick test like this:
```
<HTML>
<BODY BACKGROUND="myimage.jpg">
</BODY>
</HTML>
```
and open it into your Web browser, as shown in Figure 2.12.

Note that most JPEG files will show barely visible seams between tiles—even if you followed these steps perfectly—because the exact color information is distorted slightly during compression. Most people won't even notice this subtle effect once the tile is on your page, but if it bothers you, use a GIF image for tiling instead.

11. Once you see the tile in your browser, you may see a few spots that need touching up in Paint Shop Pro before you pronounce your work a success.

You can use essentially the same process of copying and shuffling pieces of an image to draw your own seamless tiles from scratch, or add artwork to existing tiles. Figure 2.13 is a simple example, created by painting a colored stripe onto the image and its copies, then tweaking it as described here. Figure 2.14 shows the result in Netscape.

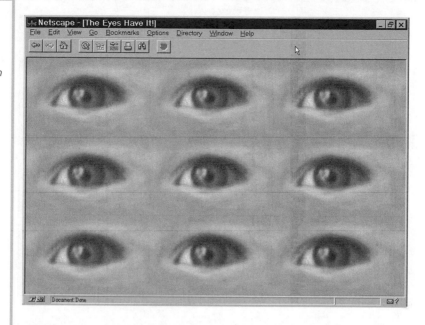

Figure 2.12. JPEG images will usually have barely visible "cracks" between tiles due to the lossy compression algorithm.

Dramatic accents like this can make the subtle seams between JPEG tiles less noticeable, too.

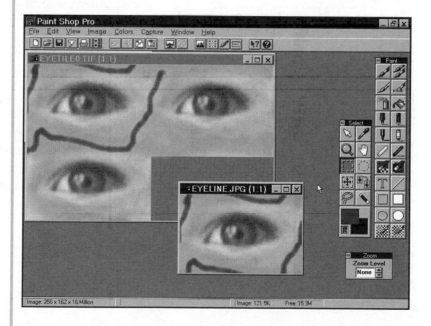

Figure 2.13. When you get the hang of tiling, you can add any number of artistic effects to your backgrounds.

Figure 2.14.
The modified tile
in Figure 2.13, as
seen in Netscape
Navigator.

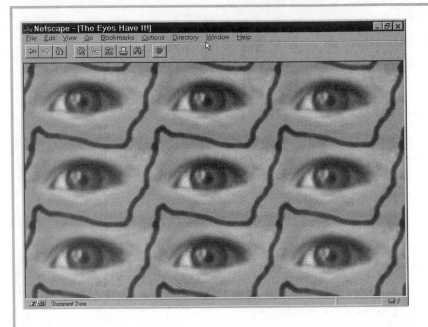

Translucent Images

When you're using not-so-subtle background tiles, it would be rather counterproductive to cover them up with a big foreground image. But of course it would be even more counterproductive not to have big foreground images announcing the content of your eye-popping site. An interesting compromise with a wide variety of applications is to create foreground images that are translucent and allow the background to show through every part to varying degrees.

You can achieve this uncommon effect quite neatly by dithering a color or gray scale image down to two colors, as shown in Figure 2.15.

Paint Shop Pro (like most other graphics programs) gives you a variety of dithering options. Ordered Dither places pixels in a regular pattern, and three types of error diffusion offer subtle differences in how they randomly place pixels. Try them all, and you'll see the difference much more clearly than I could ever explain.

Figure 2.16 shows the two variations on the image in Figure 2.15, each dithered with the Floyd-Steinberg Error Diffusion method down to two colors and saved as transparent GIFs. The difference between the left and right images is that the left one was lighter shades of gray before being dithered, so the pattern is more sparse and allows more of the background to show through.

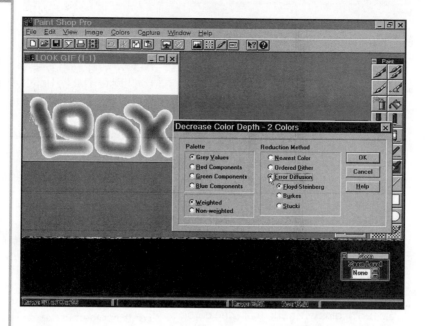

*Figure 2.15.
Ordered Dither
gives a regular
pattern, whereas
error diffusion
adds a degree of
randomness.*

If the figure were in color, you'd also see that, after I dithered each image down to two colors, I increased the color depth up to 16 colors and edited the palette entry of the black color to be light blue (in the left image) or red (in the right image). The net effect is a colored, translucent image that clearly shows both the "LOOK" logo and the background beneath it. You could also use the color replacement tool in Paint Shop Pro's paint palette to make multicolored translucent images easily.

*Figure 2.16.
Translucent,
colored images
show up clearly
but also let the
background
show through.*

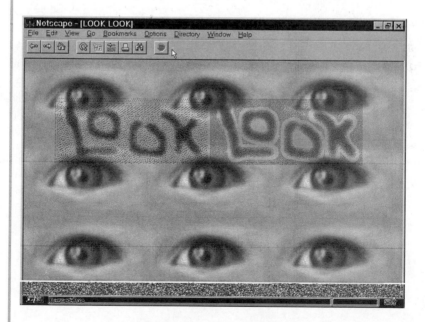

As mentioned in Chapter 1, the complexity of error diffusion dithering can significantly increase file sizes. But reducing the color depth tends to *decrease* file size, so all in all, translucent images don't usually get too big. The examples in Figure 2.13 are only about 5KB each, even though they're quite large (320×200 pixels).

Things You Probably Shouldn't Do with Tables

Tables are your most powerful tool for creative Web page layouts. The boring, conventional way to use tables is for tabular arrangements of text and numbers. But the real fun begins when you make the borders of your tables invisible, and use them as guides for arranging graphics and columns of text any old which way you please.

Tip: Tables were once only visible to users of Netscape Navigator. But now that the current version of Microsoft Internet Explorer and the next versions of every other major browser support tables, you can use them without fear of having them turn into a mushy mishmash of text before the eyes of non-Netscapers.

Note that Microsoft Internet Explorer 3.0 and the upcoming Netscape Navigator 3.0 now allow you to specify a separate background for each cell in a table. Refer to Appendix B, "HTML Quick-Reference," for the exact commands to do it. Some neat table border coloring attributes are highlighted there as well.

Laying It Out on the Table

In Figure 2.17, I've arranged some scanned handwriting with type of various sizes and colors into a table. I left the borders visible so I could make sure everything was placed the way I wanted, but before putting this on a Web page I would use the TABLE BORDER=0 command to make the lines invisible.

Listing 2.2 contains the HTML to make the table in Figure 2.17.

The <TABLE> and </TABLE> tags always start and end a table, and the BORDER attribute sets the border width. Duh.

<TR> and </TR> tags enclose each row in a table and accept the VALIGN attribute, which controls whether the contents of the row are vertically aligned to the "center," "top," or "bottom." You could also use HEIGHT to set an exact height for the row in pixels, but in this example I just let the browser automatically figure out the right height based on the tallest item in the row.

Each cell in the table starts with <TD> and ends with </TD>. The ALIGN attribute sets the horizontal alignment within the cell to either "center," "left," or "right." I used WIDTH to set the cell widths to exactly 200 or 100 pixels, and COLSPAN to indicate that each cell in the top two rows should span two columns.

That's all there is to it! I did use a few sneaky tricks: a totally transparent 100×100-pixel image called space100.gif to fill an empty cell, and an image too big to fit in its cell (more on that shortly).

*Figure 2.17.
Tables can
include text,
graphics, or a
combination of
both.*

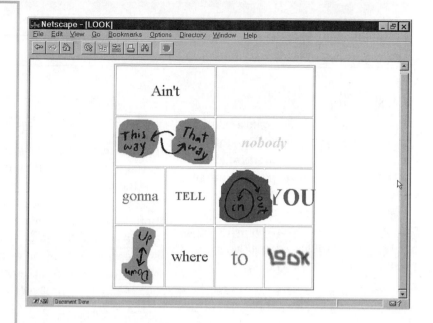

Listing 2.2. Making a table for text and graphics.

```
<TABLE BORDER=2>
<TR VALIGN="middle" COLSPAN=2>
  <TD ALIGN="center" WIDTH=200 COLSPAN=2>
    <FONT SIZE=6 COLOR="blue">Ain't</FONT></TD>
  <TD ALIGN="center" WIDTH=200 COLSPAN=2>
    <IMG SRC="space100.gif"></TD>
</TR>
<TR VALIGN="middle">
  <TD ALIGN="left" WIDTH=200 COLSPAN=2>
    <IMG SRC="thisthat.gif" USEMAP="#thisthat" BORDER=0></TD>
  <TD ALIGN="center" WIDTH=200 COLSPAN=2>
    <FONT SIZE=6 COLOR="yellow"><I><B>nobody</B></I></FONT></TD>
</TR>
<TR VALIGN="middle">
  <TD ALIGN="center" WIDTH=100>
    <FONT SIZE=6 COLOR="fuchsia">gonna</FONT></TD>
  <TD ALIGN="center" WIDTH=100>
    <FONT SIZE=5 COLOR="green"><B>TELL</B></FONT></TD>
  <TD ALIGN="center" WIDTH=100>
    <IMG SRC="inout.gif" USEMAP="#inout" BORDER=0></TD>
  <TD ALIGN="center" WIDTH=100>
    <FONT SIZE=7 COLOR="teal"><B>YOU</B></FONT></TD>
</TR>
<TR VALIGN="middle">
  <TD ALIGN="center" WIDTH=100>
    <IMG SRC="updown.gif" USEMAP="#updown" BORDER=0></TD>
  <TD ALIGN="center" WIDTH=100>
    <FONT SIZE=6 COLOR="purple">where</FONT></TD>
  <TD ALIGN="center" WIDTH=100>
    <FONT SIZE=7 COLOR="gray">to</FONT></TD>
  <TD ALIGN="center" WIDTH=100>
    <IMG SRC="look2.gif"></TD>
```

continues

Listing 2.2. continued

```
</TR>
</TABLE>
```

Nested Tables

Now suppose you want to add a column of text to the page, placed to the right of the table in Figure 2.17. No current extension to HTML allows you to wrap text to the right (or left) of a table—but that doesn't mean there isn't a way to do it! You can create another table, like the one shown in Figure 2.18, and insert the table in Figure 2.17 within a cell in that new table.

Figure 2.19 shows the two tables from Figures 2.17 and 2.18 put together. It also demonstrates a useful "bug" that you can use on purpose to create a sort of grunge-style layout effect: By putting a table in a space that's just a little too small to hold it, you can make text or images from one cell overlap into another. (Though both the table and the space to put it in are 400 pixels wide, the borders make it just a tad too big to fit.) Unfortunately (or fortunately, depending on whether you did it on purpose or by accident), this trick only fools Netscape Navigator. Microsoft Internet Explorer will automatically resize all cells to fit properly, as in Figure 2.20.

Figure 2.18. To wrap text to the right or left of a table, create another table and insert the first one inside it.

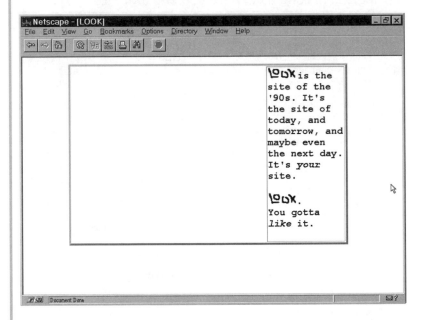

The code to create a nested table with the arrangement shown in Figures 2.18 and 2.19 would look like Listing 2.3.

Listing 2.3. Creating nested tables.

```
<TABLE BORDER=4>
<TR VALIGN="middle">
<TD WIDTH=400>
(the table in Figure 2.17 goes here)

</TD>
<TD WIDTH=160>
<IMG SRC="look1.gif" ALIGN="bottom">
<FONT SIZE=5><TT><B>is the site of the '90s.
It's the site of today, and tomorrow, and maybe even the next day.
It's <I>your</I> site.<P>
<IMG SRC="look1.gif">.<BR> You gotta<BR> <I>like</I> it.</B></TT><P>
</TD>
</TR>
</TABLE>
```

As an added touch, you'll notice that I inserted yet another graphic to the right of the nested table in Figures 2.19 and 2.20 by placing the following tag *before* the table code:

```
<IMG SRC="other.gif" ALIGN="right"
  BORDER=0>
```

The image appears on the far right-hand margin, and all graphics, text, or tables that follow are automatically placed to the left of it.

Figure 2.19. Putting a table where it won't quite fit within another table can create an overlapping post-modern effect in Netscape Navigator.

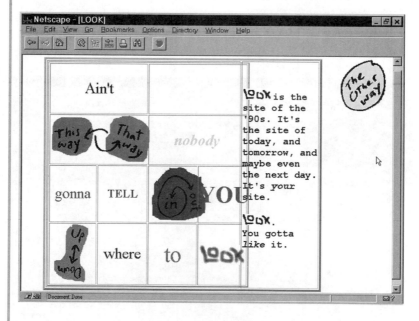

Figure 2.20.
Microsoft
Internet Explorer
is a little more
fussy than
Netscape
Navigator and
adjusts the size
of all cells to
hold any
oversized
content. (This is
the same HTML
page shown in
Figure 2.19.)

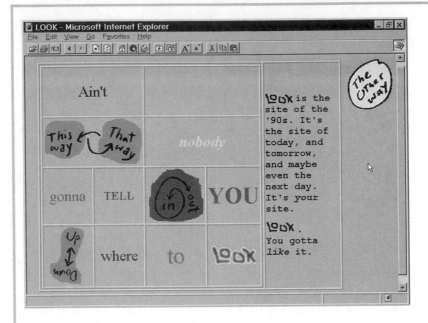

The finished "LOOK" page, complete with borderless table layouts, is depicted in Figure 2.21. But if you look at this page on the *Web Page Wizardry* CD-ROM (it's /look/look.htm), you'll see more than a figure in a book could show! The logo at the top of the page is animated in flashing colors, and each of the handwritten images is a clickable imagemap. And the best way to view the page is to start at looklook.htm instead, which will automatically load look.htm after six seconds.

Figure 2.21.
When the
borders of the
tables are hidden
and a wild
background is
added, the result
is an unquestion-
ably unique
look!

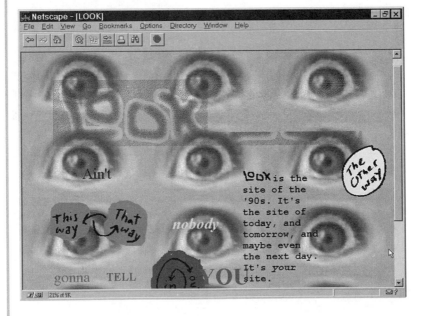

The rest of this chapter explains how to set up the clickable image maps and auto-loading pages, and Chapter 3, "Animation the Easy Way: Multi-Image GIFs," reveals how the animated GIF images were produced.

Do-It-Yourself Imagemapping

If you've ever put a page up on the Web, you know how to make an image link to another document. If you haven't, it looks like this:

```
<A HREF="whatever.htm"><IMG
  SRC="myimage.gif"></A>
```

You can also subdivide an image into regions and link to different documents, depending on which region the user clicks. This is called an *imagemap*, and any image can be made into an imagemap.

Both Netscape Navigator and Microsoft Explorer allow you to choose between two different methods for implementing image maps: *server-side image maps* and *client-side image maps*. Nowadays, all your image maps should be client-side, especially because you can easily make these automatically work the old server-side way

for users of older browser programs. I'll explain both kinds in the following sections, but first a tip that will help you with any of them....

Server-Side Imagemaps

The old-fashioned way to do an imagemap is to let the server computer where the Web page resides do all the work. When the user clicks an image that has been mapped this way, the browser program just sends the X,Y coordinates of the mouse pointer's location to a special script on the server. Usually, this script is called "imagemap" and is located in the cgi-bin directory on the server, and the HTML to implement the imagemap is just a normal anchor link:

```
<A HREF="/cgi-bin/imagemap/thisthat">
  <IMG SRC="thisthat.gif"></A>
```

Simple. But when you install a Web page including such a link, you need to tell the imagemap script which parts of the image should be associated with which link addresses. This is normally done in a *map file*. Each line in the map file is simply the word rect followed by a URL address and two sets of X,Y coordinates representing the top-left corner and the bottom-right corner of a region of the image. The first line in a map file begins with the word "default," followed by the URL address that should be used if the user happens to click outside any rectangular region defined by a rect line. A map file named thisthat.map might look like this:

```
default /top/this.htm
rect /top/this.htm 0,0,102,99
rect /top/that.htm 103,0,205,99
```

The final step in setting up a server-side imagemap is telling the imagemap script which map file to use for which image by adding a line to a system file named imagemap.conf. This file will already exist and includes entries for every imagemap defined on the server. You simply add a line with the name used in the HREF attribute of the <A> tag, a colon, and then the actual location and name of the associated map file. For example, the previous reference is HREF="/cgi-bin/imagemap/thisthat", and the preceding map file is named thisthat.map. If this map file is in a directory named /mapfiles, the line in imagemap.conf would read

```
thisthat : /mapfiles/thisthat.map
```

All this isn't nearly as difficult as it may sound if you've never set up an imagemap before, but it can be a hassle—especially if your pages reside on somebody else's server and you don't have the rights to modify system files like imagemap.conf yourself. What's worse, server-side image maps don't work

Figure 2.22.
Paint Shop Pro
can easily tell you
the coordinates
for imagemap
regions without
mucking about
with special
image mapping
utilities.

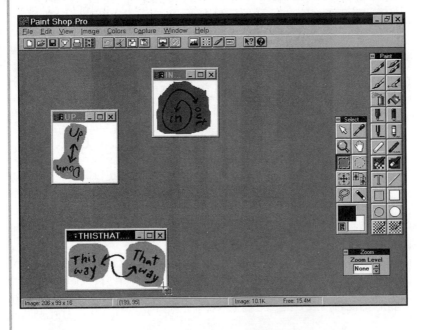

at all on Web pages located on your hard drive, a CD-ROM, or most local networks.

There are also some variations in the exact syntax for imagemap implementation, depending on the software installed on your server. So if you move your pages to a different server, the image maps may not work anymore. Yuck. Fortunately, there's now an easier and more reliable way to set up image maps.

Client-Side Imagemaps

The latest versions of all the major browsers support client-side image maps, where the association of links with specific regions in an image is handled by the browser itself instead of a server script. This means that you can include image maps in your HTML files without imposing an additional burden on your Internet Service Provider's server, and you can be more certain that they will be processed correctly and dependably.

The HTML to implement a client-side imagemap looks like Listing 2.4.

Tip: Remember that links do not necessarily have to lead to HTML documents. You could make an imagemap link to sound files, video clips, or any other media that you know the user has a plug-in or helper app to handle.

You'll find several example client-side image maps in the look.htm document on the *Web Page Wizardry* CD-ROM.

In that document (and the preceding example), the <MAP> and <AREA> tags were located in the same file as the <IMG> tag. It is also possible to put the map definition in a separate file by including that file's name in the USEMAP attribute, like this:

```
<IMG SRC="/thisthat.gif"
  USEMAP="maps.htm#thisthat">
```

Combined Client/Server Imagemaps

There is a way for you to provide client-side image maps that automatically switch to server-side image maps if the user's browser doesn't support client-side maps. With a single line of code, you can allow an imagemap to be interpreted either by the end user's software or by the server by including the ISMAP attribute in the <IMG> tag, then including both a USEMAP= attribute and cgi-bin/imagemap reference.

```
<A HREF="/cgi-bin/imagemap/thisthat">
<IMG SRC="thisthat.gif"
  USEMAP="#thisthat" ISMAP>
</A>
```

Here, as with any unrecognized tag, browsers that don't support client-side image maps will simply ignore the <USEMAP> and <ISMAP> tags and treat the preceding code like an old-fashioned server-side imagemap.

Listing 2.4. HTML for a client-side imagemap.

```
<MAP NAME="thisthat">
<AREA SHAPE="RECT" COORDS="0,0,102,99" HREF="this.htm">
<AREA SHAPE="RECT" COORDS="103,0,205,99" HREF="that.htm">
</MAP>

<-- any amount of HTML could go here -->

<IMG SRC="thisthat.gif" USEMAP="#thisthat">
```

Auto-Loading Pages

When you open the looklook.htm document on the CD-ROM, it displays a background of calm-looking eyes, and the "LOOK" logo flashes a few times (the flashing in this case is done with the LOWSRC tag, discussed in Chapter 1). Then, perhaps to your surprise, the look.htm document loads automatically and displays the LOOK home page, complete with wide-open eyes, even though you didn't click anything.

An auto-loading page can add an aura of magic to your Web site, but you sure don't need to be a magician to create one. It's simply a matter of including a tag like the following between the <HEAD> and </HEAD> tags at the beginning of any Web page:

```
<META HTTP-EQUIV="Refresh" CONTENT="6;
   URL=look.htm">
```

This is a sneaky way to send a message requesting a document, as if the user had entered its address directly. The 6 means "wait six seconds," and the URL=look.htm means load the document named look.htm. You could use any other address of a Web page or other media file, such as http://mysite.com/nextpage.html.

If the Refresh interval specified in the CONTENT attribute of a META tag is zero (0), the next page loads immediately, as soon as the current load is finished.

For most Web authors, that's all you need to know about the META tag to use it. But in case you're wondering how this somewhat cryptic tag actually works, here's the scoop:

What META Actually Does

The contents of the META tag are parsed by the server when the document is loaded, in order to create simulated HTTP response headers (in this case, a header field called foo with the contents bar). This response header is then processed in response to any client's request for the document, just as though the command had been deliberately sent by the client.

For example, the META tag

```
<META HTTP-EQUIV="Published By"
   CONTENT="SAMS.net">
```

would create the following header field:

```
Published by: SAMS.net
```

This header field may then be placed into the document by the server whenever the page is requested (depending upon the server used—not all servers accommodate this functionality).

Note that in order for META information to be handled correctly, the META tag must reside within the HEAD section of the document. This forces it to be parsed and executed *prior* to displaying the page.

By using the META field in various clever ways, you can add a lot of extensibility to your documents. In fact, that's exactly why it was put there. Because any data placed within the HEAD section of a document is parsed and executed before the page is displayed to the user, it's possible to write CGI scripts that make use of your META information and literally decide what to display on-the-fly. (CGI scripts are beyond the scope of this book, but this is a good example of where and how one might be used.)

By stringing together a series of similar pages, each containing a META refresh leading to the next in the series, it is possible to create large sequential structures, such as slideshows or multimedia presentations. This is especially effective when combined with other tricks detailed in these pages, such as audio or video embedding.

What's Next?

I hope this chapter has inspired you to be more creative than you thought you could with the HTML in your Web pages. And all the tricks in this chapter will give even more "oomph" to pages that also include the new media types covered in the rest of this book.

Before we launch into the hard-core and high-bandwidth world of serious Internet multimedia in Part II of the book, Chapter 3 will introduce you to some easier, more compatible, and less demanding ways to start putting some action into your site.

Tip: The document loaded with a META refresh does not have to be an HTML file; it can be anything at all, including any sort of media file. After the designated Refresh interval has passed, the client will fire up the appropriate helper app to display the file while the browser keeps doing its own thing in the background.

Since most viewers/players possess a Save or Save As feature, the user can keep a copy of the file by using the helper app. This could even be used to give a file to people who are unaccustomed to the Web. You might want to remind them to disconnect when they're through, however!

by Dick Oliver

Animation the Easy Way: Multi-Image GIFs

There are several ways to add some movement to a Web page. You could hire a programmer or spend a few months learning the Java language. You could use a pre-built applet or OLE component to play some sort of video or interactive media file. Or you could ask all the visitors to your Web site to go get a helper application or plug-in program to play your favorite media file format. All of these can be excellent solutions in many situations, but every one of them involves an investment of time and resources, even before you start to produce the animation itself.

Wouldn't it be nice if you could just "snap together" three or four GIF images to make a simple animated graphic, without having to deal with any extra software components or media viewers at all? And wouldn't it be great if people using older Web browsers automatically could see at least the first frame of your animation, without your having to do any extra coding or producing additional graphics files? And while we're wishing, how about an animation format that can save a cool animated icon in a 20KB or smaller file?

Believe it or not, these Utopian dreams have already become a reality. In fact, multiframe animation was built into the GIF file format way back in 1989. The compression is very efficient, and it's almost shamefully easy to make GIF animations. Every user of Netscape Navigator 2.0 and Microsoft Internet Explorer 3.0 (which means the vast majority of Internet surfers) can see animated GIFs without any additional software or add-ons. You can include these animations in a Web page exactly as if they were "ordinary" GIFs, with the <IMG> tag. Most browsers will support GIF animation in their next releases, but in the meantime, users of browsers other than Navigator or Explorer will always just see the first image in the animation.

Ease of creation and use makes GIF animations a great choice for simple animated icons and any Web page graphics that could use a little motion to spice them up. In this chapter you'll learn how to create GIF animations and how to optimize them for the fastest possible display.

Building a GIF Animation

The CD-ROM accompanying this book includes an evaluation copy of Alchemy Mindworks' GIF Construction Set, a nifty little utility designed especially for assembling multi-image GIFs.

The first step in creating a GIF animation is to create a series of images to be displayed one after the other. You can use any graphics software you like to make the images. You don't even need to use software that supports GIF to make the images; GIF Construction Set can import BMP, JPEG, PCX, TIFF, and almost any other graphics file format you throw at it.

The following numbered steps show you how to make a simple GIF animation. This animation will flip back and forth between two "LOOK" logo images, which you saw in

the look.htm document discussed in Chapter 2, "Wild Type, Far-Out Layouts, and Cheap HTML Tricks." (I created these images in Paint Shop Pro, which is also discussed in Chapter 2.)

1. Before you assemble an animation with GIF Construction Set, you may want to open the images you want to include within another graphics program, so you can refer to them as you put the animation together. Figure 3.1 shows the two images for this example open in Paint Shop Pro, with the GIF Construction Set program in the foreground.

2. To start a new animation, start GIF Construction Set and select File ¦ New. "HEADER GIF 89a Screen (640×480)" should appear at the top of the white area. This is the first "block" in the GIF file, and you will be adding additional image blocks and control blocks that will be listed below this one.

3. Click the Edit button, and the dialog box in Figure 3.1 appears. Enter the screen width and depth (height) of the largest image you want to use in the animation, and click OK. (Not sure how big your images are? Paint Shop Pro displays the width and depth of the current image at the lower-left corner of the screen.)

4. If you want the animation to loop continuously when viewed in Netscape Navigator, click on the Insert button and then click on Loop. This inserts a special control block that only Netscape Navigator recognizes, telling it to immediately

restart the animation every time it finishes. If you want to create an animation that plays only once and then stops (leaving the last image on display), skip this step.

5. Click Insert ¦ Image and choose the first image in the animation as shown in Figure 3.2. This is also the image that will be displayed by browsers that don't support GIF animation. If you want to go along with this example, select the `lookclr.gif` image in the `/look` directory of the CD-ROM.

6. A dialog box will appear saying "The palette of the image you have imported does not match the global palette for this file." Later in this chapter, I'll explain in detail the options also included in this dialog, but for now, choose "Use a local palette for this image" and click OK.

Figure 3.1. GIF Construction Set runs in a fairly small window, allowing you to see other applications— such as Paint Shop Pro—at the same time. Here, the Edit Header dialog displays information.

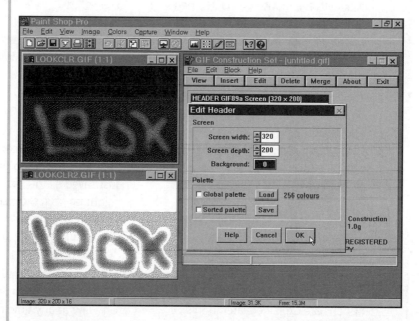

Note: GIF Construction Set is what Steven William Rimmer (its author) calls "bookware." That is, if you continue to use the program after trying it out, he asks you to "register" it by buying his latest novel, *The Order,* from a bookstore and then entering some information from the book into the GIF Construction Set registration screen.

Once you create an animation for a Web page with GIF Construction Set, I'm sure you'll agree that it's well worth the cost of a paperback novel, times 10. So go buy Steve's book—and while you're at it, why not take a break from the computer for a while and read it?

Figure 3.2.
Even in Windows
95, GIF Construc-
tion Set uses a
Windows 3.x–
style file selection
box. Tsk, tsk.
(But then again,
who really
cares?)

8. Repeat steps 5 through 7 for every image in the animation. Remember that the control block for an image has to occur *before* the image block. But you need to insert the image first and then go back to edit the control block to add transparency.

   (A little confusing? Don't worry, you'll be an old pro at it by the end of this chapter. And in the meantime, if you make a mistake, you can highlight any block and click on Delete to get rid of it.)

7. If you want the image you just inserted to be transparent, you need to press the up arrow once or click with the mouse on LOOP, then click on Insert ¦ Control. This inserts a control block in front of the image.

   Then click Edit to get the Edit Control Block dialog box shown in Figure 3.3. Check Transparent colour, and then click the little eyedropper icon button. The image is displayed, and the cursor turns to an eyedropper. Click the tip of the eyedropper on the color you want to be transparent when the image is displayed.

   Before you click on OK, be sure to select Background under the Remove by selection list. (The other options are explained later in this chapter.)

9. When all the images and control blocks are inserted in the right order, select File ¦ Save as to save the animation (see Figure 3.4). Be sure to give it a name ending in `.gif`!

10. Using your favorite Web page editor, make an HTML document with an `IMG` tag referring to the `.gif` file you just saved as the `SRC`. (A sample tag might be `<IMG SRC="lookani.gif">`.) Load the document in Netscape Navigator version 2.0 or higher to see the results.

    You can also preview the animation in GIF Construction Set by clicking on View at any time during the construction process.

I obviously can't illustrate the animation effect of flipping back and forth between two images with a printed figure in a book. But you can load the `/look/look.htm` document on the CD-ROM if you'd like to see the action.

Figure 3.3.
Control blocks
enable you to
make images
transparent or
insert a time
delay between
images.

*Figure 3.4.
Save your file
with the .gif
extension.*

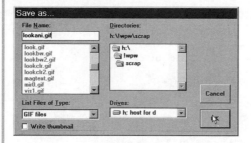

Navigator, you noticed that all the icons are animated; a vision appears in the crystal ball, the scepter flashes, the cauldron bubbles, the mirror revolves, the book pages turn. These icons are actually five separate multi-image GIFs, and the HTML code for this snazzy action-filled page (see Listing 3.1) looks just like an ordinary static Web page.

GIF Animation Tips and Tricks

If you've fired up the *Web Page Wizardry* CD-ROM at all, you've probably seen the home page in Figures 3.5 through 3.7 (called `home.htm` in the main root directory folder on the CD). If you have used Netscape

Note: If this were a page on the Internet instead of a CD-ROM, I would have included ALT attributes so that users of very old browsers or very slow modems would see some text without having to wait for the graphics to download.

*Figure 3.5.
At first glance,
and to non-
Netscape users,
this looks like a
page full of
regular GIF
images.*

Listing 3.1. The Web Page Wizardry CD-ROM Home Page (`home.htm`).

```
<HTML>
<HEAD><TITLE>Web Page Wizardry</TITLE></HEAD>
<BODY BACKGROUND="bubsmoke.jpg" BGCOLOR="black">
<CENTER>
<IMG SRC="wpwtitle.gif" LOWSRC="hat.gif"><P>

<A HREF="visions.htm"><IMG SRC="visions.gif" BORDER=0></A>
<A HREF="programs.htm"><IMG SRC="programs.gif" BORDER=0></A>
 <IMG SRC="spacer.gif"><IMG SRC="spacer.gif">
<A HREF="brews.htm"><IMG SRC="brews.gif" BORDER=0></A>
 <IMG SRC="spacer.gif"><IMG SRC="spacer.gif">
<A HREF="worlds.htm"><IMG SRC="worlds.gif" ALIGN="absmiddle" BORDER=0></A>
<A HREF="pages.htm"><IMG SRC="pages.gif" BORDER=0></A><BR>

<A HREF="visions.htm"><IMG SRC="vistext.gif" BORDER=0></A>
<A HREF="programs.htm"><IMG SRC="prgtext.gif" BORDER=0></A>
<A HREF="brews.htm"><IMG SRC="brwtext.gif" BORDER=0></A>
<A HREF="worlds.htm"><IMG SRC="wrltext.gif" BORDER=0></A>
<A HREF="pages.htm"><IMG SRC="pagtext.gif" BORDER=0></A>
</CENTER>
</BODY>
</HTML>
```

Figure 3.6. Users of Netscape, however, will quickly notice that all the GIFs are actually multi-image animations.

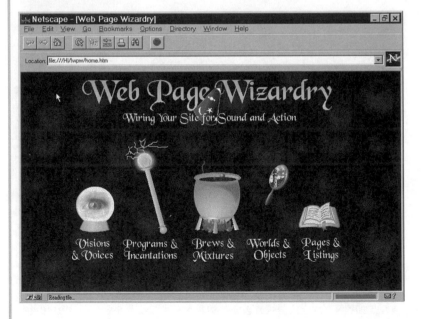

A Hand-Crafted Animation

Someone could probably do a pretty good job creating all these animations in Paint Shop Pro or another shareware graphics program, but I decided to bring in the heavy artillery and create them in Adobe Photoshop instead. Not only does Photoshop offer more advanced drawing and coloring tools, but more importantly, it lets you keep various parts of an image in separate layers that you can modify independently. This feature (which is also found in a number of other commercial graphics editors) makes drawing simple animations a breeze.

Take the spell book that flips its own pages, for example. I just sketched the first image from scratch, and then drew five views of the turning page on separate layers, as shown in Figure 3.8.

Once I'd drawn all the pages, I turned on each layer one at a time (keeping the book and background layers always on), and used Photoshop's File ¦ Save a copy command to save each view as a separate true-color BMP file.

Figure 3.7. Netscape gracefully handles the logistics of displaying five separate GIF animations all at once.

Tip: If you're wondering how I did that rotating mirror within Photoshop, I didn't. I used a modeling program (Arena Design, included in the CD-ROM with this book) to build a 3D model of the mirror and a keyframe animation of it rotating. Then I brought the images from that animation into Photoshop to add the magic window through which you can see the castle.

You'll find out more about creating 3D models in Part III of this book, "A World of Your Own: Virtual Reality." Though the emphasis there is on interactive VRML plug-ins, remember that you can use still images and animations of the 3D objects and worlds you build for regular Web page graphics, too!

Figure 3.8.
Photoshop
makes it easy to
build animations
because you can
draw just the
changes from
frame to frame
and use
transparency to
show or hide
them at will.

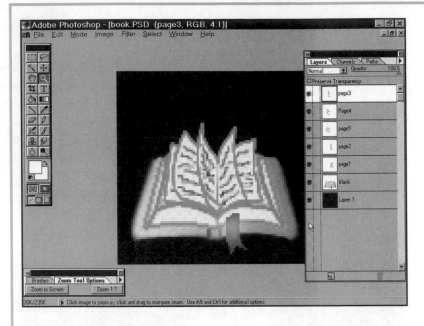

Handling Palettes

I knew that GIF Construction Set would be able to import the BMP files and dither them down to 256 colors. However, I also knew that I would get the best results by giving GIF Construction Set one file that was already dithered to 256 colors, so that it could use that file's colors as the global palette to which all other files in the animation could be matched. So I used Photoshop's Mode ¦ Index Color command to change the first image in the sequence (the book with flat pages) to 256 colors and saved that in the GIF format.

Next, I fired up GIF Construction Set, and assembled the images as explained in the step-by-step example earlier in this chapter.

The only difference between this and the earlier example is in how I handled that global palette and the dithering of the imported BMP files. For the first image in the GIF, I inserted the 256-color GIF file and chose "Use this image as the global palette," as shown in Figure 3.9. For all other images, I inserted the true-color BMP files and chose "Dither this image to the global palette," as in Figure 3.10.

Tip:

You may recall that Uncle Oliver implored you: "Don't dither!" in a previous chapter. In this case, he broke his own rule because the subtle gradations of color in these images look a lot better when dithered, and he was willing to put up with slightly larger file sizes on a CD-ROM than he might tolerate on the Internet.

But do like I say, not like I do: For most situations, you should use a nearest color algorithm in your favorite graphics program to change all images to 256 colors before bringing them into GIF Construction Set, and then choose "Remap this image to the global palette" when importing them, rather than "Dither this image to the global palette." They might not look quite as pretty, but they'll often come out a lot smaller and faster.

On the other hand, when you need the absolute best possible quality and don't care so much about size or speed, you have the option of using a separate optimized palette of colors for each image. To do this, you would choose "Use a local palette for this image" when you insert each image.

Tips on Transparency

As demonstrated in the earlier "LOOK" example, you can make the background transparent by inserting a control block in front of each image and choosing Transparent colour and Remove by Background when you edit the control block (see Figure 3.11). You can use the eyedropper tool (mentioned earlier) to pick the transparent color, or you can click on the number next to it to pick the color from the global or local palette itself (see Figure 3.12).

To make sure you pick the right color to be transparent, you can click on the View button to preview the animation. Note that the background color used during the preview can be set by selecting File ¦ Setup and picking a color from the "Edit view mode background" picklist (see Figure 3.13). You may want to choose a contrasting color (in this example, white or gray) to check the transparency value, and then choose a color similar to your Web page background (in this example, black) to see what the animation will actually look like on the page.

*Figure 3.9.
For at least one image in your animation (usually the first one), you should select "Use this image as the global palette" after you insert the image.*

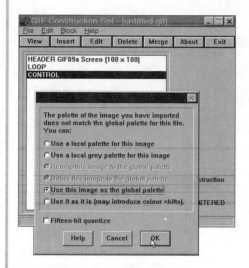

*Figure 3.10.
Once you have a global palette from one image, you can reduce file size and improve display speed by remapping or dithering all other images to that palette.*

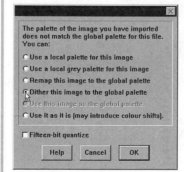

Tip: Notice that the Setup dialog box also includes some controls to fine-tune the dithering of true-color images. You'll probably never need these, but if you're not happy with the results of a dithered image, here's where you should go to fuss and fiddle with it.

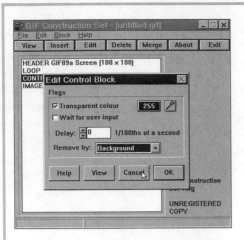

Figure 3.11.
If you want the
animation to
have a
transparent
color, insert and
edit a control
block before
each image.

Doing the Loop

In the first example in this chapter, I mentioned that you can make an animation loop continuously by clicking on Insert ¦ Loop. However, there's one more thing you need to know to create a successful looped animation, and it isn't at all obvious. Because of the way that Netscape Navigator processes and displays multi-image GIF files, you will often find that the first frame of a looping animation is skipped or only half displayed, making a noticeable jerk or some other subtle-but-annoying effect.

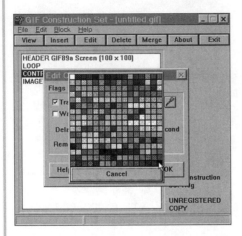

Figure 3.12.
To pull up this
color-picking
palette, click the
number next to
the eyedropper
tool (255 in
Figure 3.11).

The way to avoid this is to always repeat the first image at the end of the animation, too. Then the "jerk" becomes invisible because it occurs between two identical images. For example, Figure 3.14 shows the complete `pages.gif` animation. This actually contains only six separate images—the seventh one is a repeat of the first.

Repeating the first image does increase the size of the GIF file, and you may be willing to tolerate a little jerkiness to keep the size down. Also, in some animations, such as the "LOOK" logo example, you'd never notice or care about the jerk anyway. So, it's a good idea to try the animation without the first image repeat to see if you're happy with the results. If you are, there's no reason to make the file bigger by repeating that first image.

Figure 3.13.
The File ¦ Setup
dialog box lets
you choose a
preview
background color
and fine tune
some other picky
stuff.

Tip: One more tip on looping: If you highlight the LOOP block and click the Edit button, you can set a number of iterations for the animation to repeat before stopping. As far as I can tell, this doesn't actually work in the current version of Netscape Navigator, but it's supposed to, so they'll probably fix it in the next version of Netscape and other new browsers. Then you'll be able to have an animation that repeats, say, three times, and then stops.

One reason this will be useful is because auto-loading pages (with the `META HTTP-EQUIV="Refresh"` tag) won't do anything until all images are finished loading, and infinitely looping GIFs *never* finish loading!

Figure 3.14. For smooth animation, it often helps to make the first and last images identical.

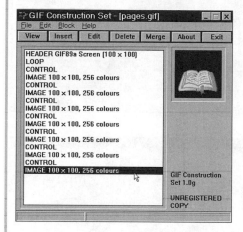

Optimizing GIF Animations for Speed and Size

There are two ways to improve the speed and reduce the size of GIF animations. One is to save only the part of the image that actually changes from one frame to the next, and insert this smaller GIF file instead of an entire replacement of the whole image. The other way is to make any part of the image that doesn't change transparent. This can also dramatically reduce the size of the file because a solid region of transparency will compress much more efficiently

than the same region filled with complex image data.

The most impressive application of these techniques would be an animation where a small moving character or object is superimposed over a complex backdrop. You could save the backdrop only once as the first image, and then insert only the images of the small changing region for subsequent images. This can easily reduce the size of the animation file by a factor of 10 or more.

I'll use a less dramatic example, though, where we'll actually only shave about 6KB off a 26KB animation file. It should be quite clear how to apply the same technique to a larger file.

Cropping the Crystal

Like the spell book, the crystal ball animation was created as a number of separate image layers in Photoshop (see Figure 3.15). Instead of saving each frame in the animation as a layer, though, in this case I used the opacity slider to vary the transparency effects between layers as I swirled the "fog" layer around with the smudge brush.

However, only the first image of the series was saved in its entirety. I cropped off the bottom part (including the gold stand) of all the other images. Figure 3.16 shows the five images used to build the animation. (I actually did the cropping in Paint Shop Pro, even though I could have done it right in Photoshop.) Note that these include a cropped copy of the first image to put at the end of the animation.

*Figure 3.15.
The crystal ball
animation was
created by
varying the
opacity of the
layers in a
Photoshop
image.*

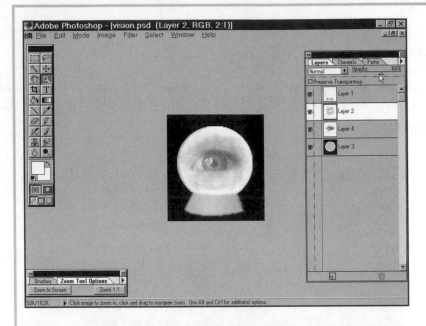

*Figure 3.16.
To make the file
sizes smaller, I
stored only the
part of the
animation that
changes from
frame to frame.*

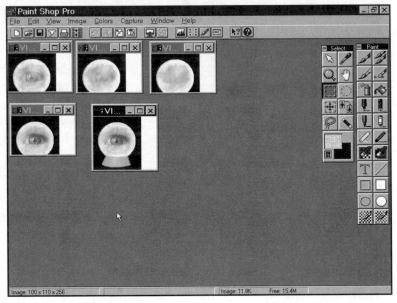

When I assembled these images in GIF Construction Set, I set each Control block to Remove by Previous Image instead of Remove by Background (see Figure 3.17). This keeps the previous image visible under any transparent areas—or areas not covered by the current image, if the current image is smaller than any of the previous ones. This way, the gold stand from the first image remains unchanged when the smaller cropped frames are displayed.

You may also notice in Figure 3.17 that I specified a Delay of 20/100 (or 1/5) of a second between animation frames. This slows the animation down enough so that the foggy haze seems to drift in and out, rather than snap back and forth like someone changing TV channels.

Figure 3.17. By setting each Control Block to Remove by Previous Image, you can leave parts of a previously displayed frame visible.

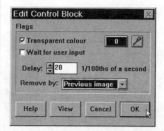

Emptying the Pot

The largest animation on the *Web Page Wizardry* home page is the bubbling cauldron. Because the big fat pot had to be dithered for the shading to look good, the animation weighs in at over 40KB—about twice as large as the other multi-image GIFs on the page.

There's a sneaky way to cut that file size almost in half. In Figure 3.19, I placed a blue rectangle over the unchanging (and biggest) part of each image except for the first one. Then when I pulled these images into GIF Construction Set, I set that blue to be transparent and chose Remove by Previous Image, as I did for the crystal ball images.

Unfortunately, this sneaky stunt only works if you don't need to use the transparency for letting the background of a Web page show around the edges of an image. (If I used the same black to block out the pot as I used for the background around the top and bottom, parts of the steam, bubbles, and fire would not get erased properly between frames.)

Tip: You can control where a smaller image appears over a larger one by highlighting the image block and clicking Edit (see Figure 3.18). In this example, both the Image left (horizontal offset) and Image top (vertical offset) values are 0, meaning that the top-left corner of the image should be placed exactly over the top-left corner of the entire animation. However, if you have a small object to place in the middle of a large backdrop, you can adjust these offsets to place the object just where you want it.

Figure 3.18. You can use the Image left and Image top settings to place a smaller image in the middle of a larger one. (Here, no offset is needed so they are both set to 0.)

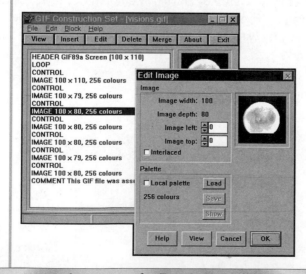

If I were posting this page on the Internet, I would probably choose to use a solid black background on the page so I could use the optimized Remove by Previous Image version of this animation (26KB) instead of the fully transparent Remove by Background version (40KB). But since this is for a CD-ROM, I splurged and went with the fancy background and the 40KB image. Even with this move of reckless abandon, all the animations on the page still only add up to 120KB, which is smaller than the static graphics on many Web pages these days.

What's Next?

This chapter has given you a very easy and highly efficient way to add simple animation to your Web pages. Part II, "Five Million Channels: Multimedia Over the Net," brings out the big toys and lets you play with sound, video, and interactive media for the Web.

Five Million Channels: Multimedia Over the Net

part **II**

Putting Multimedia on Your Web Pages

chapter 4

by Tod Foley
and Dick Oliver

For better or for worse, multimedia has come to the Web—and in a big way. In the last year, dozens of new formats for the compression or streaming transmission of audio and video data have been released publicly or incorporated into widely distributed software products. Meanwhile, the HTML Specification has evolved so quickly that two variant forms—each with its own strong and weak suits regarding multimedia content—have advanced well beyond the canonical version overseen by the Internet Engineering Task Force and the World Wide Web Consortium. In 1996 the trend seems to be picking up speed, as developer after developer rushes to lay claim to that most elusive of all digital media titles: "The Industry Standard."

The new wave of World Wide Web applications is providing multimedia developers and content creators with more bells, whistles, gongs, and interactive design options than ever possible before. The question is no longer "Can I add multimedia to my Web site?" but rather "Which tools are best for the specific type of multimedia experience I'm envisioning?" There are also many tools to choose from. This chapter provides you with a solid understanding of how to make your way through this minefield of choices, and add multimedia content to your Web pages.

Content First

Obviously, before you can place *anything* on your Web page, you first have to obtain it—or create it from scratch.

Creating multimedia of any kind is a challenging and complicated task—one which is made no easier by the fact that the very tools used in its creation are constantly changing. If you're planning to create your own content from scratch you might want to consider skipping ahead to Chapter 5, "Creating Online Audio," Chapter 6, "Do-It-Yourself Digital Video," or Chapter 7, "Creating Interactive Animation with Shockwave and Friends," right now. There you will find detailed information regarding the creation and formatting of your content. You can return to this point when you're ready to begin looking at how to place your new creations into your Web pages.

For those of us who are artistically challenged, a number of alternative ways to obtain useful multimedia assets is available. Aside from the obvious ("hire an artist"), here are a few suggestions:

✦ Stock Media

The Web itself is chock-full of useful content in all media types, and stock media clearinghouses of all shapes and sizes now exist online. At these places, you can find all the sounds, music, textures, video, and 3D models you need; just name it. Of course, prices can vary greatly from one clearinghouse to the next, so be sure to shop around. See the hotlist on the CD-ROM for links to some of the best stock media sources on the Web.

✦ Free for All

Don't feel like spending any money? Much of the material on the Internet is deliberately "anti-copyrighted" or has reverted to the public domain.

Note:
It's still a good idea to double-check with the accredited author or current owner of the content; you don't want to get sued for copyright infringement. In addition, various offices of the U.S. government have spent a good deal of time and money generating content which, by law, belongs to all Americans (any NASA footage found online, for instance); these assets are free for you to use. Consult your favorite search engine or the hotlist on the CD-ROM.

✦ Bartering for Art: A win-win situation

Want to show video on your site? Go find some videographers. Hang out in camera stores, leave a flyer on the school bulletin board, or (easiest of all) check out the online forums and Usenet newsgroups that cater to the interests of videographers. As clearly as possible, describe your site and what you want to do with it and offer to trade Web page coding or other services for permission to use art. Chances are you'll find a few up-and-coming artists who'd be more than happy to let thousands of people peruse their work online.

For the examples in this chapter, I created a Web page allowing hungry Web surfers a chance to preview the daily menu for a (fictitious) seafood restaurant. A picture of a lobster was morphed with Photomorph 2 to create a short video (see Figure 4.1). we then recorded and mixed a voice-over with Goldwave (see Figure 4.2), with some music by a friend (Dana Robinson) in the background. Finally, the sound and video were combined, clipped, and compressed with Video Action ED (see Figure 4.3).

Goldwave and Video Action ED are included on the CD-ROM with this book (Windows Sound Recorder is included with Microsoft Windows). The quality of the end result (which you can see in /downeast/ downeast.htm on the CD-ROM) isn't great, but it's about as good as anything on the Web that you can reasonably play back over a 28.8Kbps or slower modem. The point is that you don't need to own a multi-million-dollar production studio to create multimedia that looks and sounds as good as you can expect within the bandwidth restrictions of today's Web.

For more details on producing and optimizing multimedia content with free and inexpensive tools, refer to Chapter 5 and Chapter 6.

Figure 4.1. Photomorph 2 makes it easy to create interesting videos from still images.

Figure 4.2.
Any sound card
and microphone,
combined with
the Goldwave
shareware on the
Web Page
Wizardry CD-
ROM, can be
used to record
Internet-quality
audio.

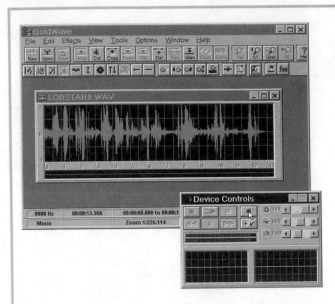

Streaming Over the Web

In the past, browsers have been limited to prerecorded and canned sequences, retrieved as full files. Video and audio files took minutes and sometimes hours to retrieve, thus severely limiting the inclusion of video and audio. The goal that everyone is moving toward is the creation of video that will be small enough to "stream" over the web.

This is to say that you will not have to completely download the clip before you can start to watch it. *Streaming* video or audio will play in real time while the data is being received.

Figure 4.3.
The CD-ROM
also includes a
complete audio/
video editor
program, Video
Action ED. Now
you have no
excuse not to
hop aboard the
multimedia
bandwagon!

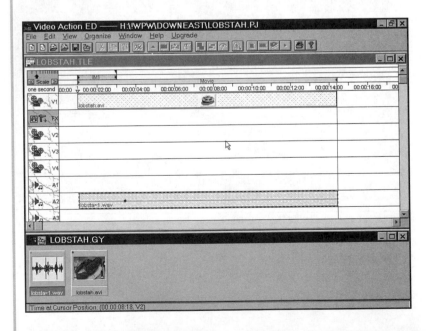

The real-time transfer of video data streams introduces new problems of maintaining adequate playback quality in the face of network congestion and client load. Nevertheless, a large number of companies are making streaming video a reality with varying levels of success.

MPEG-1 is emerging as the video file format standard because it produces video files that are typically 1/4 the size of other video formats. Unfortunately, MPEG is not currently supported by QuickTime, so at present most of the streaming video technologies are limited to PC users.

A number of packages are cross-platform at present, but they require special server software that is out of the price range of most individual users. By the time you read this, however, Apple is promising a beta release of QuickTime 2.5, and a number of other companies are also planning products to serve and receive streaming MPEG over normal modem lines. For late-breaking news on this promising development, keep your eye (and ear) on the multimedia news sites listed in Appendix C, "Online Resources and Cutting-Edge Web Sites," and the corresponding live hotlist on the *Web Page Wizardry* CD-ROM.

Meanwhile, streaming playback is now widely supported for Windows AVI and WAV files through Microsoft Internet Explorer 3.0's built-in features and Netscape Navigator 2.0 plug-ins. The examples in this chapter use these media types to demonstrate both streaming and the old-fashioned download-and-play methods of delivering audiovisual media.

Laying It Inline

When it comes to placing audio, video, and animation (as well as any other sort of data you might want to send to a browser) in your Web pages, these media are not that different at all. In fact, as far as standard HTML is concerned, the only difference between one kind of file and another is the corresponding *media type*, which is indicated by the file extension (the three or four letters following the dot at the end of the filename). Given this significant piece of information (and, of course, the data in the file itself), the browser will marshal its helpers or plug-ins to handle everything as seamlessly as possible.

The tag you use to place a file into your Web page will determine how (and if) it responds when browsed. There are a couple of things you'll have to consider when doing this—namely, which browsers you intend to serve best, and whether or not you're going to stick to the authorized, "official" HTML Spec (which is specifically designed to minimize incompatibilities and display errors among all known browsers).

In the following discussion, I demonstrate how to embed video and sound into your Web pages so that users of all major browsers can enjoy the multimedia experience.

The Public IMG

You are by now familiar with the function of the IMG tag, which is used to incorporate inline graphics (which are displayed directly "in" the page, as opposed to within the window of an external viewer). As of this writing, the IMG tag as implemented by Netscape Navigator 2.0 recognizes only GIF or JPG formats, but Microsoft Internet Explorer 3.0 allows you to include BMP images and—more significantly—AVI videos and three-dimensional VRML worlds.

Figure 4.4 shows an AVI video clip embedded in a Web page in Microsoft Internet Explorer 3.0. (The reason the interface looks a little different than your copy of Explorer 3.0 is that this screen shot was taken with a prerelease, alpha-test copy.)

The HTML code to include the video can be as simple as:

```
<IMG DYNSRC="lobstah.avi" WIDTH=160
  HEIGHT=120>
```

The DYNSRC stands for *dynamic source*, and tells Explorer that this is a motion video file instead of just a still SRC image.

If you include both SRC and DYNSRC attributes in an IMG tag, then older browsers that don't support DYNSRC will simply display the SRC image instead. This is a very painless way to ensure backward compatibility!

Two more new attributes can be used along with DYNSRC in an IMG tag, too. CONTROLS causes a set of controls to be displayed beneath the video clip. LOOP=INFINITE makes the video automatically repeat forever, while LOOP=*n* plays the video *n* times and then stops (for example, LOOP=3 would play three times). Naturally, you can also use any of the standard IMG attributes, such as ALIGN, BORDER, and so on.

To add icing to the cake, the file specified with DYNSRC= can be a virtual reality (VRML) world instead of a video, if you wish. Refer to Chapter 8, "The World Wide Web Isn't Flat" and Chapter 15, "The High-Bandwidth Site of the Future," for examples.

Note: As of version 2.0, Netscape Navigator does not yet support the DYNSRC attribute. You'll see how to handle embedded video for Netscape later in this chapter.

Figure 4.4.
The lobster looks like an ordinary image when printed in this book, but if you open /downeast/ downeast.htm on the CD-ROM, you'll see that it's actually a short video.

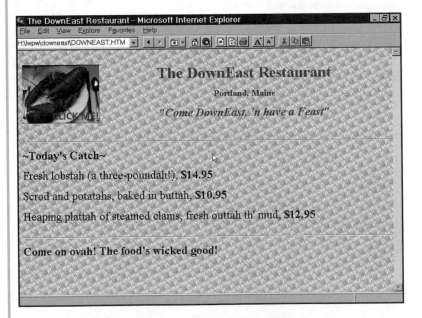

Link-and-Load

Of course, the *real* way to achieve a "click-and-download" effect is to make a link to it—simply place the filename in an Anchor tag with an HREF, as shown in this line:

```
<A HREF="/WINDOWS/MEDIA/CANYON.MID">
  Click Here to Download</A>
```

This way, of course, the associated helper program is triggered as soon as the file has finished downloading, and executes the file (in the preceding example, for instance, the MIDI helper would fire up and play CANYON). If no helper program has been specified under General Preferences (in Netscape) or the Windows Associations (in Explorer), your browser will ask if you wish to save the file.

To make the lobster video in the DownEast Restaurant sample page available to users who don't have Internet Explorer 3.0, you could enclose the IMG tag with an ordinary A HREF link, and perhaps include the words "Click me!" or something similar in the SRC image; for example,

```
<A HREF="lobstah.avi">
<IMG DYNSRC="lobstah2.avi"
SRC="lobstah.jpg" WIDTH=160 HEIGHT=120>
</A>
```

Figure 4.5 shows the result of an Internet Explorer 2.0 user clicking on the lobstah.jpg image; a separate AVI window appears, and plays back the video. Users of other browsers would see whatever AVI viewer their software is configured to use as a helper app, or they would be given the chance to save the AVI file to disk if no viewer is available.

Figure 4.5. Users of older browsers (such as Explorer 2.0, shown here) see a still image, which they can click to download and display the AVI animation. This is exactly the same page as seen with Explorer 3.0 in Figure 4.4 (/downeast/downeast.htm).

Note: Note that DYNSRC begins playing video clips as soon as they begin downloading, but users whose browsers don't support DYNSRC have to wait until the video is completely done downloading before they begin to see it.

Microsoft Background Sounds

Video files embedded with `IMG DYNSRC` can include soundtracks, but Microsoft Internet Explorer also lets you specify a background sound for a page like this:

```
<BGSOUND SRC="lobstah.wav">
```

The background sound may not synchronize exactly with video content on the page, but in situations where that's okay `BGSOUND` can offer several advantages. Not only does the background sound usually start playing sooner than video, but you can include more than one video on the page and use `BGSOUND` to provide a master soundtrack for all of them.

A particularly effective way to reduce the file sizes on your page is to use a short video with the `LOOP` attribute to repeat it several times (or continually), while a longer background sound plays. This was used in the `downeast.htm` example on the CD-ROM to reduce the total multimedia file size for the page from over 500KB (`lobstah.avi`) to less than 200KB (`lobstah8.wav` and `lobstah2.avi`), while keeping the same voice-over and a similar video effect.

To save even more space, you can specify a MIDI music file as the `BGSOUND SRC`. Because MIDI files are usually at least ten times as compact as a WAV file of the same time duration, you can use MIDI to effectively serve quite lengthy soundtracks—even to 14.4Kbps modem users.

Netscape Plug-Ins

With the release of Navigator 2.0 (and another set of Netscape-only HTML enhancements), Netscape browsers can now be extended to handle inline data of any type. This makes for a *seamless* presentation, compared to the original method of making the target app a helper for non-native media types; the non-native data is output *right into* the displayed page, rather than being sent to any external applications or opening more windows.

In order for the seamless presentation to occur, however, the user must have a *plug-in* that recognizes the incoming data type and knows what to do with it. A plug-in is like a helper that is fused into Navigator itself: Rather than executing anything external or launching files from the desktop, it adds a new set of display capabilities directly into the Netscape browser.

The Plug-ins Development Kit, available for free from Netscape, allows developers to create new plug-ins for their own products and data types. For more information, see Netscape's Web site at

```
http://www.netscape.com/comprod/
   development_partners/plugin_api/
   index.html
```

Plug-ins are already available for most common media types, including GIF, JPG, AU, MPEG, MID, EPS, and many more are in the works. Many of the most promising plug-ins make use of special encoding techniques that allow for streaming of massive datafiles (such as high-fidelity audio or video data); this makes for more immediate output and shorter download time, without degrading the quality of the user's experience.

Where to Find Plug-Ins

Netscape maintains a Web page that lists all registered plug-ins and plug-in developers. To check out the current assortment, simply fire up your trusty browser and head out to this site:

```
http://home.netscape.com/comprod
  products/navigator/version_2.0
  plugins/index.html
```

If you're serious about staying up-to-date as far as your plug-in collection is concerned, you'll probably want to stop by this page fairly regularly because new plug-ins are frequently added to the list.

Media Types and Plug-Ins

As mentioned earlier, every media file embedded within an HTML page possesses a media type, which tells the browser how the file should be handled upon receipt (that is, which plug-in or helper app the data should be passed to). Media types are automatically associated with the appropriate files (this is based upon file extensions or the existence of a self-descriptive header within the body of the file itself). The transmission process is fairly transparent while it happens—assuming proper installation, the flow of multiple media formats can be quite seamless.

Unfortunately, the programs used to process these files—plug-ins especially—are still relatively new (even by the youthful standards of the World Wide Web). In realistic terms, this means that many users will have to expend some effort to obtain and install the necessary plug-ins or helper programs before they'll be able to view your media files.

Basically, we're talking about asking your online visitors to undergo the equivalent of a software upgrade. Even though most plug-ins are easy to install and available as freeware (for the time being, at least), this is still something that many people may be reluctant to do. Fortunately, you can do a number of simple things to help make this entire process as painless as possible for your Web guests. Keep these details in mind:

✦ Different systems handle media types differently. The tone and timbre of any note played will differ depending on the hardware involved (both the audio card and the physical speaker). Likewise, the color and quality of video and graphic elements can vary between computers and browsers.

✦ Unassociated files may or may not be visible. Depending on which browser you use, which tag you happen to run across, and what the contents of that tag are, a file that has no helper program (in Netscape's General Options) or association (in Windows systems) may or may not be represented in the rendered page. By definition, the file cannot be literally displayed, so if it is represented at all, it will be by an icon. If an icon is displayed, the user will often be able to download a copy of the file by performing a Save File As.

✦ All required software should be made available. There are few things more frustrating than successfully finding your way to what sounds like a great Web site, only to find that you now need to go chasing plug-ins and helpers all over cyberspace before you'll be able to experience it. It's not very difficult—and it's certainly conscientious—to make the required software available right there on your home page, or to give visitors a link to the home page of the software's developer or publisher.

+ You might need a FAQ or newbies page. The purpose of this page is simply to welcome newcomers to your site and to explain what's going on. As long as the link to the FAQ or newbie page is prominently located near the top of your home page, it will generally function as intended, steering newcomers aside just long enough to give them a clue. This approach is somewhat of a compromise between structure and style, allowing you to make any "initiatory" information available without intruding into the structure of the home page.

+ Give credit where credit is due. This may seem like something of a side point, but it's worth mentioning: If you do make use of someone else's technology on your page, it's only fair (and often legally required) that you credit your source for it.

How EMBED Works and What You Can Do with It

Just when you think you've mastered the last HTML element you'll ever need to know, along comes another set of expansions to the specification. You might as well get used to it—HTML's rapid evolution shows no sign of stopping any time soon. Besides, they wouldn't add a new tag if it weren't a good and necessary thing, right? (Don't answer that question without donning your asbestos longjohns; this is the sort of stuff religious wars are based on....)

While Microsoft opted to add the DYNSRC attribute to the old, familiar IMG tag, Netscape chose instead to introduce an entirely new tag called EMBED.

The EMBED tag enables you to place *any* type of file directly into your Web page, but only for people who have a plug-in or helper app installed and configured to accept the media type you embed. The following line of HTML, for instance,

```
<EMBED SRC="lobstah.avi">
```

would embed a video clip named `lobstah.avi` at the current position on the page, as long as visitors to the page have an AVI-compatible plug-in or helper app. (You'll find out what happens if the user *doesn't* have an AVI viewer shortly.)

Notice that, like the IMG tag, EMBED possesses an SRC attribute, which indicates the URL of the embedded document or application. Also like IMG, the EMBED tag can take ALIGN, WIDTH, and HEIGHT attributes.

The EMBED tag also enables you to set any number of optional parameters in order to pass startup values to the program being called. For instance, the page in Figure 4.6 includes the following:

```
<EMBED SRC="lobstah.avi" WIDTH=160
  HEIGHT=120 ALIGN="left"
  ONCURSOR="play">
```

Note: Netscape Navigator 2.0 did not include a plug-in to view AVI files, so users had to install a third-party plug-in, such as CoolFusion, before they could view video clips. But the Navigator version 3.0 comes preconfigured with a plug-in for AVI files, so most new users of Netscape will be able to see embedded videos without installing any additional software.

The `SRC`, `WIDTH`, `HEIGHT`, and `ALIGN` attributes are interpreted by the browser just as they would be for a still image. However, the actual display of the video is handled by whichever plug-in or helper app each user may have installed.

The `ONCURSOR` parameter is not a standard attribute of the `EMBED` tag, so the browser simply hands it over to the user's plug-in program to interpret. If a user happens to have the CoolFusion AVI viewer plug-in installed, then CoolFusion will interpret the `ONCURSOR="play"` command to mean that whenever the user passes the mouse cursor over the video, it should restart. It is important to know that this parameter is meaningful only to CoolFusion, and that most other plug-ins have their own particular parameters that they can understand. If a user has a different AVI plug-in, or no plug-in at all for handling AVI files, then this parameter will do nothing at all. (Refer to the Web pages of each plug-in developer for information on the commands that a specific plug-in will accept as attributes in the `EMBED` tag.)

Tip: If you want to support two or more popular plug-ins for the same media type that understand different parameters, you can put parameters for each of them in the same `EMBED` tag. Any parameters that aren't meaningful to the particular plug-in a user has installed will simply be ignored.

Figure 4.6. With the appropriate Navigator plug-in installed, AVI files appear on the Web page just as if the plug-in functionality were built into Netscape Navigator.

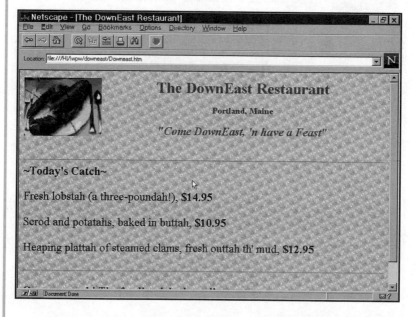

What Can Go Wrong?

EMBED works great when all the visitors to your site have the appropriate plug-in installed. But what will people who don't have the right plug-in see? That depends, unfortunately, on circumstances beyond your control as a Web page publisher.

One thing you can be certain of is this: Users of Microsoft Internet Explorer (and, for now at least, all other browsers besides Netscape) will ignore the EMBED tag completely. However, users of Netscape Navigator 2.0 may see an unsightly puzzle-piece icon and a message saying Plugin Not Loaded, as shown in Figure 4.7. If they click on the Get the Plugin button, they will be taken to a page on Netscape Corporation's Web site explaining how to get and install plug-ins and helper apps (see Figure 4.8).

Experienced Web surfers will probably find it fairly easy to navigate from the links on Netscape's "About the page you've requested" page to the site where the plug-in they need can be downloaded. But many novice users are likely to throw up their hands in confusion, and blame the problem on something they "shouldn't have done." Those people may or may not ever make it back to your Web page. To avoid this confusion, you should provide your own links to any plug-ins that visitors to your site will need, along with an explanation of how to download and install them. This should preferably be done on a home page that will be seen *before* any pages where EMBED tags are used.

Figure 4.7. When no plug-in or helper app can be found to handle an EMBED tag, Netscape Navigator displays this message.

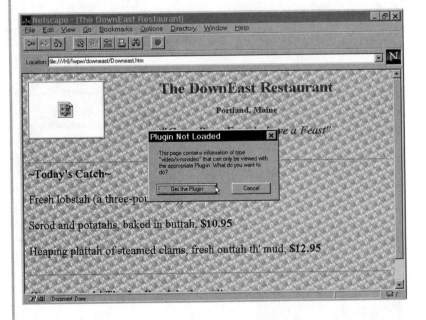

Helper Apps to the Rescue

To thicken the plot, people who already have the software they need to view your EMBED media files may see an even scarier message, announcing boldly "Warning: There is a possible security hazard," which appears in Figure 4.9. What this message really means is that the user has a helper app available on his or her system that can display the media file, and Netscape is about to run it. The alarming tone of the message is very unfortunate because the likelihood of having any security risk is actually no greater than any other time a helper app is invoked or a page is displayed.

Some novice users are sure to become convinced that they must click Cancel or risk having the monitor blow up, but what you really want them to do is click Continue, so they can watch a totally harmless video clip.

Unfortunately, there's really nothing you can do as a Web page author to control whether this message appears, or any of the configuration options discussed in the next few pages. But you should still be aware of what users may see so you can intelligently choose if and when to use the EMBED tag, and what sort of caveats to offer along with your embedded media.

The brave and reckless folk who do click Continue will see the first frame of the video clip (which is all black for the lobstah.avi example shown in Figure 4.10). When they pass the mouse cursor over the image, a message saying "Double-click to activate the embedded Video Clip" (or whatever media type you have embedded) will appear in the message area at the bottom of the Netscape window. Double-clicking as instructed starts the helper app, which will display the media embedded in the document just as if it were a plug-in (see Figure 4.11).

Figure 4.8. Clicking on "Get the Plugin" in Figure 4.7 takes you to this page on Netscape's site.

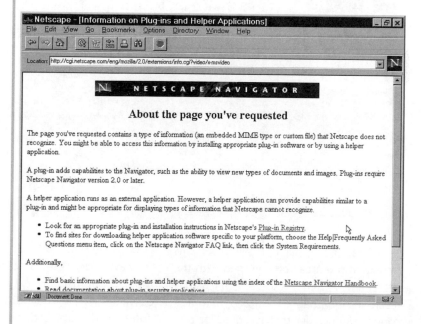

Figure 4.9.
This alarming
message may
appear in
Netscape
Navigator before
users can see
your innocent
media files.

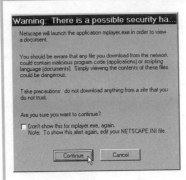

> # Note: Embedded helper apps only work in Windows 95 and Windows NT. They will not function for Macintosh or UNIX users.
>
> Also, you should not confuse this use of Windows Object Linking and Embedding (OLE) with the OLE plug-in controls discussed later in this chapter. Though they do rely on the same underlying software technology, embedded helper apps do not require any sort of Netscape plug-in to function.

Figure 4.10.
Here, the
MPLAYER.EXE
program that
comes with
Windows 95 is
displaying the
first frame of a
video as an
embedded
object.

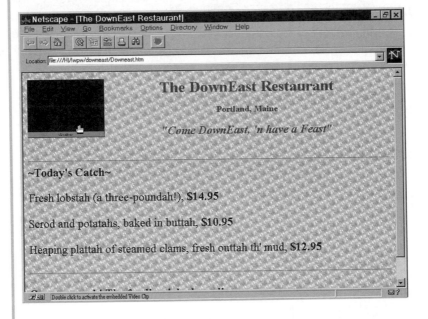

Note that the helper app will restrict its display to the area you specified with the WIDTH and HEIGHT attributes, which may result in squashed or warped output if controls are included that a plug-in wouldn't display (see Figure 4.11). You can avoid this by leaving out the WIDTH and HEIGHT attributes, but then any text or images farther down the page will not be displayed until the entire media file is done downloading—

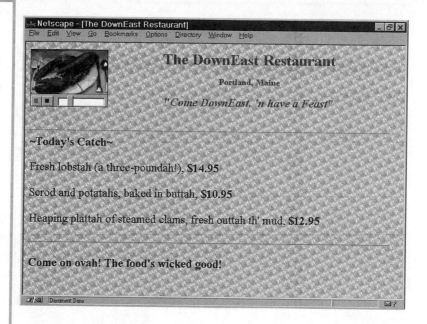

Figure 4.11.
Double-clicking
on the frame in
Figure 4.10 plays
the video, still
embedded in the
Web page.

which might be a long time if you've embedded a big video file!

You may be wondering how Netscape Navigator knows which helper app to invoke to go with each embedded media type. If you guessed that it refers to the helper app list that a user can access by selecting Options ¦ General Preferences ¦ Helpers, you're wrong! Those helper configurations are used only for media linked with an A HREF tag and are ignored for the EMBED tag. Instead, the Windows file type associations registry is used to find the appropriate application to handle the embedded media type.

Figure 4.12 shows how to edit the Windows 95 associations to control which embedded helper app will get which file types.

1. Start Windows Explorer (or Windows Internet Explorer), and select View ¦ Options.

2. Click on the File Types tab, and choose the file type you want to configure from the scrolling list.

3. Click the Edit button, and you will be able to choose the MIME Content Type and Default Extension for this file type. (Note that the "Confirm open after download" setting here only applies to Microsoft Internet Explorer and has no effect on Netscape Navigator 2.0.)

4. To change which program is invoked for this file type, choose one of the Actions and click on the Edit button. You can then specify the "Application used to perform action," including any parameters you want to have passed to that application.

Be aware that any changes you make here will affect all OLE embedding in any Windows program—not just Netscape Navigator. For example, if you change the application program associated with AVI video files, any AVI video embedded in Microsoft Word documents would be displayed with the new application from then on.

Figure 4.12.
As with all OLE
applications,
Netscape
Navigator uses
the Windows file
types registry to
associate media
types with
applications to
display them.

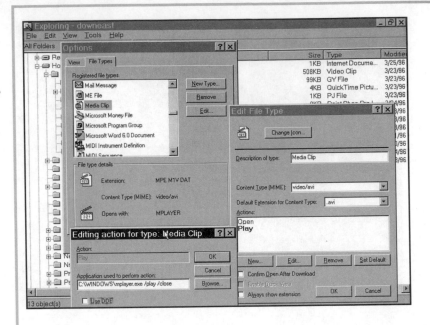

Though multimedia files are an obvious use of embedding, you can actually embed any media type for which a plug-in or OLE application is configured. In Figure 4.13, for instance, a TIF image has been embedded into a Web page and Netscape invoked Paint Shop Pro to display it. (The separate Paint Shop Pro editing window was opened only when I double-clicked on the embedded image.)

The HTML code to embed this TIF was just the same as for any other media type:

```
<EMBED SRC="lobstah.tif">
```

Unfortunately, you as a Web page author have no control over or knowledge of which file types and applications that people who visit your pages will have configured on their computers, or even how many visitors will be using a Microsoft Windows operating system. So the exotic uses of EMBED are probably best left to corporate intranets or other situations where the page publisher has some control over the intended audience's computer setup.

Supporting Non-Netscape Browsers

Because Netscape knew that its browser would be the first (and perhaps only) browser to support the EMBED tag, it created an easy way to provide alternate content for other browsers. Immediately following an EMBED tag, you can specify any amount of HTML code for other browsers, surrounded by NOEMBED (and /NOEMBED) tags. For example, the /downeast/downeast.htm document shown in the figures throughout this chapter contains the following code:

```
<EMBED SRC="lobstah.avi" WIDTH=160
  HEIGHT=120 ALIGN="left"
ONCURSOR="play">
<NOEMBED>
 <BGSOUND SRC="lobstah8.wav">
   <A HREF="lobstah.avi">
    <IMG SRC="lobstah.jpg"
    DYNSRC="lobstah2.avi" LOOP=INFINITE
    WIDTH=160 HEIGHT=120 ALIGN="left"
    BORDER=0>
  </A>
</NOEMBED>
```

Figure 4.13.
When a user
double-clicks on
an embedded TIF
file, the OLE
application
associated with
that file type is
opened.

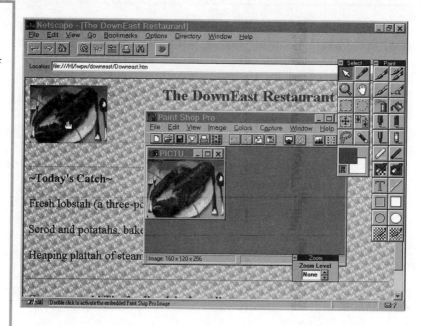

Here's how this will work in various browsers:

+ Netscape Navigator 2.0 sees only the EMBED tag and ignores everything between <NOEMBED> and </NOEMBED>. If the CoolFusion plug-in is installed, it interprets the ONCURSOR="play" command as discussed earlier. Otherwise, whatever plug-in or helper app that Netscape can find to display AVI files is used.

+ Microsoft Internet Explorer 3.0 ignores the EMBED tag and sees the BGSOUND and IMG tags. It plays the lobstah8.wav sound file in the background while it loops the lobstah2.avi video specified in the DYNSRC tag. Note that this is a different video clip than Netscape will play—it contains no sound, and is a shorter clip designed to loop over and over again as the sound plays in the background.

+ Most other browsers see only the IMG SRC attribute and display the lobstah.jpg still image. I added the words "CLICK ME!" to this image so that users with an AVI helper app can click on the image to play the lobstah.avi video clip specified in the A HREF attribute.

+ Netscape Navigator version 1.2 is actually a special problem case because it recognizes the EMBED tag but not the NOEMBED tag. It displays *both* the image specified in IMG SRC *and* an embedded OLE display or, more often, a broken image icon resulting from a failed attempt to display the EMBED tag. This can result in the dreaded Security Hazard message, or in the more innocuous but less hopeful message in Figure 4.14. Although these messages may be bothersome, the essential information on the page is still displayed successfully and clicking

Figure 4.14.
Users of the old
version 1.2 of
Netscape
Navigator may
see some odd
icons or
messages when
they look at
pages intended
for newer
browsers, but
they'll also see
the rest of your
page just fine.

on the "CLICK ME!" image will still launch an AVI helper app if one is available.

Forcing a Download with EMBED

The preceding paragraphs detail the principal uses of the EMBED tag, namely to display inline versions of the specified file, or to allow the user to launch the associated helper program in order to view/play the file. However, EMBED has a tricky side as well: The tag can be used to push just about any common type of file to the user's machine by causing the client to perform what you might call a *forced download*.

The syntax for this function is exactly the same as the typical EMBED tag, including an SRC attribute that refers to the URL of the file you want to send, as shown in this line:

```
<EMBED SRC="filename.zip">
```

There are two major conditionals on the use of EMBED for this purpose. First, it does not work with EXE files (obviously, this would be a major security risk). Second, it will work only as described here if the user has a helper application associated with the media type (file extension) in question. If no helper (or plug-in) exists on the user's machine, all the user receives is an inline picture of the default "dead" icon, indicating that Netscape doesn't know what to do with the file. When working with the more common file types, this stipulation should pose no problem at all; but if the file is of some rare type, it would be necessary to make the associated helper app available before the forced download will work.

This function is useful if you want to send a file automatically on page load (that is, as soon as a Netscape browser displays your page), or if you need to get a file to people who are unfamiliar with ftp and uncomfortable with computers in general. *The user doesn't even have to click on an icon to receive the file*, which will be automatically sent to whatever folder is specified in his or her Temporary Directory settings under General Preferences ¦ Apps.

Another thing that makes this feature so useful is that the source file (on the server) does *not* have to exist within a publicly accessible directory (as would be the case with a typical ftp); embedding the file's URL into your page effectively bypasses this necessity.

Needless to say, this function should be used rarely and responsibly.

Where Things Stand

The EMBED tag has come under fire for a number of reasons, both technical and political. As of this writing, the W3C seems highly unlikely to accept the EMBED tag; in fact, they've even drafted a sort of counterproposal that specifies a new tag called OBJECT (both Netscape and Microsoft were involved in the creation of this second proposal, though it was Microsoft's idea to call the tag OBJECT instead of the originally proposed INSERT). The OBJECT tag will do everything Netscape wants the EMBED tag to do, plus a lot more.

None of this has stopped Netscape from using EMBED as originally proposed. Indeed, the EMBED tag is an integral element of Netscape's current plug-in system, which has already won much support from users and vendors alike. Obviously, the goal for Netscape is to make sure that use of the EMBED tag becomes so common that the WC3 has no alternative but to accept it as an official part of HTML. Netscape has moved quickly and openly toward this goal, and

thanks to the dozens of third-party vendors who've already invested time and money in the creation of plug-ins for embedded media, Netscape may actually stand a chance of getting what it wants.

Microsoft, meanwhile, has decided to stick with the original unfortunately-named IMG tag and has proposed a number of additional attributes that would enable it to be used for embedding sound and AVI files, as explained earlier in this chapter.

Keep your eye on the W3C pages at `http://www.w3.org/pub/WWW/` for more on this topic—the EMBED wars are far from over.

What's Next?

In this chapter, you've seen how to embed video and sound into a Web page. But remember that the EMBED tag can be used to include a vast array of media types besides just Windows AVI and WAV files. Some of these media types are alternative audio and video formats that aim to achieve greater compression, quality, or compatibility than the Windows standard formats. Others, such as Shockwave and QuickTime VR, add a variety of interactive features that old-fashioned audiovisual media types lack.

In Chapter 5, "Creating Online Audio," and Chapter 6, "Do-It-Yourself Digital Video," you'll get some tips and instructions for producing your own clips for use on the Web. Chapter 7, "Interactive Animation with Shockwave and Friends," introduces true interactive multimedia for the Web, with the ever-popular Macromedia Director and a number of other authoring and delivery tools.

Creating Online Audio

Sounds have the power to completely alter the perceived message of the visuals they accompany. If you need to create your own source audio, there are a number of things you should keep in mind: Working with audio can be a tricky task, one made even more confounding by the limitations imposed on content on the Web in order for it to be viewed or heard reasonably over slow connections. The following quick introduction to digital audio should help you better understand how to add sound to your Web pages.

Rates and Sizes

Just as with moving pictures, the quality and convincing nature of a digital audio file is largely dependent on its speed. More precisely, this depends on the distance in time between one "sample" (or one "frame") and the next. In digital audio, this is known as the *sampling rate* and is generally expressed in kiloHertz (kHz). A digital audio device that records or plays back 11,000 samples per second (a fairly poor rate, but adequate for low-end professional audio), is said to operate at 11kHz. If the sampling rate during recording or conversion is too low, the whole thing will sound terrible.

If sampling rate can be likened to the frames of a movie, *sample resolution* might represent the number of colors available for use on the screen. While the sampling rate indicates how often a sample is taken, the sample resolution determines the degree of *detail* with which each sample is recorded; that is, the number of bits dedicated to each sample.

chapter 5

by Tod Foley and
John J. Kottler

Take for instance the ruler that you use to make measurements. Typically you will find inches on the ruler as well as $1/2$, $1/4$, $1/8$ and $1/16$ inches. If you measure the length of a pencil using inches only, you wouldn't get a very accurate measurement. However, if you measure that same pencil using $1/16$ inches, you would get a much more accurate measurement. This is the same case with sampling resolution. The finer the measurements you make (using higher rates), the more accurate the sound recording will be.

Quick Lesson on Digital Audio

A sound wave is much like a water wave; it contains highs and lows, crests and troughs. A sound wave can be recorded by measuring its highs and lows (amplitude) over a series of time. In order to capture sound digitally, an infinite amount of time must be broken into a definite number of points (this is referred to as the sampling frequency or rate). The amplitude of the sound wave at each point in time may then be measured and stored as a digital code. There are additional compression techniques where the differences between actual points on a sound wave and data points predicted mathematically by the compression algorithm are stored. By storing only these differences and not every data point, audio information can be stored using less space.

Sample size is also referred to as *bit depth*. The bit depth of an audio file indicates the number of bits that are grouped together in order to represent the "shape" of each sample. The more bits you use to record something, the more detail and subtlety you catch in your recording. The sample sizes of digital audio files are almost always either 8-bit (as in most multimedia files) or 16-bit (as in CD Audio).

Sampling rate and sample size determine both the subjective quality of the sound and the size of the sound file. For Internet audio, you will almost always want to use the lowest sample rate (8kHz) and sample size (eight bits) available. A CD-quality, 44kHz sample may sound terrific, but just five seconds of speech at this quality takes up over 350KB. Using a 14.4Kbps modem, this little track would take over five minutes to download!

Tip: Here's a general rule of thumb to help you quickly make a ballpark estimate of how big an 8-bit sound sample is. Each second of most music or sound effects produces a file size (in kilobytes) approximately equal to the sample rate (in kiloHertz). For example, a one-second sound sampled at 8kHz is about 8KB. Ten seconds at 16kHz is about 160KB.

Double those estimated file sizes for speech or complex, chaotic sounds. And, of course, double them again if you use 16-bit samples instead of 8-bit.

Of course, this is a general rule for monophonic sound. If you plan on using stereo sound, the size of the file is double what it would be for mono. Digital stereo recordings require that both the left and right audio channels be stored.

Audio File Formats

In the early days of multimedia computers, most machines (such as Apples, IBMs, Tandys, and other IBM clones) possessed their own native audio file formats. Moving audio from one platform to another—especially without loss of sound quality—was a difficult procedure. Soon enough, audio card manufacturers began to develop audio file formats of their own, each with its own specific strengths and weaknesses. As you might expect, this confused the issue even further.

However, in the intervening years, the audio side of multimedia development has stabilized considerably, and a number of cross-platform solutions have found their way into popular acceptance. Today, those with digital audio enjoy a somewhat more stable and standardized set of file formats and protocols than their counterparts in video. It's also fairly easy to locate software utilities that enable you to record, edit, or convert audio files from one format to another. Although sometimes, this process noticeably degrades the quality of the sound.

The most common file formats for digital audio on the Web are `.aiff`, `.au`, `.mid`, `.snd`, and `.wav`. Table 5.1 provides an overview of the strong and weak points of all these common audio formats.

Table 5.1. The five most common audio formats on the Internet.

Audio Interchange File Format (`.aif`, `.aiff`)—The audio file format of choice in the Mac world.
> Media Type: audio/x-aiff
> Native Platform: Apple, SGI
> Sample Size: typically 16-bit (variable from 1-bit to 32-bit)
> Sampling Rate: 16kHz
> Filesize per Minute: 960KB
> Sound Quality: Very good; close to FM radio.

Sun Audio (`.au`)—The native UNIX audio file format.
> Media Type: audio/basic
> Native Platform: NeXT, Sun
> Sample Size: 8-bit
> Sampling Rate: 8kHz
> Filesize per Minute: 480KB
> Sound quality: Fairly good; television/telephone quality.

Musical Instrument Digital Interface (`.mid`, `.midi`)—Protocol for exchanging music notation electronically (known as MIDI).
> Media Type: audio/midi, audio/x-midi
> Native Platform: N/A
> Sample Size: N/A
> Sampling Rate: N/A
> Filesize per Minute: 50KB
> Sound quality: Unpredictable; depends on listener's sound card.

continues

Table 5.1. continued

Macintosh Sound Files (`.snd`)—Nearly identical to `.au` files in performance features.
    Media Type: audio/basic
    Native Platform: Mac, NeXT, Tandy
    Sample Size: 8-bit
    Sampling Rate: 8kHz
    Filesize per Minute: 480KB
    Sound quality: Fairly good; television/telephone quality.

Waveform Audio (`.wav`)—Microsoft Windows native audio format
    Media Type: audio/x-wav
    Native Platform: PC
    Sample Size: 8-bit or 16-bit
    Sampling Rate: 8 to 22kHz
    Filesize per Minute: 480 to 1024KB
    Sound quality: Good to excellent; AM radio to CD quality.

> **Note:** MIDI (Musical Instrument Digital Interface) files are not waveform files and therefore operate differently from any of the other file types listed in Table 5.1. Created and maintained by the International MIDI Manufacturers Association—a coalition of musical instrument manufacturers and electronics firms—MIDI is a protocol that allows information to be exchanged between synthesizers, tone boxes, computers, and other compatible devices. MIDI files don't contain any sounds at all, in the sense that a digital sample such as an `.aiff` or `.wav` file can be said to contain a sound.
>
> Instead, a MIDI file consists of a stream of numbers, each of which corresponds to a specific audio event or attribute, such as voice, pitch, volume, sustain, decay, bend, and so on. Like the screen layout of an HTML document that may be viewed through various browsers, the audible result of a MIDI file's execution is *informed*—but not *dictated*—by its content. For example, some sound cards use extremely high quality digital samples of a real piano, while others synthesize a "piano" sound that resembles a baby duck as much as a baby grand.
>
> Furthermore, some MIDI devices may have a tuba or trombone sound loaded into the channel usually used for piano, so your New Age keyboard improvisation may sound like a brass band tuning up before a parade. Though MIDI sound cards are getting better every year and do generally follow the standard instrument mappings, it can still be difficult to predict exactly how a MIDI file will sound when played on someone else's machine.

Recording and Mixing Internet Audio

Now that you have some familiarity with how digital audio is stored, let's look at how to create some new audio files of your own. To create and edit audio content, you must use an appropriate tool. GoldWave is a program included on the CD-ROM with this book. This software enables you to record, edit, convert, and play digital audio on your Windows 3.x or Windows 95 computer.

After you start GoldWave, you will notice that the program produces two windows. Figure 5.1 demonstrates these two windows. The first window is the Editor window, where graphical representations of sound waves are drawn. In the lower-right corner of your screen, a second Device Controls window presents you with some familiar buttons for controlling the playback or recording process. To begin recording, you must first create a new audio file using the File ¦ New menu option. Choosing this option presents you with a dialog box, prompting you to choose the qualities of the sound you are creating.

Figure 5.1. GoldWave is an audio editing program you can use to record, play, convert, and apply numerous special effects to sound files.

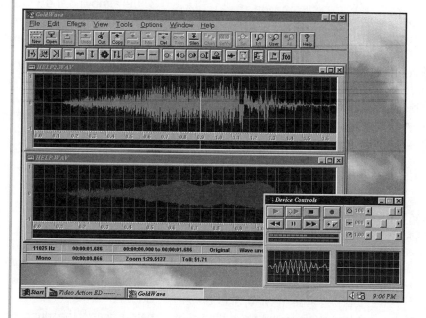

Tip: When creating Internet sound files, remember that the smaller a file is, the better. Unfortunately, as stated earlier, this requires a compromise with the quality of the sound. To minimize file size, consider creating your new sound files as 8-bit, 11kHz, monophonic (not stereo) files. This will add more noise to your sounds, but will significantly decrease the amount of storage space required for the sound file.

After you have created the new sound file, a new window is created in GoldWave's editor window. To record into this window, simply click on the red record button in the Device Controls window. The record button then changes into a purple stop button, and a vertical beam slowly progresses across the length of the new window you created. This beam is the position bar, which indicates how far along in the sound file you have recorded. Once you click on the stop button or once the position bar reaches the end of the file, the recording process stops. Whatever audio you have recorded is then converted to a graphical representation and displays in the Editor window.

Tip: Remember to check the audio settings and connections for your sound card prior to recording. You should make certain that the source you are recording is connected appropriately to the sound card. If you are using a microphone, make sure it is connected to the MIC input. If you are recording from a device, such as an external CD player or stereo, make certain that these devices are connected to the LINE input.

Most sound hardware in computers is accompanied by software for controlling the sound card. Usually, this includes mixer software for controlling the input and output levels of the sound card. Before recording, make sure that these settings are correct so that the correct input device is captured.

You can play, pause, rewind, and forward the contents of the sound file in the Editor window at any time by clicking on the appropriate buttons in the Device Controls window. You will use the play button often to audition the sound that you are creating.

Trimming the Fat

Typically, after you have captured the sound file, you need to alter it in some fashion. Most likely you will need to trim the sound file that you have just recorded. Unless you are extremely coordinated, you often must start the recording process on the computer before actually capturing the audio input. This is necessary to avoid missing the introduction of the audio clip you are attempting to record. However, depending on the length of the pause between clicking on the record button in GoldWave and beginning the audio clip, you may have a considerable amount of silence at the beginning of your audio file. Silence before or after an audio clip in a file is both annoying and wastes valuable space. Therefore, you should immediately trim the audio file you have captured.

In GoldWave, you may specify a region of the audio file by using the mouse. As you pass the mouse cursor over an audio file in GoldWave, the cursor changes into an icon of two arrows pointing toward a vertical bar between them. Place this icon at the front of the sound file where the squiggly line that represents the sound first appears and click the left mouse button.

You can then move the mouse cursor to where all of the squiggly lines stop in your audio file and click the *right* mouse button. After doing so, a range is defined that includes only the sound itself, not the silence before or after the sound. The selected range is indicated by a blue highlight in the window for the sound you are editing.

After you have selected just the sound from a sound file, choose the Edit ¦ Trim command. GoldWave discards all information that is not within the region you defined.

Adding Effects

Ranges that you define in GoldWave are important for other features than simply trimming the sound file. You can think of the highlighted section of the sound file as selecting several words in a word processing program. Any action you perform applies only to the selected region. Therefore, you can copy a section of the entire sound and paste it somewhere else later in the sound file, just as you can with text in a word processor. You may also apply a variety of special effects to the selected region of a sound.

Pump Up the Volume

Let's face it: No matter how hard you try, certain sounds that you record are going to be too quiet. You can tell this because the graphical representation of the sound does not occupy the entire height of the window in which it is drawn. To maximize the amplitude of the sound wave to fill the height of the window (or *normalize* the sound wave), GoldWave offers this feature under the Effects ¦ Volume menu command. Also included are volume commands for fading

in, fading out, changing the overall volume of the sound, or creating custom volume controls over time.

Mix Well

Another common function of sound editing software such as GoldWave is the Mix command. It is possible to take two entirely different sound files and mix them together into one sound file. The result is a single sound file that plays both of the original sounds together, at the same time. For instance, let's assume you would like to mix two sound files included with Windows: `chimes.wav` and `chord.wav`. To mix these two files together, first open the two files in GoldWave. Then select the `chord.wav` window, set the range for the sound file to include the entire sound file, and choose the Edit ¦ Copy command from the menu. With the chord sound in the Clipboard buffer, choose the other window (`chimes.wav`) and then Edit ¦ Mix from the menu. A dialog box appears, asking the volume to use when mixing the files together. A value of 100 indicates that both sounds will be the same volume when played together. Values higher than 100 instruct GoldWave to mix the sound file that is currently in the clipboard so that it is louder than the original file. Likewise, lower values indicate that the content in the Clipboard should be quieter than the original sound file. The Mix command uses the contents of the Clipboard to mix with a sound file. After you have performed the mix, the Clipboard data will remain in the Clipboard for you to paste when desired, although it is not necessary to use the Paste command with the mix effect.

Echo, Flange, and Doppler Effects

GoldWave supports numerous effects that cannot be covered in depth in this section of the book. However, the "Skiing" video example you create in Chapter 6 mixes the sound of a person yelling "Help!" into the video. Two digital audio files are included on the CD-ROM with this book: `help.wav` and `help2.wav`. The first is a simple recording of someone screaming "Help!" The second file is the same audio recording of the word "Help," but after some special effects have been applied. After playing each file, you should be able to quickly distinguish the difference.

The second audio file (`help2.wav`) applies the echo, flange, and Doppler effects to the original sound. The echo effect, as its name implies, adds an artificial echo to the sound. The flange effect, which can make your voice sound like a mechanical robot, was then applied to make the voice file sound more like two people. Finally, the Doppler effect was used to simulate the fall-off in the voice, as if the skier were moving away down the hill. Figure 5.2 shows the Doppler effect with a curve that slowly falls down. This curve is then applied to the entire region selected in the sound file.

Figure 5.2. You can create your own curves for the Doppler effect in GoldWave. In this example, the pitch of the sound drops quickly toward the end of the sound.

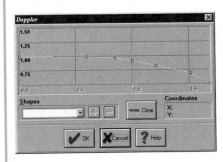

Compressing and Saving Audio Files

After you have perfected the sound, you need to save it. As with almost anything else on the Internet, saving the sound is not quite as simple as it first appears. First, you must determine which file format is best for storing the audio file. If you plan on using this file with the greatest number of computers from around the world on the Internet, you may consider using the Sun/NeXT (`.au`) format or Mac/SGI (`.aif`) format. Netscape provides an audio player that can easily play sound files of either type on any computer platform. In any case, once you have decided on the format that best matches your needs, you must save your work using the File ¦ Save option in GoldWave. A dialog box then appears, prompting you to specify the path and filename for the sound, as well as to determine what file format to use (see Figure 5.3).

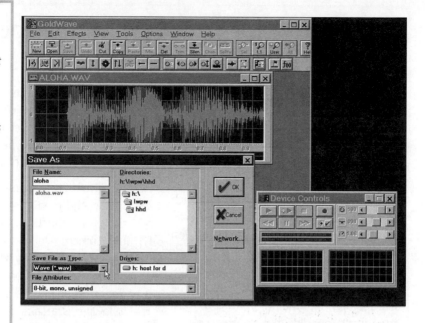

*Figure 5.3.
GoldWave
enables you to
save (and convert
between) a wide
variety of sound
file formats and
to choose
attributes such as
bit depth and
compression
type.*

Note: The Wave (.wav) file

format contains many additional file attributes that may not be found in the other audio file formats. One important attribute is MSADPCM. Using this attribute will effectively halve the size of the overall sound file. ADPCM (Adaptive Differential Pulse Code Modulation) is a compression technique that can save a considerable amount of space (and therefore time transferring the file across the Internet). As sound players that support the WAV format become available on other non-Windows computers, you may decide to use this format for storing your audio content. The GoldWave audio editor included on the CD-ROM enables you to save your files using any of these compression techniques.

Audio Conversion

No matter what platform or operating system you use, sooner or later you'll come across an audio file that you'd love to have a copy of—except for one little problem: It's encoded in a file format you're unfamiliar with, or one you have no player for. When this happens, there is something you can do (besides shrugging your shoulders and walking away): use a conversion utility.

In essence, all conversion utilities do exactly the same thing: They effectively perform a Save As… or Export command on the designated source file, creating a replica of the original data "as heard through the ears" of the target format. Because the various file formats all have different features and performance statistics, it helps to play around with them for a while, tweaking and comparing them until you get a feel for each format's particular strengths and weaknesses. Your trusty conversion utilities are your best tools for this sort of experimentation.

You can convert between most common formats within GoldWave (and most other sound editing programs), simply by opening the file you have and saving it in the format you want.

When you select a file format for output (that is, the target format), what you're really doing is telling the converter which algorithms and ranges or boundaries you want it to use in the upcoming translation process. The conversion utility then reads the file from end to end, applying a predetermined set of algorithms to the data in the file, multiplying, dividing, averaging, truncating, and rounding to the nearest equivalent, and finally saves the output of these calculations in the style of the target format.

Note: Conversion utilities can vary greatly in the amount of control they give to their users, as well as in the quality of their output. Generally speaking, they will produce translations that approach—but do not quite equal—the quality of the original. Of course, depending on the formats involved, the conversion software used, and the contents of the original (source) file, the differences between the two versions may sometimes turn out to be more drastic than you had expected. And in any case, the resulting file rarely (if ever) comes out sounding *better* than the original—unless you have some sort of rare and wondrous talent!

For this reason, it is a good idea to view or play a converted file *immediately after performing the conversion*. If the resulting file is unsatisfactory, be sure to delete it right away; this will protect you from the possibility of confusing the two files later on.

Audio Helper Apps and Plug-Ins

Helper apps are programs that are external to the browser, but which are called into action when the browser receives files of their designated media type. They are alternately known as *players* or *viewers*.

Plug-ins differ from helpers in that they insert their associated media files *inline*—that is, directly within the body of the rendered HTML document. Unlike audio helpers, audio plug-ins can generally be set up to begin playing immediately upon page load—the user doesn't even have to click on anything. The following is a sample of audio helper applications and plug-ins that are available:

✦ GSM Audio Players/Converters
   `http://www.cs.tu-berlin.de/`
   `~jutta/toast.html`

✦ Netscape Audio Player
   `http://home.mcom.com/newsref/ref/`
   `winaudio.html`

✦ RealAudio Client
   `http://www.realaudio.com`

✦ ToolVox for the Web
   `http://www.voxware.com`

✦ TSPlayer
   `ftp://oak.oakland.edu/SimTel/`
   `win3/sound/tsply100.zip`

Many of the newer helpers and plug-ins utilize a technology known as *streaming*. They receive and use audio data so that they can begin playing the file before the entire download is completed. In the past, in order to hear an audio file, you first were required to download the audio file in its entirety from the Internet. Depending on the size of the audio file, this could take some time. Streaming audio (and video) enables the helper application or plug-in to download the beginning of the file. This portion is then interpreted by the plug-in or helper application, and the audio (or video) starts playing the little data that is available. As that content is playing, additional information is downloaded from the Internet in the background. This gives the appearance of much quicker connectivity to information-rich content, such as video and audio. Streaming technology is made possible by efficient Codecs and the power of today's multithreading and multitasking operating systems.

One nice feature of streaming audio and video is that it requires no special action from the user. The user simply clicks on a link to play the audio clip, and the appropriate helper application or plug-in is invoked automatically (assuming that the program is available on the user's computer). In most cases, the only way in which streaming audio is differentiated from standard audio files is by conscious efforts made by Web page developers to place text or graphics on a page, indicating that streaming audio is available.

It is important to recognize that not all streaming technologies are created equal.

All are bound to have strong points and weak points (and in these early days of Web-based multimedia, there are still more weak points than the average TV viewer or radio listener would care to put up with). Each does a better job at compressing certain types of sound, depending on the volume, pitch, and tone of the sound, and the algorithm used to represent that sound digitally.

Note: TsPlayer is unique among audio helper apps in the previous listing. It does not play any audio files on its own. Rather, it passes audio data (in WAV format) through itself, to the actual audio helper (which may be any application that can play .wav files). This produces an effect similar to streaming, in that the audio file begins playing before the download is completed.

What's Next?

This chapter explained the basics of creating your own digital audio. Chapter 6, "Do-It-Yourself Digital Video" initiates you into the coveted art of motion video production for the Internet.

Do-It-Yourself Digital Video

chapter 6

by Janice Norton, Kit Gainer,
and John J. Kottler

So you think you want to create some video for the Internet. The first question to ask yourself is: "Do I really need video, or can I create a similar effect with less hassle?" Consider using simple animation techniques such as GIF animation, forced updates of graphics on a Web page from the server or browser (server push or client pull), or a program like Macromedia Director, Astound, or Sizzle. All of these approaches are usually much faster and easier, both for you and the people who will visit your Web site.

Likewise, ask yourself, "Which would be more effective for the amount of space required: a few seconds of video, or a slick audio production replete with sound effects and music?"

Once you are sure that video is the best or easiest thing to use for the task at hand, the question becomes, "How much and what kind of video will best suit the requirements of my intended Internet site?" For example, imagine you are designing an online demonstration of the inner workings of an engine's pistons. In this case, you could set the video to loop using a movie player, which would enable you to run your presentation indefinitely in the space of about 100KB or less. Likewise, perhaps your movie would be almost as effective, or more effective, using fewer colors. For instance, movies using 16 or 256 colors require much less space than true-color with its 16.7 million colors. Black-and-white video movies require even less.

Often, you can cut your frame rate and playback size and still create the effect you are seeking. Remember, people have to download your clip, and in most cases, users will happily trade off some quality to have the clip download more quickly.

Moreover, most people will simply not be able to enjoy high-quality video—even if they don't mind the download—because they do not have enough Video RAM to display at color depths greater than 256 colors, or a processor capable of pushing large, high-quality video images.

All this is not to suggest that you should avoid video, especially if you want it or need it. Nor is it to suggest that the average user cannot enjoy the beautiful video that you've created and transmitted over the Internet. The real issue here is to determine how to create the best effect using the least amount of bandwidth.

Before deciding how to create the desired video, you should look at the tools at hand and what effect is desired. Ideally, what you create will be a match between the tools and the concept. In many cases, you have to be clever in fashioning your concept to match the tools you have available in order to create the most powerful effect.

Video Formats

The Web changes constantly, so it is difficult to stay current with what is happening. The best way for you to stay current is to surf the Net, and one of the best sites on the Net that stays current with all the new video technologies and toys available is VideoNet:

http://www.netvideo.com/

Another great site for video technology on the Web is Kokonet:

http://cnct.com/home/koko/tech/

Here, you will find an impressive list of (and links to) all of the new plug-ins, gadgets, and gizmos. Both sites are updated frequently and offer thoughtful insight into the video revolution.

In the past, browsers have been limited to prerecorded and canned sequences, retrieved as full files. Video and audio files took minutes and sometimes hours to retrieve, thus severely limiting the inclusion of video and audio. The goal that everyone is moving toward is the creation of video that will be small enough to be handled over the Web.

The transfer of video data introduces new problems of maintaining adequate playback quality in the face of network congestion and client load. Nevertheless, a large number of companies are making video a reality with varying levels of success.

A number of different video formats are available, each with certain strengths and weaknesses. The most popular formats have spawned from the Apple for the Macintosh crowd and Microsoft for the PC crowd. Other formats have been proposed by independent organizations, such as the Motion Picture Experts Group. In the following section we will take a closer look at these formats and the various tools available for working with each.

Microsoft's AVI format

The AVI file format is the native file format for Windows. It has become a standard in the PC world. Several tools have become available that allow AVI files to be easily embedded into Web pages.

CoolFusion

CoolFusion is a freeware plug-in for Windows that streams AVI files in real time over the Net and doesn't require server software to work. CoolFusion enables you to embed AVI files directly into your HTML document and to create a variety of effects using simple tags.

Note: Streaming video is becoming popular on the Web. It is the technology that enables video to begin playing while it downloads. The resolution comes in low and details are filled in as more information is downloaded.

Note: Microsoft has recently announced a new streaming video format (.asf) specifically designed for the Web, called ActiveMovie. This format will be available as an ActiveX control and will be built into Internet Explorer 3.0.

To playback an AVI file in your document automatically when the user launches your home page, use the following syntax:

```
<EMBED src=your.avi width=176 height=144>
```

Several unique tag parameters enable you to determine the display of controls and menus and when the movie starts and stops. Table 6.1 shows the parameters that can be included in the tag line after the `height` parameter.

Apple's QuickTime

Apple's QuickTime video format, developed originally for Macintosh computers, has become very popular. The current version, QuickTime 2.1, offers many advantages over other file formats. Apple promised a beta version of QuickTime 2.5 by April 1996. Currently, Apple and Netscape are working closely to develop and integrate even more QuickTime features into the Netscape browser. QuickTime 2.1 is available for free for both the Mac and PC at

```
http://quicktime.apple.com
```

The following sections describe a few of the many tools available that enable QuickTime video to be displayed over the Web.

Table 6.1. Parameters of the EMBED tag.

Parameter	Purpose
showcontrols=FALSE	Hides the controls
nomenu=TRUE	Hides the menu
streamondoubleclk=TRUE	Displays only the first frame of the AVI clip and requires the user to click to resume the data stream
playingonrdoubleclk="close"	Enables the user to stop an AVI window
onclosestream="pause"	Enables the user to pause the AVI clip
onclosestream="resume"	Resumes the video
onrdoubleclk="play fullscreen"	Stretches your video and plays it back to full screen

ViewMovie

ViewMovie is an online QuickTime movie viewer plug-in that allows you to embed QuickTime movies in Web pages without the need for any special Web server or expensive software. It can be found at

```
http://www.well.com/user/ivanski/
   viewmovie/docs.html
```

Unfortunately, the plug-in is currently only available for the Mac, but a Windows version is in the works. Another drawback—the current version doesn't stream, but the introduction of QuickTime 2.5 may eventually make this possible. Another major problem is that the movie disappears when the window is resized; however, the controller remains, and by clicking the Play or Shuttle buttons, you can restore the movie.

Embedding a QuickTime movie is easy. Use the following syntax:

```
<EMBED SRC="qtmovie.mov" WIDTH=320
   HEIGHT=256>
```

Several parameters are available for ViewMovie also; they can be combined into one tag for multiple functions (see Table 6.2).

ViewMovie also offers a variety of other scripting functions that enable the user to create animated menus and other effects. Full documentation is available on the ViewMovie home page.

QuickTime VR

A related technology developed at Apple is QuickTime VR:

```
http://quicktime.apple.com/qtvr.html
```

This technology enables you to create virtual environments using either standard video, photographs, or 3D-modeled and -rendered landscapes or environments. QuickTime VR doesn't require any special server to operate. An index of QuickTime VR movies is available at

```
http://quicktime.apple.com/archive/
   index.html
```

Until recently, QuickTime VR required a rather expensive licensing structure, which placed this technology out of the reach of most individuals. Now QuickTime VR is free of these licensing requirements. The only expense is $495.00 for the software necessary to create your environment.

Table 6.2. Parameters for ViewMovie.

Parameter	Description
CONTROLLER=FALSE	Hides the controller
AUTOPLAY=TRUE	Plays automatically
LOOP=TRUE	Loops
KEEPASPECTRATIO=FALSE	Squeezes or stretches the aspect ratio
PLAYRATE=50	Changes the speed (with 100 meaning normal speed)

The technology works like this: With a standard 35mm camera and tripod, a real-world 360-degree scene can be photographed in a few minutes. Once photographs are scanned, QuickTime VR authoring tools automatically stitch a series of photographs together to produce a single, seamless digital panorama. Because QuickTime VR uses photographic film instead of video, colors are richer and image quality is superior. Alternatively, computer-generated scenes can be rendered using any off-the-shelf rendering package.

A single, 360-degree view of a real-world scene using video, such as navigable movies, requires tens of megabytes. A standard QuickTime VR file can be stored in 500KB; lower-resolution files can be even smaller.

MPEG

The MPEG video format is the result of an independent organization, the Motion Pictures Expert Group. They proposed the MPEG video standard format which enables high compression rates. It is emerging as the video file format standard because it produces video files that are typically $1/4$ the size of other video formats. The MPEG standard includes specifications for software and hardware.

Software-based MPEG compression will probably be the way you want to go for creating high-resolution video. Perhaps the best and easiest MPEG compressor/converter is Sparkle. Unfortunately Sparkle is currently only available for the Mac.

Sparkle

Sparkle enables you to play and convert any QuickTime movie to an MPEG movie that is playable on both Mac and Windows platforms with the click of a button. Depending on your movie size, you can see a 50 percent decrease in file size over movies compressed with other video formats. Sparkle also allows you to view both QuickTime and MPEG movies.

The latest version of Sparkle also allows you to easily associate a WAV file with your MPEG movie. Consequently, although Sparkle doesn't support sound, you can play back your movie and the sound file at the same time. (Version 2.4.5 is on the accompanying CD-ROM.)

Sparkle, besides encoding almost effortlessly from QuickTime to MPEG, also is the standard helper application for viewing MPEG movies on the Macintosh.

Other Tools

The preceding sections showed several tools that are available for placing video on your Web pages, but many other tools for handling video are available for all operating systems. Appendix C contains resources of Web links to help you find just what you're looking for, but let's look at a few more popular tools.

PreVU

PreVU is a system of plug-ins and converters allowing video to stream over the Net:

```
http://www.intervu.com/sysreq.html
```

PreVU does not require any proprietary computer or server or other software options to stream video over the Net. It can play any video encoded by the dozens of MPEG video encoders already available. Once it has streamed to the user, the video can be cached and played back a second time. Moreover, users can save the video that has been previously cached with the click of a button. (PreVU users will want to increase their Netscape Cache as much as possible to take full advantage of PreVU capabilities.)

Unfortunately, PreVU is currently only available for the PC, although the Macintosh version is promised for April of 1996; another drawback is that PreVU doesn't currently support audio, although that is promised for future versions of the product.

An excellent feature of PreVU is that it offers Web developers new embedding options. This allows the doubling or halving of the size of the displayed window, and the ability to loop the video—thus conserving bandwidth and making previously cached videos reusable. PreVU also allows the user to specify the maximum playback speed for the selected videos, making slow motion and similar effects possible without creating multiple files.

Web Page Video Tips

The best way to minimize your bandwidth is to plan all aspects of your site from the start, including the use of video as part of an overall communication strategy. A well-designed site that integrates video with other elements will be more effective and use less bandwidth.

Use the highest quality source for your video data. Higher quality video has less noise, so it compresses more efficiently. Using a higher-quality video source can cut your file size by a factor of two or more.

Keep each video short. Using long video clips not only increases the chance that you will overflow a visitor's cache, it reduces the number of concurrent visitors you can support. You want people to be impressed with your message's quality and its availability.

The smaller the video is, the better. Large video images not only eat up your server capacity, they put greater demands on your visitors' computers to decode the file. Try integrating a smaller video on a page with a larger graphic image.

Limit the number of videos on any page. If you have lots of clips, divide them into groups of three or so per page and provide an index page.

Caption every video. Captions help visitors to download only the videos they want—you both win! They're also a powerful marketing tool because people are more likely to read captions than the text of your document.

Net Toob

Currently, any 486 machine with the newest version of the Net Toob helper application can play real-time audio and video using MPEG compression.

http://tvnet.com/duplexx/netoob.html

The Net Toob video player can play MPEG files at 7.5, 15, or standard 30 fps, thus reducing file size by as much as 50 percent. This allows real-time streaming of the data across the Internet, even over 14.4Kbps connections.

Besides MPEG, Video for Windows (AVI) and QuickTime (MOV) files are playable on Net Toob, making it a single utility for all digital video formats.

VDOLive

VDOLive playback (client) software is available for Windows, Mac, and UNIX platforms for free.

http://www.VDOLive.com

VDOLive allows you to view multimedia databases, video catalogs, real-time video advertising, special interest video forums, and other video communications over the Internet in real time.

According to Xing Technology, typical file sizes of movies at a frame size of 160×120, 15 frames per second, and 24 bits per pixel can reach about 52MB of uncompressed digital video per minute. After compression, using VDOLive compression technology, compressed video requires 180KB to 960KB per minute. VDOLive's best compression rate is 10 to 50 times higher than MPEG, which requires about 9MB per minute.

VDOLive does this using two technologies. The first is a scalable compression algorithm that compresses video to a small enough file size to run over the small bandwidth portions of the Internet, but also allows the quality of the video to increase with the size and quality of the connection at the other end. Secondly, VDOLive's communications protocol is a key factor—its protocol maintains the integrity of the video as it makes its way through the complex Internet.

StreamWorks

The StreamWorks client software is free and available at

http://www.xingtech.com/

In order to see it work, all you need is a computer with a sound card (or built-in sound hardware) and a connection to the Internet. No special audio/video decoding hardware is needed, because all necessary decoding is done by the StreamWorks software. However, rather expensive server equipment and software is necessary if you wish to become a StreamWorks content provider.

StreamWorks is a set of encoder, server, and client components from Xing Technology that allows you to create live audio and video on demand for the Macintosh, PC, and UNIX platforms, over existing TCP/IP LANs and WANs networks and over the Internet.

Use StreamWorks offline audio encoders for converting WAV files to the StreamWorks MPEG audio and LBR formats. The StreamWorks server also supports any valid MPEG-1 system stream, and Xing builds MPEG encoder tools that can be used to create streams.

Squeezing It Through the Pipe: Codecs

How your video picture looks and how long it takes to stream across the Net will be largely determined by what video codec you choose when you compress the video clip.

Codecs (short for compressor-decompressor) compress the enormous amount of video information needed to display a video movie on your computer. When the user plays your video, the codec decompresses the video on-the-fly while the movie plays back.

Codecs can be *lossy* (meaning various areas of the picture are simplified), or *lossless* (meaning all areas of the video are kept intact). Lossy codecs have lower overall quality, but offer much greater compression than lossless codecs.

Numerous different types of codecs are available, both hardware- and software-based. While hardware-based codecs offer far greater compression, they also require the user to have similar hardware for playback. In contrast, software-based codecs require only similar software (which is usually free). Consequently, since the Web is worldwide and very diverse, we will only cover software-based compression solutions.

MPEG 1 and 2

MPEG is not only a video format, but a compression codec as well. MPEG (software-based version) is the most commonly used type of compression on the Internet for two main reasons: first, because freeware MPEG converters are commonly available on the Web, and second, because MPEG offers the best compression ratio of any commonly used codec.

However, MPEG does have the disadvantage of being lossy and of not enabling 8-bit compression. While 16, 24, or even 32-bit video is great, most computer users cannot display it properly. Consequently, the quality of MPEG is substantially degraded for many users. Another disadvantage of MPEG is that most of the freeware converters on the Web do not offer a facility for playing back audio along with the video image, although MPEG-1 can support audio and video tracks. MPEG-2 is designed for commercial broadcast applications and is not currently applicable to Web-based applications.

Quick Lesson on Digital Video

The term *codec* is short for compressor/decompressor. Most digital video must be compressed in order to be stored in a reasonable amount of space. Then when the stored video is played, the data must be decompressed in order to be displayed. For example, a 320×240 pixel video clip with 24-bit color depth and a frame rate of 15 fps would take up just under 3.5 MB of space for just one second of video without compression!

Several companies, such as Intel, Cinepak, and Microsoft, have designed digital video compression technologies—each with varying quality and amount of storage space saved. These compression/decompression techniques are accomplished using software, but there are several hardware-based codecs as well. MPEG (Motion Pictures Expert Group) is an example of a hardware-based compression/decompression scheme. Although with faster processors, it is now becoming possible to implement this compression algorithm using software.

The following address contains many links to software for viewing and creating multimedia content for the Web

```
http://www.cs.ubc.ca/spider/ladic/
  anim_pc.html
```

This site contains MPEG viewer software such as VMPEG Lite and simple MPEG encoding software such as CONVMPG3. Macintosh users can check out the site at

```
http://www.baylor.edu/server/providers/
  application.html
```

Cinepak

Cinepak, by Radius, is the most commonly used video codec for CD-ROM production. Cinepak, although lossy, offers very good compression and enables you to embed an 8-bit palette within a 16-bit or 32-bit movie. Embedding an 8-bit palette within your movie significantly improves the visual quality of your video when played back on a computer unable to display at higher color depths.

The biggest drawback of Cinepak is the significantly longer time it takes to compress the video. Typically, Cinepak takes between 30 seconds to two minutes per frame to compress a piece of video footage. So 30 seconds of video, captured at 10 frames per second, could take as long as 10 hours to compress!

To find out more about Cinepak, visit

```
http://www.radius.com/Cinepak/
  cinepak.html
```

Indeo R.32

Indeo R.32, a video codec solution by Intel Corporation, is very similar to Cinepak and is rapidly replacing Cinepak for CD-ROM production. Although lossy, Indeo offers very good compression and enables you to embed an 8-bit palette within a 16-bit or 32-bit movie. Again, embedding an 8-bit palette within your movie significantly improves the visual quality of your video when played back on a computer unable to display at higher color depths. Indeo's 8-bit playback quality is substantially higher than that of Cinepak, and Indeo R.32 also compresses substantially faster than Cinepak.

In comparison to Cinepak, Indeo R.32 does have a few disadvantages, however. Cinepak offers slightly smoother playback at high frame rates and slightly better compression than Indeo R.32 does. Indeo R.32 is available at

```
http://www.intel.com/pc-supp/multimed/
  indeo/
```

Indeo Video Interactive

Indeo Video Interactive is perhaps one of the most exciting new codecs available. According to Intel, Indeo Video Interactive offers these new features:

✦ Transparency Support, which enables video or graphics to be overlaid on top of another video or graphic in the background. The graphics can then be controlled in real time via a joystick, keystroke, or mouse.

✦ Local Window Decode, which gives programmers the ability to create an independent video playback window within a larger video playback display or graphics scene, thus enabling fast branching and panning.

- Random Keyframe Access, which enables placement of keyframes (used to refresh image quality within a video stream) to be placed at any arbitrary interval. This makes it possible to quickly or dynamically adjust video quality levels and frame rate during playback. This feature can offer big savings in file size and improve playback quality.
- Saturation/Contrast/Brightness controls that can be adjusted on-the-fly (as a video file is being played).
- Password protection that enables programmers to assign passwords to keyframes to protect video clips from alteration or from being played back with applications that cannot provide the correct password.
- Exceptional video quality on Pentium Processor-based systems, with full-screen, near VHS quality—comparable to software MPEG-1 players at 2X CD-ROM data rates. Indeo video interactive's scalable quality feature also enables quality to scale between several different quality levels or bands, depending on the capability of the PC's CPU to minimize frame-dropping.

As was the case with Indeo video Release 3.2, Intel continues to license Indeo video interactive to software developers for free, and on a royalty-free basis. Indeo video interactive is available for both Mac and Windows platforms and offers better compression than earlier versions of Indeo. All of Intel's Indeo codecs can be found at

`http://www.intel.com/pc-supp/multimed/indeo/`

Animation Compression

Animation compression (lossy) offers decent compression and fairly good playback speed with the added advantage of color depth settings ranging from 1-bit to 32-bit color or black-and-white. If the material is appropriate, a 1-bit or 4-bit video clip can produce stunning results and substantial file size savings using the animation compressor.

Motion JPEG

JPEG (Lossy) compression, while offering incredible compression ratios, decompresses very slowly. This compression algorithm typically requires dedicated hardware for compression/decompression. Because of its high compression ratios and because it maintains each key frame of a video, it is often used in video production.

General Codec Options and Settings

With all of these codecs, you have a choice of frame rate. With many of them, you are also given a choice of quality. (It is best to capture at the color depth and frame rate you plan to use for your final output.)

Action Sequence Settings

The settings you choose will probably depend on the content of your clip. For action sequences, you probably want to choose a higher frame rate and lower quality. Otherwise, in an action sequence, the jerkiness caused by a low frame rate would be more noticeable, while the lack of artifacting eliminated by the high-quality setting would not even be noticed (so trade these two options, as first stated, for best effect).

Non-Action Sequence Settings

With non-action sequences, do the opposite. A lower frame-rate, but with a higher quality setting, is appropriate—jerkiness will be less noticeable while artifacting will be far more noticeable.

Creating the Original Content

Unless you plan to reuse digital video from another source, the first thing you need to do to create your own movies is to get a camera. You can easily rent video cameras in most cities, but if you want to invest further and purchase a video camera for creating your own video movies, we suggest selecting a good Hi-Band 8 Video Camera with a plug-in for an external microphone.

The Hi-Band 8 format and respective video equipment for video taping uses a higher resolution than standard VHS. While

---

Debabbelizing Your Video

The best way to ensure a high-quality video for the majority of users is to do what most multimedia folks call *debabbelizing*, after the popular video processing program named Debabbelizer made by Equilibrium. This program enables you to process video and graphic files in a number of ways as well as import and export using a multitude of file formats.

To save size and produce clean video, it is important to create a common color palette to be used throughout your digital video. For instance, by optimizing your video to be used with the default colors of the system palette, machines with lower color resolutions, such as 256 colors, will not need to constantly remap colors when playing video content. This can save a lot of headache for visitors to your site. Without a common color palette, the system will experience adverse color effects throughout.

The debabbelizing process looks at each of the movie's frames and counts and notates the colors contained in each of the frames. Then it compares all of the colors used in the movie and picks the best 256 colors to represent the millions of colors contained in that exact movie, thus creating a Super Palette which can be embedded in movies.

When the movie is played back in 8-bit, QuickTime calls up the palette and resets the monitor temporarily to that color palette, eliminating much of the graininess of 8-bit playback, while not effecting the playback quality of the movie at higher color depths.

Hi-Band 8 is not quite broadcast quality, it is substantially better than VHS. When you digitize the video, the difference in picture quality between Hi-Band 8 (about $1,000) and professional equipment (about $10,000) will be non-existent. The process of converting video in its original format to a series of digital information on a computer is referred to as *digitizing*. Digitizing will be covered shortly.

Among the features of a Hi-Band 8 or other video camera, camera sensitivity is one of the most important factors to consider. The camera sensitivity is measured in *lux* (the light level at which the camera is able to pick up images). Most Hi-Band 8 cameras can shoot down to about two or three lux. The lower the lux, the darker the environment you can successfully videotape, and thus the less often you'll need cumbersome lighting equipment.

Tip:
The cheapest method of all may be to use a product called QuickCam made by Connectix. These little cameras cost only $99 (including all the hardware and software you need to get started) and are available for both Mac and Windows. The camera can be used for video teleconferencing as well as for capturing live video.

The QuickCam camera captures sound video in 4-bit black-and-white and works well in low-level light. The only drawback of the camera is that it needs to be connected to a computer. More information on Connectix and its products is available at

`http://www.connectix.com/connectix/qcchoice.html`

Similar inexpensive video devices for video-conferencing are becoming available. For low-cost video solutions, these work very well.

Lighting a Video Shoot

Good lighting and careful planning are essential for a successful video shoot, no matter how good your equipment is and no matter how low of a "lux" your camera can handle. The key to proper lighting is the "Lighting Triangle" technique.

The Lighting Triangle consists of three lights arranged in a triangle around your subject. The three lights are

✦ The *key light* is the brightest light, and it represents what is the main light source on a subject (that is, where the "table lamp" is, if you are photographing someone in a room at night).

✦ The *fill light* should be more diffused and half as bright as the key light, and placed opposite of the key light. The fill light is used to eliminate unwanted shadows on your subject.

✦ The *back light* is placed behind the subject to illuminate the top and back of the subject. The back light should also be about half as bright as the key light. Its purpose is to define your subject and separate the subject from the background.

This technique will help you shoot good quality video.

Digitizing Video

After you have captured a scene using a video camera, you must digitize it into the computer. This process varies, depending on the hardware and software you use on your computer. For instance, if you are using an Apple Macintosh computer with audio/video capabilities, you can simply connect your video source to the computer and begin recording the content digitally. However, if you are using a PC, you must first purchase a video capture card. These cards range from a few hundred to several thousand dollars, depending, of course, on the level of quality you hope to obtain. Obviously, the most expensive cards are intended for video professionals who create digital studios with their computers. However, the price of typical capture cards has dropped below $500.

Tip: When shopping for a video capture card, make sure that it is capable of digitizing motion video. There are numerous devices on the market today that accept a video signal from a source such as a video camera, but merely take a single "snapshot" photo of the source, not moving video.

If you are looking to capture single images from a video source, consider equipment such as Play Inc.'s Snappy Video Snapshot, which is available for under $200. This device attaches to the parallel port of your computer and captures very high-resolution, stable photographic images from your video source.

Most capture equipment includes software for capturing and editing video input. Adobe Premiere, Microsoft VidCap, and Video Action Pro (registered version) all offer the capability of recording and editing digital video. Later in this chapter, you will learn how to perform some basic editing functions using Video Action ED, which is available on the CD-ROM included with this book.

These programs will enable you to specify the format of the video file you want to capture. When capturing video files, you need to specify settings that can affect the final output of your video. Some of the key settings that affect the size and quality of the video include

+ The rate at which video is recorded in frames/second (fps)
+ The quality of the audio to be recorded with the video
+ The dimensions of the video window in pixels
+ The compression algorithm to apply to the video

Although ultimately you will want to create a video that is highly compressed so that it requires very little space, capture your original footage using the highest settings possible. Then, when you edit the footage with other material, you can be sure that the final, compressed video will be as clear as possible.

If you use a high ratio of compression when initially recording, those compressed files will be further compressed when they are edited and used to produce another final file. Be aware, however, that minimizing compression during the recording process will generate mammoth files. For instance, if you were to capture video without compression using 320x240 pixel resolution, 24-bit true-color, and 15 fps, files could grow substantially at about 3.5MB per second! In reality, when capturing, you will likely still need to compress the video stream; how-ever, you should use less aggressive settings for capturing original content.

A good rule to follow is to capture video using 320×240 resolution, 15fps or higher, and high quality video compression settings using an efficient codec such as Indeo or Cinepak. Typically, compression algorithms allow you to define the quality of the com-pressor by choosing values between 0% and 100%. Often, a preview window will display the effects of the video compressor using these different values. For initial compression, try capturing video with quali-ties greater than 75%.

When creating Internet videos, consider making your videos using smaller resolu-tions like 160×120 and higher compression ratios. If your videos will be using audio, use lower-quality audio settings to conserve space and bandwidth. Remember that the larger a file is, the longer it takes to transfer over the Internet. Files about 1.5MB in size may take 10-20 minutes to download using a 28.8Kbps modem!

Figure 6.1 demonstrates a video capture in progress, including the numerous option windows that Microsoft VidCap provides.

Figure 6.1.
You can capture video using any number of settings.

To begin recording video content digitally using VidCap, select Capture ¦ Capture Video Sequence from the pull-down menu. When all settings have been verified, click on the OK button to start the recording process. Figure 6.1 shows a recording in progress. Press the ESC key on your keyboard to halt the recording process.

Tip: Because it takes a moment to actually start the process, start recording first and then begin the actual video signal output. Although you can record either video noise or blank input, you can be sure that you will not miss the introduction of the video clip. You can always use video editing software to remove those blank sections of your video file.

Note: If you do use VidCap to capture your video files, it is important to remember to set the actual filename that you wish to capture video to each time you wish to record. Do this with the File ¦ Set Capture File option in the menu or by clicking on the left-most toolbar button.

Setting the capture file allocates space for recording the digital video. How-ever, if you forget to reset the capture file, you may inadvertently overwrite your previous work.

Editing Video

After you capture your video, you need to edit it. A fully functional digital video editing program called Video Action ED is included on the CD-ROM with this book. This software enables you to combine numerous video file clips, static bitmap images, and sounds together to create a final production. Video Action ED also features numerous effects that you can apply to videos, as well as transitions that make your sequences smoother. In this section, you will see how to use these basics of Video Action ED to create a skiing video.

Most video editing packages are fairly similar in that most provide the basic capabilities, unless you are using a very low-end package. If you want more elaborate effects, consider using software such as Adobe Premiere, Gold Disk's VideoDirector, in:Sync's Speed Razor, or Ulead's MediaStudio Pro.

The Video Action Screen

Now let's examine how to create a simple video production using Video Action ED for Windows-based machines. When you first start Video Action, you are greeted with two windows: a timeline in the top half of the Video Action window and a gallery in the lower half. The timeline window is similar to

Tip: If you are a Mac user with only the QuickCam camera, or with only a video capture board and no software for editing, try QuickEditor, a low-cost shareware movie editor. It is Mac and PowerMac native and offers features including 2D and 3D plug-in transitions and effects and stereo soundtrack editing. QuickEditor is available at this address:

```
ftp://sumex-aim.stanford.edu/info-mac/_Graphic_%26_Sound_Tool/_Movie/
```

Figure 6.2. Video Action ED is a powerful video editing tool.

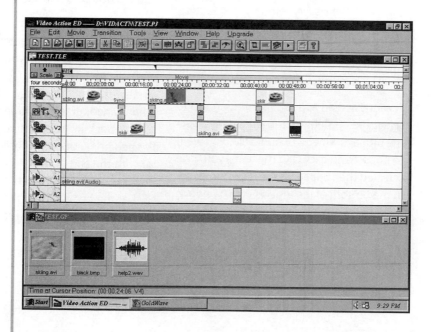

a storyboard; it enables you to position elements, such as video, audio, or pictures, at some exact moment in time. When the final movie is played, the items placed in the timeline will be played in the order in which they appear from left to right.

The second window, or gallery window, is a collection that displays all the multimedia content currently in use for the final video production. Figure 6.2 illustrates a Video Action screen in which the order of videos and transitions can be found in the timeline window at the top. The original video, a static bitmap file, and an additional audio file can be found in the gallery window at the bottom of the screen.

Collecting Content

Before you can place any multimedia elements on the timeline, you must first import them into the gallery window. To do this, click on the small button in the top-left corner of the gallery window (this button appears as a pot with four colored balls and an arrow pointing into the pot). You can also select the Organize ¦ Collect command when the gallery window is active.

A window then appears, prompting you to select the content to import. Simply select the bitmaps, videos, or audio files you want to import and click OK. The items you have selected then appear in the gallery window at the bottom of the Video Action window. A small thumbnail drawing of the original item is displayed as well.

Killing Time

Once you have imported the content necessary for your video production, you can begin dragging the items from the gallery onto the timeline. You can drag graphic material on any of the four video tracks or audio material on any of the four audio tracks. After you have dropped a video or graphic item on the timeline, it is represented by a yellow rectangle with a thumbnail of the content. The length of the yellow regions on the timeline are directly proportional to the length of the actual clip.

Similarly, you can drag audio resources from the gallery onto the timeline. These files appear as light blue regions in the audio tracks of the timeline. You can place either type of resource anywhere on the timeline. If audio and video clips overlap in the timeline, they will be played together. Any blank space in the timeline indicates "silence" in the video, represented by muted audio tracks and a black screen in the video tracks.

Let's assume you have three video clips that you want to play immediately in sequence. Let's also assume that you have a single audio file that is long enough to extend the length of the three video clips. To create a final video, drag the three video clips onto one track in the timeline, ensuring that the beginning of each subsequent clip lines up with the end of the preceding clip. Then drag the audio file onto its own audio track so that the beginning of the audio file lines up with the beginning of the first video clip.

Note: A blue rectangle with a horizontal line through its center represents an audio clip on the timeline. You can find this audio clip toward the lower half of Figure 6.2. This horizontal line specifies the volume for the sound clip at any point along the timeline. You can click anywhere along this line to create a new key point. By dragging this new key point, you adjust the volume of the audio file at that point. As you move the volume at that point up or down, notice that lines emanate from both sides of this line and connect to other key points in the audio clip. The volume of the audio clip over time is directly related to the curve of these lines throughout the timeline. By adjusting the volume, you can create effects, such as fade-outs, without reconstructing the audio file in separate audio editing software.

Trimming Clips

As mentioned earlier, it is possible that you might record signal noise or blank frames before or after the actual content you intended to record. The starting and ending positions of each video clip identified on the timeline can be adjusted. To adjust these settings, double-click on a clip in the timeline. A window similar to the one shown in Figure 6.3 appears.

Figure 6.3.
You can specify the starting and ending positions of each clip in Video Action's Clip Player and Trimmer window.

A preview of the clip you're modifying is available in the center of this window. Beneath this preview is a scroll bar that enables you to search for a specific frame in the video. Just beneath this scroll bar is a range marked by a yellow line with two red end points. This range identifies how much of the clip is being used in the timeline window.

If you find that you need to trim the beginning of the video clip, simply drag the scroll bar to the new starting position for the video clip and click on the Time In button. The range that identifies the video clip adjusts appropriately. These Time In and Time Out buttons simply enable you to specify from where you want a video clip to begin playing and where you want it to stop.

Transitions

There is nothing wrong with placing video clips right up against each other on the timeline. The clips will be played in the final movie production, but there will be no *transitions* between them; that is, when one clip finishes, the second immediately appears. Although this is not unacceptable, there may be occasions when you prefer to create a smoother transition. For example, if you have one clip that is dark and another that is bright, playing those clips back-to-back will create a flash between the dark and light clips. Depending on the effect you are trying to create, you might want one clip to transition gradually into another via a *dissolve effect*.

To make the clips run more smoothly, let's create a dissolve transition in Video Action, using the three back-to-back clips already discussed. Between the first and second video tracks in Video Action is an additional transition track. This transition track specifies what transitions are to occur between the first and second video tracks when the final movie is rendered. To create a transition in this track, simply drag one clip to the second video track so that the beginning of that clip starts before the clip on the first track finishes. The transition effect, indicated by a green region in the timeline, will be created automatically between the time the first track's video clip ends and the second track's video clip starts. The timeline window in Figure 6.2 includes five separate transitions for the movie being created.

After you have defined the transition region, you can then specify what transition you wish to use between the video clips on the first and second video tracks. To change transition effects, click once on the transition you wish to alter in the transition track. Then click on the Transition menu to display a Transition Group window. This window enables you to select from twenty different transition types including wipes, dissolves,

zooms, and even page-turns. Double-clicking on the appropriate animated icon replaces the selected transition with the new effect and displays a Transition Viewer window as shown in Figure 6.4. This transition window enables you to modify specific properties regarding the transition and to preview how the effect will appear in your movie.

If you want to create a second transition, you will need to place the starting position of the third video clip just before the end of the second video clip. However, this time you must place the third clip back on the first track. Because the transition track is applied only between the first and second tracks, all video clips included in a transition must alternate sides of the transition track.

Tip: It is possible to dissolve (gradually fade) between two digital video clips. Therefore, it is also possible to fade-out the final video. To create a fade-to-black effect, follow these steps:

1. Create a black bitmap file that matches the dimensions of your video clips using a Windows paint program.

2. Save the black bitmap file and import it into the Video Action gallery.

3. If the final video clip of your movie exists on track one, place the black graphic file at the end of the second track.

4. Make certain that the start of the black graphic file starts before the final video clip ends to create a transition between the video clip and the black graphic.

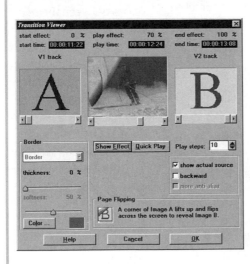

Figure 6.4. The Transition Viewer window in the Video Action editing software enables you to modify the details of a transition and to preview the results.

5. Ensure that the final transition is a simple dissolve transition (which is the default transition type).

When the final movie is created and played, the final video clip will fade to a black screen.

To add a special effect to a video clip, first select the video clip in the timeline window. Then choose the Tools ¦ Video Effects & Titler option or click the FX button on the toolbar. A window similar to that shown in Figure 6.5 appears, enabling you to select special effects and tweak the results of each effect.

Video FX

What movie would be complete without a few special effects? So you do not feel neglected, Video Action enables you to incorporate several special effects into your own digital movies. Some special effects are absolutely legitimate and necessary. For instance, if you digitize a video clip and the lighting is not suitable, you can adjust the brightness or contrast of the clip and save the modified version in your final movie. Yet there are also several cool effects, such as Old Movie, Kaleidoscope, Star Highlight, or Title Generator that can make your movies stand out.

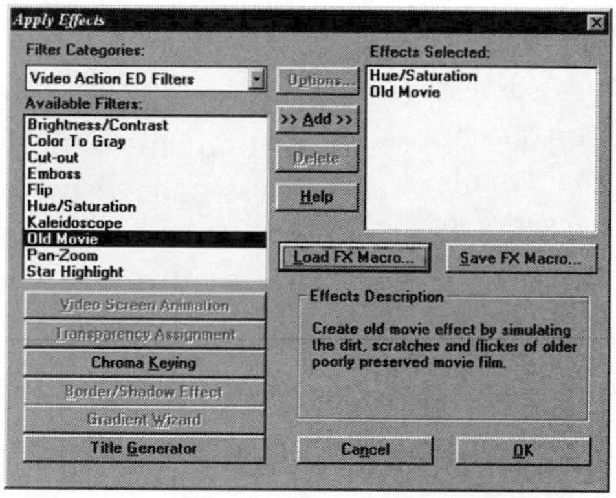

Let the Movie Roll

After you have finished designing the timeline for your digital movie and are satisfied with the layout, you can create the final movie. To create the movie in Video Action, you must first specify the settings for the final production. Settings for the final movie can be altered by selecting Movie ¦ Movie Settings while the timeline window is selected. Figure 6.6 is an example of some of the settings you can modify for video files you create.

Note: Windows 95 has made significant improvements in attempting to resolve color resolution problems and color mappings automatically. However, if you wish to control the color output of your video files on a Windows-based machine, you can use Video Action ED. In the Movie Settings window, you can specify which compressor to use when creating a final video. If you instead choose No Compression for the compression option, the color depth option will then enable you to choose from several palettes (including custom palettes) to use when rendering the final movie.

Figure 6.5. Video Action supports numerous special effects that can make your movies more compelling.

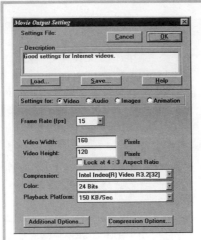

Figure 6.6.
You can specify a number of settings for the final video file that you create with Video Action ED.

When creating Internet videos, remember to keep the size of the final video file relatively small. Smaller files require less time to transmit over the Internet and are therefore more effective for the person viewing them. Adjust the settings in the Movie Settings Output window to achieve optimal compression by these means (listed settings are only suggestions):

✦ Minimizing the dimensions of the final video window: 160x120 pixels.

✦ Limiting the number of frames per second (fps) of the video: 8-10 fps.

✦ Choosing a video compressor and reducing the compression quality as a compromise to the final size of the video: Indeo, 50 percent or less.

✦ Limiting audio: 8-bit, 11kHz.

After you have established the appropriate settings for an Internet video, you must select the region of the timeline you want to export as the final movie. A yellow bar with red triangles at each end of the bar and the word Movie on it should be present near the top of the timeline window. Simply stretch the ends of this rectangle to enclose the multimedia elements in the tracks below. In other words, ensure that the beginning of the Movie meter is at the same position as the beginning of the very first video clip. Similarly, make certain that the end of the meter is at the same ending position as the last video clip.

To actually create the final digital movie, select Movie ¦ Make Movie ¦ AVI File Output. When a dialog window appears prompting for the name of the final movie file, type in an appropriate name and click OK. All the content in the timeline window is then assembled appropriately and written to a final `.avi` file.

What's Next?

This chapter has given you a crash course in creating digital video suitable for the kind of uses you saw in Chapter 4, "Putting Multimedia on Your Web Pages." In Chapter 7, "Creating Interactive Animation with Shockwave and Friends," you'll learn how to take visitors to your site beyond passive listening and viewing, into the new world of interactive media.

chapter 7

By Kit Gainer, Janice Norton, and Kelly Murdock

Creating Interactive Animation with Shockwave and Friends

The first section in this book provides great tips on getting the most out of HTML. The other chapters in this section show you how to use multimedia elements to enhance your Web pages. With this chapter, we add a bold new buzzword to the mix—*interactivity*. This not only makes your Web pages look and sound cool, but also provides visitors to your site with an engaging experience each time they visit.

These interactive tricks can be accomplished in many ways. Consider Java, JavaScript, VBScript, and ActiveX, all of which provide great control over such interaction. But for the easy path to sprucing up your Web page, Shockwave, a technology from Macromedia, can help you produce quick results without learning how to program.

Despite all the attention that Shockwave is getting on the Web, it is not the only game in town. Other similar interactive products are becoming available, so Web page creators now have many choices. Big-name companies, such as Oracle and Powersoft, are getting into the multimedia development scene with products such as Media Objects and Media.splash. You learn about some alternative packages at the end of this chapter. For now, however, the hot item is Shockwave, so let's take a good closer look....

Shockwave Is Director on the Web

The engine behind Shockwave is Macromedia's Director, which explains why so many new Shockwave sites are appearing. There are currently over 250,000 developers using Director, and Shockwave enables them to present their work on the Web.

Macromedia's Director is the premier multimedia development tool. It has been around for some time; it is the software used to produce the majority of the CD-ROM titles currently on the market. At Macromedia's Web site, you can find a gallery of examples done with Macromedia tools. Perusing this gallery will give you an idea of the type of things possible with Director and Shockwave:

```
http://www.macromedia.com/Gallery/
   index.html
```

Shockwave is a technology that enables multimedia developers to create Director movies that are embedded into Web pages using standard HTML. These pages are viewed using Netscape's Navigator 2.0, equipped with the Shockwave plug-in. You can do this by means of two key components:

+ **Afterburner**—A utility that compresses standard Director movies and formats them to be viewed by the Shockwave plug-in.
+ **Shockwave Plug-in**—A Netscape Navigator 2.0 plug-in that plays back Afterburned Director movies over the Web.

There really isn't much to Shockwave, but the promise that it holds is incredible. With this technology, multimedia professionals who develop content in Director can make the same content available on the Web.

Note: Shockwave plug-ins are now available for Macs, Power Macs, Windows 3.1, Windows 95, and Windows NT operating systems. UNIX versions are in the works.

Macromedia isn't stopping with Director, either. It has recently announced that Shockwave for Freehand and Shockwave for Authorware plug-ins are now available, which will similarly enable Freehand and Authorware users to also publish their work on the Web.

Note: Currently, Shockwave is available for the following versions: Director 4.x, Freehand 5.x, and Authorware 3.5.

Macromedia has just started shipping Director 5, which includes many enhancements and additional features. Shockwave support for Director 5 will be available very soon. Check out Macromedia's Web site for the latest news.

A Quick Look at Shocked Sites

The best way to get you excited about Shockwave is to show it in action. Sites using Shockwave, or *Shocked* sites, are growing at an alarming rate.

Naturally, the first visit should be to a site where you can obtain the Shockwave plug-in. Netscape and Macromedia both offer it at their sites, but almost any Shockwave site has a link to the plug-in. Both Shockwave and Afterburner are free of charge.

The Netscape address is

```
http://home.netscape.com/comprod/
   products/navigator/version_2.0/
   plugins/index.html
```

Macromedia's site is at

```
http://www.macromedia.com/Tools/
   Shockwave/sdc/Plugin/index.html
```

Note: Currently, Shockwave is only available for Netscape Navigator 2.0 or later. But Macromedia has said that it will make the plug-in available for all other browsers, including Microsoft's Internet Explorer, NaviSoft, CompuServe, and SGI's WebFORCE.

Macromedia has teamed up with Microsoft to make Shockwave available for Internet Explorer as an ActiveX control, so you can view Shockwave movies using Internet Explorer 3.0. Check the Microsoft and Macromedia Web sites for the latest information.

After downloading the Shockwave plug-in, run the program in a temporary directory to decompress all the files. Then run the setup program. Setup will ask you to identify the directory where Netscape is located. After installation, the files will be located in the Plugins subdirectory of your Netscape folder. Once this is complete, your browser will be "Shockwave aware" the next time you load it.

When your browser is Shockwave savvy, take a trip to the appropriately named "Shockwave Epicenter" site at Macromedia:

```
http://www.macromedia.com/Tools/
   Shockwave/Gallery/index.html
```

Here, you'll find links to thousands of Shockwave sites, and if the sheer number of sites is overwhelming, then try the Vanguard directory, which includes the sites that Macromedia thinks are better than the rest. Figure 7.1 shows the site for the Nissan Pathfinder, which leads users on an interactive adventure through Africa. Start your adventure at this address:

```
http://www.nissanmotors.com/pathfinder/
   gear.cgi
```

Macromedia's Interactive Gallery features a number of interesting works. The examples are broken up into several unique categories including First Impressions, Banners, Logos, Games, Custom Multimedia Development, and Presentations. These varied categories give you an idea of the types of uses for Director and Shockwave. Another good example seen in the gallery is a Shockwave promotional piece done by Infrared Communications, as shown in Figure 7.2

The significant promise of Shockwave is interactivity, so how about an arcade game? The Webfrog game at the Arcade Alley site (`http://www.ashock.com/html/webfrog.html`) is a great example of the kind of interactivity that Director and Shockwave can provide. This game, despite its complexity, weighs in at only 54KB (see Figure 7.3).

Figure 7.1.
From
Macromedia's
Vanguard
Gallery, Nissan
Pathfinder
enables you to
take a virtual
adventure
through Africa
via Shockwave.

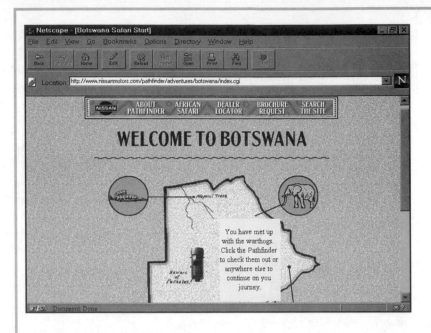

The dart game found at http://www.2-lanemedia.com/darts.htm and created by 2-Lane
Media is the same dart game that is included in WarnerActive's CD-ROM game "Panic in
the Park." The developers were able to take their existing files and run them through
Afterburner to produce a Shockwave movie that is inserted into their Web page with a
simple <EMBED> tag (see Figure 7.4).

Figure 7.2.
From
Macromedia's
Interactive
Gallery, Infrared
Communication's
Shockwave pro-
motion movie.
The movie
features red and
blue scenes that
move and flash
about.

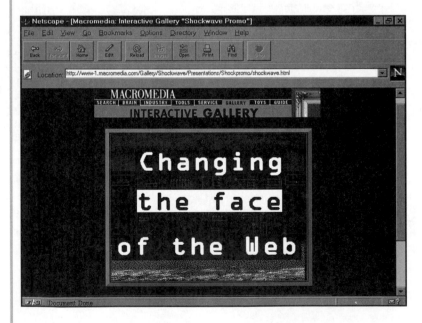

Figure 7.3.
Webfrog
Shockwave
Movie at the
Arcade Alley
Site. What is
more interactive
than arcade
games?

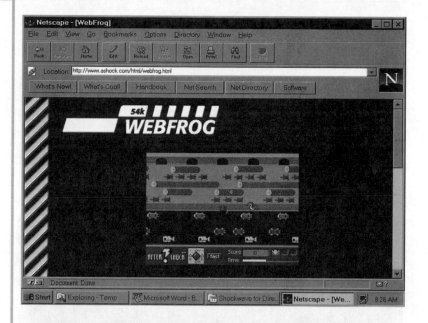

Figure 7.4.
Repurposed
content—Dart
game from the
WarnerActive
CD-ROM "Panic
in the Park."

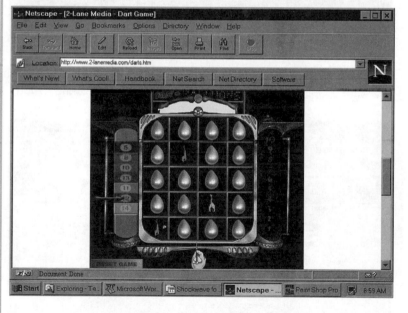

Although much of the Shockwave content is aimed at the entertainment market, education is another area that receives a lot of attention. Because it is simple to use, Director is used in many educational settings to produce interactive movies that let students learn and be creative. Figure 7.5 shows a good example of this, where at the CyberKids site, nine-year-old Wulia Bekoi shows off her original story, "My Computerized House," as a Shockwave interactive movie.

Another great list of Shockwave sites is at Director Web:

`http://hakatai.mcli.dist.maricopa.edu/director/shockwavelist.html`

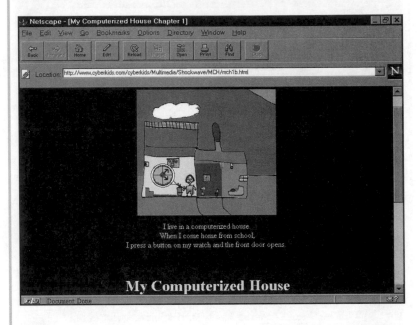

*Figure 7.5.
Shockwave
movie at the
CyberKids site
showing nine-
year-old Wulia
Bekoi's inter-
active story, "My
Computerized
House."*

The list is actually a Shockwave movie (see Figure 7.6). There are a lot of sites to look at, and more are popping up all the time, but I will leave the exploring to you.

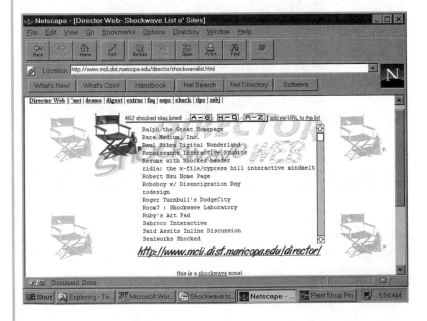

*Figure 7.6.
Another great
Shockwave jump
list at Director
Web.*

What You Need to "Shock" Your Site

As we mentioned in the preceding section, a site that includes Shockwave content is said to be *Shocked*—kind of a nifty name and one that is sure to draw a crowd. To Shock your site, all you really need are some Shockwave movies and a way to write them into your HTML file. That's it. Using the EMBED tag, the movie can be placed anywhere in the HTML file and played when a visitor with the Shockwave plug-in comes along.

The word "movie" refers to a Director animation you create. It can be simple or complex, interactive or noninteractive, and as large or small as you like.

So, where do Shockwave movies come from? They are simply Director files that have been compressed using the Afterburner utility, which converts the file into a format that the Shockwave plug-in will recognize and play on the Web.

Although Director is not required, owning a copy will let you create your own movies. Many sites are offering premade Shockwave movies to whomever wants to use them. Several such movies are included on the CD. Let's look at an example of using one of these premade movies.

The Easy (and Cheap) Way to Shock Your Site

Let's take the quick path to Shocking your site by borrowing some premade Shockwave movies. You can use one of the movies available on the CD included with this book. They can be found in the Shock subdirectory

and have the .dcr extension (which stands for compressed Director files). Regular Director files have the .dir extension.

The following example shows you how to place a Shockwave movie into your Web page. On the CD, find the file named welcome.dcr. Copy this file into the same directory that your HTML file is in. Then place the following tag in your HTML file at the location where you wish the movie to appear:

```
<EMBED SRC="welcome.dcr" WIDTH=96
  HEIGHT=22 TEXTFOCUS=onMouse>
```

Just like a GIF image, the WIDTH and HEIGHT parameters specify the width and height of the stage in pixels. Netscape automatically crops your movie to the size you specify in your tag.

> # Note: The TEXTFOCUS parameter controls how interactive movies are started. It has three options: onMouse, onStartShockwave, and never. The default is onMouse. This tells Shockwave to respond to input from the keyboard after the user clicks anywhere on the movie. The onStartShockwave option begins responding to keyboard input as soon as the movie starts running, and the never option ignores all input from the keyboard. Movies without interactivity ignore this parameter.

To substitute an image for browsers that don't support Shockwave, use the NOEMBED tag:

```
<NOEMBED> <IMG SRC="welcome.gif">
  </NOEMBED>
```

Note that the user still sees the Netscape broken image icon as well as the image you have substituted.

To see the results of embedding this Shockwave movie in a Web page, see `welcome.htm` on the CD. It should resemble Figure 7.7.

Several other simple Shockwave movies are included on the CD. Feel free to use them to Shock your Web pages.

Figure 7.7. Your first Shocked site, welcome.htm. The word "Welcome" scrolls from right to left and a voice is heard saying "Welcome."

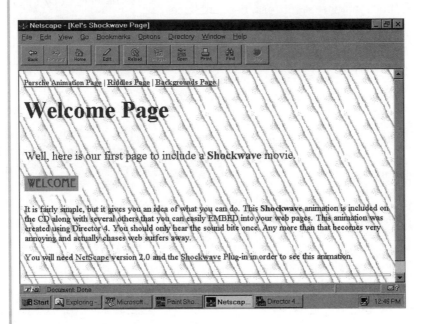

Creating Shockwave Movies with Director

The simple Shockwave movies that you can scrounge up to Shock your site are fine, but you are limited to what someone else's creative juices produced. To really have fun with Shockwave, you need Director and Afterburner.

Director is available from any software reseller, but it will cost you about $800 (the most recent upgrade costs around $300). Afterburner is easy to get; just go to

Macromedia's Web site at the following address and download it.

`http://www.macromedia.com`

It is free, along with the Shockwave plug-in.

Director is a powerful piece of software, well worth the price, but just to make sure you will be happy with it, try experimenting with the save-disabled version included on the CD. This demo version has all the features of the actual product, but you can't save the files. It is a great tool to learn how to use the product before you spend the money.

The next example walks through creating a Shockwave movie using the Director demo

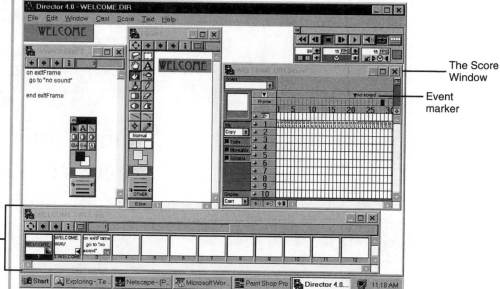

Figure 7.8.
The first look at the Director environment. The "Welcome" graphic in the upper-left corner is the stage. All windows can be moved and resized as needed.

The Score Window

Event marker

The Cast window

on the CD. You won't be able to save the movie, but a saved copy is included on the CD in the Shock directory. In the process, you will learn the basics of using Director.

First, let's look at the main windows used in Director (shown in Figure 7.8). All can be opened and closed using the Windows menu.

+ **The Stage Window** is not actually a window, but the background of the Director environment where your creation shows up. The size and position of the stage can be set using the File ¦ Preferences menu.

+ **The Control Panel Window** is used to set your background color (using the box in the lower-right corner), start and stop the animation (similar to a VCR control), and set the frame rate.

+ **The Cast Window** is where all the elements of the movie, including graphics, sounds, and scripts, are stored.

+ **The Score Window** is where your movie is actually assembled. Think of the grid as a time line that progresses from left to right as the movie plays.

+ **The Paint Window** is used to create Cast members. It is similar to other paint programs, but it offers some useful editing tools and features not found in other paint packages, such as the lasso, which "shrinks to fit" around your selection.

+ **The Scripts Window** is where you insert Lingo scripts (Director's scripting language is called Lingo) to control the interactions of your movies.

+ **The Tools Window** enables you to place text, lines, and simple shapes quickly on the stage.

Director has other windows (not shown in the figure or included in the list above) that add functionality to the environment.

Setting Up the Director Environment

Exploration and experimentation are key to learning the ins and outs of Director. Let's first set up the stage. Select File ¦ Preferences and set the size of the stage to 160×100 and the location to left 0 and top 0. This places the stage in the upper-left corner of the background. It looks like a white box.

To set the background color of the stage, select Window ¦ Control Panel to bring up the Control Panel. In the lower-right corner is a box; click and hold this button to bring up a color palette. Select black, and the stage changes to black.

Animation by Director: The Porsche Movie

Director can be used to create everything from simple animations to advanced interactive programs. In Chapter 3, "Animations the Easy Way: Multi-Image GIFs," you learned how to create animations using GIF files, but Director has the unique advantage of being able to synchronize the audio with the animation. Let's look at an example.

In this example, you import an image taken from an animation of a Porsche rendered in Caligari's TrueSpace 2.0 and use Director's animation features to make the car move across the screen.

First, by using the File ¦ Import command (or by pressing Ctrl-J), load the first image of the animation, named CDU0000.pcx, from the /Shock/Porsche subdirectory on the CD.

In the Import dialog box, notice all the different file types that you can import. They include not only various graphics files for Windows and Macs, but also audio and video formats.

Caution:

If you are authoring for the Net, don't import QuickTime or other video formats to use in your animation because they are not currently supported by Shockwave. A work-around is covered in the "Making Faux Video" section.

When importing the Porsche image, Director asks you if you want to Install a custom palette or Remap to the current one. Choose Remap to current palette, because currently, Netscape does not support custom palettes. Also, sounds must be at least in an 8-bit, 11 kHz format to be compatible with both Mac and PC formats. It is possible to make sound files of higher quality, but this makes your movie too large to download readily over the Net.

After the import, the image shows up in the Cast window. The Cast window is where all the elements of the movie are stored, including graphics, sounds, and scripts. Notice in Figure 7.8 how different elements are shown in the Cast window. Here you see an image, a WAV file, and a script.

Loading the Stage and Settling the Score

Now that you have a Cast member, you can place the image on the Stage. There are many ways to do this. The simplest is to select the thumbnail in the Cast window and drag it onto the stage area. You can easily reposition it by dragging it. Notice that its corresponding number appears in the first open graphics channel of the Score window, opened by selecting Windows ¦ Score.

Several images in the Cast window can be selected and moved to the Score at once. By holding down the Ctrl key while selecting and dragging several Cast members to the Score window, the elements line up vertically across *channels*. Likewise, holding down the Alt key aligns the elements horizontally across the columns, called *frames*.

The little numbers you see in the cells correspond to the numbered elements of the Cast window. This gives you some feedback as to where each element is located.

Each cell of the Score can contain one Cast member, called a *sprite*. A sprite is a bitmap image placed in some defined position. A sprite can be animated by rapidly changing its position in succession. Each sprite can be as large or small as you choose to make it. However, remember, the larger the image, the slower it animates.

At the top of the Score window above the cells is a little solid black square. This is the Playback head indicating which frame appears on the stage. When the animation is playing, the head moves from left to right.

To the left of the cells are 48 numbered channels that hold sprites, but above those are several special channels marked with icons as seen in Figure 7.9. If you cannot see these icons, press the blue up arrow icon directly above the right vertical scroll bar. This icon lets you roll up the special channels to save space if you wish. Now, let's look at those special channels.

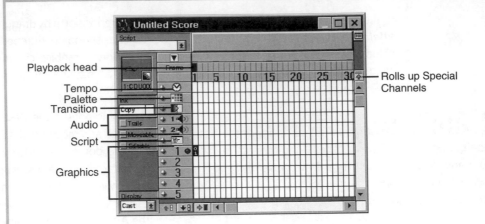

Figure 7.9.
The Director
environment as
you build the
Porsche movie.
Notice the
various channels
and features of
the Score
window.

Descending from the top, you see the following:

+ **Tempo Channel**—This channel has a clock icon. If you double-click any part of the grid in this channel, it brings up the Tempo menu. There are several radio buttons that let you control how your animation plays back.

+ **Palette Channel**—This channel enables you to set custom palettes for your movies. Currently, Netscape does not support custom palettes, so setting the palette to Windows System Palette produces the best results for both Macs and PCs.

+ **Transition Channel**—This is where you can set the transition from one frame to the next. The options here range from directional screen wipes to dissolving pixels.

+ **Sound Channels**—The next two channels are where the audio tracks are positioned. To set a sound to play in one of these channels, select the frames you want the sound to play over and choose Set Sound

from the Score menu. It presents a list of sounds appearing in the Cast window. Double-click the sound you want to play, and it appears automatically in the Score window.

+ **Script Channel**—The sixth icon from the top is the script channel. Scripts are used to add interactivity and control to your movies.

+ **Graphics Channels**—Each of the next 48 channels are for graphics. The higher the channel, the further back the graphic: Channel 1 is the furthest in the background, and channel 48 is the closest in the foreground. For example, if you have a background in channel 1, a dog in channel 2, and a tree in channel 3, you can animate the dog moving behind the tree by moving the dog across the stage. As the dog moves into the same space as the tree, it seems to pass behind the tree.

Now, back to the example. Drag the Porsche image located in the Cast to the first cell of channel 1. Notice that it appears on the Stage.

Building Cast Members with the Paint Window

Not all Cast members must be imported: You can create your own Cast members in Director using the Paint window. If you know how to use other paint packages, this window and its functions should be familiar to you.

Note: One of the new features of Director 5 is a Paint window capable of producing images with 16.7 million colors. This will enable users to touch up photographs in Director. Director 5 also supports Photoshop plug-ins such as Kai's Power Tools.

At the top of the Paint window are several buttons in a horizontal toolbar that help you manage the various Cast members. Similar buttons are found in all windows that deal with Cast members, such as the Cast, Text, and Script windows. The orange button with a diamond is used to place the current Cast member on the Stage or Score or to reposition its location in the Cast window. The pink button with a plus sign lets you add a new Cast member. The green arrow buttons bring up the previous or next Cast member. The light blue button with an "I" brings up information on the Cast member. The information dialog box lets you name the Cast members and set priorities. The dark blue button brings up any script associated with that particular cast member.

Now let's get some practice. Double-click the image of the Porsche in the cast window to load it into the Paint window. Now select the lasso tool in the upper-left corner of the toolbar and circle the Porsche. The Porsche begins to flash, meaning it is the selected object. If it doesn't do this, try holding the lasso button down until a pop-up menu appears and select Shrink.

With the Porsche selected, click Edit ¦ Copy to copy the Porsche to the Clipboard. Then press the new Cast member button (the pink plus sign) and select Edit ¦ Paste to copy the Porsche to a new Cast member. Notice that the menus change depending on which window is active. With the Paint window active, Paint and Effect menu options show up.

In the new Cast member, draw two lines that run parallel to the car to represent a road. Then use the fill tool to color it black and delete the Porsche. We pasted the Porsche in only as a guide to line up the road.

Now let's make another Cast member for the yellow median lines. Copy and paste the road into a new Cast member, and then click and hold the foreground color box below the tool buttons and select yellow. Change the line thickness and draw some dashed lines down the middle of the road. Draw the lines so that they extend about twice the distance of the road. Now use the fill tool to remove the black road.

As a final step, double-click the 8-bits button at the bottom of the Paint window and change the color depth on both the road and lines Cast members to 1-bit. This reduces the size of these Cast members by requiring Director to remember only one color, not 256.

The Text Window

Although text can be handled in the Paint window, Director has a separate window specifically for dealing with text. You access this window by selecting Window ¦ Text. The text window is pretty straight forward. You can type directly into the text window, or you can paste text directly into the window from your favorite word processing program. The black bar on the right side of the window controls how wide your text box is. You can change the width of the text box by dragging the bar.

The light blue information icon brings up a dialog box that lets you change the type of text box you want to create. Perhaps the most useful choice is Scrolling Text found under the Style menu. This enables you to create a scrolling text window with no limitation on the length of your document.

Once you have added your text to the window, you can control how it and your text box look by selecting the text and choosing the font, size, and style from the text pull-down menu located on the top pull-down menu.

Caution: Keep in mind that not everyone
will have the same system fonts that you have on your machine. If you don't want to choose one of the basic core fonts, you can keep the font you choose by selecting the text document in the Cast window and converting it to a bitmap. This command is found under the Cast menu.

Be careful, because once you do this, you will not be able to edit the text. Also, be careful because while text adds very little to file size, bitmaps do! A big text document may be only a few kilobytes, but it might be several hundred once converted.

Also consider that although you can easily create editable or scrolling text, there is no quick and easy method for creating an editable or scrolling bitmap.

Animating Your Sprite

Now that your Cast is assembled, you can place them on the Stage and animate their movements across it. The Cast members' positions in the Score are important, so drag the road and the lines into channels 1 and 2. Then drag the Porsche into channel 3. This makes the Porsche appear on top of the road and the lines as you wish. Now position them as shown as shown in Figure 7.10, with the car to the left.

To animate the car, select the cell in channel 3, frame 1 and, while holding down the Alt key, drag it to channel 3, frame 20. This copies the Porsche image into frame 20. With the cell in channel 3, frame 20 selected, move the car image on the stage off the screen to the right. Now drag over all frames from 1 to 20 in channel 3 and select Score ¦ In-Between Linear. This computes all the intermediate positions of the Porsche image as it moves from left to right.

Now animate the yellow lines between frames 1 and 20 using the same commands. Position the lines so they remain in the middle of the road. Finally, use the same command with the road to fill all the frames of the road channel up to 20. However, do not reposition the road. Test the movie by pressing the play button on the Control Panel; the car should look like it is driving to the right off the stage and the yellow lines moving to the left give an added effect of motion. To loop the movie, toggle the loop button (second button from the right) in the Control Panel to On.

Using the Score ¦ In-between Special command, you can simulate acceleration and deceleration by selecting "ease in" or "ease out" effects. Try it on the Porsche.

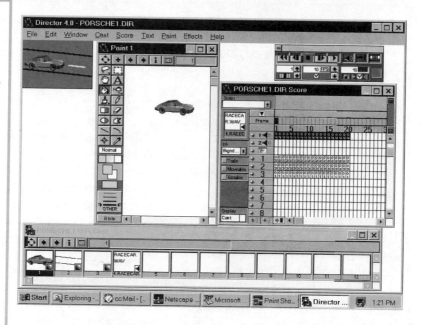

Figure 7.10.
The completed
Porsche movie
showing all Cast
members in the
Cast window and
their positions in
the Score. The
stage in the
upper-left corner
shows the movie
at frame 1.

Looks Great, But I Can't Hear Anything: Adding Music and Sound Effects

Now let's add some sound to the animation. Select File ¦ Import and load the racecar.wav file from the \shock directory. It appears in the Cast window. Now select the frames from 1 to 20 in sound channel 1, choose Score ¦ Set Sound, and select racecar.wav from the dialog box. Press the play button on the Control Panel to hear the results.

If you want to loop a piece of music located in the sound channel, select it in the Score window. An icon with the sound's name will appear in the upper-left corner. Double-click the icon, and an information box appears. Check the box that says "looped," and the sound loops continuously until it is interrupted by another sound.

If you want to stop a looped sound from playing, place a one-second silent sound clip in that channel.

Caution: When choosing sounds for your Shockwave project, keep in mind that sound is bandwidth intensive and does not compress well, so the shorter your music clip, the more effective it is. Music usually works best if you have a repetitive piece with verse and chorus.

It is also important to remember that you can't just take any piece of music and use it, even if you perform it yourself—unless you want to risk a lawsuit. Be careful not to use any copyrighted music, pictures, or text without getting permission.

Saving Your Movie

When you have completed your movie, clean it up to reduce its size. To do this, first open the Cast window and select Cast ¦ Find Cast Members. This gives you a dialog box. Select Find Cast members not used in the Score and OK. Now select Edit ¦ Clear cast member. This gets rid of any unused cast members you may have forgotten to delete while you were constructing the movie.

Next, if you are using the "real" version of Director, select File ¦ Save and Compact. Call your movie Porsche.dir. Now close your movie and you are ready to compress it into a Shockwave movie using After-burner.

Putting Your Movie on the Web

To put your movie on the Web, use the Afterburner utility. Although Afterburner is an excellent compressor, the amount of compression you get varies depending on how much sound is in the file and what type of graphics and text are used. You can usually expect approximately 50 percent compression.

Afterburner is simple to use. Just open the Afterburner application and select the Porsche.dir file. Afterburner suggests it be saved as porsche.dcr. Save the file and you're done. Your movie is now Shocked and ready to be included on your Web page. To do so, use the EMBED tag, like this:

```
<EMBED SRC="porsche.dcr" WIDTH=200
   HEIGHT=60 TEXTFOCUS=onMouse>
```

The Shockwave movie starts when it finishes loading. Figure 7.11 shows how it looks in an HTML file. Another Porsche movie made from 30 images of the original animation is included on this Web page. The next section will show how this is done, along with teaching you more details about Director.

Figure 7.11.
An HTML page enhanced with two Shockwave Porsche movies. The first is animated using Director functions, and the second is made of many images imported into Director.

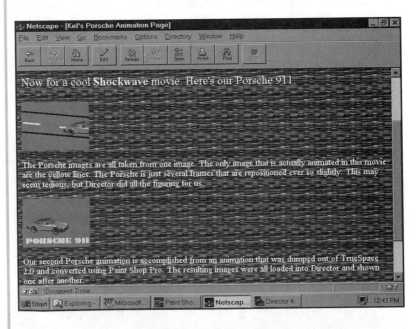

Character Animations in Director—The Walking Skeletons Movie

Now that we've seen how Director can animate simple images, let's look at how it can be used to import and control multiframe animations. In this example, you import several animated images of a skeleton walking, rendered in Photoshop and saved as both PICT (Mac) and PCX (Windows) files. Using the File ¦ Import command, load the images found in the hot directory.

When the Import dialog box is open, select the PCX (or PICT) file type and choose Import All. After the import, all eight frames of the animation show up in the Cast window, as shown in Figure 7.12.

Making the Skeleton Walk

With all your Cast members loaded, you are now ready to make the skeletons walk. In the Score window, select the first eight frames in channel number 1. Then, select all the Cast members and select Score ¦ Cast to Time. Set fps to six frames per second in the Control Panel and click the play button. You now have a character animation movie— the skeletons are walking!

Recall that each cell of the Score can contain one sprite. In this animation, each sprite is an image of the skeleton, drawn in a different position of his walk sequence.

The Alignment Tool

Perhaps the most important tool in the paint window is the alignment tool. Located in the lower-left corner of the tool palette, it looks like four arrows pointing inward. It enables you to create a consistent alignment point for any series of Cast members in the paint window. Several different sized images can be easily lined up using the alignment tool by selecting a common point on all the images.

Figure 7.12 Frame 1 of walk.dir *shows three skeletons walking. Notice the eight images in the Cast window.*

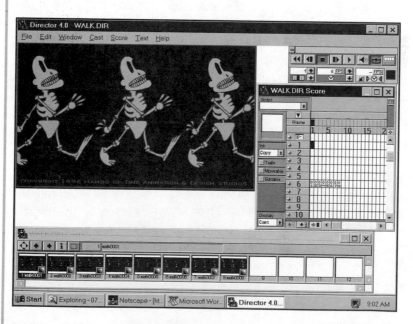

Your choice of alignment points greatly affects the playback of your animation. Take a series of images (perhaps the walking skeletons) and change the alignment points in the series to a variety of locations. If the skeletons animate from the hip bone, this is vastly different in effect than if they animate from the forehead….

To create alignment points, just select the tool, click, and drag across the image. You see a crosshair pattern. When you release the mouse, the alignment point is defined by the point where the vertical and horizontal lines intersect. You can redefine it at any time by simply repeating the process.

Let's take a closer look at the features of the Score window, the "master control" area of the entire movie or animation.

What's the Speed of Your Ink!?

Recall that the size and number of sprites you have on the stage at one time affect the playback speed of the animation; the ink effects you choose affect it as well. All sprites have an ink assigned to them. The ink you select substantially changes the speed of the sprite when it moves. These effects are set using the pull-down menu to the left of the Score window. The default

Tip: Copy ink animates substantially faster then any other ink, but of course it brings with it design challenges because of the visible "bounding box" effect. So choose this ink carefully when you are planning your design, and always design with your ink choices in mind.

ink is Copy (it is also the "fastest" ink), which means that the sprite appears on the stage as an opaque (white) square surrounding the original image you have painted or imported.

To assign an ink effect, click the sprite(s) you wish to work on either on the Stage or in the Score.

Tip: If you double-click a sprite in the Score, it selects the whole uninterrupted row of similar sprites in that channel.

To change the ink of selected Cast members in the Score, click the Ink pull-down menu, located to the left of the Score window and drag down and highlight the desired ink.

The second fastest ink is Matte, which turns all white areas of the sprite not surrounded by a colored area transparent. For example, a red zero painted on a white background set to Matte ink and placed on black background appears as a red zero surrounded by black with a white center.

The third fastest ink is Background Transparent, which means that all white areas are transparent. A red zero painted on a white background set to Background Transparent and placed on a black background appears as a red zero surrounded by black with a black center.

All the ink effects are shown in Figure 7.13. Learning to use these ink effects can be become a powerful design tool.

Figure 7.13. Eighteen ink effects to choose from! Try 'em all to see what's possible....

More Score Features

Check the Trails box to cause your sprite to leave trails. This means that the image of your sprite remains on the stage even if it is no longer in the Score; it "stains" the stage with its image (see Figure 7.14). The stain can be removed by placing another sprite on top of it, or by adding a transition effect.

Besides creating interesting visual effects, you can use trails to substantially improve playback performance. The fewer the number and the smaller the size of the sprites you

Figure 7.14. This is what happens when you turn on Trails! Play with all the ink effects and options, but choose wisely in the end because they greatly affect the look and performance of your animation.

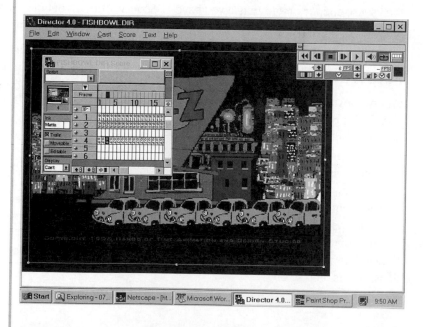

have on the Stage at any one time, the faster your animation plays back. If you have an area of the Stage that is not changing, you can place that Cast member in only the first cell of the animation and then eliminate it in all subsequent cells: The image appears to remain on the screen, but the computer can execute events happening elsewhere on the stage substantially faster because it no longer has to keep track of the Cast member you have eliminated from the Score. The remaining sprite is a visual "echo" of itself that requires no energy from the computer to be seen on the Stage.

Underneath the Trails checkbox, the Moveable checkbox enables the user to drag an image across the stage. Using this simple checkbox, you can create any number of fun activities. For example, you could create a set of blocks that a child could manipulate to construct castles or bridges, the same way he or she would with real blocks.

Below that, the Editable checkbox enables the user to change or add to text you have placed on the stage.

Know the Score!

When constructing your animation, you may find it helpful to view the Score window in a variety of ways. Click the Display pull-down menu in the lower-left corner of the score window. There are six different ways to view the Score. Each are helpful at different times. The default view is Cast, which shows the number corresponding to the number of its Cast member. Other choices show which inks are used, transitions, scripts, and so on.

Interactivity with Lingo

Now that we've shown you that with Director you can do the same tricks discussed earlier in the book, we will look at what you can do with Director and Shockwave that isn't possible with the other techniques.

Enter Lingo, to a rousing applause. Lingo is a scripting language designed especially for Director that enables the user to add scripts, which release the interactive nature of Director.

Event Markers

Before you review several simple scripts that enable you to create complex interactive multimedia, you'll need to become familiar with *event markers*.

The event marker looks like a downward carat and is located in a small box above the word "frame" in the upper-left corner of the Score window. It defines a place in the Score where something happens.

To create an event marker, click the black arrow, drag it out to the right, and release it above the frame where you want the event to take place. You might remember noticing an event marker called "no sound" in Figure 7.8.

You can move the event marker if you decide you don't like where it is placed. When it is placed, double-click it to access a dialog box that lets you name the marker. This name appears next to the event marker. Now you can refer to it in any of your scripts.

Creating Scripts

To create a script, click the Script box (in the upper-left corner of the Score window) and drag down to New. This launches the Script window. Then type the script you wish to execute and close the window.

To assign the script in the Score window, highlight the cell in the script channel where you wish the script to be executed. Next, click the Script box and drag down until you have highlighted the script you wish to be executed; then release the mouse. The script now appears in the cell you highlighted. When the playback head crosses that frame, Director executes that script.

Looping

The loop is one of the most important functions of any interactive program. It lets you control the order of the movie. Perhaps the simplest script is a jump in the movie sequence. It looks like this:

```
on exitFrame
  go to "1A"
end
```

This script causes the playback head to return to the event marker labeled A1, once the frame is completed. The A1 event marker can be anywhere in the Score, but if it is placed in a cell previous to where the Lingo script is placed, then the movie returns to this location before continuing, thus creating a loop. But, remember when creating this loop that the last frame must flow smoothly into the first or the animation looks choppy.

Any Cast Member Can Become a Button! It's All in the Script...

Any Cast member can act as a button that responds when the user clicks it. But before you can detect user interaction, you must stop the movie using the following script:

```
on exitFrame
  go to the frame
end
```

This causes the playback head to wait at that frame until the user issues another command, by either clicking a button or using a keystroke. There are numerous ways to continue the movie, but perhaps the easiest and most useful is to attach a script to a Cast member, which acts as a button.

Here are some examples of scripts attached to buttons.

```
on mouseDown
  go to "1A"
end
on mouseUp
  go to "1A"
end
```

These scripts both take you to event marker A1. The only difference is that the first script is executed when you press the mouse button, and the second is executed when the mouse button is released.

Using Scripts to Establish Links

Lingo can also be used to establish links to other Shockwave movies, or Web pages using the GotoNetPage command:

```
on mouseUp
  GotoNetPage "http://www.macromedia.com/
    Gallery/Shockwave/Custom/index2.html"
end
```

This script sends the Web surfer to Macromedia's gallery page when the mouse button is released. It is extremely useful for providing a means of building links in a Shockwave movie without having to build it in HTML.

User Message Scripts

Sometimes you will want to tell your user something without proceeding out of the current loop. The following script does this when attached to a sprite:

```
on mouseUp
  alert "Sorry, this area is unavailable
  to you."
end
```

This script displays a dialog box. Clicking OK enables the user to continue.

The if...then Command

The if...then command is one of the simplest yet most powerful commands you can use. It sets up a reaction to what the user has done. For example, to set up a counter that determines how many times a user has passed through a certain place in the script, first initialize the starting number of count.

```
on exitFrame
  set count = 1
  put count
end.
```

This command sets the variable count to 1. Then enter the following:

```
on exitFrame
  set count = count +1
  put count
  If count>8 then go to "Off limits"
  else
    nothing
  end if
end
```

Each time the playback passes by the script (the if...then) the count advances by one.

The ninth time the playback head passes the script, the if...then statement causes the playback head to go to the event marker off limits in the script.

Adding Macintosh-Specific Commands

When adding sound, keep in mind that the Windows version of Director doesn't support sound playback in both channels at the same time, but the Macintosh does. To play two sounds on the Mac but not the PC, use the following Lingo command while having a sound in sound channel 2.

```
on exitFrame
  if the machinetype = 256 then
   nothing
  else
    puppetSound "Gong"
  end if
end
```

Machinetype 256 is the code for a Windows machine. In this case "Gong" refers to an audio Cast member named "Gong." What this statement is saying is, "If this isn't a PC, play the gong sound."

The following command can be modified to display messages specific to Mac or PC users, and for a variety of different uses. The following example will hide the cursor of Windows machines and set the cursor of the Macintosh to a watch icon.

```
on exitFrame
  if the machinetype = 256 then
    cursor 200
  else
    cursor 4
  end if
end
```

What this statement is saying is "If the playback machine is a PC, then hide the cursor. If it is anything else, then set the cursor to be a stop watch."

While the scripts listed here are simple, they will allow you to quickly create rich multimedia pieces to which you can add more complex elements. They also offer the advantage of being Shockwave compatible.

The rollover Command—Background Textures Page Example

For an example of a Shockwave movie that uses Lingo scripts, let's build an Interactive Background Previewer that presents several backgrounds produced with Kai's Power Tools in an interactive format. First, import all the texture GIF images in the \shock directory and position them on the Stage set to 600 by 250 as shown in Figure 7.15. Make sure that they are located in order in channels 1–12.

Next create a text field using the Tool window under the textures. Open the information dialog by clicking on the light blue icon with an i in it and name it texture. Now open the script window using the Window ¦ Script menu option and type the following:

```
on startMovie
  global nameList
  put "Texture Name" into field "texture"
  set nameList=["Blue Ice","Blue Marble","Mottled Color",
"Goldenrod","Shaved Metal","Lavendar Pattern","Purple Freeway",
"Razor's Edge","Red Water","Ripping Claws","Sandstone","Grainy Stone"]
end startMovie

on spotTexture
  repeat with i = 1 to 12
    if rollover (i) then
      put getAt(nameList, i) into field "texture"
      exit
    end if
  end repeat
end spotTexture
```

Figure 7.15. An Interactive Background Previewer that tells you the name of the texture as you move the mouse over it and jumps to a sample page using that texture as a background when you click on it.

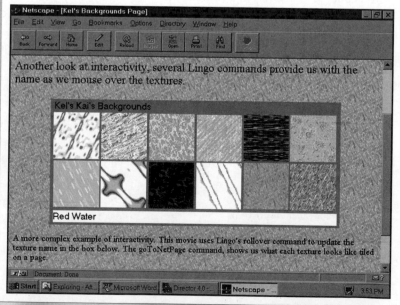

This script has two main sections: The first initializes a variable called `nameList`, places the words "Texture Name" in the text field, and sets up a list of texture names from which to draw. The second section tells Director to sample where the mouse is with the `rollover` command, and if it is over any of the 12 sprites, to display the appropriate color name in the text field. (This is why it is important to order the sprites the same as the names in the list; otherwise they won't match.)

The `repeat` command lets you place this script in one location to cover all 12 textures. You could have placed a separate script to display the name in each channel, but this method saves the extra typing. The primary disadvantage is that it requires that the computer continually poll for the mouse position, thus slowing down the performance of any ongoing animation in the movie. Now take a look at the results by pushing the play icon in the Control Panel.

Seeing a group of textures and their associated names is great, but it would be better if you could see how they look in a sample Web page. By using the `GotoNetPage` Lingo command, you can create links to other Web pages or to other Shockwave movies.

This is easily done in our example by building a script for each texture. Select the first texture (Blue Ice in channel 1) and open a new script by clicking the script selection menu in the upper-left corner and dragging it down to New. Then type the following script:

```
on mouseUp
  goToNetPage("blueice.htm")
end
```

This tells the movie to go to the `blueice.htm` page when the mouse button is released.

The `blueice.htm` page shows what the texture looks like as a tiled background.

A separate HTML page has been built for each texture, and the completed movie has links to each texture. To see this example as a Web page, look at `backgrnd.htm` in the `/shock` directory on the CD.

This short introduction to Lingo only touches the surface of Lingo. Many more commands are available, but once again, I leave you to explore them.

To learn more about creating rich Lingo scripts, check out the Lingo dictionary included with Director or go to the Macromedia site at

`http://www.macromedia.com`

or the Director user's site at

`http://hakatai.mcli.dist.maricopa.edu/`
`  director/index.html`

Advanced Director Tricks

You're getting the hang of it now, so let's look at some advanced tricks that really distinguish your Web pages.

Creating Faux Video

Shockwave does not support QuickTime or AVI video formats, so to create *faux video*, try this trick.

Import the individual frames of the video and align them using the alignment tool in the Paint window. Place them on the stage with the Cast to Time command described earlier, placing them in channel 2. Save your movie and click through it using the Control Panel.

Now select several key frames from the movie and move them into channel 1. Then, using the Paint window, edit all the frames between these key frames and replace anything that doesn't change with white.

Then select all the edited nonkey frames and change their ink to Matte. This makes the white, nonessential parts transparent, so when the video plays, only the parts of the video that have changed are updated. Finally, add the audio from the QuickTime or AVI file in the sound channel and tweak it until it matches the picture.

Although this is a labor-intensive process, the results can be quite good. The savings in file size are substantial, especially if you limit your frame rate to the minimum. You can create the illusion of video—just choose your sequences and edit them tightly. Remember, you can use the same Cast members over and over again, layering them up to 48 times without adding to your file size.

Director updates the stage from the bottom to the top (that is, from cell 48 to cell 1), so if speed is your main concern, place your Cast members in the high-numbered channels. This technique does not make a "chunky" animation run well, but it does make any animation play back a little faster.

Big Animation with Small File Sizes Using Tools

The Tool window is small, but holds a lot of power. It enables you to create movie elements quickly and is perfect for making buttons and touching up a scene. Access this window by selecting Window ¦ Tools. There are nine buttons on the tool panel. The arrow icon simply returns your cursor to the default setting, enabling you to manipulate objects on the stage. (The tool window is shown back in Figure 7.8 to the left of the Paint window.)

The other buttons let you create text (without the hassle of dealing with the text window), create lines, and create quick-draw shapes. You can define the line thickness from zero to three pixels by changing the selection at the bottom of the panel. You can also define the line color by using the paint chip selectors located in the middle of the panel. These represent the foreground and background colors of an object. Below the paint chips is the pattern selector.

The advantage of each of the aforementioned tools is that they add almost nothing (a few bytes) to the size of your file. The biggest advantage of using the tool palette is its use in coordination with 1-bit Cast members. To convert a Cast member to 1-bit, first either import it or create it using the Paint window. Then double-click "8 bits" (at the bottom-left corner). You get a menu that enables you to change your artwork size, palette color depth, and so on. To change the color depth, choose the Color pull-down menu and drag down until 1-bit is highlighted; then release the mouse. Now click OK. After you have placed the Cast member on the stage, redefine what is black and what is white using the paint chips.

You can also use the paint chips to change the color from frame to frame, thus creating a flashing sign using only one cast member.

Another way to define more than two colors for a 1-bit graphic is to cut it into component pieces (different cast members) and layer them using Matte and Background Transparent ink effects. For example, you could take a picture of a man, and divide the figure up into pants, shirt, shoes, face, a pair of arms, and so on; you can define a color pair to be applied to each of the component parts (Cast members). In that case, the figure would become five separate Cast members, which would be assembled only on the Stage itself. If carefully designed and placed, the figure appears as a cohesive and yet colorful unit. Of course, the added benefit is that all the separate Cast members can animate independently. So break up your figures thinking not only of design elements but motion requirements as well. You can also add smaller 8-bit component parts where necessary to make the image appear more lifelike.

The advantage of doing all this is that a 1-bit image is about one-tenth the size of an 8-bit image, and with many images, the 1-bit image appears cleaner than the 8-bit.

The only disadvantage is that 1-bit images and quick-draw shapes animate more slowly than do 8-bit images. Nevertheless, the savings in file size in most cases is worth the relatively minor reduction in playback speed, especially for Shockwave movies.

Adding Multiple Movies to a Page

Although there is no limit to the number of movies you can have on a page at one time, each Shockwave movie uses 50KB to 100KB of RAM. More RAM than that is required by the actual movie and the browser, so users with limited amounts of RAM will experience problems.

However, if you move from page to page, each page containing a movie, Shockwave frees up the additional RAM necessary to play the new movie by discarding the movies from the previous page. Likewise, if you are using multiple movies on a single page (as seen in Figure 7.16), it is best to have sound on only one to avoid crashing the user's computer. If you want to have multiple sound movies, avoid using looped sounds and have the sounds play only when the user clicks a button or triggers the sound by some specific action.

Figure 7.16.
An HTML page
with several
Shockwave
movies playing at
the same time.

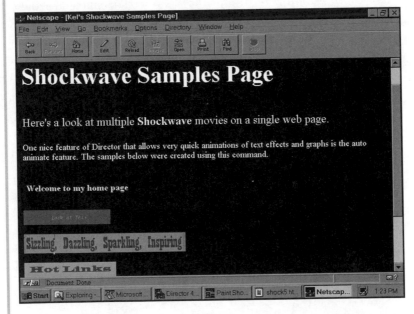

Shockwave Limitations

What we've seen is great, but the current version of Shockwave has some severe limitations. These include the following:

+ **Shockwave movies do not support QuickTime**. This may not be much of a problem because QuickTime is so bandwidth-intensive that most developers tend to avoid its use.

+ **Director doesn't support MIDI.** This doesn't mean that you can't have music, but it does mean that the substantial savings in disk space inherent with MIDI aren't available, and the developer must use WAV files for sound.

+ **Shockwave does not support custom palettes.** Consequently, graphics, if planned around the Windows system palette, may look acceptable, but skin tones and most gradients do not.

+ **Shockwave movies must be downloaded and cached in their entirety before they can play**. If your file size gets too big, Web surfers will not wait for the entire movie to download before they move on.

At this writing, Macromedia is working on these limitations and expects to fix them sometime soon. In the meantime, Shockwave represents a revolution on the Internet for cramming a lot into a little space.

Note:
Macromedia has disabled certain commands specifically in Shockwave files because of security concerns. The following Lingo functions have been disabled in Shockwave:

X-Objects—Reads and writes text files that contain information such as user responses, names and addresses, or interactive game information.

FileIO XObject—Makes multiple instances of an object in memory such as controlling Director movies on two computers from a Director movie on a central computer.

SerialPort XObject—Controls devices that play video and audio source material, such as videodisc, videotape, and audio CD players.

Resource and XLib commands, OpenXLib—Control resource files located outside a Director movie.

OpenResFile, CloseXLib, and CloseResFile—Respectively open and close an open window and close windows that can play a Director movie.

importFileInto command—Replaces a file member with a specified external file.

saveMovie command—Saves a movie to a file.

PrintFrom command—Prints whatever is displayed on the stage for a frame or range of frames.

In addition, several system-related commands have also been disabled, including:

Open—Launches and closes specified applications.

Exit Director, Quit, Restart, and Shutdown commands—Respectively restarts, and shuts down, the computer.

Filename and path properties and functions fileName of cast, fileName of window, getNthFileNameInFolder, moviePath—These commands search for documents located on your hard drive and link to external files.

pathName, searchCurrentFolder, and windows, paths—These commands search paths.

mci command—Passes specified strings to the Windows media control.

Alternatives to Shockwave

Although Director is a great program and Shockwave undoubtedly occupies the position of dominance for creating multimedia applications on the Web, it would be foolish, especially if price is your main consideration, not to at least look at some of the other packages out there.

In this section, we give an overview. However, the nature of the Web is that new technologies and sites are being added every day. Your best path is to surf around and check things out in depth at regular intervals, to stay apprised of what is current and available. Probably the best place to start your search is at the Plug-in Center on the Netscape Site at

```
http://home.mcom.com/comprod/products/
  navigator/version_2.0/plugins/
  index.html
```

Sizzler

One of the new animation plug-ins for the Net is Sizzler. Sizzler automates the process for creating faux video described earlier. However, the manual method gives you much better compression in many cases. It's is available at

```
http://www.totallyhip.com/sizzler/
  6f_sizz.html
```

Sizzler's biggest advantage over Shockwave is that it streams live, so you don't have to wait for the file to download to begin watching it. Although the plug-in is cross platform, the application itself is currently only available for the Macintosh. A Windows version of the Sizzler converter is in development at this writing and has been promised soon.

Sizzler is currently free for both the plug-in and converter applications during the beta period. Its intended price tag hasn't been revealed yet, but it is probably substantially less expensive than Director.

Unlike Director, Sizzler has an easy-to-use interface but doesn't currently allow developers to add sound and full interactivity to their files. The converter only converts PICTs and QuickTime video. Totally Hip, the makers of Sizzler, are developing these features for the Sizzler converter application and will continue to extend the functionality of the Sizzler converter.

As with Director, you can increase the performance of Sizzler by reducing the amount of images or the size of an animation using solid fills instead of gradients. Smaller files, as usual, have better playback performance. Sizzler files should range from 20KB to 400KB. Sizzler files are usually smaller than the native file but vary depending on the number, size, and complexity of the cells.

To publish Sizzler files on a Web server, configure the server to recognize the sprites by defining a MIME type. The MIME type for sprite files is `application/x-sprite`. When your server knows this, it recognizes sprite files and enables you to publish them on your Web page. For more details, refer to the readme file "Configuring Your Server" included in the Sizzler download package.

At the Totally Hip home page, you can also find an ever-increasing list of sites on the Web that use Sizzler to animate portions of their sites. If you visit some of these sites, you will notice how quick Sizzler is. The plug-in is also very small.

Figure 7.17 shows The Box Web site

```
http://www.cibernet.it/thebox/english/
    first_fly.html
```

where they have used Sizzler to catch a fly in the Web. This little critter buzzes and flies about. As the page downloads, you'll notice that it appears immediately, but only as a

bunch of gray boxes. Slowly the resolution increases until you can see it in detail. This is a good example of how streaming animation works, giving you something to look at besides a gray box until the animation finishes downloading.

Astound

Astound is another package that promises to bring animation to the World Wide Web. At this writing, the software for creating Astound documents is for Windows only, but a Mac version is promised soon. Like the software to create Astound, the plug-in is still PC only available at

```
http://www.golddisk.com/awp/index.html
```

The Astound plug-in also plays Studio M files.

Astound authoring software is currently priced at $250.00, but the Studio M software, though far less powerful, is priced at

Figure 7.17.
A fly caught in the Web using Sizzler.

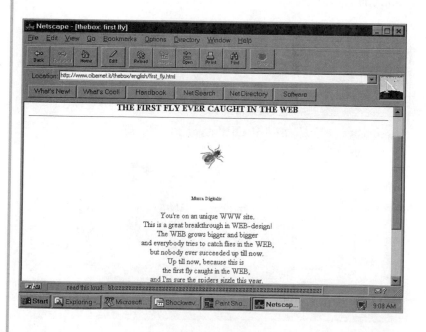

$49.00. Like Astound, Studio M is currently only available for the PC.

Astound is a presentation package with the unique ability to animate charts, graphs, and so on. You can use Astound templates or create your own. The templates have multimedia effects built in, and you can add text charts, 3D graphics, sound, video, animated clip art, and backgrounds. Astound's interactivity seems to be extremely limited compared with that of Director but is ideal for business and casual users.

Astound's Timeline window works similarly to the Score window in Director and has a feature that automatically analyzes your presentation and suggests ways to make it run more smoothly—or simply adjusts it for you.

Another advantage of Astound is that it can link to popular programs like Excel and Lotus. You can either link to an external file or import the information and create graphs and charts from the information therein.

An example of Astound in use is shown in Figure 7.18.

Studio M

Studio M works in much the same way as Astound, offering fewer transitions and templates. Like Astound, you can combine sound, graphics, video, and limited animation, but there is no provision for interactivity or linking to Excel or Lotus.

Studio M is used primarily to create virtual greeting cards for distribution through e-mail, floppy disk, or home pages. These cards can also be printed out on a color or black and white printer.

The Studio M Installer can automatically create a Web page from one of 50 customizable templates. Using the template, you can add JPEG slide shows of your own choosing and your own text. You can also create Web pages and add your Web project (ASN file) directly to your HTML document.

Figure 7.18. A standard template used with Astound to create interactive presentations for the Web. Here you see the fridge.

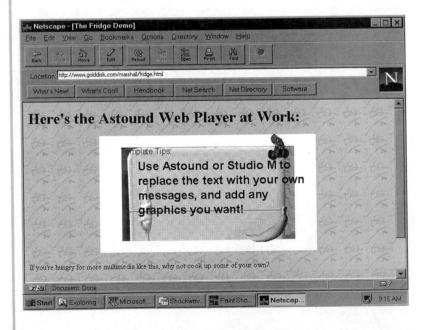

To add a project with a hypertext link for playback in the full Netscape window using Studio M, use the following syntax:

```
<A HREF="project filename.ASN">Click
    here</A>
```

To embed a project that automatically begins playing in a specific area of your Web page when your page is displayed, use the following syntax:

```
<EMBED SRC="project filename.ASN"
    HEIGHT=slide's height in pixels
    WIDTH=slide's width in pixels>
```

Astound and Studio M offer advantages over Director in several respects, especially if price is your main consideration. Astound may be just the solution for the business person who wants to convey important information over a corporate Intranet in a slick but expedient manner.

Likewise, Studio M offers a quick and affordable solution for the family or small businessperson who wants to create a spiffy

Web page but doesn't have much capital or time to devote to the process.

Powersoft's Media.splash

It's not just the little multimedia companies that are getting into the interactivity-on-the-Web craze. Powersoft, maker of PowerBuilder and other high-end development tools, has a product called Media.splash that is sure to make a splash.

Its main benefit is to tie into Powersoft's other powerful tools and use it to create sophisticated Web sites with access to databases. This makes it easy to develop dynamic Web pages with personalized content.

Media.splash works a little differently than other products. Rather than embedding the file in an HTML script, it spawns a new window for each file accessed. This has the advantage of enabling the user to run several Media.splash files conveniently at the same time. An example is shown in Figure 7.19.

Figure 7.19. Media.splash in action. Notice the separate window that is spawned to show the file. Clicking the Go button reveals the "Rhigaroo" that was created.

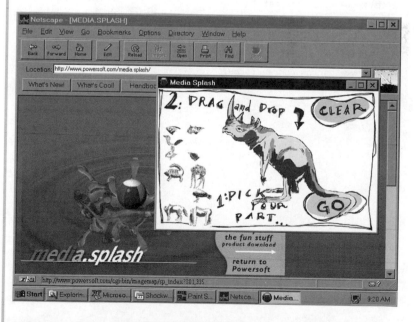

Other Options Still to Come

Still not enough? Well, don't worry, because many other products are in the preliminary phases, and they should give Shockwave and the others a run for their money. Here are some to watch.

WorldWired Inc. has been working on cT Professional, which promises a cross-platform multimedia authoring language specifically built for the Internet.

http://www.worldwired.com

Allegiant has a product called Marionet that is worth seeing. Built as a scripting engine, Marionet supports advanced features such as a unique chat protocol, automated link management, and search capabilities. Marionet can create scripts that run quietly in the background using simple English-like commands. This is the same group that introduced SuperCard for the Macintosh, so you can expect some great features.

http://www.allegiant.net

From Harrow Software, check out Formula Graphics at

http://www.harrow.com.au/formula

Finally, an up-and-coming product that seems to be getting a lot of attention is Emblaze Creator from GEO Interactive Media Group at

http://www.geo.co.il

Want more? iWorld at

http://www.iworld.com/InternetShopper/
   1Misc.html

has a good list of products in this arena. Many of these products and others are listed here with links.

What's Next?

Along with other packages, Shockwave is an exciting technology that enables users to quickly add animations and interactive presentations to Web pages.

Now that you have interactivity on your Web pages, you may wonder what could possibly be next. Well, the next section moves you to the ultimate in interactivity: using VRML. With VRML, you can build and navigate through your own worlds on the Web—in 3D!

A World of Your Own: Virtual Reality

part **III**

The World Wide Web Isn't Flat

The World Wide Web is the most rapidly evolving technology today. It is one of the few technologies that has every other software and hardware manufacturer scurrying to release something that is either explicitly for the Internet or compatible with the Internet. With more development tools that make Web page development a snap, everyone is getting into the act of creating their own pages, or personal niches of Cyberspace. However, the term Cyberspace is rather elusive. It infers that it is truly three dimensional, like the space that our planet Earth orbits in. However, as most of us know, a large extent of the content on the Web is simply two dimensional—simple screens or pages of information and graphics. Sure, some of the pictures may *appear* to be 3D, but they are not. It is not possible to rotate one of these pictures and see what's on the other side. They are simply decorations, like paintings on a wall or drawings in a notebook. Now, this has all changed with the recent introduction to the Web of the *Virtual Reality Modeling Language* or *VRML* for short. This technology literally expands the dimensions of the Web.

Certainly, you've seen some motion pictures that have brought back to life photo-realistic dinosaurs or created devious enemies made entirely of liquid metal. You've probably also seen numerous commercials that make inanimate objects suddenly move and dance. Thanks to the wonderful world of computer graphics, it's possible to create any scenario. It's possible because the complex programs that create these semi-realistic scenes rely entirely on creating 3D worlds. These programs allow trained artists the capabilities of assembling objects that occupy all three dimensions of space, not just the width and height of an object. Then these objects can be moved about in all three dimensions. When the final scenes are created, computer algorithms based on mathematical functions examine the scene and determine where to add reflections, spots of light, and shadows relevant to the objects to make them appear realistic. Typically, these mathematical calculations require an extraordinary amount of computation just to render one 3D image.

Let's say the average time required to generate a single scene is just one minute—pretty short amount of time for a complex scene. However, if we were creating a movie, then this scene would be animated. You may recall that movies are actually made up of several pictures on a tape. These pictures are assembled one right after another and each picture differs very slightly. When these pictures are passed quickly in order, the result is an appearance of motion. Production quality videos require that thirty of these pictures (or frames) pass on the screen within a second of time (30fps—frames per second). Therefore, if we were creating one second of a video using 3D software, we would need to generate thirty scenes. If each scene takes a minute, then that one second of video would require thirty minutes to create!

What if you wanted to make a minute-long video? That means you need 60 seconds of motion, where each second requires 30 scenes to be rendered. The result is 1,800 frames that require 30 hours to generate the final video, if each frame requires about a minute to create!

I hope you can now have a better appreciation of all the work it takes just to generate a minute of 3D computer animation—not to mention the countless hours required to create the 3D objects within each scene and the time spent determining how to animate each of those objects. Understanding and creating 3D worlds in a computer takes a little patience and much practice.

In this chapter, you will be introduced to 3D worlds that you can visit using the Internet. You will learn how to configure and use a 3D browser within your Internet browser, as well as find some interesting worlds on the Internet. You will also see how to create your own virtual reality worlds using dedicated development tools to lay out and convert 3D objects. Finally, you will be introduced to some areas on the Internet where you can find libraries of 3D objects that you may assemble and use in your own scenes.

In Chapter 9, "Building 3D Cyberspace," and Chapter 10, "Fancy Modeling Tricks," you will learn how to create simple and more complex 3D worlds of your own, similar to some you will see in this chapter. Although you will be introduced to the wonderful world of 3D graphics on the Web, this section of the book cannot possibly cover each nuance of creating 3D worlds. However, it will serve as a starting point that will help you to add some cool 3D attributes to your Web pages.

VRML

The Virtual Reality Modeling Language (VRML) is not entirely new. It has been around for a while, but has just recently been standardized and has sparked the imagination of developers on the Web. VRML is a language for developing 3D scenes. A file in VRML contains instructions on how to draw this scene. These instructions are then read by a VRML browser, which determines how to actually convert the instructions into 3D graphics. The process is similar to how a World Wide Web browser reads an HTML file and converts that file into the Web pages you see on the Internet. Figure 8.1 shows a

VRML world as displayed by the Live3D VRML browser.

The VRML instructions that form a complete scene are stored in a VRML file referred to as a *world*. Often these files are standard text files and end with the .wrl file extension (*wrl* is short for *world*). The file consists of commands that instruct the VRML browser how to create 3D objects. These instructions are quite simple and are similar to telling the browser to "move to this point in space" or "draw a sphere with a one meter radius." Listing 8.1 shows a sample VRML file, which will be covered in more detail in Chapters 9 and 10.

Figure 8.1. These virtual apples appear rather simple. However, they are 3D apples, so it is possible to spin them around. Also notice the apparent shine on the apples, automatically generated by the VRML browser.

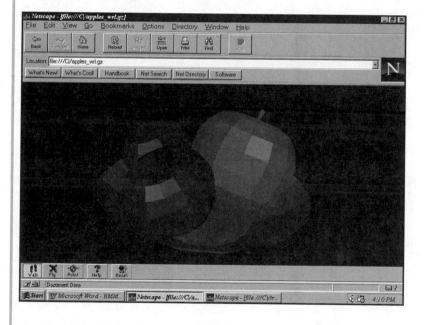

Listing 8.1. VRML files consist of textual instructions.

```
#VRML V1.0 ASCII

# WAYCOOL.WRL
# A way cool demonstration

DEF BackgroundImage Info {
    # Nice space background
    string "spacebak.gif"
}

SpinGroup {
    # Spin a cube on its Y, Z axis's
    rotation 0 1 1 -.1

    Separator {
        Texture2 {
            # Animate some text on the cube
            filename "wpwanim.gif"
        }
        Cube {
            width 10
            height 10
            depth 10
        }
    }
}

Separator {
    Transform {
        translation 10 0 0
    }

    AxisAlignment {
        alignment ALIGNAXISXYZ
    }

    FontStyle {
        size 4
    }

    AsciiText {
        string "Web Page Wizardry"
    }
}
```

The VRML browser takes these instructions and performs the actions. The browser is responsible for assembling the scene, which includes determining where to create objects, how to draw and color those objects, and how to apply lighting and shadows for the scene. The browser is also responsible for enabling the user to control how to view the scene. Most VRML browsers allow the user to either "walk," "fly," or "examine" objects in a VRML world.

Walk—As its name implies, this mode of a VRML browser enables you to simulate walking around the scene. You can move forward, backward, and left to right, but cannot move up or down.

Fly—This VRML browser mode simulates the action of flying an airplane around the scene. You can move forward and backward, as well as bank to either the left or right or move up and down.

Examine—Every browser names its modes of viewing the VRML scene differently. The "examine" mode lets you spin the objects in a VRML scene, so that you may see whatever side you wish.

Point—In certain VRML browsers, such as Live3D, it is possible to reset the center point of the world you are viewing. This "point" mode also moves your viewing location toward that new center point. For instance, in Figure 8.1, if you click on the stem of an apple, future rotations of that object would be around the center of that stem, not the center of the entire bowl.

Note: Most VRML browsers offer a convenient way to change between viewing modes. Typically, you will find buttons at the bottom of the VRML window for toggling between these modes or choices in a menu for the VRML browser. Each VRML browser implements these viewing modes differently. In addition, examining 3D worlds using these viewing modes may vary depending on the VRML browser.

There are several different VRML browsers available today. In this book, we will concentrate on the VRML browser plug-in for Netscape 2: Netscape's Live3D. The CD-ROM included with this book contains Live3D.

WorldView by Intervista Software is a stand-alone product that can be used by itself to access VRML URLs on the Web without a Web browser. Some Web browsers that do not yet support the plug-in technology found in Netscape may use WorldView as a helper application.

The Next Level of VRML

As you can see so far, creating virtual worlds in Cyberspace can be pretty effective. Imagine the possibilities. For instance, if you owned hotels, you could create 3D models of the rooms so that people who want to reserve a room for a vacation could see what your hotel has to offer. Or maybe you construct houses and would like to show your floor samples in three dimensions. Perhaps you want to track three different stocks over a period of three weeks; you could represent the results as 3D graphs and charts. Maybe you need to see 3D models of chemical compounds or simply to create 3D games. All these are just examples of what you can do with VRML.

As with any technology, though, the current technology is not powerful enough and must continue to evolve. Developers are constantly striving to improve on a technology, adding new features and functions that have been requested by those who use the new technology. Therefore, it should come as no surprise, particularly in the rapidly growing area of the Internet, that VRML is also being improved.

Currently, you can create 3D scenes that look quite realistic in the world of VRML, but that is all. The user can zoom in on an object in your scene, rotate it around in space, or click on different areas to jump to other worlds or Web pages on the Internet. Unfortunately, that is about all the user can do. In fact, as you walk toward an object in the current versions of VRML, you can walk right through the object!

VRML 2.0 will address these limitations and expand on the current instructions offered in VRML 1.*x*. In the next version of VRML, you can expect to see many new advancements—mainly because you will be able to control the actions of a VRML world programmatically via languages, such as C or Java. For instance, you will be able to simulate effects, such as fog, or play sounds that emanate from a perceived location in your 3D world. You will also be able to animate objects that take on particular programmatic qualities, such as bouncing or being pulled by gravity. It will be possible to detect when two objects are colliding in space and to take appropriate actions, such as bounce off each other or explode. In addition, although current VRML files are simple text files, they are becoming increasingly complex and require greater amounts of space or bandwidth for transfer. Newer VRML browsers support compressed versions of these VRML world files that are smaller and require less time to download from the Internet when slower connections are used.

The possibilities for these new improvements in VRML are even greater. It will be possible to create more realistic games where you can fly into things or walk into walls.

You can create virtual reality cafés or chat rooms where you can interact with other 3D individuals. Simulations will become possible that actually allow students to use a virtual screw driver to loosen virtual screws.

Live3D is incorporating some of these new features by adhering to a new standard developed by Silicon Graphics and Netscape, *Moving Worlds*. This standard contains many of the features that will be used in VRML 2.0. In this section of the book, we will look at how to implement VRML and view the results using the Live3D VRML browser.

Viewing the World

So how do you get started with VRML? Netscape Navigator 2.*x* supports a plug-in technology within the Web browser. This technology enables you to view rich forms of data in the Web browser window instead of in separate helper application windows. The result is a Web page with rich content that appears to be integrated with the rest of the document. With plug-ins, you can embed an object, such as a video, into the Web page that maintains attributes like an inline graphic. However, when you load the page, the video will play within its own window inside of the browser's window.

The same is possible with VRML via the Live3D plug-in from Netscape. Live3D is a VRML browser that enables you to view and interact with VRML worlds from a window embedded inside the Netscape browser. You no longer need to switch to a separate program to view 3D scenes. Live3D, as you will see later in this chapter and in Chapter 9, is incorporating some of the features that will be found in the next generation of VRML.

I Get Around

Moving around a VRML world takes some getting used to. Even after navigating through worlds for a long time, it sometimes still gets confusing just where you are. For that reason, most VRML browsers provide a Reset button that restores the original, default view that you saw when you first opened a scene. Let's take a look at how to get around a VRML world by opening a 3D object with Live3D. The object we'll examine comes from the Internet and can be found at the following URL address:

```
http://www.ocnus.com/models/Vehicles/
   x29.wrl.gz
```

This file uses the new compressed format for VRML files, *gzip* compression. Figure 8.2 displays the 3D object, the X-29 fighter jet, as it appears when first loaded in the VRML browser.

As you can see from Figure 8.2, there is a nice gleam of light reflecting from the top of the aircraft. This indicates that the light source is somewhere above where you are "standing" in Cyberspace. To move toward or around this object, simply hold the left mouse button down and move the mouse at the same time. Depending on the mode your browser is set to (walk, fly, or point), you will move toward the object. Tables 8.1 through 8.3 show the possible mouse movements involved with each VRML mode of movement, while Figure 8.3 illustrates how the VRML object appears after walking toward it and slightly to the front of it.

Figure 8.2. The X-29 Fighter Jet is loaded and is at its default position in the Live3D VRML browser.

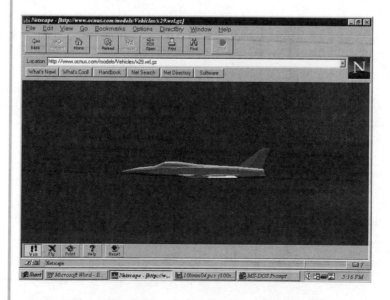

Table 8.1. Mouse movements in the walk mode of the Live3D VRML browser.

Mouse Action	3D Action
Holding Left Button/Move Forward	Walks toward the object.
Holding Left Button/Move Left/Right	Rotates your view to the left or right. Imagine spinning on the heel of your foot while continuing to look straight ahead.
Holding Left Button/Move Backward	Walks backward away from the object.
Holding Right Button/Mouse Movement	Rotates the objects in the scene around the center of the scene. This center may be reset using the point mode.

Table 8.2. Mouse movements in the fly mode.

Mouse Action	3D Action
Holding Left Button/Move Forward	Tips your viewing angle downward. This action moves your relative position down as well.
Holding Left Button/Move Left/Right	Rotates to the left or right. This is similar to the walk mode, unless the "Bank when Flying" option is enabled in Live3D. Then, the objects will appear to move as if you were tilting while turning.
Holding Left Button/Move Backward	Tips your viewing angle upward. This action moves your relative position up as well.
Holding Right Button/Mouse Movement	Rotates the objects in the scene around the origin of the scene. This origin may be reset using the point mode.

Table 8.3. Mouse movements in the point mode.

Mouse Action	3D Action
Holding Left Button/Move Forward	Walks toward the object.
Holding Left Button/Move Left/Right	Rotates your view to the left or right.
Holding Left Button/Move Backward	Walks backward away from the object.
Single left button click	Resets the center of the object at the position of the mouse pointer.
Holding Right Button/Mouse Movement	Rotates the objects in the scene around the origin of the scene. This origin may be reset using the point mode.

Figure 8.3.
After using the
controls
described in
Tables 8.1
through 8.3, the
same jet fighter
can be displayed
from the front of
the aircraft.

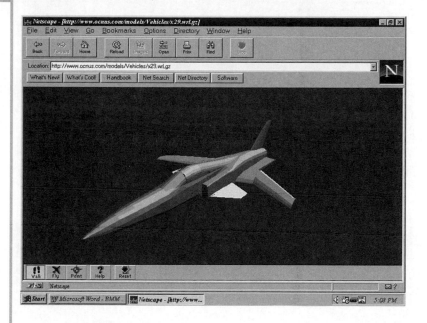

Figure 8.3.
After using the controls described in Tables 8.1 through 8.3, the same jet fighter can be displayed from the front of the aircraft.

Spin It Around

Tables 8.1 through 8.3 specify that the combination of holding the right mouse button and moving the mouse in any direction will rotate the objects in the VRML scene in that direction. This is one way of examining the objects. Figure 8.4 shows the same jet fighter you have been examining so far in another position after it has been rotated. As the objects move around, you may notice that you are moving the mouse cursor against the sides of your monitor, without any more room to move. In this case, you cannot rotate the objects any farther. Try releasing the mouse button, moving the cursor to the opposite side of the monitor, and then repressing the right mouse button and moving the mouse to rotate the objects farther.

You may cause the objects within a scene to rotate completely on their own without your having to continually control the mouse. To make an object begin rotating or orbiting, simply hold down the right mouse button as if you were going to inspect the object. Quickly move the mouse in a direction while holding down the button in a sweeping motion, almost as if you were brushing a bug off your desk.

The objects will begin rotating freely in the direction you moved the mouse. Of course, if you swept the mouse as if you were brushing off a *big* bug, then the objects are probably spinning uncontrollably on the screen! It will take some practice and control to get the objects to spin properly. The speed at which the objects spin is proportional to the speed at which you flick the mouse.

Figure 8.4.
You can also
freely rotate an
object in VRML.
In this case, the
jet fighter has
been rotated in
order to view the
bottom-right side
of the aircraft.

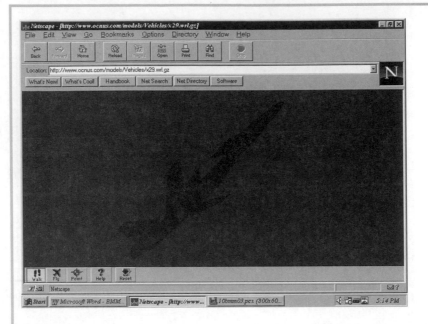

Watch Where You're Going

As you can see in Figure 8.4, it is difficult to make out the features of the airplane. This is because the light that you saw reflecting off the fuselage of the aircraft before was coming from above and slightly to the left of the aircraft. In Figure 8.4, you are looking at the bottom-right portion of the same plane. Therefore, you are seeing the side that is in the shadows that are created by the plane itself.

Although this is accurate, there may be times when you would rather be able to see all sides of an object, regardless of other lights in the scene. Fortunately, you may turn on your "headlight," which is comparable to lights that you may turn on when you are driving an automobile at night. Instead of relying on other light sources defined in a scene, all light is directed from a single headlight that follows the direction

you move in Cyberspace. Imagine wearing a coal-mining helmet with the lamp on the front. As you examine the VRML scene, the objects will be lit as your helmet's light falls on them. Figure 8.5 demonstrates viewing the same aircraft from the same position; however, the headlight has been turned on to view the details of the underside of the craft. Shortly, you will see how to enable this feature in the Live3D VRML browser as well as numerous additional options.

Changing Options

Live3D features numerous options that enable you to control the VRML scene you are viewing. You may right-click at any time inside of the VRML window to display a pop-up menu. Figure 8.5 shows the pop-up menu used to enable the headlight. This menu also enables you to configure other settings or perform the following particular actions.

Figure 8.5.
With a headlight
lit, it is possible
to see the detail
missing in the
shadows.

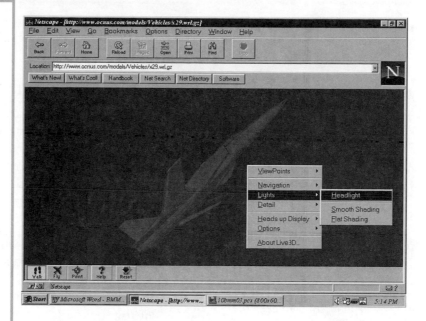

ViewPoints—Displays a list of other viewpoints from which you can examine the VRML scene. These are optional camera angles that must be set up by the person who developed the VRML scene. When more than one perspective has been designed for the scene, they will be listed in this submenu. Clicking on any of these camera positions displays the scene from that camera's view.

Navigation—Enables you to change the qualities of the scene as you move throughout the world. Some options in this submenu include the ability to change modes, enable the illusion of banking when turning in the fly mode, and enabling/disabling collision detection, and the animation between viewpoints.

Lights—From this submenu, you can enable/disable the headlight, as well as choose how shading should be handled for the objects that are rendered in Cyberspace.

Detail—There are three simple levels of detail for objects drawn by VRML browsers, such as Live3D. Usually, you will want to display the scene using a *solid* option, which paints the surfaces of the 3D objects. However, painting the surfaces requires some computation power and time. If you are using a slower computer, you may decide to use a *wireframe*, which is similar to a skeleton of the objects. Only the connecting lines between points that make up the objects are drawn, not the surfaces. Finally, a *point cloud* is merely the collection of points in space, that when connected, form a *wireframe* or *solid* rendering of the objects.

Heads Up Display—When viewing a scene in Live3D, you may choose to display additional controls in the window. These controls include navigation help text that overlays the objects in the window, cross-hairs that clearly show where you click in the window, and a status bar that appears across the top of the window, indicating the download progress.

Options—Finally, the options submenu from the Live3D pop-up menu enables you to adjust other advanced parameters of the Live3D window. Most of these options are for enhancing performance or conserving valuable screen space. Experiment with each of these options to see how they affect a VRML scene on your computer.

Around the World Wide Web

Now that you know what VRML is and how to control your VRML scenes with Live3D, let's examine some sites on the Web that may be of particular interest to you. Each of the examples covered in this section of this chapter demonstrates an interesting site and explains why each is interesting.

One of the first places you should visit when trying to learn more about or find some specific information regarding VRML is Yahoo. The following address takes you directly to the VRML section of the Yahoo database:

```
http://www.yahoo.com/
Computers_and_Internet/Internet/
World_Wide_Web/
Virtual_Reality_Modeling_Language__VRML_/
```

As new information is added to the Web, you will be able to find it easily here.

VRML Information Sites

There are literally hundreds of sites around the World Wide Web that contain information regarding VRML, and this number is constantly changing. It's impossible to pretend to cover all of these sites in a single chapter of a book, but we will cover a few that prove interesting.

If you are interested in learning about the standards for VRML or reading the meeting notes from each session of the standards committee, here are a few sites that may interest you:

VRML Forum & Repository—Founded by the originators of VRML, this Web site enables you to follow and contribute to discussions revolving around the technology. It also provides links to a VRML Repository at San Diego's Supercomputer facility, where you can find utilities, such as 3D modeling software, conversion programs for changing AutoCAD files into VRML objects, and other useful information. Figure 8.6 shows only a portion of the information related to VRML available at this site. The URL for this site is

```
http://sdsc.edu/vrml
```

You may also access the VRML Repository directly using the URL:

```
http://vrml.wired.com
```

Figure 8.6.
The VRML
repository
contains useful
links to software
and other VRML
information.

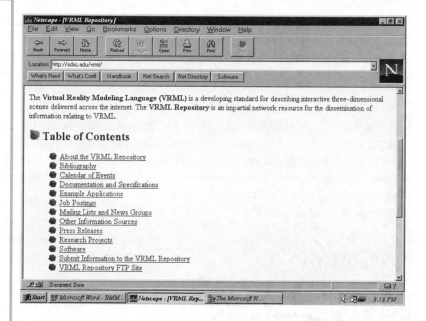

VRML Architecture Group—If you are interested in finding out more about the meetings that are being conducted regarding VRML, you should visit the VRML Architecture Group's Web site. Here you can see all of the notes from each of the meetings conducted by the VRML Architecture Group. You can also learn about the proposals for processes involving the nomination of future VRML versions. Figure 8.7 gives you an idea of the type of information you will find at this site.

Figure 8.7.
The VRML
Architecture
Group is
instrumental in
determining the
future directions
of VRML.

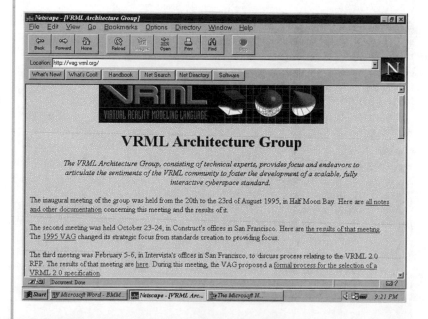

The URL for this site is:

`http://vag.vrml.org`

Some Cool Worlds

We discussed some possibilities for using VRML; however, we did not mention that it can be used to simulate trips to other places in the world (or out of this world). Here are a few sites that are pretty cool because they are either very practical or employ some features of VRML very nicely.

VirtualSOMA

Did you ever want to take a tour of San Francisco? Well you can meander through "South or Market Street Area," or SOMA for short. Planet 9 Studios created a complete virtual city that accurately copies the city of San Francisco. You can visit Planet 9 Studios at the following address

`http://www.planet9.com`

This site is interesting because the final results can look stunningly realistic. Each building in the virtual city is simply a cube of varying dimensions. However, what makes this scene realistic is the use of textured surfaces. As you will learn in Chapter 10, it is possible to "wrap" a graphic file around the surfaces of a 3D object. Each of the buildings on the street in VirtualSOMA includes scanned photos of the actual buildings.

Figure 8.8 displays Planet 9 Studios' Web site, which includes numerous pictures of the completed VirtualSOMA model and information on how it was created.

VRML Spaceship

Meridian's Web site is full of VRML models that its developers have created. Most of the models are fairly straight-forward. However, their examples make great use of worlds within worlds. To illustrate this, their example of a starship at this site

`http://www.merid.com:80/vrml/starship.wrl`

Figure 8.8. Realistic-looking virtual worlds can be created in VRML with the use of textured surfaces as shown here in VirtualSOMA, Planet 9 Studios' VRML model of San Francisco.

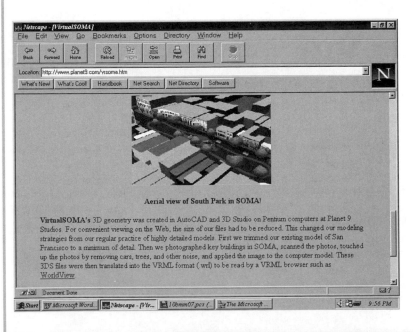

appears rather simple from a distance, as shown in Figure 8.9. On closer investigation, though, Figure 8.10 shows you that there is more to be found inside this spaceship.

VRML Hotel Room

Imagine that you are going to visit another country and you need to make hotel reservations. Wouldn't it be nice to first get an idea of what the hotel rooms look like before you make your decision? Squirrel

Figure 8.9.
An object that appears simple from far away, like this spaceship, may have more detailed objects hiding inside.

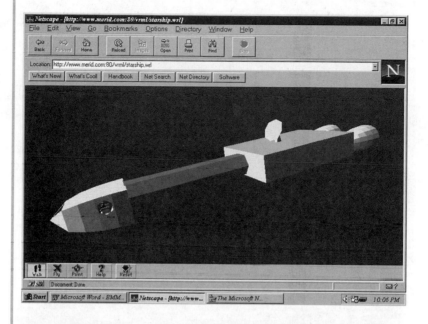

Figure 8.10.
Entering the spaceship through its window, you can find the pilot. If you enter the center of the ship, you will find two other shipmates.

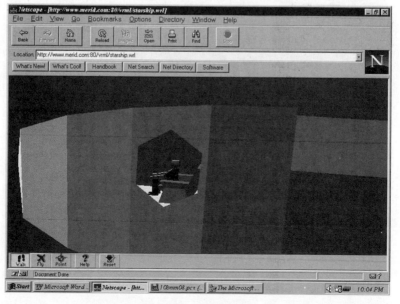

Virtual Reality VRML has a model of a hotel room that allows you to "try before you buy." The room can be found with additional VRML objects at this site:

```
http://www.squirrel.com.au/austresorts/
  Bedarra.wrl.gz
```

Figure 8.11 shows the hotel room. This particular scene is rather complex (there are additional rooms in the VRML file that are not shown in this figure), so be patient as the scene is transferred and then rendered on your machine.

VRML Site of the Week

As mentioned earlier, hundreds of sites on the World Wide Web are supporting VRML. So how can you continue to find the coolest ones? One way is to visit the VRML Site of the Week. This site updates information weekly to provide you with links to some of the most interesting sites with VRML on the Web.

Figure 8.12 shows the home page for this site, which can be found at:

```
http://www.virtus.com/vrmlsite.html
```

Grafman's VRML Gallery

If you are looking for examples that create dynamic VRML files and use some of the enhanced capabilities of Live3D, then visit Grafman's VRML Gallery. One example is a roller-skater that moves around randomly on the screen. When you first visit this site, you can choose the skater's color, and her outfit is dynamically created after you make your selection.

Figure 8.13 demonstrates the virtual skater. You can access this site using the following URL:

```
http://www.graphcomp.com/vrml/
```

Figure 8.11. Using VRML, you can look at a hotel room before you decide to stay the night.

*Figure 8.12.
Some of the best
sites on the Web
are posted at the
"VRML Site of
the Week."*

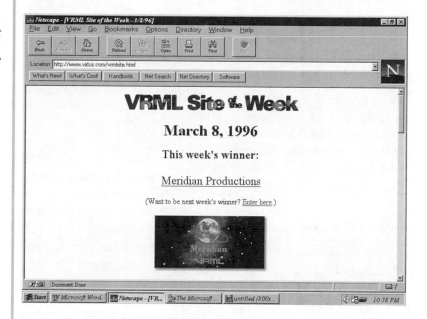

*Figure 8.13.
The color of this
moving skater's
outfit is
dynamically
created based on
the color values
that you select.*

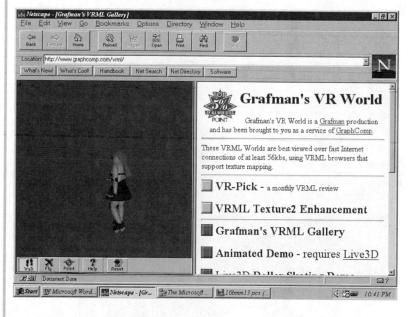

Netscape's VRML Weather

Of course, the Netscape site contains numerous examples of VRML models that are best used with its product Live3D. One such example is a VRML interface for determining the weather. Figure 8.14 shows how you can find out the weather for any part of the world. In the top-right corner of the browser, you will see a 3D model of the earth, complete with the moon and several weather satellites in orbit around the earth. If you rotate the earth using the right mouse button as discussed earlier in this chapter, you can spin the world to choose the area of the world for which you wish to receive weather information.

By clicking on a continent, such as North America, you will see a recent satellite image for that region in the window at the bottom of the screen. This is a highly practical example of how to use VRML effectively. If you wish to see this page, jump to the location:

```
http://www.netscape.com/comprod/
  products/navigator/live3d/examples/
  weather/weather.htm
```

Of course, there are other equally impressive examples at Netscape's site. To access them easily, simply key in the following URL:

```
http://www.netscape.com/comprod/
  products/navigator/live3d
  cool_worlds.html
```

Build It and They Will Come

Now that you have had the opportunity to see different VRML sites on the Web, you undoubtedly would like to create your very own niche in Cyberspace. In Chapters 9 and 10, you will learn in detail how to create virtual worlds using the VRML language. This will include how to position objects and add lighting, as well as how to create brand new objects. In this chapter, you will be presented with a few sites that contain VRML object libraries from which you may borrow objects for your own worlds. You will also learn how to assemble a scene using Arena Design VRML by Andover Advanced Technologies, which is included on the CD-ROM with this book.

Figure 8.14. To see the weather anywhere in the world, you can spin the VRML globe and click on a continent to get a satellite image.

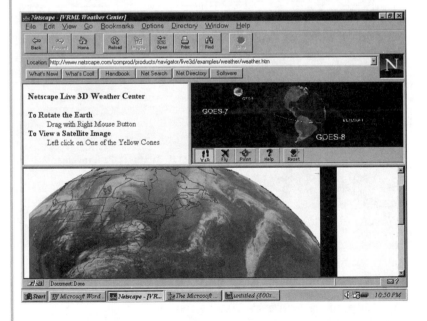

Finding Prebuilt Objects

Creating unique 3D objects takes time and requires a trained eye. Fortunately, you do not need years of experience creating 3D objects with CAD systems in order to work with VRML. There are numerous sites on the Internet that provide hundreds of premade VRML objects that you can simply download and embed in your own VRML worlds. You can use several of the Internet search engines to find Web sites or ftp sites that contain VRML objects, but the following is a list of several locations to get you started:

- ✦ New College of California: vrmLab

    `http://www.newcollege.edu/vrmLab/`

- ✦ Ocnus' Rope Company

    `http://www.ocnus.com/models/`
    `models.html`

- ✦ Squirrel Virtual Reality

    `http://www.squirrel.com.au/`
    `virtualreality/`

- ✦ Grafman's VRML Gallery

    `http://www.graphcomp.com/vrml/`

- ✦ OFF2VRML

    `http://coney.gsfc.nasa.gov/Mathews/`
    `Objects/off2vrml.html`

- ✦ Department of Computer Science, The University of Edinburgh

    `http://www.dcs.ed.ac.uk/generated/`
    `package-links/objects/vrml.html`

- ✦ Construct

    `http://vrml.arc.org/`

Note: Most sites allow you to reuse their 3D worlds, as long as it is not for commercial profit. However, these policies vary widely depending on the owners of that site. Be sure to investigate any policies or guidelines listed at a site or contact the owners of a site before using VRML objects in your own pages.

There are additional sites on the Web that are repositories for other 3D objects. Although these objects are not native VRML files, you can use a conversion program to

Tip: If you are viewing a VRML object at a site and wish to save it, you may choose Save As... from the File menu in the Netscape browser. This will copy the VRML world (.wrl or .gz) to your computer's disk.

However, when copying worlds that use textured surfaces, you must make sure that those graphics files are copied as well. If the world you are viewing is a .wrl file, you can easily open this file with WordPad or another word processor that can read standard ASCII text files. Search the entire file that you saved for the word *Texture2*. Remember the filename that appears on a line near the results of each search you perform. You will need to download those graphic files from the Internet, as well, in order for the scene to appear correctly.

If you need to access a compressed VRML world file (.gz), then use the Winzip extraction utility found on the accompanying CD-ROM to decompress the file. Then view the results in a word processor.

make them suitable for VRML browsers. One site, Viewpoint Datalabs: Avalon, on the Internet contains countless 3D objects in other formats that can be converted to VRML rather easily:

```
ftp://avalon.viewpoint.com/pub/objects/
```

or

```
http://www.viewpoint.com/avalon/
  objects.html
```

Tip: You do not necessarily need to copy VRML worlds from a site on the Internet. You may also use VRML's WWWInline node (discussed in Chapter 10) to place a VRML object from the Internet directly into your scene. The WWWInline node allows you to enter the URL to jump to the location of an object that you've embedded in your scene.

Conversion Mania

As convenient as it is to have libraries of VRML objects on the Internet, there cannot possibly be an appropriate 3D object for every person's need. You will unquestionably want a more unique object at one time or another for your personal world. But what if you are not a computer graphic artist and do not want to attempt drawing in three dimensions? If you know someone who is experienced with other 3D applications, such as AutoCAD, or if you can find other 3D objects in formats other than VRML, then you can use those 3D objects for your scene as well.

In order for you to use AutoCAD, 3D Studio, or other 3D files in your VRML world, you simply must convert those files into VRML

files. This can often be accomplished quite painlessly through the use of a good conversion application. The program WCVT2POV converts files in numerous other formats to a compatible VRML file. With a conversion utility such as this, a whole new world of opportunities are available for your VRML scenes. Check out this site for WCVT2POV

```
http://www.povray.org/povzine
```

The chances of finding additional 3D objects of a type that can be read by this conversion program is greater. Therefore, you have a better chance of being able to get the 3D clip art that you need for your VRML world. However, if you still cannot find a particular object that matches your needs, you can always resort to employing someone who knows how to model a 3D object in 3D Studio or AutoCAD. You can then take that person's model and convert it to VRML to suit your needs.

Most converter programs are fairly straightforward to use. You simply open a file in one particular format and then save it back as another format, such as VRML. Between those two steps, you may be able to change properties for the object, such as being able to rotate it or change colors. Let's take a simple example to demonstrate using a converter. This exercise uses WCVT2POV.

Included on the CD-ROM is a series of sample 3D files. If you open the `dolphins.raw` file into the WCVT2POV program, you would see three dolphins as shown in Figure 8.15. Immediately, you see that there is a problem. There are supposed to be three dolphins, yet at the current angle, it is nearly impossible to distinguish between them.

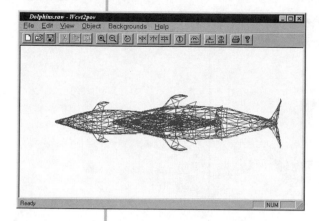

Figure 8.15.
There are three dolphins in the `dolphins.raw` *file, but you can't distinguish between them.*

The first action you perform is to rotate the dolphins 45 degrees along their x axis. This is equivalent to tilting them upward. To do this, choose the Object ¦ Rotate option. A second window appears, asking you to enter the amount of rotation for the object along its x, y, and z axes. Simply key in the amount of rotation to perform on any axis and click the OK button.

Secondly, to further distinguish each dolphin, let's assign a different color to each. Let's make the top red, the middle green, and the bottom blue. WCVT2POV features a color assignment dialog box that allows you to do this easily. From the Object menu, you can select the Colors... choice. A window then appears listing the individual objects in the top-left corner of the window; in this case, three separate dolphins. To assign colors, simply select an object from this list and then choose an appropriate color from the Group Color list that appears in the top-right corner of that same window. The results are shown in Figure 8.16.

The final scene can then be saved as a VRML file and then read by the Live3D VRML browser in Netscape 2 to yield the results

found in Figure 8.17. As you can see, it is simple to use a vast array of other 3D models as VRML objects in your personal worlds.

Assembling a Scene

Once you have gathered all of the objects that you wish to place in your own VRML world, you need to actually assemble them together into a scene. In Chapters 9 and 10, you will see how to assemble VRML worlds using the syntax of the VRML language. However, if you wish to simply place objects in a scene, you may find it more convenient to use a 3D modeling tool. Arena Design VRML (on the CD-ROM) enables you to easily import objects, such as VRML objects, lay them out in your virtual world, and save the results as a virtual world. Most 3D programs require practice and patience to master. This section of the chapter will not cover every nuance of the designer program, but rather will introduce you to the software so that you can begin to effectively experiment with VRML worlds of your own.

Importing VRML Objects

When you have decided on the objects you wish to place in your scene, you may begin importing them into Arena Design VRML. To import an object into the designer, choose File ¦ Import Scene. A dialog box appears, allowing you to import a 3D file. You may import a VRML file, as well as 3D Studio, AutoCAD, or Windows metafiles. When you have selected a file to import, that object is displayed in the designer's window, as shown in Figure 8.18.

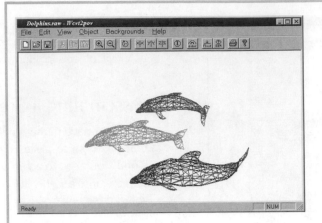

*Figure 8.16.
Each dolphin is
easier to see
after the scene
has been rotated
and each
dolphin has its
own unique
color.*

Associating Objects Together

If you wish to keep these objects together, you should make sure that they are associated with each other. In the designer, this means that you must merge the objects together as one object. The benefit of this is that you can modify all three objects at once. In some cases, complex objects are actually created by numerous smaller ob-

jects. If you want to move the more complex object, you may be only moving a smaller subset of the object—if you haven't fused all the objects together. In this exercise, you'll move, rotate, and color all the objects at once. Therefore, you must bind them together. To do this in the designer, choose the Object ¦ Hierarchy… option. A window similar to the one shown in Figure 8.19 appears.

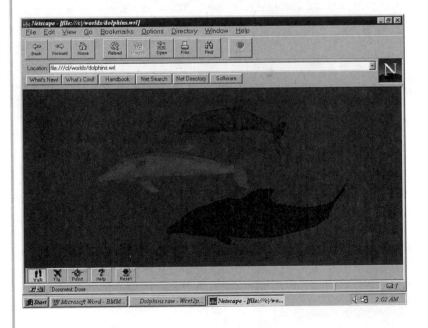

*Figure 8.17.
The final VRML
file generated by
the conversion
program appears
more clearly
when displayed
with a VRML
browser.*

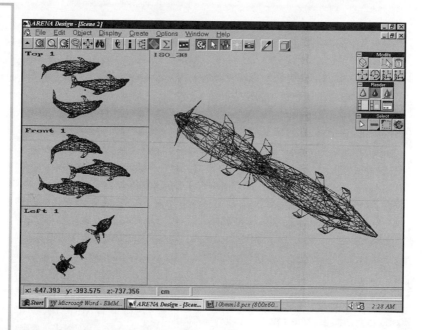

Figure 8.18. After importing the VRML file for the dolphins, you see the wireframe images of the objects in three dimensions.

Figure 8.19. You can browse objects and create relationships between them with the object hierarchy window.

beneath this group object. These geometric items (Dolph01, Dolph02, and Dolph03) were merged together by simply dragging the name of each geometric item on top of the group item. If the group item did not already exist, you could simply click on the New Object button to create a new one. Once all the geometric items are associated within a group, they may be modified together as a single object.

Changing Properties of Objects

Each object in a scene may have different attributes from other objects in the scene. For instance, one object may be blue, another one may be red. One object may contain a textured surface to give the appearance of water, while another may give the appearance of fire. All these attributes may be modified by using the object hierarchy window shown in Figure 8.19. By double-clicking on the name of an object in the window, you will see a window that enables

As you can see by the list shown in Figure 8.19, there are numerous objects that make up this scene: mainly five lights (four point lights and one infinite light), a camera angle, and three dolphin objects. The list shown in Figure 8.19 displays the results of merging all three dolphins together into one complete object.

You may notice the item highlighted in the list in Figure 8.19, Dummy_160. It is not really a geometric object in this scene, rather it is a collection type. Each of the geometric objects that are associated together under this grouping are displayed in the outline

you to change properties for the object itself. An example of this window is presented in Figure 8.20.

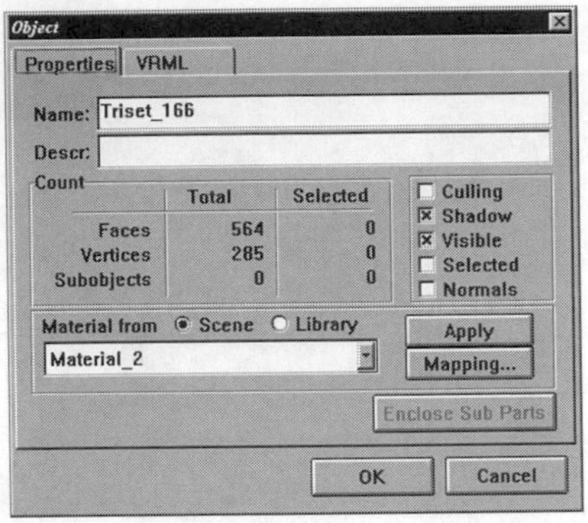

Figure 8.20. You can change properties for each object in a scene, such as the material it uses or the URL the object should link to in VRML.

You can determine certain qualities for the object, such as whether it produces shadows, in the Properties tab of this dialog box. You also may determine what material the object should use. To change the material for an object to use a textured map from Design VRML's texture library, you simply click on the Library radio button in the dialog box. The list beneath this selection is then populated with different types of material, such as glass, wood, water, and fire, as well as numerous colors. To change the object's material, simply choose it from the list, and then click on the Apply button.

Note: You *must* click the Apply button in the object window shown in Figure 8.20 if you wish to save the changes you have made for a material selection. Clicking the OK button alone does not automatically apply the material for an object.

A separate VRML tab is available for changing some characteristics of objects specifi-

cally to support VRML. In this tab, you can specify a URL that will allow you to click on the object to jump to another Web page or VRML world when you view the entire scene using a VRML browser. You may also specify alternative text to be displayed when your cursor is passed over a linking object in VRML. Typically, if you do not include a description, the VRML browser will simply display the URL that an object will link to. You may clarify this with more descriptive text.

Selecting Objects

Near the right side of the toolbar for the designer's window, you will find several icons: a paint brush with paint, a selection arrow, two arrows that point to each other, a sun, and a camera. These are toggle buttons that enable/disable numerous additional floating tool palettes. For most of your work, you may find it most convenient to enable each of these tool palettes because you often use them interchangeably. Figure 8.21 shows the position and contents of these toolbars.

The Select tool palette has four buttons: a small arrow head, a plus or minus symbol, a rectangle with a red-tabbed corner, and a globe. These tools enable you to select different objects within your 3D scene. For instance, with the arrow head, you can click individual objects in the scene to be selected. The plus/minus button determines the behavior of selections as you click on objects in the scene. If you choose the additive mode, all objects that you click on will be selected. Likewise, the subtractive mode will deselect each object that you click on. The combination of a plus and minus symbol indicates a toggle mode, where each object you click on will either be selected or deselected each time you click on it. The rectangle with a red-tabbed corner indicates a bounding rectangle select tool. By selecting this tool, you may stretch a rectangle around all the objects in a scene that you want to select. Finally, the globe icon invokes a select all function, working appropriately based on whether you are in an additive, subtractive, or toggle mode for selection.

Tip:
If you click on objects in a scene, yet they do not become selected properly, check the selection style button in the Select tool palette. If a minus or plus/minus button appears, you may need to change that to the additive selection mode.

Modifying Objects

After you have effectively selected the objects to be changed in a scene, you may use the designer's Modify tool palette to change additional qualities for the objects selected. The tools included in this palette are Move, Rotate, Scale in Two Dimensions, and Scale in Three Dimensions. You can click on any of the buttons in this tool palette to activate the appropriate action you wish to perform on the objects in a scene. You can also hold down the left mouse button on any of these buttons to reveal further options for each tool.

When performing any of these actions, simply pick the tool from the tool palette and then click on an object or group of objects in the scene that you wish to affect. A 3D bounding rectangle appears, representing the object or objects you selected. You may then move your mouse to move, rotate, or scale the box, depending on the action you have chosen to perform. When you have finished, you simply click the mouse button again to stop the action.

Figure 8.21. You can render the scene in Arena Design VRML in order to test shading, lighting, colors, and textures for the objects.

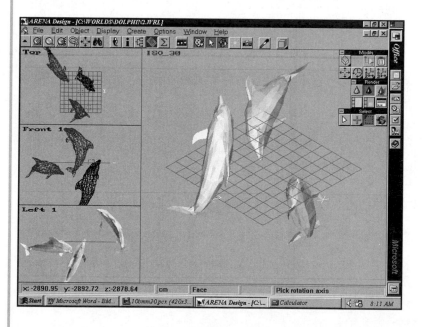

Note: Controlling objects in 3D space takes some getting used to. As a default, Arena Design VRML uses four separate windows for navigation. The right window represents the x/z plane, which is basically how close or far away an object is and how far to the left or right it may be positioned. The three supporting windows that are tiled on the left side of the scene layout window help you to determine how high each object is or if it is centered by representing left, front, and top views of the same scene.

Although different views are displayed in each of the different windows, you may also modify the objects using these separate windows. This becomes especially useful when attempting to line up objects on top of each other.

A more complete understanding of the three dimensions is covered in Chapter 9.

Testing and Saving the Final Scene

After rotating, moving, sizing, and applying different materials, you probably would like to see a preview of what the final scene looks like. To do this, simply click on the Update View button in the Render tool palette. This quickly renders the contents of the currently active window. You may also choose the quality of the render by selecting one of the three varying quality cones at the top of the Render tool palette. To change options for rendering or to render only a portion of a window, you may select those appropriate tools in the second row of the tool palette. Figure 8.21 shows a scene that has been rendered in Arena Design VRML.

When you have finished tweaking the scene, you will of course want to save it for use in your VRML browser. This simply requires that you choose the File ¦ Save as... option. A window prompts you to enter the filename you wish to use. To save a scene as a VRML file, make certain that the List Files of Type option near the bottom of the window is set to VRML.

Tip: If you become unsure of what a particular button in a tool palette does, let your mouse rest over the button for a few seconds. More descriptive "tip" text automatically appears near the button.

Caution: If you use textured surfaces for materials in your scene, you may need to modify by hand the VRML file created by Arena Design VRML. Each of the bitmap files for textured materials is found in a material directory in the Arena Design VRML directory. To compound problems, these materials are in the standard Windows bitmap format (.bmp). This is convenient when you are adding new textures, but not so convenient when you want to generate VRML files.

If you wish to use these texture bitmaps in your VRML scenes, you will need to convert the bitmap files to .gif files and save these files in the same directory as the VRML world you created with Design VRML. Then use WordPad or another suitable word processor that handles standard ASCII text files to search for and replace each instance of .bmp with .gif. You should also verify the paths for each texture graphic file to insure that they match the location of your .gif files, especially when the entire scene is transferred to the Internet.

What's Next?

In this chapter you have been introduced to the complex world of VRML. You learned what the language is, where to find 3D objects for it, how to create your own scenes, and what is coming for future generations of VRML. In the next chapter, you will become intimate with the language of VRML and adept at controlling objects' three dimensions. In Chapter 10, you will further expand your knowledge of VRML to create realistic worlds.

The world of VRML is a continuously evolving world, where each new feature sparks a fire of creativity. I hope VRML has sparked enough interest in you that you will begin to use it in your own Web pages and continue to develop the Web in a new dimension.

Building 3D Cyberspace

chapter 9

by John J. Kottler

Virtual reality and three-dimensional interfaces are quickly becoming the newest and hottest buzzwords in the computer industry. Nowhere is this more evident than in their presence on the Web. Hundreds of sites that are dedicated to exploiting 3D worlds are now available. The Virtual Reality Modeling Language (VRML) has become the standard language for building these complex worlds.

Modeling in three dimensions is not nearly as simple as it looks. It often requires years of practice to build the skills needed for creating truly original 3D designs. Ask a person who works with 3D products, such as AutoCAD or 3D Studio, and they will quickly tell you that it takes a good amount of time to become acquainted with the new technology and even longer to become a master at it.

Several tools are available to help modelers, those people who create unique 3D models, to compose their works. Some programs aid in the creation of 3D objects from a two-dimensional source. Others are coupled with dedicated hardware digitizers, such as a 3D tracing pen, which an artist uses to trace an actual 3D object. In addition, there are dozens of methods available for assistance with the animation of these 3D worlds, including sensors that are attached to human performers, a process referred to as motion capture.

In Chapter 8, "The World Wide Web Isn't Flat," you were introduced to VRML and the capabilities possible with this new Web technology. In this chapter, you will learn how to create your own virtual worlds and attach them into your own Web pages. The VRML standard is complex and evolving continually. Therefore, this chapter is dedicated to covering only an introduction to the language. The next chapter will cover in depth some enhanced features of VRML.

3D Architecture 101

Before venturing into the world of VRML, it is important to familiarize yourself with basic components of 3D space. As you well know, real space consists of three dimensions: width, height, and depth. For instance, to measure a box, you measure each of these attributes of the box. In the world of mathematics, these coordinates are thought of along three separate axes: X, Y, and Z, which represent the width, height, and depth, respectively.

Each object in space can be referenced by values along these three axes and can contain information regarding its width, height, and depth as well as its location. For instance, if you were to place a box in a corner of a room, you would be required to specify its location using values along the horizontal, vertical, and depth axes.

The *origin* is the center of VRML's universe. It is simply the point where all three axes in Figure 9.1 intersect. More precisely, it is the point where the value on each axis is equal to zero. Each point to the left, to the right, above, below, closer, or farther away can be indicated by its distance from this point.

For those who don't remember or slept through some of their geometry courses, let's review some basic components. The smallest element is a point. As you'll remember (or maybe not), a point contains no width, height, or depth. It is an abstract concept and in fact does not even qualify as one dimensional! A point is simply a dot, a speck that identifies a location in space. It is not an object because it cannot be measured in any way other than location.

The next step up in geometric elements is a line. Lines are actually a series of points that exist consecutively in a row. They can span across the horizontal, vertical, depth, or any combination of these axes. In geometric terms, lines are infinitely continuous, without a beginning or ending point. Yet in a virtual world, line *segments* are used since they contain definite starting and ending points. These line segments construct polygons which make up 3D objects.

Finally, there are planes, which are a series of points combined together to form a surface, like a thin panel of wood. The surface is formed by a series of points that are connected side by side to each other, but not on top of each other. Like lines, planes are infinite in nature. Although they span two dimensions, they continue infinitely in each direction of those two directions. However, for computer systems and 3D objects, *bounds* are placed on the edges of these surfaces. These bounds then force the object to be two dimensional because both a width and height can be measured. Particular shapes for surfaces created by these bounds are *polygons*.

When objects in 3D space are assembled, they are actually a series of two-dimensional

Figure 9.1. Space is measured using three axes: X, Y, and Z. (For the Z axis, + is coming toward you and – is moving away.)

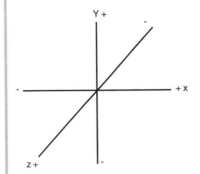

surfaces interconnected. Therefore, creating a 3D cube in space is similar to constructing a cardboard box. A simple box is made up of six sides. Assuming that you are making a cubical box, each side is a square. Each square is then assembled along the edges to form the box as shown in Figure 9.2. As you can see from this description, the box is hollow. The same holds true for 3D objects in VRML space.

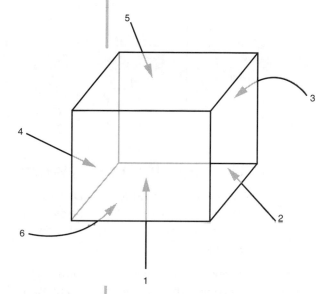

Figure 9.2.
A cube is created by connecting six square sides together.

As the World Wide Web Turns

Another important concept of 3D programming is the rotation of objects. Just as objects can be defined and located along three dimensions, they can also be spun around those same three axes. Figure 9.3 demonstrates each of these rotations.

You can think of each of these axes as rods that penetrate through the center of the object you wish to rotate. If the object is a block of wood, six rods would come from the center of the block: one from the top, bottom, left, right, front, and back sides. Imagine grabbing each end of one rod, for example the front and back rods, and spinning the rod with your fingers. This will effectively rotate the block in either a clockwise or counterclockwise motion.

A Roller-Coaster Ride

As just mentioned, there are three axes on which an object can rotate. The first is the X axis, or the horizontal axis. Rotation that occurs on this axis is often referred to as *pitch.* Pitch can be compared to the way an airplane arches upward when taking off from the ground or a roller-coaster rises and falls, where the nose of the car constantly rotates upward when climbing or downward when descending.

Objects can also *roll*, or rotate along the Z axis. This can be compared to the way in which an airplane banks when making a steep turn (when you look out one window and see the ground but see the sky out the opposite window!). This can also be compared to some of the newer roller coasters that twist their riders around.

Another axis, the Y axis, refers to the way in which an object is spun. This is similar to the way you move your head to the left or right. This type of rotation is referred to as *yaw* and is common with aircraft as well. You could think of yaw as the effect of an airplane being steered on a runway, the way it turns as it approaches the actual airport. It is also comparable to the rotation of the Earth around its axis. Although not directly associated with most roller coasters, *yaw* is comparable to that spinning in your head you may notice after getting off one!

Figure 9.3.
Objects can be
rotated three
dimensionally as
well in virtual
space.

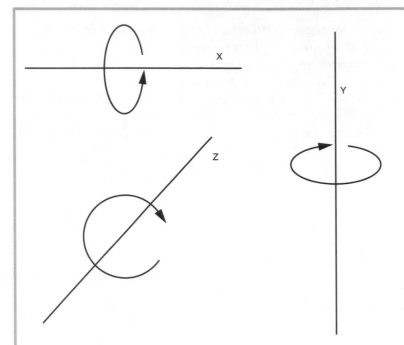

Gimme a Light

After you create objects in space, you need to light them. Think about it: You cannot walk around a room that you are unfamiliar with at night without either a light on or putting on steel-tipped boots. You would be bumping into everything, unless you knew exactly where each piece of furniture was—simply because you wouldn't see it. The same holds true for virtual objects in 3D space. You must provide a light source; otherwise, you will never see any of the objects you created.

This is similar to the aircraft example in Chapter 8, in which you were introduced to lighting a scene with a headlight. You saw in this example that it was difficult, if not impossible, at certain angles to see any detail of the aircraft. This was because of inadequate light.

The Light from Everywhere

Fortunately, most VRML browsers provide a default light source, one that radiates equally from all directions similar to that shown in Figure 9.4.

A nondirectional point lamp provides lighting comparable to that of an incandescent light bulb. Although a single lamp is provided by the VRML browser, you can specify additional light sources. These light sources can be placed anywhere in 3D space and given a variety of colors.

Life in the Spotlight

You can also create spotlights similar to those used in stage productions. Another type of spotlight is your average flashlight. When you turn on your flashlight, you are casting a well-defined circle of light onto an object. You can clearly control the direction

*Figure 9.4.
A nondirectional
point lamp
radiates light
equally in all
directions.*

are adjusting the focus of the beam that lights an object.

Rendered Unconscious

When an object is defined, placed in space, and given appropriate lighting conditions, the computer must create the object. The quickest method by which a computer can generate this object is to create a skeleton of the 3D object. This skeleton is merely the lines that connect the points of the object together. No surfaces, colors, or textures are applied. This type of rendering is aptly referred to as a *wireframe* of the object, because the object appears to be nothing more than a set of wires connected together. In Chapter 8, Figure 8.16 showed simple wireframes of dolphins. Figure 9.2 also illustrates a simple cube using just the lines, a type of wireframe image.

As you can see, you can peer right through the image. There are no surfaces applied; therefore, it is difficult to determine which are the sides of the object or which pieces of the object are behind others. Although wireframes do not produce a highly realistic image, their speed makes them the preferred method for designers who want to get a quick feel for what the object may look like. When creating 3D objects, artists can view the objects from various perspectives in order to better understand the positioning of each object as well as its appearance in a scene. Wireframes are also particularly useful when animating an object. Wireframe objects can be compared to the simple black and white sketches that an artist does while planning a cartoon.

in which light will be projected. This is similar to the world of VRML, where you can easily determine additional lights that focus on a particular spot of an object.

This is another example in which you must use the rotational capabilities discussed earlier to help position the beam of light cast from a spotlight. You can focus the result of a spotlight, so you must control the direction in which the beam travels.

Spotlights add realism to a scene and just as with nondirectional lights, you can specify a unique color for each spotlight. In addition, because you can control the direction in which a spotlight beams light, you can also specify the diameter of the circle produced by the light. You can easily adjust the size to be either small (like a penlight) or wide (like an automobile headlamp). In a sense, you

Applying the Coating

When an object has been generated and verified in its wireframe form, the surfaces of the object are painted. In the example of a cube, each face of the cube would be painted, so you could no longer see through the cube. If the cube were simply painted the same color on each face with the same intensity of light, and if there were no distinguishing lines, the edges would no longer be visible. The object would no longer appear as a cube but rather as a distorted, two-dimensional design.

This process of applying varying amounts of light to the polygons that build a solid image from the wireframe skeleton is often referred to as *rendering*. Depending on the process selected for shading a 3D object, rendering can take a few seconds to a few days.

The Quick and the Dirty

To avoid making 3D objects appear as if they are two dimensional, the surfaces are shaded on the basis of the amount of light striking each surface. There are several different methods of shading 3D objects. Each successive method requires more processing power to complete and thus, either takes much longer or requires incredibly fast computer systems.

Flat shading is the quickest for rendering a 3D object. Unfortunately, because of the quickness of flat shading, often the realism of a scene is sacrificed for speed. For instance, let's assume that a sphere is being generated on the screen and that a light source is located in front of and above the sphere. The amount of light that may strike the top corner of the sphere is calculated and used to paint the entire face of the object. The result is an object that looks more like a circle than a sphere.

The Great Gouraud

Obviously, flat shading is inadequate for creating 3D worlds that look realistic. Therefore, another level of shading has been introduced, *Gouraud shading*, which causes some of the polygons that make up a sphere near the top-right to be brighter in color. Polygons immediately surrounding the center of this light spot would get increasingly darker as their distance from the center of the spot increases, until they match the color of the sphere. However, as the apples in Chapter 8 Figure 8.1 depict, this is not a fine shading. Often, you will notice the edges of the polygons that make up the sphere. Although this still does not produce the most realistic results, it is easier for a computer to generate quickly.

What's Wrong with Phong?

If Gouraud is not realistic enough (and for most users, it's not), another shading algorithm known as *Phong shading* may work. Phong shading builds on Gouraud shading and takes it one step farther. In addition to calculating how shading should be applied to surrounding polygons, it also averages the values for shading between those polygons. The result is an image that is much more realistic, but pays the price of realism with speed. Because many more areas of the object are being calculated at once, the process can take longer to complete.

Follow That Ray!

Ray tracing is the highest form of shading available to the 3D world of computers. This process, found in computer animation in movies or television commercials, creates highly realistic results, so much so that even a discerning eye may be fooled. As you might imagine, the rendering process is extensive. The path of each ray of artificial light is traced through the virtual scene. Depending on the equipment used and the complexity of the scene, this rendering process can take anywhere from a few hours to several days.

Note: Typical VRML browsers implement wireframe and Gouraud renderings of 3D objects. Some browsers also implement Phong shading. However, because of the dense number of calculations required for ray tracing, this type of rendering is reserved typically for high-end workstations. Most VRML browsers do not implement this automatically.

The mode you wish to use to view 3D objects may be selectable in the VRML browser. In Live3D, the rendering option may be selected in the Options menu when you right-click the mouse button inside of the VRML browser window.

Creating Your World

So now that you have some familiarity with the general concepts of 3D objects, how do you create them? In this section, we'll look at how to create some simple objects in VRML. First, let's remember that a VRML file or world (.wrl) is simply a text file that is sent from a Web server to a client PC. When a Web browser receives this file, it immediately invokes a helper application or plug-in to handle the new content—in this case, a VRML browser. It is the job of the VRML browser to parse through the information in the VRML file and create the actual 3D world.

Although it is simply a text file, the text within that file makes up the VRML language. VRML shares many of the same qualities of other languages. The method in which VRML files are read, parsed, and then displayed is analogous to interpreted languages such as BASIC. A BASIC program is also constructed from textual commands that are read and translated into computer functions when the program is used.

How to Start a VRML File

Many languages contain their own commands and structures that carry out the functionality of that language. Although somewhat like English words, these commands or the combination of these commands may need to be further clarified. In this case, special lines of code within a program or VRML world known as *comments* can be added. Comment lines in VRML are denoted by a "#" character at the beginning of the line. All text after that character is considered commented text.

Although convenient and highly recommended, comments are not essential to the development of computer programs or worlds in Cyberspace; however, the first line of VRML code in a world file *must* contain the following comment:

```
#VRML V1.0 ASCII
```

This instructs the VRML browser that the file is compliant with a particular version of VRML and that it contains its source code in ASCII, or basic text format. This comment is the only type that is not ignored by the VRML browser.

Separators

When creating graphical objects in a VRML world, you must specify each one individually. However, there may be many attributes associated with that object, such as color, position, and type. All attributes of an object are grouped together in a *separator*. The concept of a separator in VRML is similar to those plastic separators you may be accustomed to in the grocery store checkout line. Let's assume you are purchasing some groceries and wish to keep your groceries separate from your friend's groceries behind you. You place all your items on the conveyor and put a separator between your items and your friend's items. Although you may have different items in your purchase, they are all grouped together as your purchase.

The same holds true for separators in VRML. One object (or purchase) may contain several items, such as the type of object being constructed, its color, and its position, but VRML knows to group these items together.

The separator function in VRML looks like this:

```
Separator {
    # … VRML code …
}
```

You'll notice that the separator function, as well as many other functions in VRML, uses curly braces ({ and }), which identify a particular portion of the VRML code to be considered with that separator. Therefore, you can also think of separators as grocery baskets. The size of your grocery basket (identified by the leading and trailing braces) enables you to place items into the basket. Items in your basket are separate from items in another shopper's basket. It's also important to remember always to specify both the starting and ending braces. If not, the results are similar to creating half a shopping cart, from which the items can spill all over the floor!

Nodes

The actual items within a separator are considered *nodes*, called so because they can be arranged in a hierarchical structure. For instance, you may have one object that is considered the *parent*. Two additional objects may be embedded in that parent's structure and are thus considered its children. This is similar to a tree, which starts at the trunk and expands into branches, smaller twigs, and leaves. Each part of that tree is a node.

If you were to create a simple tree using separators in VRML, it would look something like the code in Listing 9.1. This sample relates two leaves to a branch and that branch to the trunk of the tree.

Listing 9.1. Parts of a tree can be treated as nodes that are related.

```
Separator {
    # Trunk
    Separator {
        # Branch 1
        Separator {
            # Leaf 1
        }
        Separator {
            # Leaf 2
        }
    }
    Separator {
        # Branch 2
    }
}
```

You will see shortly that every item in a separator, such as an object's color and location, is considered a node in VRML.

Tip: You may notice that sections of VRML listings are indented. This helps to make the code easier to read. In general, commands within a set of braces (" { } ") should be indented, in much the same way you would do this in programming languages.

Note: The first letter of each node in a VRML file must be capitalized. The actual parameters for a node may be all lowercase.

Hip to be Square

After all this discussion, you're just about ready to draw your first VRML object. You're going to draw a very basic object: a cube. As we discussed earlier, each object in the 3D world must be made up of points that are connected by lines to create a wireframe. Then this wireframe is painted to create a complete image. Fortunately, VRML provides some very basic objects from which you may choose to assemble your world. Toward the end of this chapter, you will see other places where you can obtain VRML objects to use in your world as well.

Instead of assembling all the points necessary for a cube yourself, VRML offers a cube function. Although it is referred to as a cube, it is possible to specify unequal width, height, or depth measurements to create different blocks. VRML provides four basic shapes: cube, cylinder, sphere, and cone. This in itself seems fairly limited, but it is possible to assemble these shapes together to create more complex designs. Of course, you can also model completely unique objects.

Let's draw a cube in the center of the screen, the origin of the three axes (see Listing 9.2).

The source code in Listing 9.2 can be written using a standard text-based word processor such as Notepad or Wordpad. Although several applications are available that ease the creation of such VRML files, you can create VRML files manually, typing the appropriate commands into those files.

Listing 9.2. A cube can be created easily in Cyberspace.

```
#VRML V1.0 ASCII

Separator {
    Cube {
        width 10
        height 10
        depth 10
    }
}
```

Reviewing the Results

The VRML code in Listing 9.2 produces a simple cube in the middle of a virtual world. Since Listing 9.2 does not yet specify a specific location for drawing the cube, its default position is the origin, or the center of the screen. When you have entered VRML source code, you must save the file as a .wrl file. To view how your world looks, you must then run either a standalone helper application or open the file as a plug-in in Netscape 2.0 by choosing File ¦ Open File. In either case, when you have opened the file with your VRML browser, the cube will appear in the center of your space.

You will quickly notice certain defaults provided to you by the VRML browser. First, the background is black (or close to it) by default. The 3D objects painted in space are white and a nondirectional light source is provided. Figure 9.5 depicts this cube in Netscape's VRML Live3D browser.

Positioning Objects

Of course, not all objects will be created in the center of the universe. You will want to be able to move one object to another location in Cyberspace. The important aspect to remember here is that you are moving an object *relative* to the center of the universe you are creating. At this point, you are probably feeling the power, the ability to create a universe!

So how do you change the location at which an object is to be displayed? Every new object is created at the origin by default, so you are technically *translating* that object in space. You *transform* that object from one location (the origin) to its new location. To accomplish this, VRML provides the Transform node. This node expects three parameters, indicating how far to move an object along the X, Y, and Z axes. These three values are simply separated by spaces in the VRML Transform node. Listing 9.3 moves the cube you just created 5 units to the right, 5 units down, and 10 units forward.

Any objects that follow the Transform node are offset by the units specified by the translation parameters of the Transform node. In Listing 9.3, the cube is the only object affected by this transformation.

Guilt by Association

As mentioned earlier, objects can be related to each other. Often this is done intentionally by VRML developers to maintain relationships when objects are transformed. It is also suitably used to apply characteristics to many objects at once, such as painting several objects the same color.

Figure 9.5.
The cube created
in Listing 9.2 is
displayed by a
VRML browser
with default
settings.

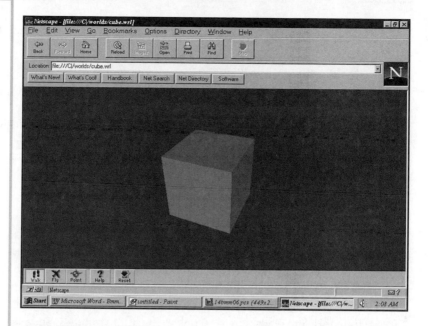

Note: The values for the X, Y, and Z coordinates of a transformation are determined by the distance away from the origin. Positive values on the X axis move the object to the right, and negative values move it to the left. Using positive values with the Y axis moves the object up, and negative values move it down. Likewise, values are either positive or negative on the Z axis to indicate objects that are closer or farther away, respectively.

When creating objects without explicitly specifying new positions for that object, the default position is at the origin. The origin is effectively the center of the screen.

Listing 9.3. The cube is now created away from the origin.

```
#VRML V1.0 ASCII

Separator {
    Transform {
        translation 5 -5 10

    }

    Cube{
        width 10
        height 10
        depth 10
    }
}
```

One important thing to notice about these associations involves the `Transform` node. The transformation node was introduced to move objects away from the origin, or the center of the VRML universe you are creating. This is the case—except when hierarchical relationships are formed: When a child object is created and directly related to another object, its origin is not the center of the universe but rather *the object from which it is inherited*.

To illustrate this, let's place a cone 10 units high with a five-unit radius on top of the cube you created in Listing 9.3. If the cube were created at the true center of the VRML universe, this cone should be translated to a new position on the Y axis. Because the cube and cone are both 10 units high, the new Y coordinate for the cone would be 10, since the position indicates the center of the object. In this case, the cube is 10 units high, and its vertical center is at 0. Since it is 10 units high, the top of the cube should be at +5 units (the bottom is at -5 units). Likewise, the cone is 10 units high, and its center would be half of its height or 5. When adding the centers of the cube and the cone together, you find that the new Y coordinate is 10.

Objects are located relative to the center of their core; because both objects are 10 units high, there are 5 units between the core and the top or bottom edges of each of the objects. Now, if you first translated the cube to its new position as shown in Listing 9.3,

what coordinates would you use to place the cone on top of the cube? The natural inclination at first is to translate the cone to the coordinates 5, 5, 10 (10 units above the translation for the cube). This would be correct if the cube and cone were not related. However, you would like these objects to be associated, forming a singular object. Listing 9.4 demonstrates how to do this in VRML and Figure 9.6 shows the result.

It's "In-Material"

Now that you know how to create basic objects and place them in Cyberspace, let's discuss how to make these objects look different by applying different color and texture attributes. So far each object you've created shares the same white color. Now let's make the cube yellow and not too shiny and the cone blue with a shiny, semitransparent coating.

To change the qualities of an object, VRML uses the `Material` node. This node works similarly to the `Transform` node in that it specifies the qualities of an object within a separator (or its children). It accepts numerous parameters, of which you use four. Listing 9.5 colors your cube yellow and its cone blue.

Color Your World

The color with which an object is painted is considered its `diffuseColor`. This attribute specifies the color to use when light strikes the surface of the object. A close relative to `diffuseColor` is `emissiveColor`. The difference is subtle, but potent: This attribute specifies a color for an object just as `diffuseColor` does, but it specifies the color

Figure 9.6.
A cone has been
added on top of
the cube.

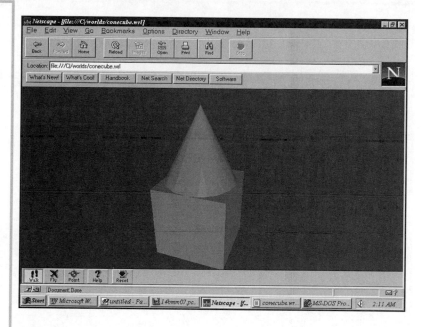

Listing 9.4. A cone is related to the cube and placed on top of it.

```
#VRML V1.0 ASCII

Separator {
    Transform {
        translation 5 -5 10
    }

    Cube{
        width 10
        height 10
        depth 10
    }

    Separator {
        Transform {
            # Since the following cone is associated with the
            # cube, its default position is the same as the
            # original cube.  Therefore, you simply need to
            # transform the cone's Y position.
            translation 0 10 0

        }

        Cone {
            bottomRadius 5
            height 10
        }
    }
}
```

that is to emanate from the object. This is most suitable for creating artificial lights like those in a hallway.

Listing 9.5. The cube has been colored using the `Material` node.

```
#VRML V1.0 ASCII

Separator {
    Transform {
        translation 5 -5 10
    }

    Material {
        # Choose a bright yellow
        diffuseColor 1 1 0
    }

    Cube{
        width 10
        height 10
        depth 10
    }

    Separator {
        Transform {
            translation 0 10 0
        }

        Material {
            # Choose a bright blue
            diffuseColor 0 0 1
            # Make it real pretty
            shininess 0.9
            # Make it somewhat transparent
            transparency 0.5
        }

        Cone {
            bottomRadius 5
            height 10
        }
    }
}
```

Tip: Don't confuse `emissiveColor` with lights in VRML. The `emissiveColor` property creates the artificial glow of a light but does not act as a light itself. It therefore does not cast shadows on any surrounding objects. To accomplish this, consider placing lamps within the object (at the same location as the object) to complete the effect. Remember, you never see lamps, just the effects they leave behind.

As you can see from the example in Listing 9.5, each color property contains three color values: the amount of red, green, and blue light to combine. The intensity of light for each ranges between 0 and 1. Therefore, to create the color white, you would use the values 1 1 1. To create black (the absence of light), you would use 0 0 0. A medium red is 0.5 0 0. Table 9.1 shows some common colors and their corresponding values.

Table 9.1. Common values for color choices in VRML.

Color	VRML Value		
White	1	1	1
Black	0	0	0
Red	1	0	0
Green	0	1	0
Blue	0	0	1
Yellow	1	1	0
Purple	1	0	1
Cyan	0	1	1
Orange	1	0.5	0
Light Gray	0.75	0.75	0.75
Medium Gray	0.5	0.5	0.5
Dark Gray	0.25	0.25	0.25

Tip: If you are familiar with choosing colors for text or link colors in HTML documents, then you are already familiar with choosing colors in VRML. HTML documents expect color values to range between 00 and FF, hexadecimal. You know that if you want to create green text in an HTML document you would use the value, #00FF00. The same goes for VRML, except that maximum values are 1.0 (FF in HTML documents) and minimum values are 0.0 (00 in HTML documents). Therefore, a bright green would be represented in VRML as 0 1 0.

A Web Helper application has also been included on the CD-ROM that accompanies this book that will aid in selecting colors and in the conversion of color codes.

If you're a little confused about color selection, try out the Color Selection application included on the CD-ROM accompanying this book. It will help you to pick colors and determine values to use in your HTML or VRML documents.

So Clear It Shines

Shiny objects are alluring. That's the sole reason for the dozens of waxes and polishes that are available on the market just for your automobile! However, besides creating a mood or capturing your eye, shine enables a VRML developer to create objects that appear to be metallic.

The blue cone in this example (Listing 9.5) uses the shininess attribute to give the cone a healthy sparkle. The shininess parameter expects a value between 0 (dull) and 1 (shiny). Of course, you do not have to choose an all or nothing approach; if you would like to have a little shine, choose a smaller value such as 0.25. For this example, the cone drawn will use a high amount of shine.

Besides simply adding shininess to an object, you can also determine its transparency. The transparency attribute of the Material node accomplishes this in VRML (0 = opaque; 1 =

transparent). Again, like shininess, you can adjust the transparency of an object by using incremental values between 0 and 1.

Rotation

Obviously, placing and coloring objects in Cyberspace is crucial to creating a virtual world. However, it is equally important to consider rotating those objects in space. Typically, you control the rotation of objects as you use the VRML browser to walk or fly around objects or spin them on any of their axes. However, you can also control how each object is rotated in space relative to other objects in space or the origin. The same Transform node that you used earlier to place objects at different positions in space contains another property for setting how much an object is rotated. Listing 9.6 rotates a cube 45 degrees toward the viewer and then pivots that cube in the new position 45 degrees clockwise. The results are shown in Figure 9.7.

It is important to notice that these rotation commands simply rotate the object *before* it is drawn so that it is positioned correctly. The Transform node does not animate objects. To learn more about performing actual animated rotations, see Chapter 10, "Fancy Modeling Tricks."

If you were sleeping in your trigonometry class, or concentrating more on your love interest in the front of the room than on your studies, you may have missed the class on converting degrees to radians. As you may or may not recall, radians are a variation on determining angles. One-half of a rotation around a circle (180 degrees) is equivalent to pi, and a complete rotation around a circle is 2 × pi. This helps to explain why the formula for the circumference of a circle, or the perimeter *around* a circle, is 2 × pi × radius.

VRML expects to find rotational measurements in the form of radians. The next question you may ask, if you don't

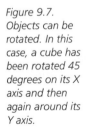

Figure 9.7. Objects can be rotated. In this case, a cube has been rotated 45 degrees on its X axis and then again around its Y axis.

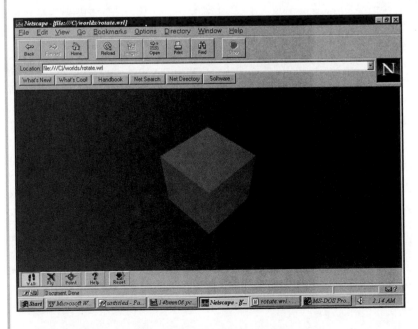

remember much from math, is how to convert degrees into radians and vice versa. Use the following formula:

```
radians = (pi*degrees)/180
```

Listing 9.6. Objects can be rotated in Cyberspace.

```
#VRML V1.0 ASCII

Separator {
    Transform {
        # Rotate the cube 45 degrees
        # toward the viewer (X Axis)
        rotation 1 0 0 .79
        # Addition translation commands
        # could be added here as well.
    }

    Transform {
        # Rotate the cube 45 degrees
        # around its Y axis.
        rotation 0 1 0 .79
    }

    Material {
        # Choose a bright yellow
        diffuseColor 1 1 0
        shininess 1
    }

    Cube{
        width 10
        height 10
        depth 10
    }
}
```

Or use the conversion program available on the CD-ROM included with this book that converts radians to degrees and vice versa.

Now let's examine the rotation property in the Transform nodes of Listing 9.6. Notice that the rotation property accepts four parameters: X (pitch), Y (yaw), Z (roll), and the amount (radians). You must first specify in which direction you wish to spin your object. By placing a 1 in either the X, Y, or Z columns, you indicate that you wish to rotate the object on that axis. The fourth parameter specifies how much you want to rotate that object. Values for the amount of

rotation must be in radians and can be either positive or negative to spin the object toward the positive end of the axis or in the opposite direction.

Be careful when attempting to rotate an object in several directions at once. It is possible to indicate that you want to spin an object on multiple axes at once. However, it is important to notice that simply setting more than one axis to 1 during a single rotation will not achieve the same result as two separate rotational transforms.

Combining axes in a single rotation statement, such as rotation 1 1 0 .79, may not achieve the desired result. In the previous example, it seems that using such a statement would accomplish your desire to pitch and yaw the object by 45 degrees. However, Figure 9.8 shows the result: not quite what you had pictured.

Figure 9.8. Attempting to rotate an object on more than one axis at a time may create undesirable results.

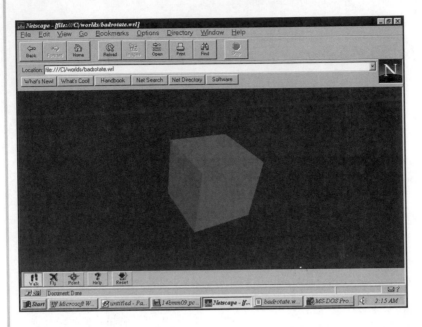

Shedding Light on the Subject

So far we have been discussing the placement of objects relying on the default lighting conditions presented by the VRML browser. It was hinted at earlier that other lights can be added to a VRML scene to add realism. The VRML language enables you to add one of three different types of light sources to your world: point lights, directional lights, and spotlights.

Point Light

Point light is one that radiates beams equally in all directions. It is similar to an incandescent light bulb found in a lamp. This node expects four properties:

✦ **on** Most likely you will never reset this property, but it is possible to turn a virtual light on or off with this "switch."

✦ **intensity** Some lights are brighter (or more intense) than others. You can set the intensity of a light source between 0 (extremely dark light) and 1 (incredibly bright light).

✦ **color** Just as you can specify the color of objects painted in your world, you can also tint a lamp to any color you choose. This color field accepts three parameters that instruct how much red, green, and blue light to mix. Values range from 0 to 1, just as they do in the Material node discussed earlier.

✦ **location** Additional light sources can be placed anywhere in

Cyberspace. You must specify the coordinates of the lamp just as you would specify the translation coordinates of the `Transform` node.

Directional Light

Directional light is light in which the rays are parallel to each other, similar to the effects of a spotlight. Think of rays of light from a directional light as traveling through a cylinder. The resulting beam is concentrated on a single location identified by parameters passed into this node. Use the following attributes to describe a directional light source:

+ **on**   Again you can choose to either turn this light on or off by passing either TRUE or FALSE.

+ **intensity**   As with point lights, you can specify how bright a directional light may be, where 1 indicates the most intense.

+ **color**   To create a mood or heighten realism, you can apply a particular color filter to this light. Again, colors are determined using the same process for creating colors as in the `Material` node.

+ **direction**   When a directional light has been established, you can specify the direction in which you want the rays to flow by passing in appropriate X, Y, and Z values. The source of the light is dependent on the most recent transformation node.

+ **orientation**   The direction in which a beam of light is cast can be specified by its orientation. This

function accepts four parameters. The first three indicate the axis on which the light should be rotated. These three axes are the X, Y, and Z axes, respectively. A value of 1 indicates that the light should be rotated on that axis. Otherwise, a value of 0 should be present. The final parameter indicates the amount of rotation in radians.

Spotlight

Spotlights are similar to directional lights. The biggest difference is that the light radiates outward in a conical fashion from a spotlight. These lights include all the parameters discussed in the directional light section, plus the following values:

+ **location**   The source of the spotlight.

+ **dropOffRate**   The edges of the spotlight are not as bright as the center of the beam. You can control how quickly the light fades as it spreads outward.

+ **cutOffAngle**   Because spotlights spread in a conical fashion, you can specify how far the light should spread in radians.

+ **orientation**   The direction in which a beam of light is cast can be specified by its orientation. This function accepts four parameters. The first three indicate the axis on which the light should be rotated. These three axes are the X, Y, and Z axes, respectively. A value of 1 indicates that the light should be rotated on that axis. Otherwise, a value of 0 should be present. The final parameter indicates the amount of rotation in radians.

What's Next?

In this chapter, you have received an introduction to VRML, a robust language for creating complex 3D scenes. We covered the basics of 3D modeling, adding objects to a scene, moving those objects, coloring and adjusting the attributes of objects, rotating objects, and adding additional lighting sources. In the next chapter, we will review some more complex VRML capabilities, such as dynamic VRML files and see how to use additional tools, such as conversion applications or 3D modeling programs, to facilitate creating your virtual worlds.

Fancy Modeling Tricks

chapter 10

by John J. Kottler

In Chapter 9, "Building 3D Cyberspace," you were introduced to the Virtual Reality Modeling Language. In that chapter you learned about modeling in three dimensions and creating simple objects in VRML. In this chapter, you will build on the experience you have gained so far to build far more complex and realistic worlds. You will gain an understanding of how to make your three-dimensional objects more realistic-looking with features of the VRML language such as texture mapping and differing levels of detail.

This chapter introduces you to more flexible implementations of VRML, such as linking VRML objects in a world to other VRML worlds or resources on the Web, such as hypertext pages. We will also cover how to create custom objects that can be placed in Cyberspace. Before the close of this chapter, you will see how VRML worlds can be more "alive" by using server-side scripting that dynamically creates VRML worlds and by learning some of the new features that will be found in the next generation of VRML. You will be introduced to each of these topics through a complete example of an online bank, the "First Bank of Cyberspace."

The standards for the next generation of VRML or VRML 2.0, have yet to be solidified. However, a solution offered by both Netscape and Silicon Graphics referred to as *Moving Worlds* will very well impact the standard. Because we have discussed the use of the Netscape browser heavily in this book, we will continue to examine Netscape's solutions for future VRML enhancements, which in this case is Moving Worlds. Toward the end of this chapter, you will see how to implement some of the functionality that Moving Worlds offers to VRML developers. For examples of Moving Worlds, refer to Chapter 8, "The World Wide Web Isn't Flat."

In this chapter, the source code that follows can be found on the CD-ROM included with this book. Again, as with Chapter 9, you may create VRML code by using a simple text-processor such as Notepad. Many of the GIF files used in the examples that follow can be found on the CD-ROM as well.

Making It Realistic

Chapter 9 reviewed the basics of VRML and creating simple scenes using the language. However, you probably noticed immediately that the examples left much to be desired. We created simple cubes, cones, and spheres, and even assembled some of these pieces together. But the reality is, most of these objects did not look all that realistic. For instance, with the information you have gained so far, you can create a simple scene such as the entrance to a bank that features steps and pillars. Figure 10.1 shows what this scene might look like using typical objects included in VRML.

This entrance is created with simple cubes to create the basic building, steps, and overhang. Two cylinders are also placed to represent the columns. However, this entrance for a large bank does not appear very realistic. The pillars and steps are arranged in the right locations, but it hardly resembles the majestic marble steps you might have in mind for a bank entrance. How can you improve this scene to make it look more realistic?

Wrap It Up

To make objects in Cyberspace appear more realistic, it is sometimes appropriate to add *textures* to objects. A texture is simply a pattern that can be applied to the surface of a 3D object. You can think of a texture as a picture that is "wrapped" around the outside of an object. For example, let's assume you want to wrap a gift with paper that contains a marble design. You would take that paper and wrap it evenly and neatly

Figure 10.1. You can use simple objects in VRML together to create more complex scenes such as this entrance to a bank.

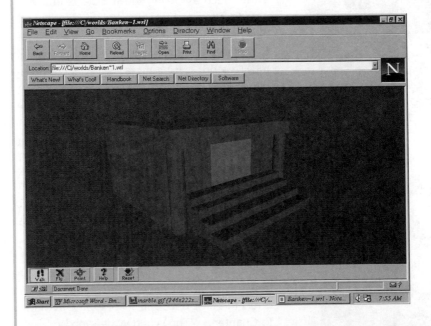

around all sides of the box. VRML does essentially the same task. The "paper" you choose to wrap an object with is the *texture* and can be defined either by a picture file (such as a GIF file) or by numbers in the VRML source code that represent a picture. (Although you can represent pictures by using numbers in your VRML code, it is difficult to implement and can be compared to trying to actually describe a painting to your friends.) VRML takes this texture and neatly wraps it around any VRML object, such as cubes, cylinders, cones, and spheres. It can even apply textures to custom objects that you create.

To make the bank entrance appear even more realistic, let's add a nice marble texture to the pillars and cross beam. Figure 10.2 shows the same 3D bank entrance from Figure 10.1 with a new marble look.

The Texture2 node is all that you need to wrap textures around objects in VRML. As mentioned in the preceding section, you can specify the texture by including numeric representation of that texture in your VRML code. However, it is much easier to simply wrap a predrawn graphics file around your VRML objects. Therefore, the only parameter that you need for the Texture2 node is the filename attribute. This parameter accepts the URL that identifies the "surface" bitmap graphic. Listing 10.1 creates the VRML object displayed in Figure 10.2, complete with marble surface. The source code as well as the marble texture for this example can be found on the CD-ROM included with this book.

Figure 10.2. Adding a marble texture makes the entrance to a bank look more appealing.

Listing 10.1. The `Texture2` node applies to all the VRML elements beneath it.

```
#VRML V1.0 ascii

Separator {
    Material {
        # Choose a medium green color
        diffuseColor 0 5 0
        # Make it shiny, since Marble is shiny
        shininess 1
    }
    Texture2 {
        # Make it marble
        filename "marble.gif"
    }
    Transform {
        translation 10 0 0
    }
    # Draw the pillars
    Cylinder {
        radius 1
        height 10
    }
    Transform {
        translation -20 0 0
    }
    Cylinder {
        radius 1
        height 10
    }
    Transform {
        translation 10 6 0
    }
    # Draw the beam over the pillars
    Cube {
        width 22
        height 2
        depth 2
    }
    Transform {
        translation 0 -5 -10
    }
    # Draw the Bank building
    Cube {
        width 22
        height 13
        depth 18
    }
    Transform {
        translation 0 -2.5 10
    }
    # Draw step 1
    Cube {
        width 18
        height 1
        depth 2
    }
    Transform {
        translation 0 -1 1
    }
```

```
    # Draw step 2
    Cube {
        width 18
        height 1
        depth 3
    }
    Transform {
        translation 0 -1 1
    }
    # Draw step 3
    Cube {
        width 18
        height 1
        depth 5
    }
    Transform {
        translation 0 -1 1
    }
    # Draw step 4
    Cube {
        width 18
        height 1
        depth 7
    }
}
```

Note: Applying textures to 3D objects overwrites material properties such as the object's color. For instance, even if you set the color of a sphere to be yellow and the texture mapped onto the sphere is blue, the resulting 3D object will be the blue color of the texture. However, if you are applying textures using transparent bitmaps, the original material color of the object will be seen through the transparent spots.

It is important to notice that textures are warped in order to wrap successfully around an entire VRML object. For instance, when wrapping a texture around a sphere, the original picture you use to apply as a texture on the sphere will be warped or pinched more towards the top and bottoms of the sphere. The texture also stretches entirely around the object. That is, the left side of the texture wraps completely around the object it is applied to until it meets the right side of the texture. The same applies to the top and bottom edges of that same texture.

Up Close and Personal

You have seen how textures applied to VRML objects make those objects appear more like their real-world counterparts. Another trick used to make objects in Cyberspace appear even more realistic is through the use of *level of detail* (LOD). Although this sounds nebulous, the theory is quite straightforward.

Imagine that you are walking down a sidewalk and you see two people coming from the opposite direction. At first, they appear in the far distance, and it is nearly impossible to determine any specific features. Those people could be anyone. As they approach, you begin to notice the color of their clothes and perhaps their hair, but although their faces are becoming clearer, you still do not recognize them. Finally, as they approach even closer, each person's facial features become more evident, and you can begin to see their clothes, eye color, and other features very clearly now. This is an example of different levels of detail. When the person is over 150 meters away, you might only recognize that the object is a person. Somewhere closer, maybe 50 meters away, you begin to see characteristics such as hair color and clothing. Around 5 meters away, you can see much more detailed facial features.

Let's apply the same techniques to the First Bank of Cyberspace example, which you'll continue to develop through the rest of this chapter. From a distance over 150 units away, you might only see the building and be able to recognize the pillars in the front. Somewhere between 50 and 150 units away, you see that there are words written over the archway, but cannot quite make them out. Less than 50 units from the bank entrance, you can clearly read that the words are "First Bank of Cyberspace."

So how do you develop different levels of detail in the VRML language? Level of detail, or LOD for short, is simply implemented via another VRML node: LOD. This node enables you to define a range of different levels of detail. This range is identified via the range attribute of the LOD node. In reality, this range attribute is specifying an array of values to be used by your VRML world.

For the banking example, I mentioned that you might want to show the basic bank when a user looks at the VRML world at a distance greater than 150 units. As the user approached the bank and is between 50 and 150 units from the bank, the name of the bank should appear abstract above the pillars. In this example, make it *very* abstract, a simple white rectangle. Finally, when the user is less than 50 units from the bank, the text should appear. With these criteria, this example requires three different levels of detail. The following syntax is necessary to create the appropriate LOD:

```
LOD {
    range [50,150]
}
```

The range attribute of the LOD node in VRML specifies *transition points*. A transition point is similar to a fence—a divider between two levels of detail. Therefore, when you specify one value range for a LOD, your VRML source file must provide for *two* possible instances: before that transition point and after that point. In general, you must specify one range value for every level of detail, plus an additional one. In the banking example, you'll want three levels of detail, which requires two transition points. The first transition point (50 in the LOD line above) infers that there is one level of detail when the user is closer than 50 units from the object and another level of detail between 50 units and 150 units. Finally, the third level of detail is used when the user is more than 150 units from the object.

After you have set the ranges for differing levels of detail in your virtual world, you must create the VRML code to be executed for each one. This VRML code should display different objects, depending on the current level of detail. Typically, when a user views objects closely, the detail increases with the appearance of more objects or more suitable textures. In the example, you can use the code in Listing 10.2 to make unreadable text appear as the viewer moves closer to the bank, and then when the viewer is very close, show actual letters.

Listing 10.2. Three different levels of detail are created for the bank: One up close for reading the name of the bank, and two positions farther away.

```
LOD {
    range [50,150]

    # Within 50 units of the bank,
    # show text for sign.
    Separator {
        Material {
            # Choose a bright white color
            diffuseColor 1 1 1
            shininess 1
        }
        FontStyle {
            size 1
        }
        AsciiText {
            string "1st Bank of Cyberspace"
            justification CENTER
            width 18
        }
    }
    # Between 50-150 units, just show a
    # rectangle representing the text
    Separator {
        Material {
            # Choose a bright white color
            diffuseColor 1 1 1
            shininess 1
        }
        Cube {
            width 10
            height .5
            depth .1
        }
    }
    # Further than 150 units away, hide
    # sign completely
    Separator {
        Cube {
            width 0
            height 0
            depth 0
        }
    }
}
```

Links Away!

So far, the 3D worlds you have created are just objects floating in space. There are no dynamic attributes applied to any of these objects. To make these objects more interactive, the VRML language provides hyperlinks to other VRML worlds or HTML documents. You can define each individual object in your 3D scene as a link to someplace else at your Web site.

The WWWAnchor node is used to create these links in Cyberspace. This node affects all objects that are within its beginning and ending curly braces ({}). It accepts one parameter that specifies the URL that the link is to connect to and a separate param-eter that provides more descriptive text for the link.

In the bank example, it would be helpful to create a link on the front doors of the bank. As your visitors approach the bank, they can then click on the doors to go inside. In reality, you'll want to link to another VRML scene that displays the inside of the bank. On the inside, which we will describe shortly, you can create a simple animation and have live stock updates. You can also provide links on the inside of the bank that enable your visitors to read news, such as current interest rates. Listing 10.3 implements a link on the doors of the bank that links to a second VRML file: Inside.wrl.

Listing 10.3. Objects in a WWWAnchor node become hotspots that link to another resource on the Web.

```
Separator {
    WWWAnchor {
        name "Inside.wrl"
        description "Go inside the bank."

        Material {
            # Choose a dark gray color
            ambientColor .2 .2 .2
            shininess 1
        }

        Transform {
            translation 0 5 -4
        }

        Cube {
            width 8
            height 6
            depth .1
        }
    }
}
```

Caution: In Listing 10.3, the WWWAnchor node links to another VRML world called Inside.wrl. In this case (and on the CD-ROM), the linked VRML file exists in the same directory as the original file from which it is linked. You will be required to adjust these paths accordingly for your applications.

In Listing 10.3, the cube that creates the black front door of the bank is included in the WWWAnchor node and becomes a hotspot. When you pass your mouse cursor over this doorway, the cursor changes to indicate that a link exists. If you include a description line in the WWWAnchor node, that line of text appears over the hotspot in your VRML world. Figure 10.3 gives an example of the screen with additional descriptive text over the doorway.

When you click on a link in a VRML scene, you will be transferred to another location on the Web. This location, specified by the name attribute of the WWWAnchor, can link to any Web resource. Typically, it will link to another, relevant hypertext (HTML) document, or additional VRML scenes. Linking to other scenes creates the illusion of more complex scenes. For instance, when you click on the bank doors, another VRML scene displays and shows the inside of the bank. This not only makes the scene appear more complex, but offers a programmatic means of controlling the environment.

In Your Own World

Although you can create fairly complex scenes by combining VRML's built-in objects, there will be times when the simple assembly of cubes, cylinders, or spheres is insufficient to create a specialized object. At these times, it is essential to create original

*Figure 10.3.
Links can provide
"doorways" to
other Web
resources such
as HTML pages
or other VRML
worlds.*

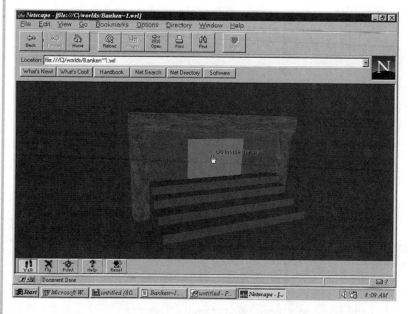

objects in VRML using the `Coordinate3` and `IndexedFaceSet` nodes. These two nodes enable you to create an object of *any* type. However, it is much more difficult to create these objects.

Fortunately, several tools are available that enable you to create 3D objects easily. Such tools as AutoCAD, 3D Studio, Caligari TrueSpace, and X-Treme 3D, are modeling tools available for Windows machines. These tools enable the designer to draw objects and be able to see exactly where each point drawn exists on each of the three axes at the same time. There are also several tools available to convert files created by these or other tools into VRML files. This is by far a simpler method of creating complex, nonstandard VRML objects.

Although it is easier to create complex models in VRML using a 3D modeling tool, it is possible to create these objects using standard VRML. It is important to at least understand how VRML implements complex objects. There might be occasions in the future where you want to create these objects dynamically using server scripts. Creating dynamic VRML files will be discussed later in this chapter.

Coordinate3

You might recall from Chapter 8 that each object in VRML consists of points in space that are connected together by polygons. A cube, for example, consists of eight points in space (at each corner of the cube) and six faces that connect those points. It is possible to create unique objects using the same approach. In this case, you specify the coordinates of your object and then the faces that connect those points together.

The `Coordinate3` node enables you to create a group of points in 3D space. This node contains the `point` attribute, which is actually an array of points. Each point in this group is designated by its appropriate X, Y, and Z coordinates. Each complete point is also separated by a comma, because each point exists in an array. These points are always created relative to the origin.

Let's make a not-so-unique shape in the world of geometry, yet one that is not built-in to VRML: a pyramid. In this case, create a pyramid with a square bottom, similar to those found in Egypt. Therefore, the object consists of four points at the base of the pyramid and another point at the top. Listing 10.4 shows how these points can be defined in VRML.

Listing 10.4. A pyramid object using the `Coordinate3` structure.

```
Coordinate3 {
    point [
        0 0 1,
        -1 1 0,
        -1 -1 0,
        1 -1 0,
        1 1 0
    ]
}
```

Connect the Dots

After the points have been constructed in 3D space, you need to connect the dots. Actually, you are choosing the sides of the object that you are creating. The polygons will be drawn using the points that you specify.

In reality, when computers render an object in a scene, each face is made up of many triangles. Computers can generate triangles more quickly than other geometric objects, and therefore, triangles are chosen to optimize rendering times for images. The triangles are combined to form other geometric shapes. For instance, a single face of a cube is actually created with two triangles as shown in Figure 10.4.

Figure 10.4. Polygon surfaces of a 3D object are actually constructed from several triangles.

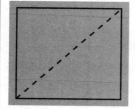

When you are ready to play "Connect the Dots" with your custom VRML object, use the `IndexedFaceSet` node. As this node implies, you specify a set of "faces" or surfaces for your object. The `IndexedFaceSet` node expects the coordinates that make up a single triangle that contributes to the overall face of the surface. However, because you already specified the X, Y, and Z coordinates for each point of your object with the `Coordinate3` node, you can simply reference those points. Points that you chose with the `Coordinate3` node are stored in an array.

You can choose the points to make up a triangle by identifying each element of the point array constructed by the `Coordinate3` node. For the pyramid, six triangular polygons must be selected from the total point array: one for each side of the pyramid and two to make up the square base. Figure 10.5 illustrates how to create the 3D pyramid using the six triangles. Listing 10.5 demonstrates the `IndexedFaceSet` node used for creating the polygons necessary for the pyramid object.

Figure 10.5. A pyramid's five surfaces are constructed from six triangles. Each point is labeled 0 through 4, indicating the points created with the `Coordinate3` node.

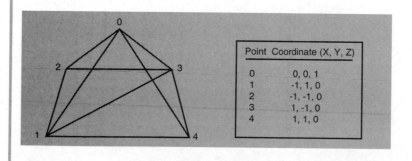

Point	Coordinate (X, Y, Z)
0	0, 0, 1
1	-1, 1, 0
2	-1, -1, 0
3	1, -1, 0
4	1, 1, 0

Listing 10.5. The `IndexedFaceSet` node specifies the triangles that connect the dots created with the `Coordinate3` node.

```
IndexedFaceSet {
    coordIndex [
        0,  1,  4,  -1,
        0,  1,  2,  -1,
        0,  2,  3,  -1,
        0,  3,  4,  -1,
        1,  3,  4,  -1,
        1,  2,  3,  -1
    ]
}
```

Tip: Newer versions of VRML do not require that you break the surfaces of a custom object into triangles. With these versions, the pyramid example could use the `IndexedFaceSet` as shown below. Notice that the base of the pyramid (a square) has all four points connected at once, not broken into two separate triangles. This will likely be the standard in the future, because it makes 3D modeling somewhat simpler for the VRML designer.

```
IndexedFaceSet {
    coordIndex [
        0,  1,  4,  -1,
        0,  1,  2,  -1,
        0,  2,  3,  -1,
        0,  3,  4,  -1,
        1,  2,  3,  4,  -1
    ]
}
```

As you can see from Listing 10.5, each point created from the `Coordinate3` node is referenced in the `coordIndex` section of the `IndexedFaceSet` node by its position in the array of points. Because every 3D object must somehow be created from triangles, there will only be three points chosen for each triangle or line of code in the example.

Each triangle is separated by a `-1`. Figure 10.5 shows the triangles listed in Listing 10.5 and the points from Listing 10.4.

Although this process for creating unique objects appears fairly straightforward, it becomes quite tedious when you're attempting to design even more complex designs. A pyramid consists of five sides that can be easily parsed into triangles. Imagine, however, trying to create a more complex shape, such as a spring. It would take quite an amount of time to determine all the coordinates necessary to simulate the shape of a coiled spring, and then even more time to figure out how to map a surface onto the spring! Fortunately, there are several applications available that aid in the construction of complex 3D models. There are also numerous programs available that enable you to convert 3D models from other non-VRML tools into a VRML file. Also, because the World Wide Web is so vast, there are hundreds, if not thousands, of 3D VRML objects available on sites around the world.

It's Alive!

This virtual bank, the First Bank of Cyberspace, is beginning to take shape. Now you should provide some information that visitors see when they enter the bank. For the "inside" of the bank, you should create at least a few objects. First, make a very simple desk. On this desk, add a simple rectangle object with a newspaper cover on the rectangle. That object will link to news and other information about the bank. You should also create a simple stock graph in another corner of the desk. The graph will track (artificially for this example) a few stocks over time. On the opposite side of the desk, place a rotating pyramid, which simply displays an advertising message. The final scene would appear as it does in Figure 10.6. You could get carried away and create teller windows to perform transactions and offer other banking facilities, but for this example, the newspaper, stock graph, and advertising pyramid should be sufficient.

Creating the scene takes just a little work. First create large walls for the inside of the bank. The desk simply requires a long rectangle for the desktop and four smaller rectangles for the legs of the desk. On top of the desk, add a single rectangle and map a newspaper texture onto it. In addition, place the pyramid on one corner of the desk and wrap an advertising slogan around the pyramid. Finally, don't forget to add another door, this time to lead back to the outside of the bank. Although this example is creating a bank, you could easily add more buildings to the scene and have a complete "cyber-town."

Now for the fun part (the stock graph), you'll simply use random values for stock prices. In reality, you would want to create a script on the server that fetches current prices from a stock service on the Web. However, for this example, random values will be sufficient. The stock chart should be added to the opposite corner of the desk. It can be

Figure 10.6. The inside of the bank provides a desk with a newspaper, an advertisement pyramid, and a dynamic stock graph.

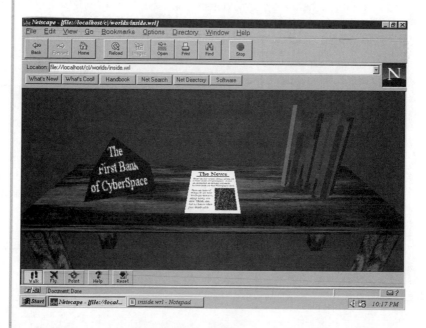

somewhat on the small side, because you can zoom in on it in VRML. The actual stock graph is created dynamically by a script on the server every time your visitors enter the bank. This script determines stock prices and updates the appropriate section of the VRML file accordingly, to create a dynamic graph that is continuously refreshed with the newest stock trends.

Making It Easier

A great way to do this is to simply update a small portion of a VRML file. Although this sounds complex, it really isn't. You should follow these basic steps:

+ Write an original VRML file and save it on your server. Use a filename that makes sense such as `My Scene.original`.

+ Add a comment line to the original VRML file such as `"### INSERT LIVE VRML CODE HERE ###"`. This helps to identify where a dynamic object should be added to the final VRML scene.

+ When your site invokes a server script to view the dynamic VRML scene (by clicking on a link to view the scene, for instance), that script should copy the original VRML file (`My Scene.original`) as the final VRML file that will be sent to the user's Web browser for display.

+ During the copy process, the script should insert the new VRML code into the section marked by your comment, `"### INSERT LIVE VRML CODE HERE ###"`.

+ After dynamic code has been added to the final VRML file, the rest of the original file should be copied.

This process makes updates of VRML scenes much easier. Let's say, for instance, that you spend time creating a VRML scene and then decide you need to add dynamic information to it. Then several months later, you need to update the scene, yet maintain that live, dynamic data. This can take a considerable amount of time. However, if you are using a server program to create the dynamic VRML scene, this requires rewriting that program. If you use the process just outlined, you simply need to redesign the scene, copy the redesigned VRML file to the server, and make sure that the `"### INSERT LIVE VRML CODE HERE###"` line exists in the correct spot. Isn't that easier?

The Server Script

You might recall that server scripts are often used to create dynamic Web pages. This is done using the standard output commands of a server scripting language such as PERL, C, or another language that is available on the operating system your server uses. The server program simply prints output to the standard console output on the server machine. This output is automatically read as input to the client's Web browser. Therefore, a server script can send any type of information over the Internet to a user's computer. It must be formatted properly, though, in order to be viewed correctly. Often HTML files are created dynamically via such server programs. But VRML files are simple ASCII text files as well. Therefore, there is no reason why a server program cannot create a VRML document to be fed to a Web browser. For the stock price example, the content should be created dynamically by a server program that can read current stock prices. As we already discussed, to make things simpler, you should be updating only a section of the final VRML file sent to the Web browser.

The best way to update a section of a VRML file is to have an original VRML file that exists on the server. In that file, add comments that clearly denote the region in the VRML file that should be updated. Then, your server program should read each line of the *original* VRML file and write that exact line into a *new* VRML file that will be viewed by the Web browser. In a sense, you are copying the file line-by-line. However, there is one important difference: Because you placed comments in strategic locations in the original VRML file, you can easily find where to insert dynamic information.

When reading each line from the original VRML source file, test each line using an IF condition in your scripting language. Compare the line read in and see if it matches the comment that indicates the dynamic region of your VRML. If so, stop copying lines of the original file and begin writing the new dynamic VRML code in the file that is sent to the Web browser. When you've finished writing the dynamic portion of your VRML code, continue copying each line of the original VRML file into the final destination file. Listing 10.6 shows a simple Visual Basic program (which can be a server program on a Windows 3.*x*, Windows 95, or Windows NT machine) that uses these steps to create the dynamic stock example. As you can see by the listing, the actual stock prices are

randomly generated, although in the real world you would want to query the actual prices. Figure 10.7 shows the final graph created using the code found in Listing 10.6. This figure however, does not label stock prices. In reality, labels should be added to indicate individual stocks as well as the dates on which these measurements were made.

Tip: To save processing time on the server, you might consider running a server script that dynamically updates a VRML scene and saves the results to a file, instead of piping the new data through the Internet to a client computer. This script could be run on the server at a given interval (say every 15 minutes for the stock example) to refresh a VRML file. Then when a user accesses that VRML scene, it will already be prepared and simply be passed to the user. This will make the scene appear to be generated more quickly if your server script is rather complex.

In order to simulate an Internet client/server relationship on a standalone computer, it is easier to have the server program (Listing 10.6) create the final VRML scene as a new file. That new file can then be loaded into your Web browser or VRML browser. To simulate this working on your computer, simply run the server program `stocks.exe` found on the CD-ROM to generate a VRML file. Then load that final VRML file into your Web or VRML browser. When the final VRML is browsed, the newest stock information will be updated and displayed in the graph on the desktop inside the bank.

Figure 10.7. Listing 10.6 dynamically updates a VRML scene to provide this sample of three separate stock prices over time.

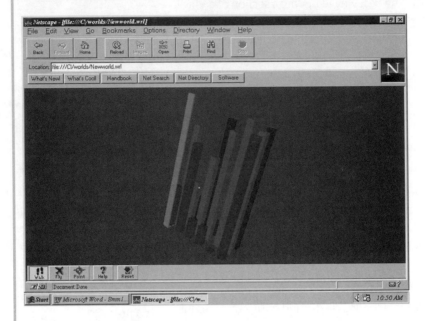

Listing 10.6. A server script can copy an original VRML file and dynamically update only a section of it.

```
Sub Stocks ()
    ' Get good and random values
    Randomize Timer

    ' Open the original VRML file for input
    Open "original.wrl" For Input As #1

    ' Start writing to the final VRML file to
    ' be displayed in VRML browser.
    Open "newworld.wrl" For Output As #2

    ' Read through the entire original file
    While Not EOF(1)
        Line Input #1, src$
        If src$ = "### INSERT LIVE VRML CODE HERE ###" Then
            ' We found where to insert the new
            ' dynamic VRML code.  So start writing
            ' it out.
            Print #2, "### HERE'S THE DYNAMIC VRML ###"
```

```
' We're going to track 3 stocks for six days.
' The for loop creates the six days worth (0-5).
For z = 5 To 0 Step -1
    ' Each iteration of the loop is a day.
    ' Create 3 random prices for the 3 stocks that day.
    price1 = Rnd * 10
    price2 = Rnd * 10
    price3 = Rnd * 10

    ' The prices are recorded as the height of
    ' the bars in the scene.  To keep the bases
    ' of all the bars the same, the Transform
    ' node must push the bars upward 1/2 their
    ' overall height.  They must be pushed along
    ' the Z axis as well to create multiple "days"
    ' of data without overlap.

    ' Write out stock #1's bar
    Print #2, "Separator {"
    Print #2, "   Material {"
    Print #2, "      diffuseColor 1 0 0"
    Print #2, "   }"
    Print #2, "   "
    Print #2, "   Transform {"
    Print #2, "      translation -1 " + price1 / 2 +
         " " + Str$(z)
    Print #2, "   }"
    Print #2, "   "
    Print #2, "   Cube {"
    Print #2, "      width .5"
    Print #2, "      depth .5"
    Print #2, "      height " + price1
    Print #2, "   }"
    Print #2, "}"
    Print #2, "   "
    Print #2, "   "

    ' Write out stock #2's bar
    Print #2, "Separator {"
    Print #2, "   Material {"
    Print #2, "      diffuseColor 0 1 0"
    Print #2, "   }"
    Print #2, "   "
    Print #2, "   Transform {"
    Print #2, "      translation 0 " + price2 / 2 +
         " " +Str$(z)
    Print #2, "   }"
    Print #2, "   "
    Print #2, "   Cube {"
    Print #2, "      width .5"
    Print #2, "      depth .5"
    Print #2, "      height " + price2
    Print #2, "   }"
    Print #2, "}"
    Print #2, "   "
    Print #2, "   "

    ' Write out stock #3's bar
    Print #2, "Separator {"
    Print #2, "   Material {"
```

continues

Listing 10.6. continued

```
                Print #2, "    diffuseColor 0 0 1"
                Print #2, "  }"
                Print #2, " "
                Print #2, "  Transform {"
                Print #2, "    translation 1 " + price3 / 2 +
                          " " + Str$(z)
                Print #2, "  }"
                Print #2, " "
                Print #2, "  Cube {"
                Print #2, "    width .5"
                Print #2, "    depth .5"
                Print #2, "    height " + price3
                Print #2, "  }"
                Print #2, "}"
                Print #2, " "
            Next

            Print #2, "### THE END OF DYNAMIC VRML ###"
        Else
            Print #2, src$
        End If
    Wend
    Close

    End
End Sub
```

A Whole New World

You have come a long way and now know quite a bit about modeling 3D objects in VRML. The nodes that we have covered so far are typical to VRML 1.*x* standards that are well known and documented today. Now let's take an overview of some of the advanced features that you will begin to see in VRML 2.0, especially with Netscape's Live3D plug-in for Netscape Navigator 2.0.

There are several key elements lacking in today's VRML standard. Some things are simple, such as background pictures. Others are more complicated, such as motion, video, and sound. These are just some of the components you will begin to see in the next generation of Cyberspace. In the not-so-distant future, you will see numerous improvements to make virtual reality on the Web seem more like reality. As the VRML browsers and standard evolve, VRML will ultimately be used for simulations, conferences, and games. Some of the improvements that are coming soon in Live3D include these features:

+ Support for background graphics that paint the walls beyond the scene.

+ Animation support such as rotation of objects.

+ Scripting support for languages such as Java and JavaScript.

+ Support for animated graphics files on surfaces of a VRML object.

+ Implementation of sound and spatial sound.

- ✦ Motion and collision detection between objects in a world.
- ✦ Compression of `.wrl` files to reduce bandwidth.
- ✦ Streaming audio and video support.

As you can see, this is just an example of the newest technologies being introduced into the next version of VRML. Silicon Graphics is a principal developer of the Moving Worlds specification and will further introduce special lighting effects, such as fog, and more real-time 3D modeling. As personal computers continue to evolve through innovations, such as enhanced 3D graphics cards, faster processors, and other multimedia advancements, these advanced effects will become possible on these machines as well.

The new VRML 2.0 specification will be extraordinarily complete, and therefore, much more complex than current VRML 1.*x*. Covering the entire scope of the newest version of VRML would clearly span beyond the scope of this book. However, certain elements that are available now in Live3D from Netscape are too substantial to pass over. We will touch lightly on a few improvements in VRML scenes that can be created for Live3D.

> # Tip:
> If you want to stay on top of VRML, visit `vrml.wired.com`. This site contains numerous resources regarding VRML. It includes full documentation for VRML 1.*x* and the standards for Moving Worlds. It also contains other useful resources, such as conversion software and discussion forums.

Back It Up

As realistic as some VRML scenes look with proper texture mapping on the actual 3D objects, there is something lacking in VRML 1.*x*. If you browse several VRML worlds, you might come across a common look between them all, the dark gray or black background. There has not been a way to add more exciting background textures—until now. Live3D offers the following node syntax for adding a GIF image as a background for your VRML scene:

```
DEF BackgroundImage Info {
    string "backgrnd.gif"
}
```

You simply use the `BackgroundImage Info` node and specify the filename or URL where the VRML browser can find the background texture. Notice that the graphic file specified is tiled in the background of the VRML browser window much like the `BACKGROUND` option in the HTML `<BODY>` tag. Later in this chapter, Listing 10.9 will demonstrate the use of a background.

Round and Round She Goes

Another limitation of traditional VRML has been the lack of animation. Live3D and Moving Worlds will support new animation and collision detection routines. Complex animation and collision detection will require the use of a scripting language, such as C or Java, for implementation. However, it is possible to create simple rotational animation using the new `SpinGroup` node. Objects that are set to spin with this command continue to do so in the background, even as you walk or fly through the scene.

The DEF command can be used to name a portion of your VRML file. Most commonly, it is used in conjunction with a Separator node, such as:

```
DEF MyCube Separator {
    Cube {
        width 10
        height 10
        depth 10
    }
}
```

Naming a section of your VRML file enables you to use that section again elsewhere with the USE command. Later, another section of a VRML file could be

```
Transform {
    translation 5 2 1
}

USE MyCube
```

Another cube would be placed at the new location in Cyberspace. In the case of Live3D, the DEF command can also be used for special features.

The SpinGroup node affects all objects that are enclosed in its leading and ending braces ({}). This node can use a rotation attribute to specify how to rotate objects. The rotation option of the SpinGroup node requires that you specify which axis you want to spin objects around as well as the degree of rotation. You might remember from Chapter 9 that Listing 9.6 demonstrated that you must specify which axis to rotate the object around by either marking a 1 (rotate) or a 0 (don't rotate) in the X, Y, and Z columns. The amount of rotation is actually measured in radians and determines how much to spin objects. With the SpinGroup node, however, this rotation amount actually determines the speed at which objects rotate. Lower numbers indicate slower rotation speeds, while higher values indicate faster speeds. Listing 10.7 demonstrates how to rotate a cube around both its Y and Z axes.

Adding Text

As convenient as geometric objects are in Cyberspace, there is always a need for text as well. The AsciiText node enables you to add strings of text to your VRML scene. In the node, simply set the string attribute, which indicates the text you want to display. You can also set the justification property of this node to LEFT, CENTER, or RIGHT to justify the text. The FontStyle node can also be used with the AsciiText node to provide greater flexibility on the text displayed by modifying attributes such as the font's size. Listing 10.8 adds simple text to a VRML scene.

Listing 10.7. Objects can be continuously rotated in the background using Moving Worlds' SpinGroup node.

```
SpinGroup {
    rotation 0 1 1 -.1

    Cube {
        width 10
        height 10
        depth 10
    }
}
```

Listing 10.8. Text can be added easily to your VRML worlds.

```
FontStyle {
    size 4
}

AsciiText {
    string "Web Page Wizardry"
}
```

Axis Alignment

Sometimes, objects have a way of disappearing in VRML. Take, for instance, some simple text like that shown in Listing 10.8. Text is not very deep at all. Although it is rendered in a 3D scene, the text does not contain depth. Text drawn on the scene is very thin, like paper. Now think about taking a piece of paper with both of your hands and tilting it away from you. If you are looking at the piece of paper straight-on and hold this piece of paper so that it is perfectly parallel to the floor, it becomes incredibly thin—almost to the extent that you cannot see it, especially if you are far away.

The same phenomenon occurs in the virtual world. If the text object created in Listing 10.8 is displayed in a VRML browser and rotated away from you, the text would appear to get increasingly squatty until it becomes nothing more than a thin line. At times, this can become annoying. For instance, if graphs of information are displayed in VRML, and the user rotates the graphs around, some of the legends might become unreadable or disappear as the scene rotates.

To prevent this from occurring, Live3D supports the `AxisAlignment` node. This node locks the X, Y, and Z rotational axes of an object. `AxisAlignment` uses an attribute named `alignment` to specify how object rotation should be locked. When the `ALIGNAXISXYZ` value is assigned to the `alignment` property, rotation is prevented on all three axes. Movement and zoom is not affected, though. Therefore, to lock text on all three axes, the following code can be placed before the `AsciiText` node, but in a text object's separator:

```
AxisAlignment {
    alignment ALIGNAXISXYZ
}
```

Adding Animation

In the future, you will see advancements that will enable you to map a video file as a texture for a VRML object. This will enable you to play a video on the face of a cube, for instance. You can also add animated textures to your objects using animated GIF images and the Texture2 node. A similar concept was covered in Chapter 3, "Animation the Easy Way: Multi-Image GIFs," where you learned how to create animations using the GIF file format. You can apply a similar technique to create animations on the surfaces of your VRML objects. Figure 10.8 shows how to create the GIF file necessary for animated textures. The process involves the following steps:

1. Determine how many frames you require for your animation.

Figure 10.8.
You can combine multiple frames into a GIF file to create animated textures in VRML.

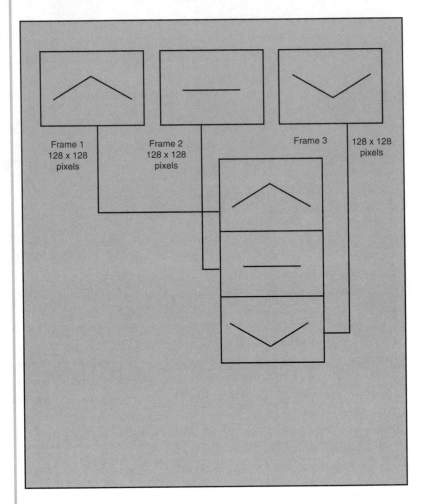

Frame 1
128 x 128
pixels

Frame 2
128 x 128
pixels

Frame 3   128 x 128
pixels

New GIF File
(128 pixels by 384 pixels)

2. Draw each frame of the animation using the same size, square graphic file. For instance, 138 pixels by 138 pixels.

3. After saving each frame, you must create a new GIF file that is as wide as one frame (in pixels) and as high as one frame (in pixels) *multiplied* by the number of frames in the animation.

4. Paste each frame drawn into the new GIF file from top to bottom, in the order in which they should be animated.

5. Save the new GIF as a file.

6. Reference the new GIF file in the `filename` attribute of a `Texture2` node.

Live3D will take care of animating the frames on the surfaces of the object that you apply in the `Texture2` node.

Putting It All Together

Listing 10.9 demonstrates how to use all of the features covered in this section on Moving Worlds and Live3D and Figure 10.9 shows the results of Listing 10.9.

In addition, the `SpinGroup` node is used in the bank example that you have been examining throughout this chapter. This node spins the pyramid on the desk inside of the bank. Some promotional information is wrapped on the pyramid, and the rotation of the object draws attention to it. The final VRML files for the First Bank of Cyberspace can be found on the CD-ROM included with this book.

Embedding the Results

Netscape Navigator 2.*x* supports the capability to embed rich data types directly into the content in the Web document displayed in the browser window. This eliminates the need to control rich content via separate programs that typically work outside and without the browser. Your VRML files can be easily embedded into Web pages using the `<EMBED>` HTML tag. You merely need to specify the name of the VRML file to display and the size of the VRML browser window with the `<EMBED>` tag. Listing 10.10 demonstrates how to correctly embed a VRML file in your Web document.

Embedding objects in a Netscape 2 browser window is convenient because they are more integrated with the rest of the content on an HTML Web page. Each embedded object appears to be part of the page, like inline GIF graphic images. Because of this feature, the Web page developer has much more flexibility in designing a page with rich content.

Listing 10.9. A simple example can use all of the Moving Worlds nodes discussed in this section.

```
#VRML V1.0 ASCII

# WAYCOOL.WRL
# A way cool demonstration

DEF BackgroundImage Info {
    # Nice space background
    string "spacebak.gif"
}

SpinGroup {
    # Spin a cube on its Y, Z axes
    rotation 0 1 1 -.1

    Separator {
        Texture2 {
            # Animate some text on the cube
            filename "wpwanim.gif"
        }
        Cube {
            width 10
            height 10
            depth 10
        }
    }
}

Separator {
    Transform {
        translation 10 0 0
    }

    AxisAlignment {
        alignment ALIGNAXISXYZ
    }

    FontStyle {
        size 4
    }

    AsciiText {
        string "Web Page Wizardry"
    }
}
```

Tip: Although often applied to textual objects, there is no reason why the AxisAlignment node cannot be used with other VRML objects. This is a useful node that can lock some objects of a VRML world, while allowing others to rotate.

Listing 10.10. After you have completed your VRML world, embed the results into your HTML Web document.

```
<HTML>
<BODY>
Here's a stunning VRML file, right in the middle
of your browser window!<PRE>


</PRE>
<CENTER>
<EMBED SRC="waycool.wrl" WIDTH=320 HEIGHT=240>
</CENTER>
</BODY>
</HTML>
```

Figure 10.9. The VRML code in Listing 10.9 creates an interesting scene.

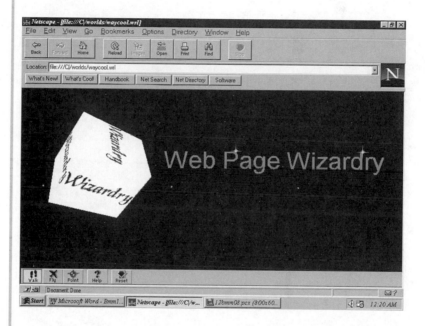

What's Next?

These past few chapters introduced you to VRML and some of its capabilities. As already mentioned, not every nuance of the VRML language could be covered completely in this book. To continue to learn more about the future of VRML, visit the vrml.wired.com site. To learn more about Netscape's Live3D and Moving Worlds speci-

fication, visit Netscape at www.netscape.com or Silicon Graphics at www.sgi.com.

You should now be ready to create some dazzling 3D worlds of your own that you can embed on your own Web pages. Experiment with some of the concepts covered in this section of the book and see how you can make your own cool VRML scenes that are alive and dynamic.

In the Driver's Seat: Interactive Programs

part IV

ActiveX and Object Linking and Embedding (OLE)

The first thing you should probably get right about OLE is how to pronounce it. The accepted way of saying OLE is "olay," *not* "O-L-E." If you know this, you're already well ahead of many Web site developers in this area.

OLE stands for Object Linking and Embedding. The technology was developed by Microsoft and is still currently available only on the Windows family of operating systems (3.1, 95, and NT). OLE was a buzzword in the computer industry long before Java was even at the coffee bean stage. And though Java has stolen the scene as the Internet programming language, OLE has been adapted to work with Web browsers and is making a potentially strong comeback. When a technology has the size, money, and power of an industry leader such as Microsoft behind it, you should always keep abreast of where it's at and where it's going.

OLE for Web pages is in an even more preliminary position than Sun's Java. As a result, this chapter won't necessarily give you all the definitive answers on OLE, because many open questions exist. We'll show you the current state of the technology and how it is being used and implemented on Web pages at this writing. We'll show you the different options for making OLE work on your Web pages and what the future promises. Most importantly, we'll give you the basics of OLE so you're ready to adapt to and accept the technology when it achieves critical mass in the near future.

chapter 11

by Brian K. Murphy

Why OLE Is so Awesome (and Looks so Simple)

Unlike Java, OLE was conceived and developed at a time when the Internet was but a bastion of research scientists, students, and computer hobbyists who had the time and patience necessary to navigate a user-unfriendly, text-only interface. There was no World Wide Web, or even Gopher for that matter. The idea of the network as being the center around which computers would primarily work was not widely held and accepted.

Microsoft created OLE as part of its development of the Windows operating system environment. The idea was to make programs more object oriented, meaning that programs could be broken down into components and shared among different applications. Thus, when you wanted to edit a spreadsheet you had included in a Word document, you could simply select it. The components from Excel that were necessary to accomplish that task would be loaded into Microsoft Word. The need to exit one program and start another to perform different operations was dra-matically reduced.

Holy OLE—Microsoft's Little Miracle

OLE proves that Microsoft does have the ability to use its powers for good. OLE was originally supposed to be a means by which software applications could enable their various components to interact with one another and function together seamlessly.

Today, with the advent of the Internet, the plans for OLE have broadened significantly, and now it is seen as one of the technologies that will bring true real-time interactive applications to Web pages. What was once possible only in stand-alone software suites will now be available on Web pages over the Internet.

As discussed subsequently, Microsoft continues to develop OLE and adapt it to the modern realities of the Internet through the use of its cutting edge ActiveX technology. The Web may not be what OLE was originally designed for, but the capabilities it brings will certainly fool most people on that count. It may not rise to the level of healing the sick, but it is still pretty cool.

OLE and ActiveX Versus Java—Not Necessarily Either/Or

After you have read the previous section, you may say to yourself, "Gee, that sounds exactly like what people say about Java." It is true that both OLE and Java hold the keys to providing interactive multimedia and applications on the Internet. However, it doesn't mean that one has to be chosen or utilized to the exclusion of the other.

OLE and Java can peacefully coexist on the Web and, in fact, even on the same Web page. Many developers will be creating both Java and OLE applications for Web pages, and each will have its own benefits. As more examples of each type become available, you'll need to evaluate for yourself which will work best.

Experimenting with both Java and OLE on your Web pages will quickly show you that each has its place in the world of interactive multimedia on the Internet.

OCXs–OLE Custom Controls

OLE will typically find its way into an interactive Web page through OLE custom controls, or OCXs. OCXs are small embedded applications that accomplish discrete tasks for a user or application. Microsoft's recently announced ActiveX is really just a newer implementation of OCXs.

As you'll see later in this chapter, OCXs help provide the basic interactive building block for developing an interactive Web page. OCXs are basically the smallest usable components of a software application, such as buttons, graphics engines, and so on. By combining them and making them work together, you can craft a rich multimedia page.

Even as I write this, though, the technology and terminology for OCXs stand on the verge of massive change. This change is ActiveX, and it may be the most important

development to date in using OLE objects on the Internet.

ActiveX

Microsoft has redeveloped and repositioned OLE controls into a new offering called ActiveX. Like its predecessor, ActiveX promises to enable Web designers and developers to build dynamic content for the Internet. ActiveX includes the possibilities of animation, 3D worlds, video, and other multimedia.

Microsoft was the first to announce an ActiveX component with ActiveMovie, an audio and video playback ActiveX control that enables Web surfers using the Internet Explorer 3.0 to play video directly in the browser window. This is just one of the many ActiveX controls likely to flood the Web over the next few months.

Not only will ActiveX be supported by the Internet Explorer 3.0, but it will also work with the most popular Web browser, the Netscape Navigator, currently through the use of plug-ins and in future versions through native support for ActiveX. Over 70 companies have already announced support for ActiveX; it looks to be a real force in the future of the Web.

For the latest on ActiveX, shown in Figure 11.1, turn to Microsoft's Web site at

`http://www.microsoft.com/internet`

Here, you can find the latest technical information on ActiveX and the location of all the coolest new ActiveX controls.

ActiveX controls can be implemented using the `<OBJECT>` tag discussed subsequently, which will be supported by future versions of Netscape and the Internet Explorer.

Figure 11.1.
Microsoft's
ActiveX Web
page.

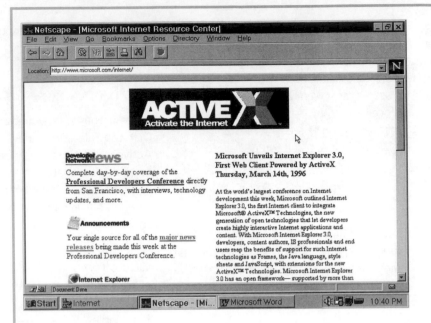

Adding OLE and ActiveX to a Web Page

OLE and ActiveX are still infant technologies when it comes to the Internet, so remember that it is somewhat of a moving target. We attempt here to give you the most up-to-date information, but it is by no means the last word on exactly how the final versions of these technologies and standards will turn out.

By learning the basics and understanding the technology, you should be able to adapt your pages to whatever bumps in the road to OLE and ActiveX may be created by Microsoft and Netscape in their browsers.

OLE and Your Web Browser

The OLE capabilities of Web pages are directly related to the OLE capabilities of the Web browser used to view them. As a result, it's important to understand what OLE technology is available in today's browsers and how it can be used to enhance your pages.

Not All OLE Is Alike

Obviously, any Web page designer has to know what types of clients are on the market and what they contain in the way of capabilities. The problem in evaluating Web browsers when thinking about adding OLE is that not all OLE is the same.

Most older OLE-compatible Web browsers communicate with other programs using the OLE architecture, meaning that you can embed a link that launches the Netscape browser in a word processing document. However, it does not mean that the browser has the potential for viewing the type of dynamic, interactive content discussed here.

Look for Web browsers that highlight their capability to interpret embedded ActiveX or OLE controls. The terminology OLE is the same, but the technology most certainly is not.

HTML 3.0 and Support for OLE

Although the present situation with OLE and the Web is somewhat fractured and confusing, the future holds a great deal of promise for standardizing how Web developers and browsers handle OLE. The World Wide Web Consortium (W3C), an industry working group, is putting together the standards for what will be HTML 3.0. One of the specific problems the group is addressing is the placing of multimedia and interactive objects like OLE controls into Web pages.

The W3C group that studied how to add OLE and other multimedia objects to Web pages included representatives from Netscape, Microsoft, Sun, and Spyglass. The committee has proposed a new tag for working with these types of objects: the <OBJECT> tag. Check the organization's Web site (http://www.w3.org) periodically for updates on their progress if you're interested in keeping current.

The <OBJECT> tag will enable Web developers to specify the properties for initializing objects to be inserted into HTML documents, as well as the program or code that will be used to display the information. Under the <OBJECT> tag, objects can be OLE controls, components, applets, plug-ins, media handlers, or just about anything that has been or will be developed in the near future.

The <OBJECT> tag is offered as a more robust alternative to the IMG tag currently used to place graphic images in Web pages. More flexible and complex, <OBJECT> enables you to include rich multimedia objects on your Web page. The only limits on viewing the objects are a particular user's choice of Web client.

Listing 11.1 shows how a typical OLE object might be implemented on a Web page using the new <OBJECT> tag.

Listing 11.1. The OBJECT tag from HTML 3.0.

```
<OBJECT
      id=clock
      type="application/x-oleobject"
      data="http://www.mcs.net/
       time.html"
      code="http://www.mcs.net/~bkmurph/
       controls">
   </OBJECT>
```

The id element is intended to allow other controls on the same page to interact with one another by referencing each control's id. The data points the object or control to the location of the data it will rely on for performing its functions. The code element is to point to where the actual control or program is located.

In addition, the <OBJECT> tag will have a variety of other elements that will make it easy to work with OLE objects on your Web pages, much like the APPLET tag. (For more information on the APPLET tag, refer to Chapter 12, "Finding and Using the Hottest Java Applets.")

Of course, the <OBJECT> tag is completely unsupported by any Web browsers available at this writing. Fortunately, there are some OLE options out there that can be used to add interactive multimedia to your pages. The problem here is not choice but standardization and compatibility. However, the problems you encounter should be worth the payoff in terms of a cutting-edge Web page that delivers jaw-dropping impact to Net surfers.

Netscape OLE and ActiveX Options

Netscape's new architecture makes it flexible and adaptable for working with OLE and ActiveX objects by using third-party plug-ins. Netscape has always been a cutting, if not bleeding, edge Web browser. Beta testing has already begun on version 3.0 of the Netscape Navigator, and it is quite possible that it will contain native support for OLE objects and controls.

Until Netscape has native support, however, plug-ins are available for adding OLE functionality to your Web pages. The plug-ins and their accompanying demos demonstrate the potential that OLE can provide to the Internet.

Unfortunately, many of the examples on the Net today are not necessarily adaptable to current Web pages because the technologies they use are still in development. Soon, there should be a greater degree of standardization so you can get a better practical grip on how to integrate OLE objects into your Web pages. Until then, it is still useful to look at how it's being implemented today.

There are currently two plug-ins available for Netscape that enable you to add OLE and ActiveX controls and objects to your interactive Web pages. NCompass and OpenScape have different ways for bringing about their results, but each is impressive in its own right.

NCompass

NCompass was originally a stand-alone Web browser that provided the ability to interpret embedded OLE controls on Web pages. Its developers, however, quickly saw the future and adapted the product as a plug-in for version 2 of the Netscape Navigator, which can now handle OLE and ActiveX controls.

The NCompass plug-in is available for downloading from

```
http://www.excite.sfu.ca/NCompass
```

The specifications for the plug-in and how it will handle OLE and ActiveX objects embedded in Web pages are still in development. However, there are some fairly impressive demonstrations of using OLE and ActiveX controls on a Web page available now from NCompass.

A Basic Demonstration

When you first load the Demos page at the NCompass site at

```
http://oberon.educ.sfu.ca/NCompass/
   home.html
```

you are presented with the Web page depicted in Figure 11.2. The NCompass plug-in allows for full integration of OLE controls with other HTML enhancements like frames.

In this example, there are actually two separate embedded OLE custom controls that (1) provide a MIDI musical soundtrack in the background, and (2) present an animated rotating cube that can be controlled with your mouse by interacting with the Web page. Listing 11.2 contains the HTML code that was used to implement this frame on the NCompass page.

Figure 11.2.
The NCompass
home page uses
an animated OLE
control.

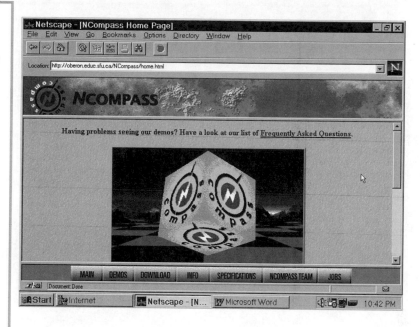

Listing 11.2. An embedded OLE control.

```
<embed SRC="symphony.opf" WIDTH=1 HEIGHT=1>
<CENTER>
<TABLE BORDER=4 CELLPADDING=0 CELLSPACING=0>
<TR ALIGN=CENTER>
<TD><embed SRC="newlogo.opf" WIDTH=400 HEIGHT=240></TD>
</TR>
```

The code uses the `<EMBED>` tag used by Netscape to place any multimedia object that will rely on a plug-in application to be displayed in the browser window. Netscape does not yet support the `<INSERT>` tag discussed previously. The NCompass plug-in relies on OLE controls that are part of an object properties file (*opf*).

When opf OLE controls become more widely available, it will be easy to plug them into your existing Web pages. The `<EMBED>` tag is easy to use with Netscape. The only options are to specify the URL for the file to embed next to `SRC=` and then identify the width and

height of the object to be displayed. All in all, it's an extremely basic way to add the rich functionality and interactivity of OLE custom controls to your pages.

An Interactive 3D Robotic Arm

Several other demos on the NCompass page present more great examples of just how easy all of this can and will be for Web developers. From the demo page you can get the Web page containing the interactive 3D robotic arm shown in Figure 11.3.

Figure 11.3.
NCompass's 3D
robotic arm
demo.

By clicking the arrow buttons on the right, Web surfers can control the movement of the 3D rendered robotic arm on the left in the Web page. The potential for interactive applications that this demo shows is enormous. The example uses two OLE custom controls, one for the button controls and the other for the 3D robotic arm. The NCompass plug-in enables the two controls to communicate with one another to bring about the interactive experience on the page.

An Embedded Video File

Another NCompass example demonstrates how multimedia files can be more effectively integrated with Web pages using OLE controls. Figure 11.4 shows an AVI video file that has been embedded as an object in the Web page using OLE controls.

In the previous example, the NCompass plug-in loads the video file and begins playing it immediately on downloading it from the file server. As you can see, playback is embedded directly into the Web page and provides a more integrated viewing experience than you would normally get from watching a video file through an external helper application. When the file has stopped playing, it can be restarted by simply clicking the still picture. This is a nice preview of the multimedia capabilities that OLE controls will provide for your Web pages.

Crass Commercialization

Some people are intent on programming Web pages that are actually designed to make money for their designers. Without endorsing any such money-grubbing model for Web pages, I will point out how OLE custom controls can help a Webmaster add interactive multimedia touches that make crass commercial messages easier to swallow for the casual Web user.

*Figure 11.4.
An embedded
OLE control
integrates a
video file
seamlessly into
this Web page.*

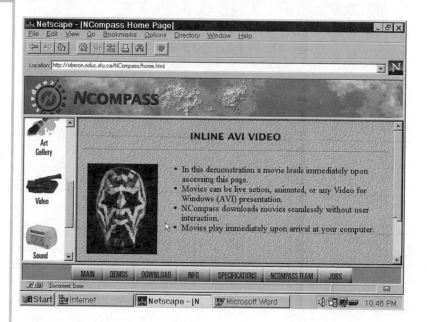

The demo created by NCompass shown in Figure 11.5 presents an embedded billboard that can be placed on a Web page displaying numerous graphic advertisements with smooth inline transitions from one to another. In addition, background sounds and music can be added for an even more compelling reason to buy the products or visit the associated Web sites.

*Figure 11.5.
NCompass shows
how OLE can be
used to make the
mundane seem
interesting.*

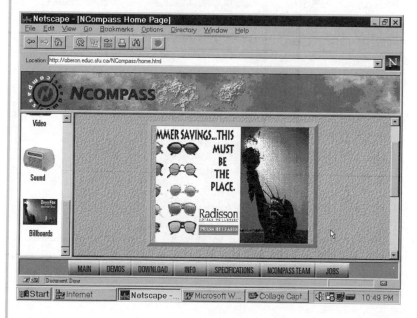

Interactive 3D Applications

On a less commercial note, the Art Gallery demo that the folks at NCompass have put together further demonstrates the interactive potential of their plug-in and OLE. As shown in Figure 11.6, the Web page presents a rotating 3D cube that has a different artistic masterpiece on each side.

Web users can click the cube to make it move closer or farther away in the Web browser. You can also use the mouse buttons to rotate the cube and view your masterpiece of choice. This demo is intended to demonstrate how to make interactive 3D applications in Web pages using OLE controls. It may not be long until you can set up a DOOM Web page that does more than give information about the game, but lets people actually play the game on your page.

OpenScape

OpenScape is a Netscape plug-in available from Business@Web at

`http://www.busweb.com`

OpenScape, shown in Figure 11.7, also provides programming developers with a runtime development kit for developing OLE objects and components. For the Web page developer, the site contains many enticing examples of why OLE objects should be included in your Web pages.

OpenScape, like all the technologies discussed in this chapter, is still under development; widespread examples of its implementation may be hard to come by in the immediate future. However, as their Web pages show, Business@Web has developed an excellent OLE plug-in that expands the functionality of the Netscape browser.

Figure 11.6. NCompass uses its masterpiece, an Interactive 3D OLE control, to show other masterpieces.

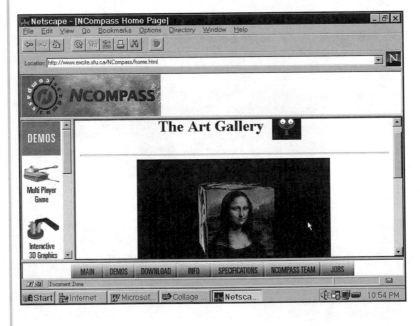

Figure 11.7.
Business@Web is
the home to the
OpenScape plug-
in for Netscape.

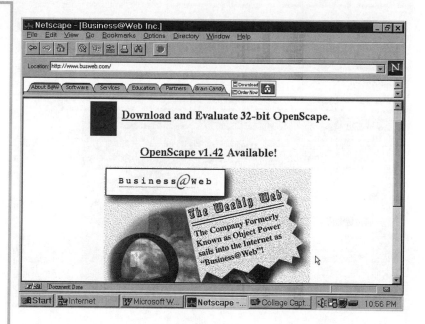

The Stock Ticker

Figure 11.8, developed by the people at Business@Web, illustrates the broad potential of what OLE can bring to your Web pages. The embedded OLE object is not just a stock ticker, but also a Microsoft Excel spreadsheet that can be activated in the Web browser with related data that can then be altered or manipulated.

The following is an excerpt of the HTML code that is behind this Web page:

```
<h3>Instruction</h3>
```

To show the full functionality of the embedded Excel spreadsheet, enter the user name "user" and the password "user" and then click the Update button. This demonstrates the power of combining an embedded object with Enterprise data.

```
<EMBED src="/software/components/
  QUOTES.OPP"
width=645 height=393
form="frmStockQuotes">
</body></html>
```

OpenScape relies on the <EMBED> tag in the same way that NCompass does to place OLE objects on the Web page. However, you can see from the SRC reference that the file types used by the programs are entirely different and unique to each plug-in.

Tip: With both the NCompass and OpenScape plug-ins, Web users can view and interact with embedded OLE objects on a Web page. However, because each plug-in uses unique file types, they are not compatible with one another: The NCompass plug-in cannot be used to view embedded OpenScape OLE objects or vice versa. You should specify on your Web pages which plug-ins or browsers are necessary for viewing any OLE objects you have embedded in your pages.

Figure 11.8.
An embedded
stock ticker and
spreadsheet are
viewable using
OpenScape.

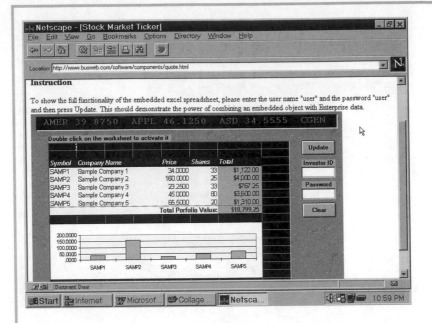

The Stock Ticker demonstrates how OLE objects can be used for businesses interested in establishing Web pages over an intranet that provide heightened functionality and interactivity for users on the network to conduct business.

A Calendar Component

Another demo on the Business@Web site further demonstrates how powerful OLE objects can be in providing full-fledged application usefulness to users' desks in the context of a Web page. The Calendar Component shown in Figure 11.9 is a scheduling program that shows a month's worth of planned events at a time.

Users can set up their own profiles for the Calendar Component and enter their own data. Then, when entering the Web page, they are prompted for a user name and password, which will load the correct data into the object. An application that once

would have been considered a stand-alone product can now be integrated as simply part of a Web page.

A look at the source HTML code for this page (see Listing 11.3) again shows the simplicity of the mechanics of placing the object on a page.

Once again, the <EMBED> tag provides the necessary information for directing the Netscape browser to using the appropriate plug-in for displaying the OLE object in the browser window.

OLE Yahtzee!

The OpenScape demos wouldn't be complete without identifying at least one way that the technology could be used for pure fun. Luckily, Business@Web provides a demonstration diversion with an OLE version of Yahtzee! called Optzee, as shown in Figure 11.10.

Listing 11.3. The source for an OpenScape object.

```
<BODY>
<H3>OpenScape Calendar Component</H3>
<H4> Login as "guest" with the password "guest", or create your own account -
Click on any of the days of the week to view event details</H4>
<EMBED SRC="/software/components/Feb.opp"
WIDTH = 517 HEIGHT = 331 FORM = "The_Month">
</BODY>
```

Figure 11.9. An OLE object can have the functionality of some stand-alone software products.

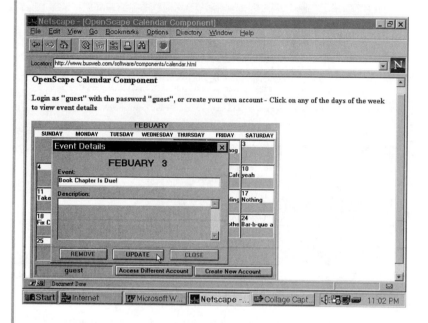

The game prompts you to enter your name so that you can compete against the scores of users worldwide. If you don't know the rules of Yahtzee! then just use trial and error on this one. The game is as simple as the HTML code that was used to put it on the Web page:

```
<H2> The Game: </H2>
<EMBED src="/software/components/
  OPTZEE.OPP"
width=516 height=260 form="GameBoard">
<H2> Instructions: </H2>
```

Again, OpenScape's reliance on the `<EMBED>` tag makes it easy for Web page developers to put a little fun in their pages and their visitors' days.

Microsoft Explorer 3.0

As discussed previously, Microsoft has recently announced its development of a new implementation of OLE controls for Web pages called ActiveX. The OLE controls using ActiveX technology will be first supported by Microsoft's own capable browser, the Internet Explorer, in version 3.0 of the software. A beta version of the Internet Explorer supporting ActiveX objects is available from Microsoft's home page at

```
http://www.microsoft.com
```

An alpha version of the Internet Explorer that supports embedded OLE controls is shown in Figure 11.11. The example is crude but shows that Microsoft is well on its way to providing integrated OLE support to the Internet Explorer. The OCX displayed in this sample page is a simple object in which you can dial the line around the circle.

which is the forerunner to the <OBJECT> tag for the HTML 3.0 standard discussed previously. Microsoft appears ready to adopt this open standard and is clearly poised to make it part of version 3.0 of the Internet Explorer.

Figure 11.10. An OLE Web version of the classic game Yahtzee!

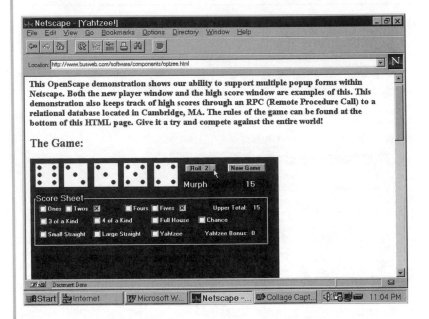

An interesting discovery with this alpha version of Internet Explorer and the sample OLE Web page is revealed by looking at the HTML source. Listing 11.4 shows the HTML code used to produce the sample Web page shown here.

You can see from the code that the object is being embedded using the <INSERT> tag,

Microsoft invented OLE, so it is probably a good idea to keep a watchful eye on its browser and the protocols it uses to embed and use OLE controls on Web pages. As discussed previously, it is clear Netscape and other companies will embrace ActiveX and make their browsers fully compatible with these objects.

Listing 11.4. A simple example of embedding an OLE control.

```
<HTML>
<HEAD>
<TITLE>Control Home Page</TITLE>
</HEAD>
<BODY>
<H1>Sample control page</H1>
An example of an embedded control:
<INSERT CLSID="{06889605-B8D0-081A-91F1-00608CEAD5B3}" HEIGHT=080 WIDTH=200>
</BODY>
</HTML>
```

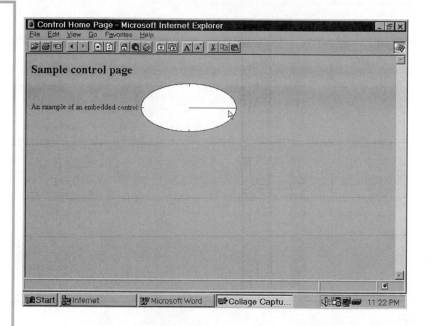

Figure 11.11.
An alpha version
of Microsoft's
Internet Explorer
shows that the
browser will
support
embedded OLE
objects.

Necessity and Bandwidth Considerations

Placing interactive OLE objects on your Web pages will significantly increase the size of documents and files to be downloaded to a user's page. Do not unnecessarily clutter a page with OLE objects just to show that you know how to use the technology.

Tip: Most Internet users access the Web at a rate of not more than 28.8Kbps over dial-up phone lines. OLE objects can add more overhead to sometimes already stretched bandwidth for users. Selective use of OLE objects will increase access times for Web users without sacrificing interactivity and a dynamic multimedia page.

OLE objects, unlike images, are not displayed until they have been completely loaded into the Web browser. What results to a Web user is an increase in perceived download times for these objects versus normal graphics, even though their file sizes may be roughly the same. Always keep in mind the patience and attention span of your average Web surfer in determining how much is too much and how long is too long for downloading your pages.

How and Why to Use OLE for Web Interactivity

The ways OLE can be used on Web pages are limited, like most things on the Web subject, only by your imagination and creativity. We'll cover a few basic examples that only hint at the possibilities of what can be accomplished by combining OLE and Web pages.

A Spreadsheet Example for Business

The developers of OpenScape at Business@Web have created a Web page with an embedded Microsoft Excel spreadsheet at

```
http://www.busweb.com/software/
    components/excel.html
```

The sample Excel spreadsheet in Figure 11.12 shows a blank expense account that could be filled in by an employee over the Web.

By selecting one of the cells on the expense account form on the Web page, a Microsoft Excel worksheet is activated, as shown in Figure 11.13. The tight integration of real-world business applications and the Web that OLE provides can offer businesses and individuals new alternatives for accomplishing even the most basic tasks in their work.

Figure 11.12. A sample expense account form that can be made part of a Web page through OLE.

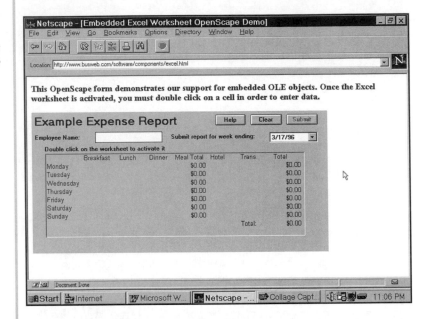

Figure 11.13. Selecting a cell in the embedded OLE object brings up a Microsoft Excel worksheet.

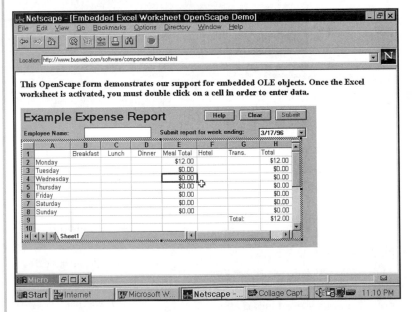

A Game Example for Pleasure

After you have your employees fill out their expense reports using the Web, you may want to reward them for all their hard work. What could be better than an online multiplayer game to relieve a little stress from the everyday working world? An example of just such a game, as shown in Figure 11.14, can be found at the NCompass demo page at

```
http://www.excite.sfu.ca/NCompass
```

Duel is an amazing example of the complexity of applications that can be delivered using OLE on Web pages. It is a multiplayer interactive game that takes advantage of Microsoft's latest DirectX gaming technology to increase playability and performance.

It's easy to see how online arcades could be developed on Web pages using OLE objects that bring the type of fun and action that Duel has already shown is possible on Web pages.

Figure 11.14. Even a high-tech game can be embedded into a Web page through the magic of OLE.

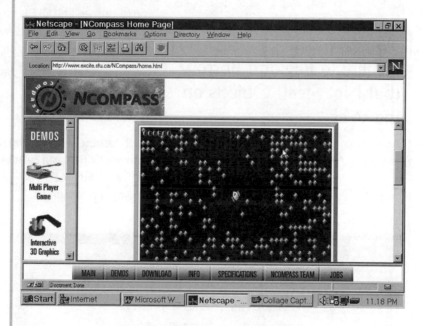

Places to Find the Best Reusable Objects

The best place to start your search for OLE objects that you can integrate into your Web page is at the Microsoft home page at

`http://www.microsoft.com`

You can find links there to information on OLE and ActiveX, with links to developers and Web pages using these technologies.

Where to Beg and Borrow (but Not Steal) Objects on the Web

Anytime you're looking for objects, you can always try NCompass at

`http://www.excite.sfu.ca/NCompass`

to see the latest demos and samples for public use. The same goes for the creators of OpenScape, Business@Web, at this address:

`http://www.busweb.com`

These companies know that for their products to be widely accepted and used there must be lots of Web pages using compatible OLE objects. As a result, you should be able to find at least some objects to get you started.

The Web is a treasure trove of information and resources, and OLE is no exception. You can try the OLE Controls WWW Server as shown in Figure 11.15. Visit this site:

`http://142.232.132.45/ocx/default.htm`

Here you'll find links to shareware and freeware OCXs.

A rich resource for locating reusable objects from developers is a relatively new mailing list called InetOLE. You can subscribe by sending a message to

Figure 11.15.
The OLE Controls
WWW Server
may be your
source for
reusable objects.

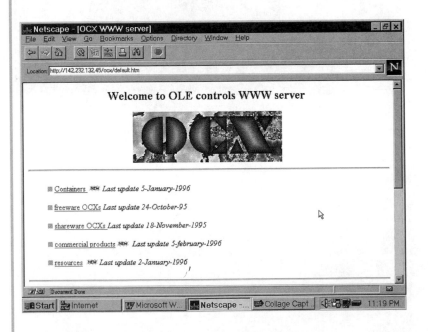

```
inetole-request@ncsa.uiuc.edu
```

with "subscribe" in the message.

An excellent commercial service for locating reusable objects is at the OLE Broker, shown in Figure 11.16:

```
http://www.olebroker.com
```

If you don't want to pay the subscription fees for the OLE Broker service, the site does have some free conferences available that might at least give you a lead or two.

Figure 11.16. The OLE Broker has free conferences in addition to its subscription services.

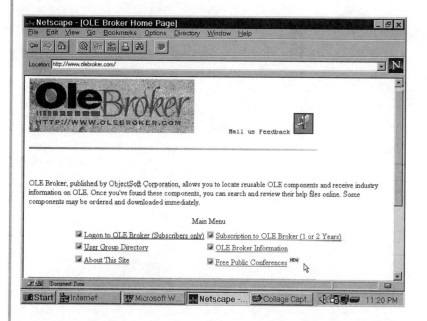

What's Next?

In the next chapter we look at the technology that has grabbed many of the headlines away from OLE in the last year or so—Java. If you have always wanted to add Java applets to your pages without knowing how to write them yourself, then the next chapter is exactly what you are looking for. We'll show you where to find the best Java applets and how to get them into your Web pages with as little pain as possible.

Finding and Using the Hottest Java Applets

Probably no advancement in Internet technology has been as hyped and anticipated as Java. As almost the entire human race probably knows by now, Java is a programming language developed by Sun Microsystems and designed to be platform independent, network-centric, and paradigm shifting. Java brings a high level of interactivity to previously static Web pages. Users can access advanced applications and features without having a typical software package installed on a local hard drive.

Java opens a new world of multimedia interactivity that every Web designer should be prepared to integrate into his or her site. With Java, you can add multimedia and interactivity to your own Web pages. You can even play a game of Pac-Man, as shown in Figure 12.1.

This chapter shows you the basics of Java and how to incorporate Java applets into your Web pages in creative and cost-effective ways.

chapter 12

by Brian K. Murphy

Figure 12.1.
The ancient
game of Pac-
Man brought to
life on the Web
with Java.

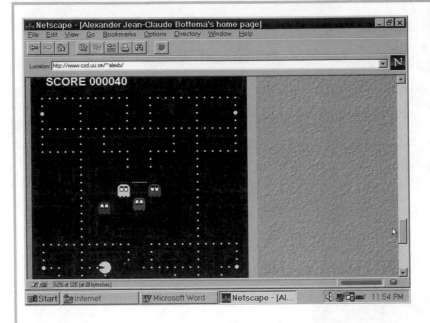

What Nonprogrammers Need to Know About Java

Not everyone has the background and education necessary to develop and write Java applets for interactive Web pages. However, just as you don't have to be a professional photographer or musician to add graphics and sound to your site, you shouldn't be dissuaded from using Java applets because you're not a computer programmer.

You don't need to get bogged down by the technical aspects and requirements of writing Java applets to begin using them in designing your Web pages. However, a brief background on the Java language and how it works should give you a better understanding of what goes on behind the scenes to give your site the new flashy features that Java applets can provide.

An Overview of Java and Programming Basics

Java is defined by the folks at Sun Microsystems (`http://www.javasoft.com/allabout.html`) as a "simple, object-oriented, network-savvy, interpreted, robust, secure, architecture-neutral, portable, high-performance, multithreaded, dynamic language." Some people simply call it the Internet programming language. Java enables programmers to write a single program that can be accessed regardless of an end user's platform or the type Web browser.

Java is an extremely safe language; there is no serious threat that any viruses could be transferred to users' computers over the Internet. Java has been widely adopted and has become the standard for delivering applications in real time over the Web.

The potential for Java applets is almost limitless. Java provides a framework for developers to create interactive applets in the same way that programming languages enable developers to create applications, such as spreadsheets or word processors, that run on your computer under DOS or Windows. The difference is that when you use Java applets, you don't need to buy and install the particular application—you simply visit the Web page. Imagine being able to access any application you want whenever you want it by using the Internet. This is what Java applets promise to help deliver.

Java Applets on Your Web Page

Now, before you go out and start plastering Java applets all over your Web page, you should consider some basics relating to where your pages are stored, the server and how they are accessed, and the client.

Server Considerations

In this chapter we discuss only those applets that have already been compiled into a Java class file; issues such as compiling the Java applet on a UNIX server versus compiling on your Windows 95 machine are not addressed. The Java *class file* is the equivalent to what you are familiar with as an executable or `.exe` file on your computer. The big difference, though, is that Java class files are architecture neutral or platform independent.

Architecture neutral means that you can place the Java class file on your Web server, regardless of what operating system is running (UNIX or Windows NT). From any server,

the Java applet performs identically for any Web browser that accesses the class file— no matter what platform the client Web browser has on the client end—no matter what platform the client uses to access the file. Thus, you needn't worry about making sure that a particular class file has been compiled for the system used on your server; that should have no impact whatsoever.

Another thing to consider is file size. Most simple applets are small, in the 3–5KB range. Other, more complex applets can get to 50–100KB and even larger. Some applets, such as animators, use additional resources beyond the simple Java class file that also need to be uploaded to your server.

In the case of animators, small GIF files that constitute the animation (like the tumbling Duke in Figure 12.2—one of the first Java applets) need to be saved on the server. Sometimes this requires 30 or 40 small GIF images that could begin to eat up a significant portion of server space. If you have only limited space on a server or are charged by the amount of space you use, be sure to examine closely the applets you plan on using and all their related files. If you find yourself wanting to use lots of Java applets but you're lacking the necessary server space, take a look at the section later in this chapter that shows you how to use applets located on other servers in your Web page.

Client Considerations

Obviously, when you create your Web pages, you need to be aware of which Web clients will be accessing your pages. It seems rare these days to find a Web page without the obligatory "Viewed Best With" plug for the Netscape Navigator or Microsoft Internet Explorer.

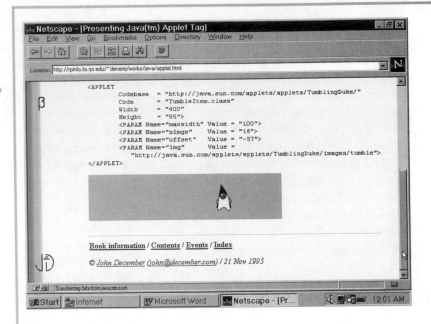

Figure 12.2. The Java mascot Duke in a tumbling animation from the Web page of noted Java author and expert, John December. The animation takes up more space than meets the eye.

Although Java has been almost universally accepted and adopted by everyone in the Internet industry, there are currently only two browsers available that have the capability for interpreting, or viewing, Java applets. Luckily, one of those browsers is Netscape Navigator 2.0, available from Netscape at `http://www.netscape.com`. Netscape is far and away the most widely used Web browser available. Netscape and Sun have worked closely on providing Java compatibility, and this should ensure that the leading browser will work great with the Java applets you plan to make part of your Web pages.

The only other browser that currently supports Java applets is the Hot Java browser from Sun. Hot Java was the first prototype Java browser and originally demonstrated how Java applets could make the Web more alive and interactive. Both Netscape Navigator 2.0 and Hot Java rely on the same characteristics for the APPLET tag to place

Java applets into an HTML document. As a result, you can write your Web pages without fear of incompatibilities between different browsers for the time being. I discuss the specifics of the APPLET tag later in this chapter.

Many other companies have licensed Java from Sun for incorporation into their Web browsers. Most notably, Microsoft plans to incorporate Java support into a release of its Internet Explorer in the near future. It is hard to predict what types of potential problems may arise from using today's Java applets with tomorrow's Web browsers; however, the fundamentals will remain the same.

You should also note that it will probably be some time before online services, such as American Online or Prodigy, provide native support of Java in their proprietary Web browsers. If you plan on directing your Web pages toward users of either of these services, you may want to consider maintaining separate Java-enhanced and non-Java pages that Web surfers can choose between when visiting your site. Many sites have adopted this approach, and it may make sense to you depending on the particular intended audience of your pages.

Tip:

Because of the potential confusion that may result from either new Web browsers or new users, you should indicate somewhere on your pages that the site is enhanced with Java and is best viewed with the browser you think works best with the page, such as Netscape Navigator 2.0, as demonstrated in Figure 12.3. That way users who are using incompatible browsers will understand why the page may not have all the features or functionality that it touts. Chapter 4 also discusses how to use these and other types of good manners for Web developers, such as including links to downloading the latest version of the appropriate browser.

Secrets of the APPLET Tag

You can use Java applets without being an expert in or even knowing much about the underlying Java language. However, if you expect to add Java applets to your Web pages to increase the interactivity and multimedia impact they present, you need to know what the APPLET tag is and how to go about writing it into your HTML documents.

A simple, very basic APPLET tag would look like the following, when written into a typical HTML document:

The APPLET tag provides several important functions in relation to adding Java applets

Figure 12.3. Identifying a Java-enhanced page that is optimally viewed with Netscape.

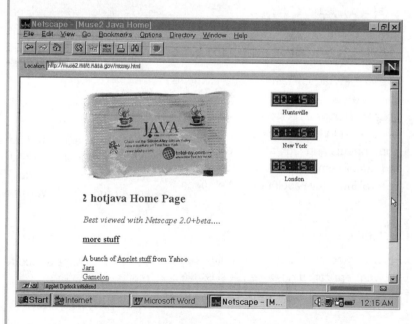

Listing 12.1. A basic APPLET tag in HTML.

```
<APPLET    CODEBASE="Applet location"
           code=AppletName.class
           width=XXX
           height=XXX>
    <param name=x value="x">
    </APPLET>
```

to your Web page, the most important of which is that it embeds the applet into your page much the same way that the IMG SRC tag embeds a picture file into your document. The APPLET tag goes even further, though, and gives you a higher degree of control over a Java applet than you are accustomed to with a typical Web image.

Let's walk through the parts of the APPLET tag from the simplest to the more complex commands and uses. By knowing just the basics, you'll be able to run Java applets on your pages in no time! If you take the time to learn more about the APPLET tag and the applet you want to use, you can add your own customizations to make some applets more specific and integrated with your page.

Classes, Sizes, Values, and More

The APPLET tag contains unique elements that you need to remember when coding your Web pages. Let's divide the elements of the APPLET tag into its practical components and look at how each of the individual commands fit into placing and controlling a Java applet on a Web page.

Classes

As discussed previously, Java applets come in what are called *class files*. A class file is best understood as the executable file that runs the Java applet and issues the command to make the magic work. Java applets are not subject to the old 8.3 DOS naming convention and follow the format of AppletName.class. Obviously, the first step to adding a Java applet to your Web page is knowing the name of the class file and its location.

Note: You need to be extremely careful when entering the necessary data for a particular Java applet into the APPLET tags in your Web pages. The Java language is case sensitive, and this can lead to troublesome results if you are not careful. It can be very aggravating to spend hours trying to get a Java applet to work on your Web page only to find that you typed Appletname.class into the APPLET tag and not AppletName.class.

Let's start with the location of the applet class file that you want to use to make your Web page snappy. It's probably a good idea to create a subdirectory called classes in the same location where your HTML documents are stored. So, if you have a Web page located at

http://www.willynilly.net/java.html

you should create a subdirectory that would then be at the URL

http://www.willynilly.net/classes/

A lot of the applets on the Net that come with ready-to-go HTML and APPLET tags assume that the classes are stored in this classes subdirectory. The location of the applet is important for the first element of the APPLET tag, CODEBASE.

Tip:

A good way to learn about how other Web designers have utilized portions of the APPLET tag on their pages is by using Netscape's View ¦ Document Source command as shown in Figure 12.4. You can closely examine the particular locations, elements, and values that have been entered for a particular Java applet. To copy the APPLET tag to work from as a model, simply highlight it with your mouse and press the Ctrl+C keys. You can then paste it into your text or Web editor to begin your own modifications.

CODEBASE—Where the Applet's At

CODEBASE is important because it establishes where a particular Java applet is located relative to the other elements on the Web page. If you do not specify a CODEBASE location, then the default is to look for the Java applet class in the same directory as the HTML document. It is a good idea to organize your Web pages cleanly and to utilize the CODEBASE element to point to a directory dedicated to storing your Java applets. The CODEBASE element is also important for pointing to Java applets within your Web page, which is discussed later in this chapter.

When you enter a location next to CODEBASE, place the relative location in quotation marks. If you are using a subdirectory located off

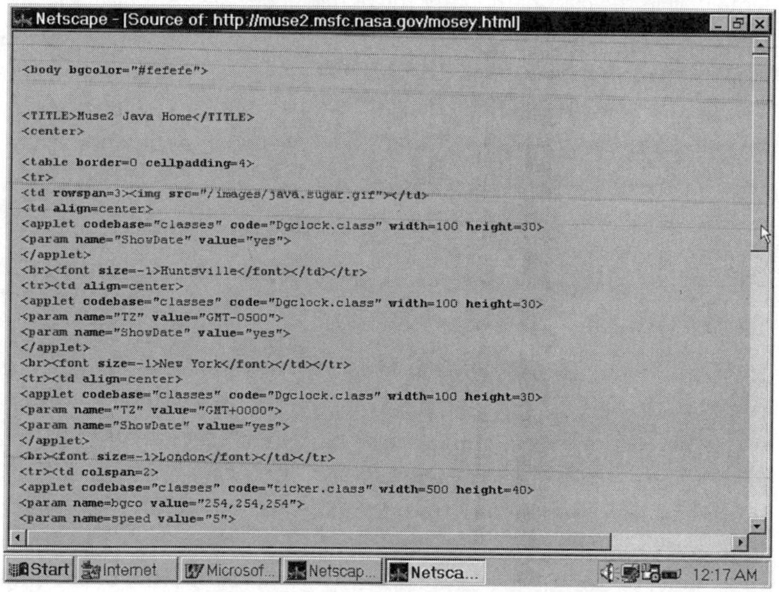

Figure 12.4.
Viewing the source code in Netscape.

```
Netscape - [Source of: http://muse2.msfc.nasa.gov/mosey.html]

<body bgcolor="#fefefe">


<TITLE>Muse2 Java Home</TITLE>
<center>

<table border=0 cellpadding=4>
<tr>
<td rowspan=3><img src="/images/java.sugar.gif"></td>
<td align=center>
<applet codebase="classes" code="Dgclock.class" width=100 height=30>
<param name="ShowDate" value="yes">
</applet>
<br><font size=-1>Huntsville</font></td></tr>
<tr><td align=center>
<applet codebase="classes" code="Dgclock.class" width=100 height=30>
<param name="TZ" value="GMT-0500">
<param name="ShowDate" value="yes">
</applet>
<br><font size=-1>New York</font></td></tr>
<tr><td align=center>
<applet codebase="classes" code="Dgclock.class" width=100 height=30>
<param name="TZ" value="GMT+0000">
<param name="ShowDate" value="yes">
</applet>
<br><font size=-1>London</font></td></tr>
<tr><td colspan=2>
<applet codebase="classes" code="ticker.class" width=500 height=40>
<param name=bgco value="254,254,254">
<param name=speed value="5">
```

Start | Internet | Microsof... | Netscap... | **Netsca...**   12:17 AM

the root directory where your main Web page is located, then you need only put the subdirectory name; otherwise, enter the full URL, as in

```
CODEBASE="http://ww2.willynilly.net/
  Java/"
```

code—What the Applet Is

The next element of the `APPLET` tag deals directly with the Java applet class that you want to use in your Web page. The `code` element of the `APPLET` tag identifies the name of the Java applet class file that will be accessed and customized with the data from the `APPLET` tag.

As shown previously, in Listing 12.1, the standard Java applet naming conventions produce a class file called `AppletName.class`. Simply fill in the class name after the equal sign on the `code` line and you're done. However, I can't emphasize enough that the class name is case sensitive. That should be the only conceivable issue that could ever arise relating to the `code` element.

Sizes—Using Width and Height

No matter what anyone tells you, when it comes to the `APPLET` tag, size matters. Two of the simplest elements of the `APPLET` tag also can be used for creative purposes. The `width` and `height` elements can be useful tools for you in placing your own special touch on a run-of-the-mill Java applet.

The `width` and `height` elements come immediately following `code` in the `APPLET` tag. It probably won't be difficult for you to figure out what the elements do from their names, but there are some issues of which you should be aware when you enter the corresponding numbers for these items.

Width—Don't Make Your Applet Too Fat

Java applets embedded into a Web page have the flexibility to take up really as little or as much space as you want. The `width` element enables you to specify the amount of screen space that a particular embedded applet consumes when loaded into a user's Web page.

The first thing you should know about both the `width` and `height` elements is exactly what the numbers that you enter for these mean: Are they inches, feet, miles? Actually, they represent the number of pixels on the screen on which the Java applet appears. There is no standard conversion I can give you for pixels per inch because of the varying types of resolutions and sizes of monitors available for today's PCs.

The best way to understand pixels is as a portion of your computer's video resolution. If you are running Windows 95 in 800×600 mode, it means that there are lines of 800 pixels across the screen and lines of 600 pixels running down the screen. If you have only 640×480 mode running, then the pixels represented on screen are proportionally fewer. Thus, if you enter a width of 600 in the `APPLET` tag, the applet takes up the width of the screen on a 640×480 screen, but only three-fourths of the width on an 800×600 screen.

The value you enter for the width depends on the function of the Java applet you plan to embed in the page. Figure 12.5 shows a simple animation Java applet with a width of 112 intended to give a slight accent to the page and takes up only a small portion of the browser window. In contrast, Figure 12.6 shows a Java applet that replicates an LED advertising sign that stretches for the width of the entire window with a value of 540.

Tip: Unlike text that you place on a Web page, a Java applet cannot wrap around or squeeze itself into the browser window of every Web surfer who visits your site. If wide Java applets are important to your site, you may want to warn visitors at the top of the page what size the browser window should be set to, and you may even consider including a graphic guide in the form of a bar so that the proper adjustments can be made while the Java applet is loading.

The width element is an easy one to play and experiment with. Some applets require specific width values to operate properly.

For example, later in this chapter we'll look at an advertising billboard applet that requires the applet width to match that of the alternating ad images. Make sure you take a look at the documentation that accompanies a particular Java applet to see if it has any mandatory settings for the width and height elements of the APPLET tag. Otherwise, have a little fun and try using ridiculously narrow and wide settings with different applets to come up with new effects for your page.

Height–Making Applets Short and Tall for One and All

The height element is obviously the vertical counterpart to the width element in the APPLET tag. All the issues and tips discussed previously apply with equal force to entering the number of pixels you want to use for the height of an applet. It's important to

Figure 12.5. A petite animation takes up little screen real estate.

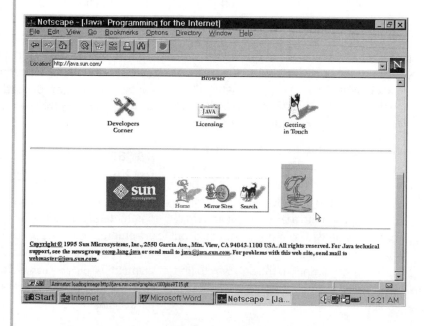

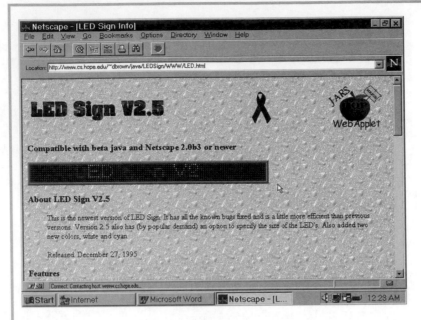

remember that some applets require you to enter specific values for the `height` element, so check any available documentation for the applet closely.

Use common sense when determining what proportions to use for your applets. I wouldn't recommend setting the `width` and `height` elements at `50` and `300`, respectively for a ticker applet, unless you want the Web surfer to see only one letter of the scrolling text at a time. Then again, for your particular application, this may be exactly the effect you are looking to create.

When setting the `height` element for an applet that uses text, be sure that the size of the text font and height of the applet bear some relation to one another. For example, a ticker applet with a large height and small font size will lead to a good deal of dead space on your page. Again, experimenting with various numbers is the only way to find the correct balance for an individual Java applet.

Values

Let's talk for a moment about applet family values. The `APPLET` tag enables you to add user-defined values for different parameters that Java applets can then access when performing their functions. For example, the `APPLET` tag for the Nervous Text applet shown in Figure 12.7 contains a parameter text value of `"Elvis has left the building"` that results in the text's appearing through the applet. Note that quotation marks are necessary around the parameter value.

param name–Different Values for Different Applets

You need to enter values for different parameters for a particular applet. The values are entered using the `param name` element of the `APPLET` tag. The standard format for this element is `param name=` followed by the name of the particular parameter, such as `param name=text`.

Figure 12.7.
Elvis is all shook
up with Nervous
Text.

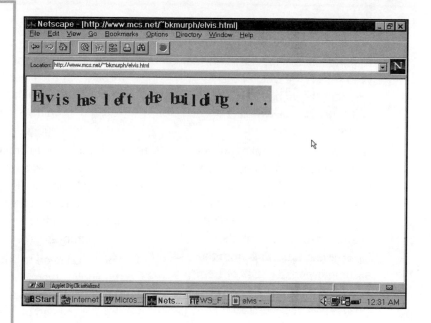

The next step is to enter the value for the parameter. This is done simply enough by following the `value=` portion of the `param name` line with your particular values or input, making sure to place them in quotes. Extending the previous example, this would yield the line

```
<param name=text value="Mr. Bill">
```

to have the value `Mr. Bill` used for the `text` parameter set up by the particular Java applet.

It is difficult to talk about `param name` elements and corresponding values without specific examples of Java applets. Every Java applet has a different variety of potential parameters available and a different selection of what values can be used with those parameters. Be sure to review all documentation for any applet you plan to use to familiarize yourself with all the options for the parameters and their corresponding values.

We'll look more closely at particular parameters and values for specific applets when we get into some examples using Java applets later in this chapter.

Anatomy of the APPLET Tag

Let's take a quick look at how all this works together using a real-world Java applet and a Web page scenario. Breaking it down into its basic parts will let you see how it all comes together. You can use a simple text editor, such as Windows Notepad to do this exercise. Start with a blank Web page called Coffee Talk.

1. The Coffee Talk Web page will be stored on your Web server at the URL:

   `http://www.yourdomain.net/`

2. Name the HTML document for the Coffee Talk Web page `coffee.html`. The URL for the Web page becomes

   `http://www.yourdomain.net/`
   `coffee.html`

3. You will be using a Java applet or two for the page, so create a subdirectory called `classes` on your Web server. The URL for this directory should be `http://www.yourdomain.net/ ~bkmurph/classes`.

4. Next, you need to make sure you have the files for the applet you want to use in your Web page. You should use the Nervous Text applet for your heading, to give it that "caffeinated" feel. Grab the `NervousText.class` file from the accompanying CD-ROM or from Sun Microsystem's Java site at `http://java.sun.com/applets/ applets/` and save it to your local hard drive.

5. Upload the `NervousText.class` file to your subdirectory on the Web server. The file is then located at `http://www.yourdomain.net/classes/ NervousText.class`.

6. Now, you're ready to start off your Coffee Talk Web page by writing the `APPLET` tag that enables you to use the Nervous Text applet as your page header.

7. Start by typing in `<APPLET` to identify the `APPLET` tag for Web browsers that will access your page.

8. Next, type in `CODEBASE="classes"` because that is the directory storing the Java applet.

9. Then type in `code=NervousText.class`, being sure to get the case correct throughout the filename. This identifies the Java applet Nervous Text that is on my server and will bring your page to life.

10. Now you need to enter a width for the Nervous Text applet. You shouldn't plan on using too much text for this applet, so a width of 300 pixels should be sufficient for your purposes. Enter `width=300`.

11. You'll also need to enter a height for the applet. Type in `height=150>` and see how that looks to start. I added the > at the end because this ends the basic `APPLET` tag.

12. The Nervous Text applet has a parameter that enables you to enter the text you would like it to make nervous. The name of the parameter is `text`, naturally, so I enter `<param name=text`.

13. I want the Nervous Text applet to jazz up the title of my Web page Coffee Talk. So, next I type in `value="COFFEE TALK!">`, using caps for greater effect.

14. I'm finished with entering the necessary information for the applet, and so I enter `</APPLET>`.

Finally, Listing 12.2 shows the `APPLET` tag I've entered for the Coffee Talk Web page looks like when I'm finished:

Listing 12.2. The COFFEE TALK! Page implementing the exercise.

```
<APPLET    CODEBASE="classes"
           code=NervousText.class
           width=300
           height=150>
<param name=text value="COFFEE TALK!">
</APPLET>
```

Figure 12.8 shows how the Nervous Text applet appears in the Netscape browser window when using the settings from the APPLET tag. Of course, this looks fairly generic because no other elements, such as text, graphics, and links, have been added to the Web page.

The applet as it is coded now is just a building block for the page you are developing. Let's take a look at how you can use other, more familiar HTML commands with the APPLET tag to get the design results you want out of your Web site.

The APPLET Tag and HTML

The Java applet is only a building block in your Web page construction. The character-istics of the APPLET tag discussed in the preceding sections provide you with the basics on how to enter the information necessary to get the applet to appear on your Web page and to control some of the parameters of the particular applet. however, the APPLET tag is not limited to simply putting an applet on your page. You can use it in conjunction with other HTML commands to create the environment you want on your page.

Don't hesitate to use all the HTML tricks you have learned, in conjunction with a Java applet on your Web page. Matching background colors of the page and the Java applet can result in a nice transparent look if you want, or you can add horizontal bars to set off the applet by itself.

Figure 12.8.
The Nervous Text applet serves as an appropriate header for this Web page.

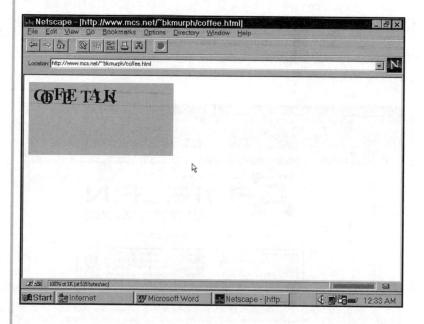

Applet Alignment

You can place an applet in your Web page using HTML the same way you can with any graphics image. Probably the most popular placement option in HTML is centering, by using the CENTER tag before and after the applet to place it in the middle of the browser window.

Another thing you can do is align how the applet looks in relation to text around the program by adding an `align=` element immediately after the height element in the APPLET tag. The values for align can be left, middle, right, and so on.

Applets Suitable for Framing

Java applets can work extremely well in a Web page when used in conjunction with frames. As you can see in Figure 12.9, you can have an applet running an animated icon in one frame while presenting a variety of information and options in other frames on the Web page.

When using Java applets inside frames on a Web page, make sure that the size of the applet and the size of the frame are in correct proportion to one another. Framing an applet follows the same procedure for framing any other type of HTML element, such as text or a graphic.

The key to working with an applet on your Web page is to forget that it's a cool interactive program component and just treat it as you would a normal graphic.

Installing and Controlling Java Applets

Java applets are so simple to install on your Web server that it's almost a stretch to call it "installing." Simply copy the `*.class` file to the classes or other subdirectory on your Webserver. Some applets, however, require that you make further subdirectories for

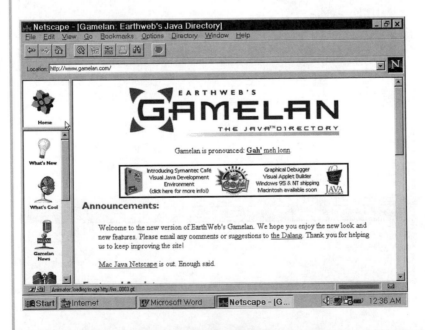

*Figure 12.9.
The upper-left
frame contains
an animated Java
applet.*

related files. For example, many Java applets use graphics files as part of their presentation. Typically, you should copy all the related files into the directory where the `*.class` file is located. However, always check any available documentation to see if you should do otherwise.

It is becoming more common for applet authors to provide all the necessary files and documentation in a standard compressed zip format. You should use the WinZip extractor, which is available on the accompanying CD-ROM, to extract all the necessary files. Many times the necessary subdirectories are mirrored in the structure of the zip file. WinZip automatically reconstructs that directory structure onto your hard drive. Then just upload it to your Web server.

How to Use Applets on Your Pages

The limits for how you can use applets on your Web pages are dictated only by the types of applets that are available. Java is still a developing language, and more applets are being created daily and released on the Net. Later in this chapter I'll show you where to look for the latest, coolest applets.

The thing to remember about Java applets is that you should use them to enhance the content and presentation on your Web page. You should always keep the focus and audience of your page in mind and let the technology complement that without overshadowing it.

How to Use Java for Business Pages with Examples

If you're putting together a Web page for your own business or someone else's, the types of applets you probably want to use are dramatically different than if you were putting together a personal home page. Let's take a look at some hands-on examples that you can implement into a business Web page, and then I'll point out some excellent business pages that you can use as a guide for further development.

The Dynamic BillBoard Applet

It seems you can't come across a Web page these days without some form of advertising located on the page. At least with Java applets, you can make mundane advertising a little more exciting. A great applet for accomplishing just that is the Dynamic BillBoard applet, available on the accompanying CD-ROM and on the Web at

http://www.jars.com.

The Dynamics BillBoard applet tool is relatively easy to set up and install and enables you to have different images rotated onto your Web page using a variety of transition special effects. Thus, if you are selling ad space on your site, you can maximize your profits by rotating different sponsors' ads. If you watch an NBA game, you'll see a similar effect on the ad boards that surround the court. The Dynamics BillBoard applet also lets you associate an URL with each image so that a Web surfer can select an ad and jump to the related Web site for that advertiser.

The Dynamics BillBoard applet consists of the main `DynamicBillBoard.class` and several additional class files that provide the necessary transitions between the images. You'll also need the graphic GIF images that you want to rotate using the billboard. All the class files and sample GIF images for this demonstration are available on the CD-ROM. Make sure that all the images you use for this applet are the same height and width in pixels.

For this example, assume that a bookstore owner has set up a Web page and wants to add a Java applet that will help sell some of his best titles. The GIF images on the CD-ROM contain seven different book covers, numbered 1 through 7 for this exercise. (The GIF images you use need not be numbered this way and can have any name you choose.)

The parameters available for this applet are the total number of billboards, the individual billboard images and associated URLs, the types of transitions available between images, and the delay between transitions.

Listing 12.3 shows the `APPLET` tag for the HTML document in Figure 12.10.

The `height` and `width` values for this applet must match exactly those of the images being displayed. In this example, the images are 125×155 pixels. The `align=middle` element enables the tag line to be positioned in the center and on either side of the applet for a nice appearance. The `delay` value is in milliseconds, and it represents the lag time you want between images. The `billboards` parameter indicates the total number of images that will be used by the applet. The `billx` parameter is the individual images for use by the applet. Note that the first parameter is `bill0`, and then it goes up to one less than the billboard's value, in this case, `bill6`. The `billx` parameter enables you to enter the image name, and then after a comma, a related URL. Finally, the `transitions` parameter enables you to specify which transitions you want the applet to use by setting the number of transitions and the class files that contain them.

Listing 12.3. Dynamic BillBoard Example.

```
<HR SIZE=4>
<CENTER>Check Out All These Great Titles
<APPLET CODEBASE="classes" code="DynamicBillBoard.class"
width="125" height="155" align="middle">
<param name="delay" value="2000">
<param name="billboards" value="7">
<param name="bill0" value="1.gif,http://www.mcp.com/samsnet/index.html">
<param name="bill1" value="2.gif,http://www.mcp.com/samsnet/index.html">
<param name="bill2" value="3.gif,http://www.mcp.com/samsnet/index.html">
<param name="bill3" value="4.gif,http://www.mcp.com/samsnet/index.html">
<param name="bill4" value="5.gif,http://www.mcp.com/samsnet/index.html">
<param name="bill5" value="6.gif,http://www.mcp.com/samsnet/index.html">
<param name="bill6" value="7.gif,http://www.mcp.com/samsnet/index.html">
<param name="transitions" value="6,ColumnTransition,FadeTransition,
TearTransition,SmashTransition,UnrollTransition,RotateTransition">
</APPLET> From Sams.net, The Internet Book Leader
</CENTER>
<HR SIZE=4>
```

Figure 12.10.
Advertising seven
books in the
space of one.

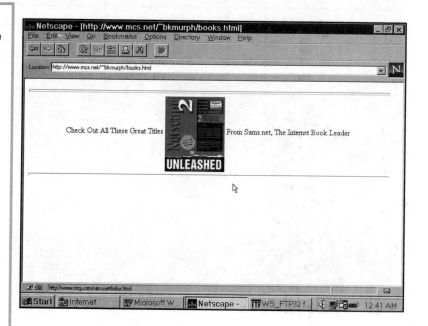

The applet is centered and has horizontal bars at the top and bottom. It can be easily plugged into the bottom of the page on the bookstore owner's Web site. The orders should start pouring in any day now.

Real Businesses, Real Applets

Many companies on the Web have embraced Java applets and have incorporated them nicely into their pages. Taking a look at these sites and then selecting the View | Document Source command in Netscape reveals the applets they're using and the values they have selected. You should be able to locate and download the applet class files from the location in the CODEBASE element and experiment with your own pages.

The Multimedia Newsstand, shown in Figure 12.11, an excellent site overall, is located at

`http://mmnewsstand.com/index.html`

It uses several Java applets to enhance its appearance. Along the top of the page is a Java scrollbar that has a plug-of-the-day saying. At the bottom of the page is a billboard applet similar to the one in the preceding section. The source for this document is laid out well, and you should be able to find the APPLET tag information with no problems.

Nando.net at `http://www.nando.net/nt/` is shown in Figure 12.12 and has a Java-enhanced version of its online newspaper, the *Nando Times*, that implements Java

Figure 12.11.
The Multimedia
Newsstand uses
several Java
applets to deliver
its message.

applets as originally and creatively as any information provider on the Internet. A news ticker applet scrolls the latest headlines while another applet loads up-to-the-minute pictures of the latest-breaking stories in news and sports. This site is definitely bookmark-worthy, and you can always rely on it to be on the cutting edge when it comes to Java applets and HTML development in general. It's a great example of how applets can be used to take your site to the next level.

Figure 12.12.
Nando.net uses
advanced
applets to deliver
updated news
and pictures to
its Web site.

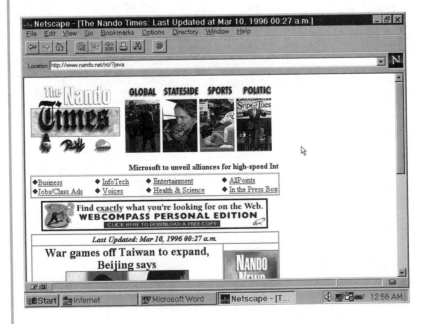

How to Use Java for Personal Pages with Examples

Many people have used Java applets to spice up their own Web pages and to give them a professional feel and heightened interactive experience. You can add animations, sounds, scrolling text, and more that yell out to Web surfers. You can also add games, puzzles, and simple diversions.

A nice and relatively sophisticated applet is Guest Book, which enables visitors to send e-mail directly to you and enables you to see when people visited your pages. It's easy to set up and adds a nice touch to the page.

The guestbook.class file and associated GIF file are located on the accompanying CD-ROM. As you can see from the following APPLET tag, it is relatively easy to fill in the values for the title and your e-mail address—and you're done.

```
<APPLET CODEBASE="classes"
code="guestbook.class" width=125
height=100>
    <param name=IMAGEURL
value="icons155.gif">
    <param name=RECEIVER
value="bkmurph@mcs.net">
    <param name=TITLE value="MurphWeb
Guest Book">
    </APPLET>
```

A Guest Book button then appears on your Web page, and when users select it, they get a window, shown in Figure 12.13, that enables them to send an e-mail to the address specified in the APPLET tag. When you use this applet, you'll receive the e-mail with a re: line indicating that it's a Guest Book entry and telling you the exact time that it was sent from the Web page.

Figure 12.13. The Guest Book applet, from Rocco V. D'Andrea, brings up a message window for Web visitors.

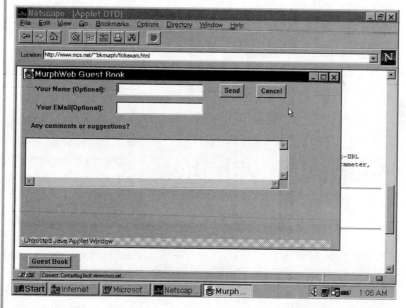

Too Much Java Makes You Jittery

Don't go too far overboard when adding Java applets to your Web page at first. Java is still in development and can be somewhat unstable if you have more than a few applets running at one time on a page. Also, remember that the vast majority of your page's viewers will be accessing it at 28.8Kbps or less. Although Java applets are usually manageably sized, it is important to remember that, unlike images, the entire applet must download before users begin to see anything. For users who have become accustomed to at least seeing a portion of an image immediately with Netscape, this can make 30 seconds seem like an eternity.

Java is great because it is interactive and live. If you have too many applets on one page, you can create a confusing mishmash of action without any focus. Be careful to add applets so that they don't overwhelm a Web surfer with sounds and actions coming from a different corner of the screen every second or two.

Directions to the Machines with the Hottest Java

The first step to using the best Java applets is obviously finding the best ones. New applets are coming out all the time and from a variety of sources all over the Internet. You should also know *how* to get the applets in addition to knowing where to get the applets. Often the applets are clearly marked and easily available for downloading, but sometimes you need to be a little creative to use a Java applet on your Web page without violating anyone's software copyright.

How to Borrow a Cup of Java from a Web Page

If you think you'd like to try out an applet you see on another Web page, you can find it easily enough even if there is no direct link on the page to the Java applet's class file. If you use Netscape's View ¦ Document Source command, you can look at the CODEBASE and code elements to find out where the applet resides on the Web server. Enter the URL for the directory where the Java class file is located. A list of files should appear. Simply hold down the shift key and select the appropriate Java class file, and it will be downloaded to your local hard drive.

When Pointing May Be Polite

Sometimes applet authors do not make their applets freely available to people for use on other Web pages. But there is still a way you can use a Java applet without running afoul of copyright laws and the applet's author: Point using the CODEBASE element in the APPLET tag.

For example, suppose you'd like to add the Nando.net applet shown in Figure 12.12 to your personal Web page, but Nando.net doesn't freely distribute it to everyone. You don't want to copy the applet without approval, so have the applet embedded in your Web page, even though it will be downloaded directly to the surfer's computer from Nando.net's server.

The CODEBASE element lets you specify the directory location of an applet. The CODEBASE value can be a valid URL on the Internet. You can copy the APPLET tag that is used on the Nando.net page and then make adjustments to the CODEBASE value so that it points to the full URL where the applet is stored.

When you replace the values in the APPLET tag with full URL addresses, you end up with the code in Listing 12.4.

You can even alter the parameter values to suit your tastes; for example, make the text bigger and a different color or make it scroll faster. What you end up with is a news ticker on your personal Web page, as shown in Figure 12.14, with very little effort.

Listing 12.4. Pointing wisth CODEBASE.

```
<APPLET CODEBASE="http://www.nando.net/java"
CODE="TextScrollerApplet.class" WIDTH=515 HEIGHT=30>
<PARAM NAME=remoteText VALUE="http://www.nando.net/nt/tickertape.txt">
<PARAM NAME=text VALUE="TickerTape data file down. Check Back Later.">
<PARAM NAME=speed VALUE="20">
<PARAM NAME=dist VALUE="5">
<PARAM NAME=font VALUE="TimesRoman">
<PARAM NAME=size VALUE="24">
<PARAM NAME=style VALUE="Bold">
<PARAM NAME=alignment VALUE="Center">
<PARAM NAME=textColor VALUE="Red">
<PARAM NAME=backgroundColor VALUE="Grey">
<BR CLEAR=0>
</APPLET>
```

Figure 12.14.
Borrowing the
Nando.net news
ticker for a
personal Web
page.

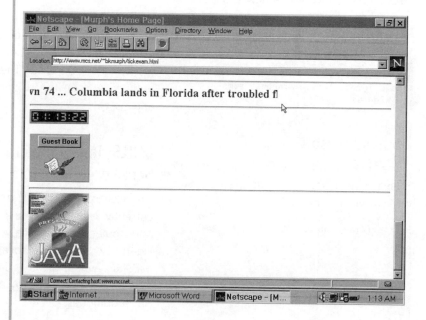

Java Applet and Information Resources— Filling Your Applet-ite

Although Java is a relatively new technology, it has already been widely accepted across the Net and a bevy of sites with information and resources are available to help you find cool new applets that you can make part of your Web page.

Also, quite a few Usenet newsgroups keep up-to-date with new applet developments, so check out the following sites occasionally or visit them regularly:

```
comp.lang.java
comp.infosystems.www.browsers.ms-
  windows.
```

Sun's Javasoft

The primary authority for information on Java is available from its creator, Sun Microsystems, Inc. at

```
http://java.sun.com
```

In addition to the vast amount of documentation and links to other resources, you'll find quite a few useful and freely available applets to download. Also, be sure to check out the $1 million Java applet contest that Sun has sponsored to spur developments using this new technology.

Gamelan

Gamelan was the first comprehensive site for information and resources about the Java programming language. It is considered the definitive Web site when it comes to locating applets. Some even refer to it as "the Yahoo! for Java applets."

Gamelan (`http://www.gamelan.com`) is itself an example of a well-designed site that implements Java applets with animated icons. The site is well organized and provides a wealth of data about applets available in a variety of categories and applications (see Figure 12.15).

If you can't find an applet on Gamelan, it's probably not worth finding. The applets Gamelan indicates are cool usually and are well worth checking out. The site is regularly updated and on the cutting edge of Java applets.

JARS: Java Applet Rating Service

An excellent site for finding the best applets currently available on the Web is JARS: the Java Applet Rating Service, which is shown in Figure 12.16. JARS is located at `http.//www.jars.com`. It provides Java applets ratings based on reviews by an independent panel of judges.

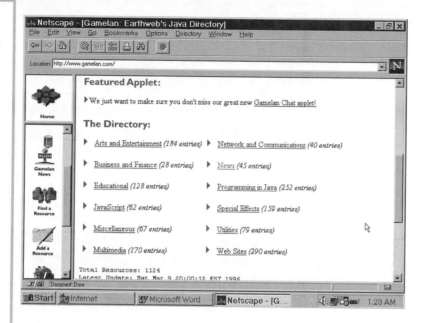

Figure 12.15.
Gamelan is the
place to find any
and all applets.

The JARS site contains listings of what have been judged the best applets on the Web. You can review different lists of all the top applets. The lists contain direct links to each of the applets and also indicate whether source code for the applet is made publicly available. You can find what is new and good in the world of applets without necessarily having to surf through hundreds of Web pages every week.

Figure 12.16.
JARS plays the
role of Siskel
and Ebert for
Java applets.

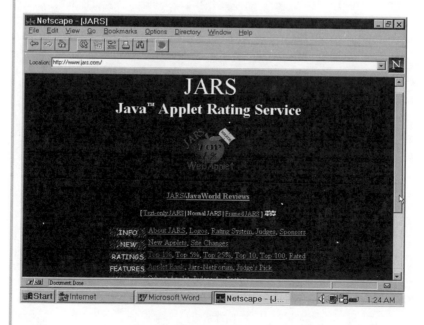

One of the most valuable aspects of the JARS site is the Applet Bank link on the main page. The link takes you to the Java Applet Locator, as shown in Figure 12.17. JARS' Java Applet Locator is an excellent categorized applet listing for finding the right Java applets for the Web page project you are currently putting together.

As you can see from Figure 12.17, by using the Java Applet Locator, you can quickly locate financial, chat, or even Easter-related applets that can help you enhance your Web page. You can help make the site even better by suggesting new categories for applets that will make searching for applets more convenient.

The JARS site is well designed and extremely easy to use. You should definitely place it under your Java bookmarks and check back regularly for links to and reviews of all the latest Java applets on the Web.

Applets.com

Applets.com is another good resource for Java applets, as its name implies. Check it out on the Web at

http://www.applets.com

If nothing else, it is certainly the easiest URL to remember for these purposes.

What's Next?

Now that you have a handle on how to get Java applets up and running on your Web page, we're going to take a look at how you can bring together all your interactive and multimedia elements on the Web page. We'll be taking a look at JavaScript and how it works as the multimedia glue to keep Web pages together, as well as other ways to make your page literally shake, rattle, and hum.

Figure 12.17. The JARS Applet Locator helps you zero in on the applet you are looking for in no time.

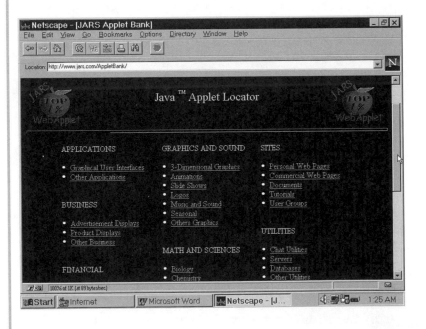

Combining Multiple Media Formats

The most amazing thing about the Internet is the sheer volume and variety of raw information available. The most amazing thing about the Web is how it takes all this raw information and places it in an easy-to-use and easy-to-navigate form. The most amazing thing about today's browsers, such as Netscape Navigator, is the amount of multimedia they can use to make the information come alive on your Web pages.

If you're thinking about designing a new Web page or redesigning an old one, you have to be thinking about multimedia. As the number of Web sites and pages increase exponentially almost daily, it is more important than ever to create pages that are rich in both content and presentation. If you look at a top-notch Web site like CNN (http://www.cnn.com), shown in Figure 13.1, you'll find a page loaded with content that includes inline images and links to even richer multimedia in the form of audio and video files. It's a good example of taking great content and making it even better with multimedia additions.

chapter **13**

by Brian K. Murphy

Figure 13.1.
CNN shows that
multimedia can
take a site with
great content
and make it
even better.

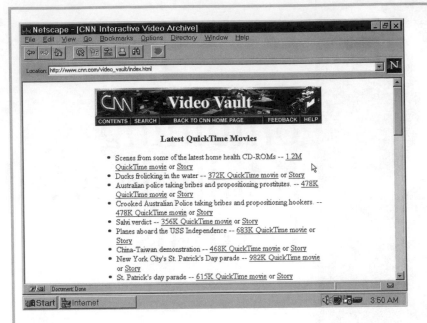

The number of multimedia file types you can use in your Web pages is almost staggering. The new version of Netscape Navigator enables third-party software developers to create plug-ins to provide additional functionality and compatibility with the base browser. The result has been an almost literal feeding frenzy of multimedia application vendors creating plug-ins delivering file compatibility for a wide range of graphic, audio, video, and interactive file types. There are almost too many choices in this area.

Another advance in the new version of Netscape is the implementation of frames, as demonstrated in Figure 13.2. Frames are an easier way to combine different multimedia files on a page in a simpler, more

elegant fashion. They also provide a more organized presentation for links to multimedia files.

In this chapter, I'll help you sort through what's available and show you how to put the best multimedia file types available to work for you on your pages. We will take a look at Javascript and the promise it holds to create quick interactions within your Web page. You'll also learn what to consider and what to avoid when adding multimedia. You'll navigate through the sea of multimedia file types and learn how to make your site glitzy but not garish. *So let's put the "multi" back in "multimedia" by mixing and matching file formats and media types as you choose.*

Figure 13.2. AudioNet's Jukebox uses Netscape frames to organize its multimedia content and ease access to the many CDs it has available online.

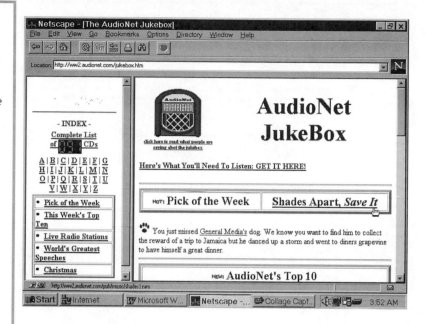

Embedding Multiple Media Types on the Same Page

As more advances are made in Internet and Web technology, it can be somewhat difficult to keep abreast of exactly what developments have been made, let alone figure out how to integrate them into your Web page. More companies are rushing every day to bring better graphics, audio, and video to Web surfers in less time.

One of the keys to keeping your Web page fresh is to keep yourself open to adding new media types and getting different media types to work together so that the whole is greater than the sum of its parts. As little as nine months ago, users would have thought your site was a multimedia extravaganza if you had RealAudio files available. Today even the dullest of dull sites have RealAudio to enhance their pages. And with the advent of RealAudio 2.0, you'd better be able to keep up with the times by embedding RealAudio files into your Web pages, as shown in Figure 13.3. You may not always be on the cutting edge of new media types, but you can remain fresh by rethinking how present media files can be used more creatively together on your Web pages.

Designing Your Web Page with Multimedia in Mind

The Web hasn't yet supplanted television as the most prominent entertainment and information medium in America's homes, but it certainly is well on its way. As you design the pages of the future, keep in mind your potential audience and what will grab its attention.

*Figure 13.3.
With RealAudio
2.0 (http://www.
realaudio.com),
you can embed
RealAudio files
directly into your
Web pages.*

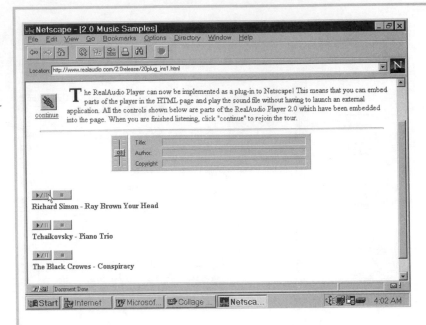

Web surfers are prone to switching sites as quickly as channel surfers with a remote control. Their attention spans are similar, so your attempts to keep Web users tuned in should factor in that reality. The best way to get and hold people's attention is by using the entire multimedia arsenal as effectively as possible. For example, the ESPNET SportsZone, as shown in Figure 13.4, uses everything from Java applets to video files to make sure that it's the only site sports addicts rely on for their daily dose of coverage.

*Figure 13.4.
The ESPNET
SportsZone uses
Java applets and
has links to
audio and video
files that are
meant to (and
do) keep Web
surfers attentive.*

Tip: When you start developing a new Web page, gather all the materials you have on that particular project, regardless of the medium. If you're developing a Web page for a company, it likely has promotional video tapes or radio ads that can be used as multimedia building blocks. When you have all the analog multimedia, you can convert it to digital and then think about what original multimedia file types you'll need to create for the Web site.

You should consider carefully the installed browser client base when you develop a multimedia plan. Obviously, Netscape is king on the Web and controls about 85% of the browser marketplace. However, the more important consideration revolves around what the most popular plug-ins and helper applications are.

Client Considerations— Plug-Ins and Helper Apps

Plug-ins and helper applications are software components that act as viewers or interpreters for virtually all the multimedia files you can include on a Web page. Browsers such as Netscape have built-in support to display images, but their multimedia (actually, not much "multi" to it) capabilities generally end there. But users can add support for any number of media types by adding plug-ins or configuring helper apps to view or listen to video, audio, animation, music, or other files.

Some file types are supported by several plug-ins or helper apps that can be used to display their multimedia. Other file types are unique or proprietary to a specific program and can only be accessed and readable if that program is installed and configured on the computer.

It doesn't take much research on the Web to figure out what the most popular plug-ins and helper apps are and what file formats they support. Look at Stroud's Consummate Winsock Apps page (see Figure 13.5) at this address:

http://cwsapps.texas.net

or the plug-in portion of the BrowserWatch page, shown in Figure 13.6, at

http://www.browserwatch.com

Both contain extensive links to helper apps or plug-ins that handle multimedia files. You'll find reviews of the programs and links to their respective Web pages.

Tip: If you want to ensure that a Netscape plug-in is widely installed before using a specific multimedia file type, pay a visit to the plug-in developer's Web page. Normally, plug-ins that are widely supported will have links to sites that implement the file types that take advantage of the plug-ins. For example, RealAudio maintains an extensive set of links to sites using its technology, as shown in Figure 13.7. If all that is available on the developer's site are demos the company has created, with no links to other pages, be somewhat cautious about using that file type if your goal is to reach a wide audience. However, you can always be a trailblazer or at least use the plug-in's file type on a small portion of your page as it gains wider acceptance.

Furthermore, by clicking on the various links, you can find examples of how other developers used the file type that the plug-in supports.

Figure 13.5.
Stroud's
Consummate
Winsock Apps
page has an
excellent and
comprehensive
list of available
multimedia plug-
ins for Netscape.

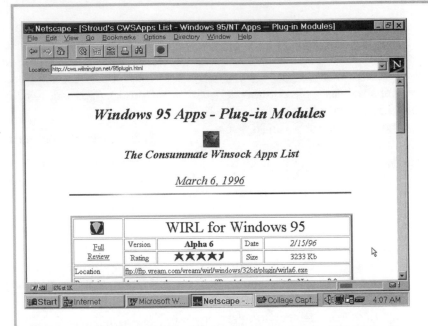

Figure 13.6.
Watch the
BrowserWatch
for reviews of
new multimedia
plug-ins.

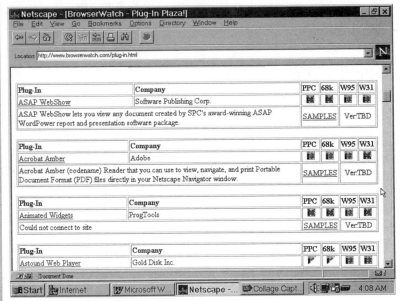

Figure 13.7.
The RealAudio
Web site
contains an
extensive set of
links to sites with
RealAudio format
files available,
indicating the
popularity of the
technology.

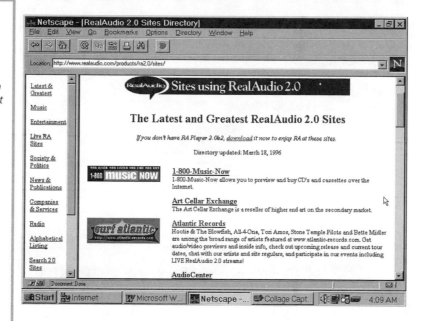

Reviewing the plug-ins and helper apps will also offer you an opportunity to consider the vast array of file types available. For example, you undoubtedly are aware that you can include links to WAV audio files or QuickTime video files on your Web pages.

But you may not know about inline Scream animations, shown in Figure 13.8, or inline real-time videos from VDOLive, as shown in Figure 13.9. Both are Netscape plug-ins that you would have discovered at Stroud's or BrowserWatch.

Figure 13.8.
You can
implement
Scream
animations
through a
Netscape plug-in
and provide an
added multi-
media boost to
your pages.

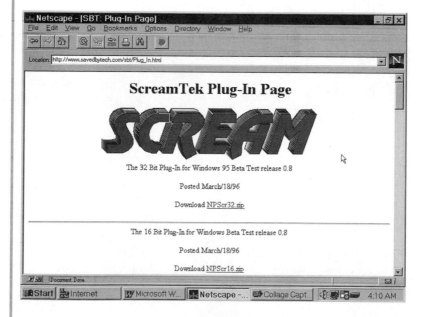

Figure 13.9.
The VDOLive
plug-in brings
real-time video
delivery to your
Web pages.

One of the keys to what works well on your site is to figure out what works well on other people's sites. Take it upon yourself to download as many Netscape plug-ins and helper apps as you can and to explore the pages that use each type. A day spent exploring what is available will help you a great deal when you decide what to include in your pages. It's one thing to read about real-time audio or OLE controls, but it's quite another to actually experience these multimedia files firsthand.

A good starting point for exploration is the Cool Site of the Day, as shown in Figure 13.10 at this address:

```
http://cool.infi.net
```

or Project Cool at

```
http://www.projectcool.com
```

More often than not, these "cool sites" involve some degree of multimedia integration.

Avoiding a Multimedia Mishmash—Bandwidth and Aesthetic Considerations

When a variety of fonts first became available on computers, many desktop publishers took the opportunity to include every available typeface in their documents. The result was quite awful most times, with a stylistically incoherent jumble of type families and faces that just didn't flow together. The same kind of danger is present when designing Web pages with multimedia file types.

A good rule of thumb with fonts is never to use more than three different typefaces on any one page, and it's probably a good idea to avoid using more than three multimedia file types on a single Web page. If you pile on Java applets, VDOLive videos, Shockwave movies, and VRML worlds, you may end up with a confusing and time-consuming (for downloading) page that is ineffective in doing what you intended.

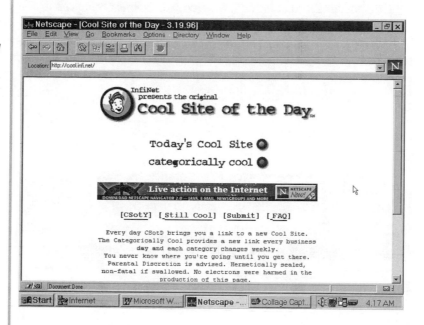

Figure 13.10. The Cool Site of the Day is a good place to start an exploration for multimedia sites on the Web.

The Bandwidth Problem— Different Pipes for Different People

Bandwidth and multimedia on the Internet go hand in hand. The more bandwidth available, the more multimedia is used to fill it. The more multimedia available, the more bandwidth is needed to support it. Each is constantly driving the other. You can call it a Catch-22 or chicken-and-egg problem, but Web page designers must consider it.

It has become increasingly popular to offer Web users variable options for different pages based on the type of bandwidth with which they are connecting to your site. As shown in Figure 13.11, surfers visiting the Internet Underground Music Archive (IUMA)

are initially presented with a welcome screen and an option for a low or a high bandwidth version. Such a solution is good for the near future as we move through a transition from slower connections to more prevalent ISDN and cable modem connections.

Another way to account for the bandwidth problem is to limit the number of multimedia files you plan on having loaded inline on your page. If, in addition to graphics, your page loads inline videos, OLE controls, and Java applets, you may be pushing some people's patience to the limit. You can always limit the inline files and use links instead, so that users have more control over which files they want to download from the site.

Figure 13.11. It's a good idea to offer high and low bandwidth versions if you have a site that uses multimedia enhancements extensively.

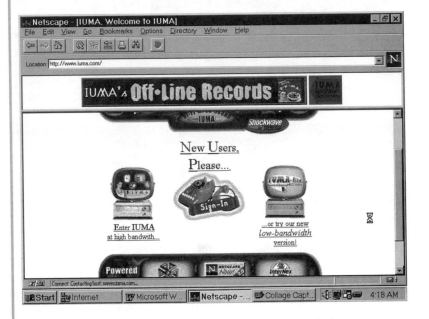

Multitasking Multimedia— Media that Play Together Stay Together

When placing more than one multimedia file, it is important to know whether the files can be viewed simultaneously in the page. The question is really one of multitasking, and the answer can be somewhat difficult. However, the answer is also readily apparent the first time you load your page and the files don't cooperate with one another in your browser.

Genuine problems will arise if you use two media objects on one page that access the same hardware resources. For example, you could potentially run into problems if you have two separate Java applets that both attempt to play back sound at the same time. This could create a hardware conflict resulting in audio playback failure or the Web surfer's computer hanging as it attempts to play back both files.

There are some definite workable and winning combinations that have proven themselves suitable for inclusion on the same Web page. VRML worlds and Macromedia Shockwave movies can be placed on the same page, creating a heightened interactive experience for visitors to your Web pages. The Cybertown Virtual Freeway, shown in Figure 13.12, is available at

http://www.cybertown.com

It demonstrates the impressive results possible by combining these file types on one Web page.

The Virtual Freeway uses an embedded navigable VRML world of a simulated freeway. Adding to the reality of this experience is a Shockwave movie embedded just below the VRML window that presents an animated steering wheel and plays back audio of a car

engine running. As you navigate through the VRML freeway, the audio and animations of the Shockwave dashboard continue.

Another excellent example of using different multimedia file types also involves VRML, this time paired with RealAudio 2.0 files:

http://www.marketcentral.com

SteelStudio's Virtual Overdrive site uses VRML to present a classic Chevy on an interactive freeway and adds a car radio that can select radio stations from around the world that employ RealAudio files.

The site lets you get a virtual feel for cruising down the road by combining two popular interactive multimedia files. You can imagine the number of variations you can use to enhance your own Web pages by thinking up your own multimedia recipes for success.

Figure 13.12. The Virtual Freeway shows how VRML and Shockwave can peacefully coexist on a Web page.

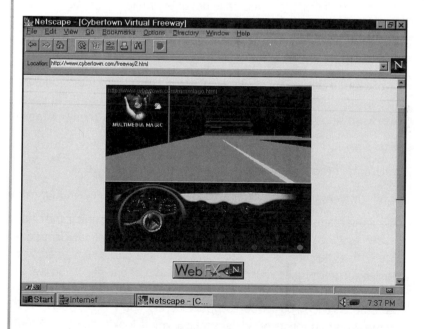

Figure 13.13. Virtual Overdrive uses VRML and RealAudio for a trip in a Chevy with music from around the world.

JavaScript as Web Page Glue

JavaScript is the radical new Web programming language developed to provide more control and flexibility to Web page designers while enhancing their ability to create live, interactive multimedia Web pages. By using JavaScript, you can exercise control over how your Web pages look and behave in a way that was previously arduous, if not impossible, to achieve.

JavaScript is a close relative to Java, but doesn't require the more complicated programming knowledge of its older sibling. To see some examples of JavaScript in action, check out the JavaScript Applets page shown in Figure 13.14 or see the many examples on the CD-ROM.

```
http://www.flinet.com/~rummy/javahtml/javasc1.html
```

Netscape's official site for JavaScript information is located at

```
http://home.netscape.com/comprod/products/navigator/version_2.0/script/index.html
```

The site contains not only examples, but also an authoring guide and links to other JavaScript resources. (See Figure 13.15.) Like Java, you can either use JavaScript passively by plugging what others have developed into your Web pages or become an active programmer using the language to create your own unique JavaScript applets. If you want to get up to speed quickly and thoroughly on all the possible permutations for using JavaScript, check out Sams.net's *Teach Yourself JavaScript in a Week* (ISBN 1-57521-073-8) by Arman Danesh. Without getting too involved, let's take a simple look at how JavaScript is used.

Figure 13.14.
The JavaScript
Applets page
provides a
comprehensive
list of sites using
JavaScript.

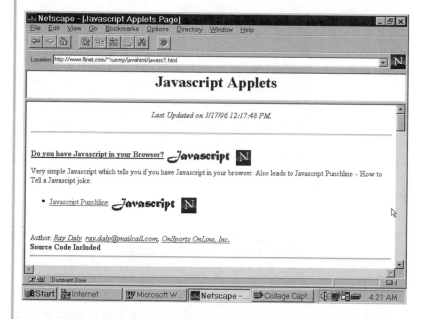

Figure 13.15.
Netscape
maintains a
JavaScript page
that provides
plenty of
resources to get
up to speed
quickly.

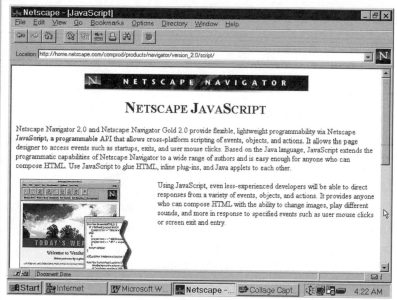

Simple JavaScript Program—Hello World!

A popular example used for introducing a new language is the "Hello World!" progam. This example is perhaps the easiest program you could ever write. It simply displays the words "Hello World!" on-screen. Although terribly simple, it illustrates some introductory points of JavaScript. The HTML file looks like this:

```
<HTML>
<HEAD>
<SCRIPT LANGUAGE="JAVASCRIPT">
        document.write("Hello World!");
</SCRIPT>
</HEAD>
<BODY>
...
</BODY>
</HTML>
```

As you can see, the JavaScript application code is embedded in the HEAD section of the HTML document. However, you can place the JavaScript code anywhere in the document. Notice the single line of code between the <SCRIPT> and </SCRIPT> tags. This line is the command that writes output to the screen. Yes, it would be just as easy to write the line in HTML, but this is only an example of how to use JavaScript. Let's move on to something more complicated.

The next example does some math. First, add a variable called TipAmount that gets multiplied by 15 percent. The results are printed out using the write statement again.

```
<HTML>
<HEAD>
<SCRIPT LANGUAGE="JAVASCRIPT">
    var TipAmount;
    amount=20;
    TipAmount=amount*.15;
    document.write("A 15% tip for
    $",amount," would be:
    $",TipAmount);
</SCRIPT>
</HEAD>
<BODY>
...
</BODY>
</HTML>
```

Without getting into a lot of programming details, this example outputs the results along with text—something you can't do easily with HTML. The HTML code above displays the following on-screen:

```
A 15% tip for $20 would be: $3
```

Loops

There are several different ways to perform loops in JavaScript: the for loop, the for-in loop, and the while loop. Let's look at an example using the for loop.

Any line of code that appears immediately after the for loop is done the number of times the loop occurs. If you want to include more than a single line of code to be looped, you must enclose that block of code with beginning and ending braces ({ }). The following loop prints the words Web Page Wizardry! 10 times on-screen:

```
<HTML>
<HEAD>
<SCRIPT LANGUAGE="JAVASCRIPT">
    for (i=1; i<=10; i++){
        document.write("Web Page
        Wizardry!");
}
</SCRIPT>
</HEAD>
<BODY>
...
</BODY>
</HTML>
```

This will continue until the variable i equals 10, and then the loop will end. The i++ command increases the value of i by one each time it is encountered.

Alert Boxes

Alert boxes can be added to quickly give the user a message in a dialog box as seen in the following example.

```
<HTML>
<HEAD>
<SCRIPT LANGUAGE="JAVASCRIPT">
    alert("This is a sample alert
    box");
</SCRIPT>
</HEAD>
<BODY>
...
</BODY>
</HTML>
```

This simply presents a dialog box with the text, This is a sample alertbox, in it. These boxes can be used not only to present information, but also to receive user input. A similar box called the prompt box allows the user to input information. A confirm box gives a dialog box with an OK button and a Cancel button.

if and if...else Statements

The if statement evaluates a statement and executes the code in brackets if it is true, or skips it if it is not true.

```
<HTML>
<HEAD>
<SCRIPT LANGUAGE="JAVASCRIPT">
    welcome=true;
    if (welcome){
        alert("Welcome to My Home
        Page");}
    else {
        alert("My Home Page");}
</SCRIPT>
</HEAD>
<BODY>
...
</BODY>
</HTML>
```

This script causes a dialog box that says, Welcome to My Home Page, before loading the rest of the page. Pretty simple, but it can be used to add some neat functions to your Web page.

JavaScript Events

JavaScript can detect certain actions taking place on the screen. These are called events and include such things as mouse clicks, loading and unloading a form, or moving the mouse over an element. These events can be used to build interactivity into your Web pages. Let's look at an example using the page load event.

```
<HTML>
<HEAD>
...
</HEAD>
<BODY onLoad="alert('This page has just
  loaded. Welcome.');">
...
</BODY>
</HTML>
```

Notice how this script doesn't need the <SCRIPT> tags. Event scripts can be placed with standard HTML tags.

This is just a quick look at a few of the functions available in JavaScript. Many more commands are available that enable scriptors to build complex interactive Web pages. JavaScript has its roots in programming, so be aware that learning JavaScript goes beyond HTML in complexity and functionality. Now let's look at what is on the horizon.

LiveMedia and the Future

Netscape recently announced that future versions of its Navigator software will include support for a new technology it is developing called LiveMedia. LiveMedia is an open standard designed to enable Netscape and other vendors' real-time audio and video products to interoperate. The list of companies announcing support for the technology reads like a Who's Who of Internet multimedia pioneers: Progressive Networks, Adobe Systems, Digital Equipment Corp., Macromedia, NetSpeak, OnLive!, Precept, Silicon Graphics, Inc., VDOnet, VocalTec, Xing, among others.

"How'd They Do That?" Examples

The best way to learn about adding multimedia to your Web pages is to look around and see what else is available on the Net right now and what impresses you. It's hard to imagine a more fun research job than surfing cool multimedia sites for inspiration for your own Web pages. The extent and variety of Web pages on the Net today is staggering, and the vast majority implement multimedia in one fashion or another. The key is to use yourself as a compass for what works and what doesn't.

By experiencing these sites firsthand, you can develop your own sense of taste for what should and should not be used in adding multimedia to Web pages. You can then take this taste and adapt it into your style for writing and presenting your own pages on the Web.

The most valuable tool in learning how to make advances to your Web pages is the View ¦ Source command on the Netscape browser. You can use it to bring up a window, as shown in Figure 13.16, and examine HTML code. Bill Dortch's hIdaho site is shown in the figure, and Dortch has some neat programs for JavaScript—freely available—to make JavaScript programming easier. By working from others' examples, you can quickly learn new tricks for your own Web pages.

LOVE–The Page, Not the Emotion

LOVE is a page developed by Group Z in Belgium and is an interesting site, although even I'm not quite sure what exactly it is supposed to mean. However, it is an impressive display of a creative use of multimedia. You really never know what the next click of the mouse will bring you. Note also that the site makes extensive use of both Netscape frames and JavaScript. The site takes some time to explore, and you really have little control over where it takes you, but it can be an interesting and informative trip. Shown in Figure 13.17, it is available at this address:

```
http://adaweb.com/adaweb/influx/GroupZ/
   LOVE/love.html
```

Figure 13.16.
The View ¦
Source command
in Netscape may
be the most
valuable tool a
Web developer
can have.

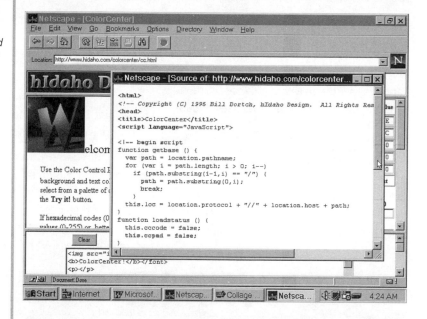

Figure 13.17.
LOVE is an
unusual site with
some interesting
examples of
JavaScript.

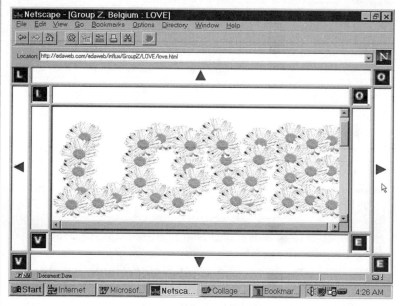

VRML Fighter–VRML and Java

A happy marriage between VRML and Java applets is definitely possible, as demonstrated by the VRML Fighter (see Figure 13.18):

```
http://www.netscape.com/comprod/
  products/navigator/live3d/examples/
  fighter/fghtentr.html
```

VRML Fighter is a demo created by Netscape to show the potential for its Live3D technology in combination with Java applets. The HTML code used to implement it is in Listing 13.1.

As you can see from the code, this is very basic and simple. Using the <EMBED> tag for the VRML world and the <APPLET> tag for the Java applet results in a combination of an Internet gaming experience on the page.

VRML Fighter demonstrates the possibilities for combining multimedia. It creates a live interactive gaming environment that can be accessed and enjoyed in the Web browser, simply by joining together the best of the two technologies—VRML and Java.

Figure 13.18. The VRML Fighter showcases the potential of Live3D and Java applets working together.

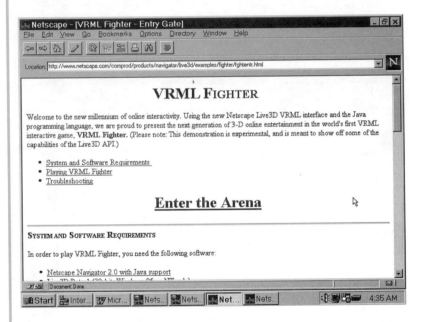

Listing 13.1. The HTML code for Netscape's VRML Fighter.

```
<center>
<EMBED SRC=fighter.wrl HEIGHT=200 WIDTH = 450>
</center>

<center>
<applet code="fighterEngine.class" width=200 height=75>
</applet>
</center>
```

"Up To The Minute" from CBS

The CBS news program "Up To The Minute" has an excellent Web site that provides a broad range of multimedia content. On its VDOLive enhanced pages at `http://uttm.com/welcome2.html` (see Figure 13.19), you can not only find embedded VDOLive files from broadcasts, but links to RealAudio files.

Getting the VDOLive file embedded in the page is a simple task. The following code shows how the `<EMBED>` tag was used on the UTTM page to integrate the VDO file:

```
<embed src="http://www.vdolive.com/
  vdofiles/cbs1.vdo"
  autostart=true stretch=true width=180
  height=160 align=bottom>
```

The RealAudio files on the site are not embedded but accessed through hyperlinks. It's important to note why this is done: Embedding RealAudio files in a page that has a VDO file embedded in it could create one of the hardware conflicts discussed in the preceding section.

What's Next?

Now that all the tools and tricks of multimedia have been covered, we will take a look at a real-world example of these elements in action. The final section will show you how to build an advanced, visually stimulating Web site specifically for lower bandwidth connections. We will then look to the future and high bandwidth possibilities.

Figure 13.19. The "Up To The Minute" Web site uses embedded VDOLive clips and RealAudio files for maximum multimedia exposure.

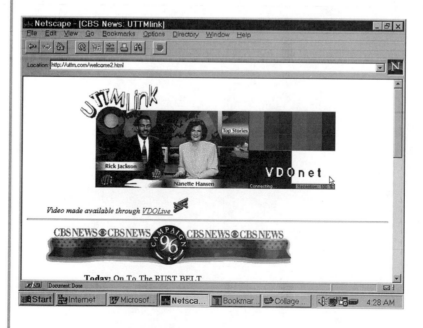

Putting It All Together: Complete Sample Sites

part V

by Dick Oliver

The Home Page of Your Dreams, Today!

If you've read the previous 13 chapters—or even skimmed the table of contents—your mind is probably reeling from all the choices and possibilities for your own Web pages. This chapter gives you some complete, hands-on examples of how to make those choices and combine those possibilities intelligently in real-world situations.

The four sample sites presented in this part all feature real people and businesses. You'll get the inside story on how and why both the multimedia and more conventional elements were used to meet their needs and goals. There is a personal site, a promotional page for an "offline" business, an online business site, and a CD-ROM-based site for a musical group. Between all of these, almost all of the technologies and techniques discussed in this book are put into action.

All these sites are included in their entirety on the CD-ROM with this book, so you can borrow all the techniques and even some of the content for your own projects. (Obviously, you can't use the logos, names, personal pictures, and copyrighted text or music. But you do have permission to use backgrounds, icons, and general design elements. When in doubt, contact me at dicko@netletter.com or contact the people whose names and e-mail addresses are on the pages to ask for specific permission.)

Making a Personal Page More Personal

Sound and action are not just for high-budget, high-bandwidth sites run by giant media moguls. In fact, one of the most popular uses of multimedia on the Web today is for personal home pages. The function of a personal home page is mostly to allow people you meet online to get some idea of who you are, and for you to have some fun making a "page of your own." If you're job hunting or you happen to be a public figure, your home page may take a more serious bent. But the sound of a human voice and some animation makes anyone's page convey more of a sense of who they are—or who they would like to be!

An Overdue Makeover

I run some popular Web sites, frequent a number of mailing lists and the occasional online chat room, and write books about the Internet. But until recently, my home page was of the old-fashioned snapshot-and-a-few-lines-of-text variety. So I decided to see if I could spice it up using only free or ultra-cheap tools and without taking much time out of my busy schedule.

Figure 14.1 and Listing 14.1 show the result, after a couple hours of messing around with it. I'll explain the decisions I made and why.

Putting a Good Face on It

The first thing I thought about was the background and layout. I wanted something that looked big and bold (like me <grin>),

*Figure 14.1.
My home page
(/dicko/
dicko.htm on the
CD-ROM or
http://
netletter.com/
dicko/ online)
flips through four
pictures of me,
so nobody has to
tolerate any one
view too long.*

but that was very fast to make and very fast to load and display. So I decided to just make a black-and-white background strip with solid white at the top and solid black down as far as my pages were likely to scroll. The strip is called /dicko/strip.gif on the CD-ROM, and because it's mostly solid colors, the big 20×2000 pixel image compresses to less than 1KB. A ragged edge adds a little zest without increasing the file size significantly.

Next, I considered the graphics. The obligatory snapshot of my face seemed too static, so I made an animated sequence of snapshots instead, and doctored them up in Paint Shop Pro to prove what an artsy kinda guy I am. Then I used GIF Construction Set to make a multi-image GIF that flips to a new goofy picture of me every 0.6 seconds (see Figure 14.2). A title graphic scanned from my handwriting and some scans of my and my daughter's body parts complete the "DickO look."

Tip: I really wanted to make the file sizes small on my page, because it will live on my high-volume commercial site where I have to pay for every byte that somebody downloads. So I did something very sneaky with all the pictures. I decreased the color depth to 16 grayscales (using "nearest color" remapping, *not* "diffusion" dithering). This cut the files to a fraction of their original size. Then I used Paint Shop Pro to colorize them to the 16 colors of my choice and then *increased the color depth to 256 colors again*.

Both Netscape and Microsoft Explorer do a much better job displaying most 256-color images than 16-color images, so the visual quality most people see is quite a bit better at the higher color depth. However, because there are still only 16 unique color values being used,

Figure 14.2.
A cheap hand scanner and two inexpensive shareware programs (Paint Shop Pro and GIF Construction Set) were all I needed to put together a stylistic animation for my home page.

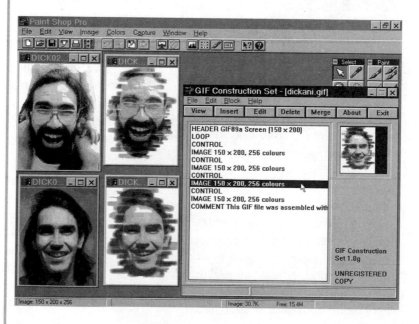

the compressed file still comes out much smaller than before I brought the images down to 16 colors and back up again.

This trick allowed me to squeeze four relatively large (150×200-pixel) photos into a 28KB GIF file. Before doctoring them, *each* of the 256-color, 150×200 GIF files was over 28KB!

The Webmaster's Voice

Most of the links on my home page lead to graphics, text, and other sites I've produced. But the links next to my two-year-old daughter's ear are the parts that probably give the most personal experience of meeting me and my family. The sound of someone's voice—even if compressed and distorted a bit—seems to reach a place in the soul that no amount of graphics can touch.

Recording voices is easy enough. In fact, for a personal home page, it would be overkill to use more than a simple recording utility, such as the Windows Sound Recorder and the chintzy microphone that came with my sound card.

The resulting WAV files could be posted as-is, or converted with a shareware sound editing program, such as CoolEdit, to the AU format so Netscape Navigator 2.0 could play them without requiring any plug-ins. But I wanted to include fairly lengthy sound samples, such as "my favorite poem" and keep the number of bytes to transfer to an absolute minimum. So, I chose to use the RealAudio encoder (Figure 14.3) to compress the sound for real-time playback. A 327KB, 8-bit WAV file compresses to about 15KB worth of RealAudio audio and starts playing immediately when the user clicks on the links (Figure 14.4).

The disadvantage of using RealAudio is that not everybody has a plug-in or helper app to play back the .RA files. But hey, it's my home page and it's no big deal if somebody can't hear my voice. They can go to http://www.realaudio.com/ and download the plug-in if they're really intent on hearing me, and I tell them so on the bottom of the page. But of course a used car site pumping out plaid-voiced sales talk might prefer the more universal AU format.

The other obvious choice would have been ToolVox, a similar plug-in which generally achieves better compression and higher quality than RealAudio. But right now, more people have RealAudio—especially the helper app, and I've gotten kind of used to it. By the time you read this, ToolVox will probably be taking the lead in number of users, so you should seriously consider it as an option for your lengthy sound files. There are other up-and-coming formats, too, but most haven't gained much widespread support yet, and sound quality is still pretty shaky over modem lines. (You'd think a modem hooked to a telephone line could carry telephone-quality voice pretty easily, but there's more to it than that. See Chapter 5, "Creating Online Audio," for all the technical details.)

Notice that I refrained from putting an AVI home video up on my personal Web site. As everybody's bandwidth increases and digital video editing software keeps dropping in price, that might become a viable option. But for now, it would just be too many pixels to push through a poor suffering server just for my personal home page.

Listing 14.1. /dicko/dicko.htm.

```html
<HTML>
<HEAD><TITLE>Dick Oliver's Home Page</TITLE></HEAD>
<BODY BACKGROUND="strip.gif" TEXT="white" LINK="red" VLINK="red" ALINK="white">
<IMG SRC="dickani.gif"> . . . <IMG SRC="dickog.gif"><BR>
 .<P>
So what can you do when you're too dumb to become a physicist or mathematician,
and not quite crazy enough to qualify for free food at the asylum?
Write books, I figure. And software. And what the heck maybe some newsletters
and Web pages, too. But enough about me already.
On to these far more interesting topics:<BR>
<CENTER>
<TABLE>
<TR>
<TD><IMG SRC="see.gif"></TD>
<TD>
<FONT COLOR="cyan"><I>See...</I></FONT><BR>
<A HREF="work.htm"><FONT COLOR="cyan">My work</FONT></A><BR>
<A HREF="family.htm"><FONT COLOR="cyan">My family</FONT></A><BR>
<A HREF="house.htm"><FONT COLOR="cyan">My house</FONT></A><BR>
<A HREF="hotlist.htm"><FONT COLOR="cyan">My hotlist</FONT></A>
</TD>
<TD>
<IMG SRC="hear.gif"></TD>
<TD>
<FONT COLOR="yellow"><I>Hear...</I></FONT><BR>
<A HREF="voice.RA"><FONT COLOR="yellow">My voice</FONT></A><BR>
<A HREF="brillig.RA"><FONT COLOR="yellow">My favorite poem</FONT></A><BR>
<A HREF="ecooro.RA"><FONT COLOR="yellow">My daughters</FONT></A><BR>
<A HREF="dog.RA"><FONT COLOR="yellow">My dog</FONT></A>
</TD>
<TD>
<IMG SRC="get.gif"></TD>
<TD>
<FONT COLOR="red"><I>Get...</I></FONT><BR>
<A HREF="news.htm">My newsletter</A><BR>
<A HREF="books.htm">My books</A><BR>
<A HREF="software.htm">My software</A><BR>
<A HREF="fools.htm">My foolishness</A>
</TD>
</TR>
</TABLE><BR>
Happy? Disgusted? Lonely? Enlightened? Just plain stupid?<BR>
Why not send some e-mail to
<A HREF="mailto:DICKO@netletter.com">
<FONT COLOR="green">DickO@netletter.com</FONT></A>
to tell me about it?<P>
NOTE: To hear the voices, you'll need the
<A HREF="http://www.realaudio.com/">RealAudio player</A>.<P>
</CENTER>
</BODY>
</HTML>
```

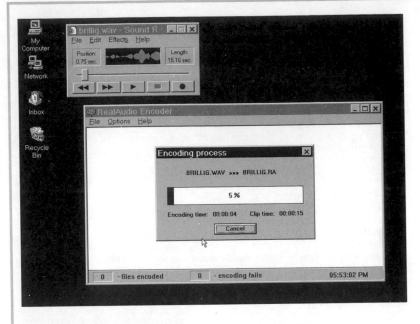

*Figure 14.3.
It doesn't take a
state of the art
recording studio
to put your voice
on the Web.
These free
programs (the
Windows 95
Sound Recorder
and RealAudio
Encoder) will do
just fine.*

*Figure 14.4.
The RealAudio
helper app
works with any
browser, and
plays back
without long
download
delays. (There is
also a RealAudio
plug-in available
for embedded
playback.)*

An Attention-Grabbing Business Page

Now let's look at a simple business site. Though the goals and concerns of a business are obviously a bit different than those you might have for your personal pages, many of the same decisions need to be made. How can you get big, attention-grabbing graphics while sucking up as little space and time on the server as possible? How can you convey a unique and memorable image without distracting too much from the more prosaic information content?

Festive Java

For the Hawaiian Hard Drive home page in Figure 14.5 and Listing 14.2, we chose a flashy but fun look, mostly conveyed by a large masthead graphic. But the most memorable part of the page is the freeware Java applet underneath the masthead, which creates moving waves of text with rainbow colors flowing through them. This applet, created by Integris Network Services (and included on the CD-ROM in this book), can be freely used by anyone willing to put a link to Integris on their page.

Having seen and played with lots of nifty little special-purpose Java applets like this one, it is always a delight to actually have a reasonable excuse to use one on a real page. This one seemed like a perfect way to set a festive "Hawaiian mood" without resorting to touristy clichés like palm trees and pineapples, which might turn off many of the Hawaiians for whom this page is intended.

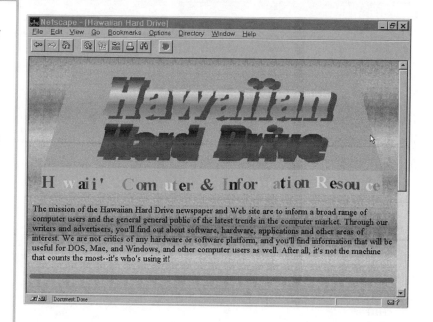

(Hawaiian Hard Drive is a free computer newspaper distributed on the islands, and this site offers its readers and advertisers an online version.)

Note: In-word spaces in the following code are intentional. They're necessary due to the width of some characters.

Listing 14.2. /hhd/hhd.htm.

```
<HTML>
<HEAD><TITLE>Hawaiian Hard Drive</TITLE></HEAD>
<BODY BACKGROUND="HHD.JPG">
<CENTER>
<IMG SRC="HHD2.GIF" ALT="Hawaiian Hard Drive"><BR>
<APPLET code="RnbText.class" width=710 height=50>
<param name=text value="H aw aii's C om puter &  Inform ation R esource">
</APPLET> <P>
</CENTER>
<EMBED SRC="aloha.wav" WIDTH=2 HEIGHT=2>
<NOEMBED><BGSOUND SRC="aloha.wav"></NOEMBED><BR>
<FONT SIZE=4>The mission of the Hawaiian Hard Drive newspaper and Web site
is to inform a broad range of computer users and the general general public
of the latest trends in the computer market. Through our writers and
advertisers, you'll find out about software, hardware, applications
and other areas of interest. We are not critics of any hardware or
software platform, and you'll find information that will be useful for DOS,
Mac, and Windows, and other computer users as well. After all, it's not the
machine that counts the most—it's who's using it!<P>
<CENTER>
<HR SIZE=10 NOSHADE>
```

continues

Listing 14.2. continued

```
<APPLET code="RnbText.class" width=120 height=50>
  <param name=text value="Features">
</APPLET><P>
<B><A HREF="webpage.htm">Making Your Own Web Page</A><BR>
<A HREF="virus.htm">A Computer Virus Primer</A><BR>
<A HREF="protect.htm">Software Copyright Protection</A><BR>
<A HREF="dtp.htm">Explore the World of Desktop Publishing</A></B>
<P>
</FONT>
<HR SIZE=10 NOSHADE>
<ADDRESS>
<FONT SIZE=3>
Hawaiian Hard Drive<BR>
94-547 Ukee Street #308<BR>
Waipahu, HI 96797<P>
(808) 677-2464<P>
<A HREF="mailto:PDeptula@aol.com">PDeptula@aol.com</A>
</ADDRESS><P>
All stories are copyright, 1995-1996 by their authors.<BR>
The Java Applet on this page was designed by
<A HREF="http://www.crl.com/~integris">Integris Network Services</A>.<P>
</FONT>
</CENTER>
</BODY>
</HTML>
```

If you scroll down the page (Figure 14.6), you'll notice that another occurrence of the same RnbText.class Java applet is used again for the heading "Features." Once you include a Java applet on a page, no extra download time is incurred if you include another copy elsewhere. Note that visitors to your site will, however, need more computer power to keep both applets working at once. With small applets like this one, that isn't much of a concern—but you should avoid including more than one big, graphics-intensive applet on any page.

Generally speaking, you need to be more careful about overburdening the user's computer with too much to do than being careful about the speed with which applets download. This applet, for example, is only 3KB but takes quite a bit of resources to constantly update long strings of text.

Tip: Even though the latest versions of Netscape Navigator and Microsoft Explorer both support Java applets, many older and more feeble browsers still don't. So you should always make sure that any text displayed by a Java applet (or OLE component) is not strictly necessary for your page to make sense.

The Hawaiian Hard Drive page, for example, still looks fine when the words "Hawaii's Computer & Information Resource" and "Features" don't appear (see Figure 14.7).

Whenever you use modern enhancements such as Java applets or embedded media, it becomes especially important to test how your pages look in other common browsers

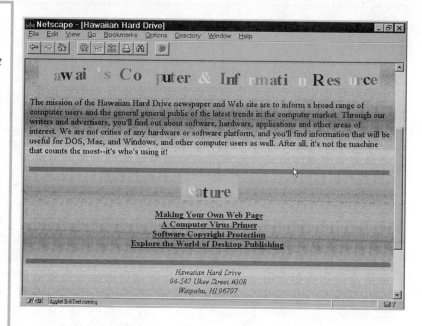

Figure 14.6.
If you include
more than one
copy of an applet
on the same
page, it still
needs to be
downloaded
only once.

besides Netscape Navigator. Figure 14.7 shows the page as it looks to Microsoft Internet Explorer 2.0 at 1024×768 resolution (the previous figures are all at 800×600 resolution, which is by far the most common today).

Figure 14.7.
In Microsoft
Internet Explorer
2.0 (shown here
at 1024×768
resolution), Java
applets don't
appear.

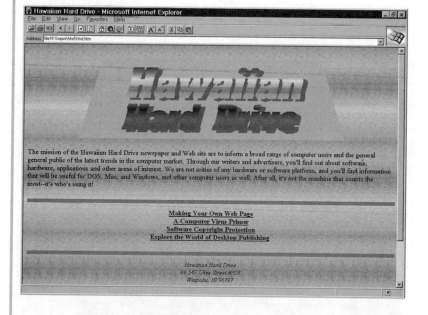

Most graphics that look good at 800×600 will look fine (though perhaps a bit small) at 1024×768, but often don't fare so well at the 640×480 resolution in Figure 14.8. As a rule of thumb, you should always make sure that all graphics, applets, and embedded media at least show enough information at 640×480 to be easily understood. Testing your pages at all three of these common window sizes is very important.

Most commercial online services have switched to Microsoft Explorer and Netscape Navigator instead of their old clunky browsers, too. So you can be assured of looking good to over 90% of the people on the Web if you test your pages with those two browsers. However, I'd highly recommend testing both with the current version (currently Explorer 3.0 and Navigator 2.0) *and* with the version before the current one (Explorer 2.0 and Navigator 1.2), because a lot of people are quite slow to upgrade once they get used to using something.

Tip: If you add an old text-based copy of Lynx for DOS to your list of test browsers, you can be sure to please virtually everybody—even the many vision-impaired people who use speech or Braille-reader enabled copies of Lynx to surf the Web.

Even if you don't test with Lynx, you can greatly enhance the readability of your pages for text-based browsers or users with slow modems by always including ALT= attributes in your IMG tags (for example, `<IMG SRC="hhd.gif" ALT="Hawaiian Hard Drive">`). This is an especially good idea if you use graphics for the title of your page, and even more so if the graphics are larger than 5KB or so.

A 13KB image such as the Hawaiian Hard Drive title may seem compact by modern multimedia file standards, but it will take about 13 seconds to load

Figure 14.8. The page doesn't look quite as perfect at 640×480 resolution, but the important information still shows.

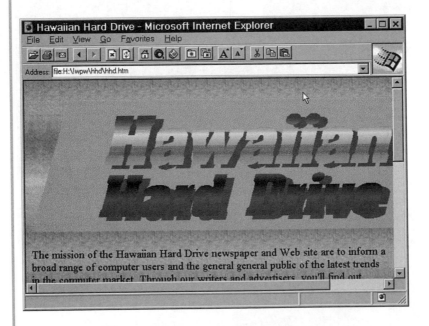

over a 14.4Kbps modem. So using ALT= can make the heading appear that much sooner for users of those modems.

Aloha!

If you have Microsoft Internet Explorer, or Netscape Navigator and a WAV-compatible plug-in, the Hawaiian Hard Drive page says "Aloha!" when you load it. Adding a little spoken message like this is pretty much a no-brainer: just record the sound with Windows Recorder or whatever software you like, and put a BGSOUND tag (for Explorer) and an EMBED tag (for Navigator) in your page like this:

```
<EMBED SRC="aloha.wav" HEIGHT=2 WIDTH=2>
<NOEMBED><BGSOUND SRC="aloha.wav">
   </NOEMBED>
```

The WIDTH and HEIGHT values make any display that your plug-in tries to put up so tiny that nobody will pay any attention to it. (Did you notice the tiny little white square just before the text starts on the /hhd/ hhd.htm page in Figure 14.5? I didn't think so.)

The NOEMBED tags aren't actually necessary yet, but including them is a good idea because you never know when a browser is going to start supporting both the Netscape and Microsoft extensions. The NOEMBED tags will ensure that any browser capable of playing the sound with the EMBED tag will definitely ignore the BGSOUND tag, and not try to play it twice or become otherwise confused.

Tip: If you prefer, you could insert a MIDI music file instead of a WAV sound file. The advantage of MIDI is that it is much more compact, so you can embed a lengthy song. The disadvantage is that the song must be instrumental (with no human voices), and the quality of the playback depends greatly on the quality of each listener's sound card. What sounds sensational on your $300 wavetable card and home stereo speakers may sound rather sickly on most people's el-cheapo multimedia kits.

I actually test MIDI files for the Web on the noisiest bargain-basement sound card and tinniest headset I have; If the music sounds good with that setup, I know it'll sound good on *any* setup.

For more details on using the BGSOUND and EMBED tags, refer to Chapter 4, "Putting Multimedia on Your Web Pages."

A Flashy and Flexible Online Business Page

One of the reasons we kept the Hawaiian Hard Drive site relatively simple is that it's primary purpose is to enhance and publicize an existing "offline" business. As a secondary endeavor to the printed newspaper, cost and time savings were at least as important as a strong presence on the Web.

Now we'll look at a business site where a bit more perfectionism might be in order: The Background Underground is a small Web site that serves as the sole worldwide sales outlet for a small selection of Web-related CD-ROM products. This site isn't there to "support" a business—the site *is* the business.

Small Is Beautiful

As with the other pages discussed in this chapter, a major priority in designing The Background Underground was keeping the size of the files to a minimum.

Tip: For a business site, a little figuring goes a long way toward making intelligent design decisions.

For example, before the redesign and name change from "Over the Rainbow," this site was getting around 5,000 hits per week. At current rates, that translates into a cost of about a dollar per month for every kilobyte on the page. So when I designed the page, I could equate some real financial numbers with previous sales figures to know how much bandwidth to budget.

Your mileage will vary, and other costs are usually involved for maintaining a good site. But if you design pages for any size commercial site, you should at least figure out the cost-per-kilobyte at projected levels of traffic so you have some idea how much your design choices actually cost *before* you make them.

As important as small file sizes are, it is even more important for an online business to successfully communicate what it offers. And more important than that is to offer something (preferably free) that will attract people to the site. The Background Underground manages this by giving away the best of its wares (background textures for Web pages and other uses) for free, and selling CD-ROMs packed with more backgrounds for those who just can't get enough of the stuff.

So what does this page need to say to its visitors? First, it needs to say, "Here's where you can get background textures free." Second, it needs to show them that the textures are attractive and unique. These two messages need to appear very quickly; the ability to click away at a moment's whim makes the Web the ultimate "short attention span theater."

To get the point across in a dramatic way, the page in Figures 14.9 and 14.10 uses a 26-image GIF animation. A new tiled image appears once per second, surrounding a prominent masthead. (In older browsers that don't support GIF animation, just the first image appears.) As Listing 14.3 reveals, the large graphic is made up of many small copies of the same multi-image GIF.

*Figure 14.9.
The colorful
border around
this masthead is
composed of 24
copies of a single
60×60-pixel
image (see /bgu/
bgu.htm on the
CD-ROM).*

*Figure 14.10.
The little tile is
actually a GIF
animation, so
the masthead
border changes
every second.*

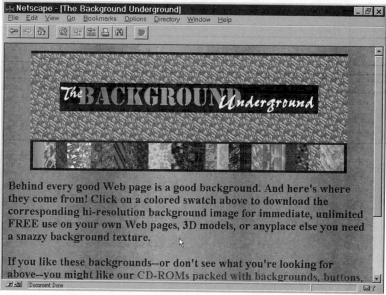

Listing 14.3. /bgu/bgu.htm.

```
<HTML>
<HEAD><TITLE>The Background Underground</TITLE></HEAD>
<BODY BACKGROUND="rainbow.jpg">
<CENTER>
<IMG SRC="topline.gif"><BR>
```

continues

Listing 14.3. continued

```
<IMG SRC="bgani.gif"><IMG SRC="bgani.gif"><IMG SRC="bgani.gif"><IMG
SRC="bgani.gif"><IMG SRC="bgani.gif"><IMG SRC="bgani.gif"><IMG
SRC="bgani.gif"><IMG SRC="bgani.gif"><IMG SRC="bgani.gif"><IMG
SRC="bgani.gif"><IMG SRC="bgani.gif"><BR>
<IMG SRC="bgani.gif"><IMG SRC="bgu.gif"
ALT="The Background Underground"><IMG SRC="bgani.gif"><BR>
<IMG SRC="bgani.gif"><IMG SRC="bgani.gif"><IMG SRC="bgani.gif"><IMG
SRC="bgani.gif"><IMG SRC="bgani.gif"><IMG SRC="bgani.gif"><IMG
SRC="bgani.gif"><IMG SRC="bgani.gif"><IMG SRC="bgani.gif"><IMG
SRC="bgani.gif"><IMG SRC="bgani.gif"><BR>
<IMG SRC="select.gif" USEMAP="select.map"><P>
</CENTER>
<FONT SIZE=5><B>Behind every good Web page is a good background. And
here's where they come from! Click on a colored swatch above to download
the corresponding hi-resolution background image for immediate, unlimited
FREE use on your own Web pages, 3D models, or anyplace else you need
a snazzy background texture.<P>
If you like these backgrounds--or don't see what you're looking for
above--you might like our <A HREF="bguorder.htm">CD-ROMs packed with
backgrounds, buttons, and beautiful Web page accents</A>.<P>
Then be sure to check out Gini Schmitz'
<A HREF="http://netletter.com/cameo/hotlist/hotlist.html">
Texture and Background Wonderland</A>, a hot hotlist of the best background
and Web page graphics sites on the Internet.<P>
</FONT>
</BODY></HTML>
```

Tip: Notice that there is *not* an embedded MIDI music file with this page, or with the GIF animation page on the CD-ROM. There's a good reason for this: Have you ever tried listening to music while looking at something rhythmically blinking, totally out of sync with the music? To paraphrase Charlie Brown: "Aaaaagh!"

If you want music and motion on the same page, please make a video clip or Shockwave movie where you can synchronize everything well enough to save your viewer's sanity! See Chapter 5, Chapter 6, "Do-It-Yourself Video," and Chapter 7, "Creating Interactive Animation with Shockwave and Friends," for help.

As usual, we employed some tricks to get a big brilliantly colorful image without using big graphics files. The GIF animation is actually tiny—just 60×60 pixels. Also, each of the images in the animation is just 16 colors. So the entire animation of 26 images turns out to be only 53KB. Because GIF animations start displaying when the first image is done downloading, the animation begins almost instantly and continues changing regularly at one-second intervals from then on.

Because each little 60×60 image is a reduced-size background tile, arranging 24 of them next to one another around the masthead makes them look like a giant 660×180-pixel animation with hundreds of unique colors! That this pops up in less than three seconds over a 28.8Kbps modem seems (to those of us who are used to waiting for huge graphics files) nothing short of miraculous.

By the time visitors look away from the first paragraph of text and the colorful animation, the interlaced 23KB image map underneath the masthead has completed loading—and they probably didn't even notice that it took over 10 seconds to do so.

Small Is Flexible

Another magical result of using tiles as decorative elements is that you can use the same tiles on a related page in a different arrangement. For example, the order form in Figure 14.11 omits the bottom row of tiles below the masthead to save space. But it will still load with almost no wait at all, because all the components that make up the assembled image will be in the browser's memory or cache from the previous page.

This not only saves time for visitors to the site, it saves money for the site owners because no additional graphics files will be downloaded from the server. So we get two thematic mastheads for the price of one! To sweeten the bargain just a little more, we even used a lone copy of the animated tile as a navigation button at the bottom of the order form (see Figure 14.12).

Breaking Up

All these snap-together graphics look great as long as the user has a big enough window to hold the entire assemblage. However, things tend to get a bit strange with smaller windows, as demonstrated in Figure 14.13. In this case, the "accident" is kind of neat looking in and of itself, and doesn't do anything bad enough to worry about. But if you design with tiles, be sure to test what happens in small windows to make sure that your page is still legible.

Figure 14.11. Because the tile animation and masthead are already in the browser's cache from the main page, the graphics on this order form appear instantly.

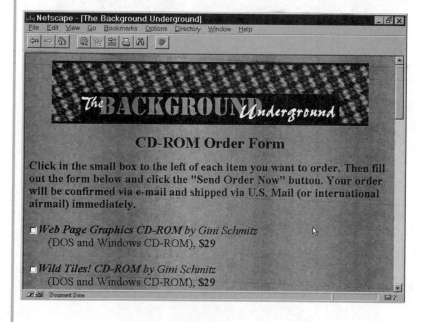

Figure 14.12.
A single copy of
the animated tile
from the
masthead border
makes a nice
icon for the
bottom of the
page, too.

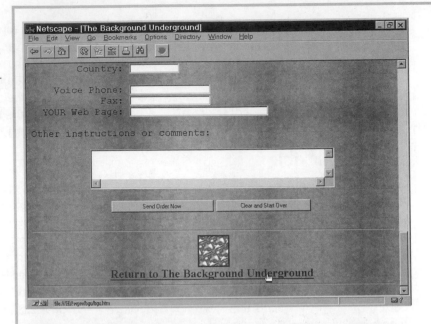

Figure 14.13.
When squeezed,
designs made
from small tiles
can fall apart.
But at least they
usually fall apart
in interesting and
attractive ways!

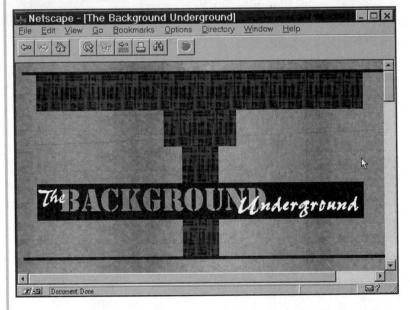

Even if you don't sell or give away background tiles, you may find a lot of potential uses for repeating tiles in Web page designs. There aren't many easier or more effective ways to get huge graphics or animations that download as fast as tiny ones do.

And by the way, just in case you need some background tiles to play with, we've included a selection of free tiles on the CD-ROM with this book, accessible from (where else) the Background Underground home page at /bgu/bgu.htm. If you want even more backgrounds, check out The Background Underground online at:

http://netletter.com/bgu/

I promise to add some more bells and whistles to the site by the time this book goes to print, so you'll discover more graphics and animation tricks there, too.

To Shock or Not To Shock?

Many of the effects on the pages presented in this chapter could be achieved quite easily—perhaps *more* easily—using Macromedia Director and Shockwave. Theoretically, "shocked" sites could wipe animated GIFs, embedded sounds, and image maps all into obsolescence with one fell swoop.

But in the real world, you need to invest a lot of money and time to get Director and either learn to use it or hire a seasoned "Director director." And in the real world, the percentage of Web surfers who have the Shockwave plug-in installed is still fairly low (albeit climbing fast). There is also a certain amount of time overhead involved in initiating the plug-in and downloading enough of the Shockwave movie to start playing, even with the new streaming animation feature.

The bottom line is that, for the vast majority of Web pages, developing Director animations would be like taking a helicopter to the grocery store.

This doesn't mean that I don't think Shockwave is a major contribution to the welfare of all humankind. Of course it is. For example, I'm developing a site for a high-end jewelry company where we need flying logos and interactive zooming and the whole nine yards. For stuff like that, Director has no real competition (see Figure 14.14).

If you're looking to invest some serious development effort into one or more major sites, or you just spent hundreds of dollars for Director and feel like you ought to use the darn thing for heaven's sake, better turn to Chapter 7 now.

For your first few small-business or personal home pages, though?… Get real.

Figure 14.14.
Don't underesti-
mate the
learning curve,
but once you get
the hang of it,
Director gives
you nearly
unlimited power
for producing
animated Web
sites.

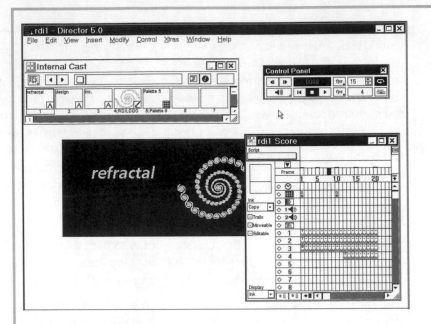

What's Next?

Now that we're on the topic of reality and major sites, a warning: Better install the Netscape Live3D virtual reality plug-in and those new 300-watt Bose speakers for the next chapter. The pages in this chapter were strictly practical, for today's Web site. Chapter 15, "The High-Bandwidth Site of the Future," as you might have guessed, steps into the ultimate multimedia entertainment site of tomorrow.

The High-Bandwidth Site of the Future

chapter 15

by Dick Oliver

The mantra of successful multimedia CD-ROM developers and marketers has been, "It's the content, stupid." In other words, the beauty and utility of the content matter a lot more than how much content there is, how fast it displays, or how many technical bells and whistles you add to it. The same mantra rings true for the Web.

After you've got the content, there are essentially three other factors to consider: bandwidth, bandwidth, and bandwidth. The number of bytes per second that fly from your site to most of your visitors is by far the most significant factor in determining what you put on your pages today.

In this chapter you'll see a site that isn't very practical, given the current bandwidth of the modem-toting masses. However, literally hundreds of companies are rushing to provide high-bandwidth connections via TV cables, ADSL (Asychronous Digital Subscriber Lines), and "copper optics" technologies, satellite services, and pumped-up cellular connections. If even a few of them succeed, the kind of site you see here will become commonplace.

In the meantime, we have the luxury of a CD-ROM drive at hand so you can enjoy the music and video as if you had your own T1 line straight to the site and were its only bandwidth-hogging visitor.

Raw Materials

If you're going to make a multimedia site, you've got to start with some multimedia. For the examples in this chapter, I started with an AVI music video, a WAV sound file, and a simple logo in a WMF graphics file.

All this content was produced by The Sponge Awareness Foundation, or SAF—a couple of mildly deranged young men with too much recording equipment on their hands. Their songs have gotten some national play on the *Dr. Demento* radio show, and the video was used as a sample file on some digital video software CD-ROMs. Continuing in the spirit of that proud heritage, a cutting-edge Web site on the *Web Page Wizardry* CD-ROM seemed in order. (In case you're wondering, no, I'm not one of the two SAF members—despite the coincidence of also being a mildly deranged young man with too much equipment on my hands.)

Capturing Graphics

Notably lacking from this formidable arsenal of content were any thematic icons or background textures, but then again, videos contain a lot of pictures, right? So, I just used the Capture ¦ Area command in Paint Shop Pro to steal some frames from the AVI video, and then painted out the backgrounds to make transparent GIF icons, as shown in Figure 15.1. (Paint Shop Pro is a shareware graphics program included on the CD-ROM with this book and discussed in Chapters 1,"Bigger, Faster, Better Graphics" and 2, "Wild Type, Far-Out Layouts, and Cheap HTML Tricks.")

Figure 15.1. Paint Shop Pro can capture anything you can display on your screen for use as a Web page graphic, including the frames in this AVI video.

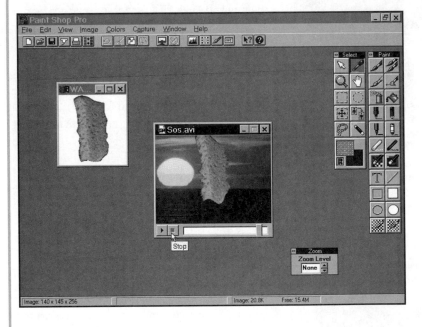

Without too much work, you could use Paint Shop Pro to carefully paint the background out from around icons like the dancing sponge in Figure 15.1. But this is the ultimate modern site, so I allowed myself to indulge in the power of Adobe Photoshop's color range selection feature, which made the job much easier and faster.

It's up to you to decide if you're going to be doing this sort of thing often enough to justify the big bucks for Photoshop or another pricey commercial graphics program. Most Webmasters will find it easier and faster to use Paint Shop Pro than to take the time to learn (and pay for) Photoshop.

Instant Backgrounds

A seriously rocking band like SAF clearly requires a seriously rocking background for its Web page. I snagged a thematic design from the climactic ending scene in the music video, where the "Land Where Sponges Never Die" morphs and warps into oblivion. Now, I could have used the paint-and-paste technique described in Chapter 2 for making tilable backgrounds, but there's an even quicker way to tile abstract designs such as this one. Figure 15.2 and the numbered steps that follow it describe how.

1. Open any graphic in Paint Shop Pro, and do any cropping or image manipulation you want. Make sure it is a 256-color or 16-color image, and not a true-color image. (The

Figure 15.2. The Mirror and Flip commands were used to turn part of this video frame into a background graphic.

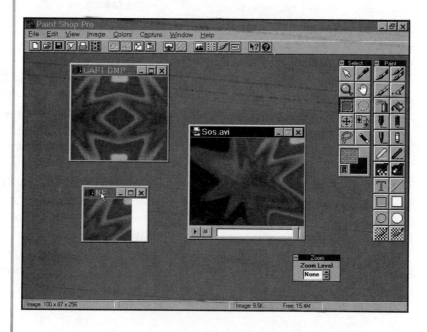

Mirror and Flip commands in step 4 work slightly differently for true-color images, for some strange reason.)

2. Select Image ¦ Enlarge Canvas and enlarge the image to twice as wide and twice as tall as it is now. (Remember, the dimensions of the image are always displayed in the lower-left corner of the Paint Shop Pro window.) Make sure that Center Image is *not* selected, and click OK.

3. Use the rectangular selection tool to carefully select the original image area, and select Edit ¦ Copy.

4. Select the following commands, in this order:

   Image ¦ Mirror

   Edit ¦ Paste ¦ Into Selection

   Image ¦ Flip

   Edit ¦ Paste ¦ Into Selection

   Image ¦ Mirror

   Edit ¦ Paste ¦ Into Selection

5. You should now have an abstract design that will tile seamlessly as a background! Before saving it, you may want to change its size; select Colors ¦ Adjust to lighten or darken it, and perhaps select Image ¦ Normal Filters ¦ Blur More to make the edges less severe.

The final tile is `/saf/theland.jpg` on the CD-ROM and is pictured in all the rest of the figures in this chapter. I used the same technique to turn part of the sky of the "Land Where Sponges Never Die" into another background tile, `/saf/theland2.jpg`. This is used behind the spinning three-dimensional virtual reality logo in `/saf/saf3d.htm`.

A 3D Virtual Reality Logo

By the way, did I mention yet that there's a spinning 3D virtual reality logo in `/saf/saf3d.htm`?

Sure, we could have just put the SAF logo graphic at the top of a home page and called it good. But how about one of those much-too-cool interactive virtual reality thingamabobs instead? Huh? Huh? Now we're talking.

Way Cool, but Way Easy

The sophisticated way to pull something like this off would be to go into Arena Design VRML (or hack together some VRML by hand) to model each line and shape in the logo with shiny 3D shapes and surfaces. But doing a fairly complex logo that way would probably involve paying a 3D modeling guru (like me) more money than SAF made on their entire 1992 Crumbling City tour of upstate New York. So, yeah, let's think "way cool." But let's think "way easy" (and "way cheap") while we're thinking "way cool," okay?

Time for the old transparent-bitmap-on-a-box trick! Check out the absurdly simple VRML file in Listing 15.1. Could a single cube at the default size possibly be cool enough to honor the SAF? You bet. As Figure 15.3 demonstrates, this brain-dead VRML cube actually turns out to make brain-boggling rotating transparent logos in front of a dramatic moving backdrop.

Listing 15.1. /saf/safcube.wrl

```
#VRML V1.0 ascii
DEF BackgroundImage Info { string "THELAND2.jpg" }
Separator {
    Texture2 { filename "saf.gif" }
    Material { diffuseColor 0 0 1 }
    Cube {}
}
```

Figure 15.3. The simple cube described in Listing 15.1 becomes a complex interactive rendering when embedded in a Web page (/saf/ saf3d.htm).

Embedding VRML in a Web Page

To see the cube in action, open the /saf/saf3d.htm document. If you have a VRML-enabled browser, you'll see the logo in Figure 15.4, and you can move it around by grabbing it with your mouse. (With Live3D, the left button zooms and pans while the right button rotates.) If you don't have a VRML-enabled browser, you'll see the 3D-looking image in Figure 15.5, but mouse clicking and dragging will have no effect on it.

*Figure 15.4.
At first, the cube
looks like a
regular two-
dimensional
logo, but when
you grab it with
your mouse, you
can spin and
zoom around as
shown in Figure
15.3.*

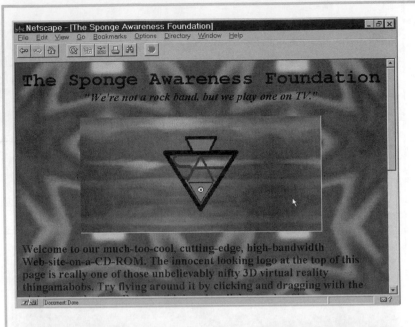

*Figure 15.5.
This image, as
seen in Internet
Explorer 2.0, is
only a simulated
snapshot of a 3D
object. It doesn't
move no matter
what you do.*

Microsoft Internet Explorer 3.0 and Netscape 2.0 plug-ins, such as Live3D, use two different HTML commands to embed VRML worlds into a Web page. Here's how to add the `safecube.wrl` to a page so that both of these browsers will treat it the same:

```
<EMBED SRC="safcube.wrl" WIDTH=500 HEIGHT=240>
<NOEMBED>
<IMG SRC="safsub.gif" DYNASRC="safecube.wrl" WIDTH=500 HEIGHT=240>
</NOEMBED>
```

If you're using Netscape with any VRML plug-in, the EMBED tag will work. Otherwise, the IMG tag will try the Microsoft-style DYNASRC attribute to insert a 3D world. If both of these fail (meaning you don't have a VRML-enabled browser), the IMG tag will just display the safsub.gif image in Figure 15.5.

Tip: To make the safsub.gif image, I used Paint Shop Pro's Capture ¦ Area command to take a screen shot of Netscape Live3D while it was displaying the VRML cube. This is a handy way to give non-VRML users at least a peek at what they're missing!

Links Ahoy!

After whetting visitors' appetites with this virtual reality treat, we gave them some links to the multimedia parts of this multimedia site (see Figure 15.6). As you look over the code for this whole page in Listing 15.2, you may note that we staggered the icons through a creative use of the IMG ALIGN="left" attribute. The only other formatting tricks used on this page are some font size and color changes to make the text readable over such a loud background.

Figure 15.6. Staggered icons, made with IMG ALIGN="left", add a little more variety to this otherwise ordinary list of links (/saf/saf3d.htm).

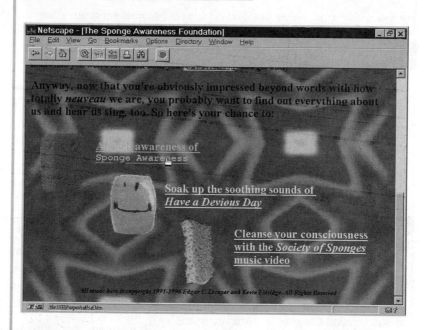

Listing 15.2. /saf/saf3d.htm.

```
<HTML>
<HEAD><TITLE>The Sponge Awareness Foundation</TITLE></HEAD>
<BODY BACKGROUND="theland.jpg"
  TEXT="black" VLINK="silver" LINK="yellow" BGCOLOR="red">
<CENTER>
```

continues

Listing 15.2. continued

```
<TT><FONT SIZE=7><B>The Sponge Awareness Foundation</B></FONT></TT><BR>
<FONT SIZE=5>
<I><B>"We're not a rock band, but we play one on TV."</B></I></FONT><P>
<EMBED SRC="safcube.wrl" WIDTH=500 HEIGHT=240>
<NOEMBED><IMG SRC="safsub.gif" DYNASRC="safecube.wrl"
WIDTH=500 HEIGHT=240></NOEMBED><P>
</CENTER>

<FONT SIZE=5><B>Welcome to our much-too-cool, cutting-edge, high-bandwidth
Web-site-on-a-CD-ROM. The innocent looking logo at the top of this page is
really one of those unbelievably nifty 3D virtual reality thingamabobs.
Try flying around it by clicking and dragging with the right mouse button.
Bet you think we're slick now, hey?!

<FONT SIZE=4>(You do if you have Live3D or another VRML plug-in installed,
that is. Otherwise, you can click till the cows come home and you won't see
much until you <A HREF="http://home.netscape.com/">go to Netscape</A> and
get one. Or if you're using an old-fashioned  VRML helper app, you can
<A HREF="safcube.wrl" click here to view the 3D logo</A>.)<P></FONT>

Anyway, now that you're obviously impressed beyond words with how totally
<I>neuveau</I> we are, you probably want to find out everything about us
and hear us sing, too. So here's your chance to:</B><P></FONT>

<A HREF="saf.htm"><IMG SRC="engorged.gif" ALIGN="left" BORDER=0><BR>
<H2>Absorb awareness of <BR><TT>Sponge Awareness</TT></A></H2>
<A HREF="devious.htm"><IMG SRC="devious.gif" ALIGN="left" BORDER=0><BR>
<H2>Soak up the soothing sounds of <BR><I>Have a Devious Day</I></A></H2>
<A HREF="sos.htm"><IMG SRC="warped.gif" ALIGN="left" BORDER=0><BR>
<H2><B>Cleanse your consciousness with the <I>Society of Sponges</I>
music video</A></H2>
<BR CLEAR="all"><P>
<CENTER><FONT SIZE=2>
<I>All music here is copyright 1991-1996 Edgar C. Lecuyer and Kevin Eldridge.
All Rights Reserved</I></FONT></CENTER>
</BODY>
</HTML>
```

Yet Another GIF Animation

If you've read Chapter 3, "Animation the Easy Way: Multi-Image GIFs" and Chapter 14, "The Home Page of Your Dreams, To-day!" you've probably figured out that I *like* GIF animations. It probably won't be a big surprise, then, when you load `/saf/saf.htm` or click on the `Absorb awareness of Sponge Awareness` link in the `saf3d.htm` document.

Sure enough, I couldn't resist. Figures 15.7 and 15.8 confirm that the image at the top of `/saf/saf.htm` is just what you expected: flashing colors, winking eye, that kind of

Figure 15.7.
An ordinary
boring logo on a
party site like
this one? No
way (/saf/
saf.htm).

thing. I won't list the HTML for this page because it's nothing too special. Chapter 3 will give you the skinny on how to make GIF animations like this if you haven't become addicted to them already.

Figure 15.8.
Even a tiny touch
of color
animation can
add a lot of spice
to a bland page
of text (/saf/
saf.htm).

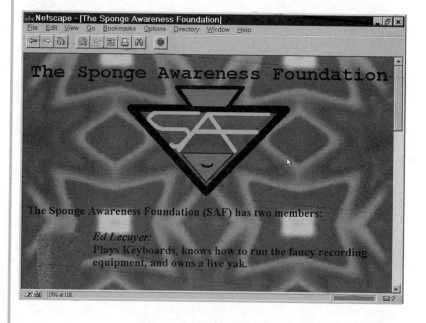

Sound Check

Making a full-length song play when a page loads is no different than playing a quick sound bite like the "Aloha!" discussed in Chapter 14. The simplicity of Listing 15.3 is proof that it doesn't take rocket science to blast rock and roll through a Web page.

Notice that both the Netscape EMBED tag and the Microsoft BGSOUND tag are included, and that a link is also provided for people who only have a helper app such as Windows Media Player.

The only other thing to notice about this document is that the 400-pixel width of the background combined with a centered graphic make a lovely symmetrical design when viewed at 800×600 resolution (see Figure 15.9). This doesn't look as nice at other window sizes, but so many people use 800×600 resolution that effects like this are well worth cultivating.

Figure 15.9. People who view this page at 800×600 resolution get an extra nice visual layout to complement the music they hear.

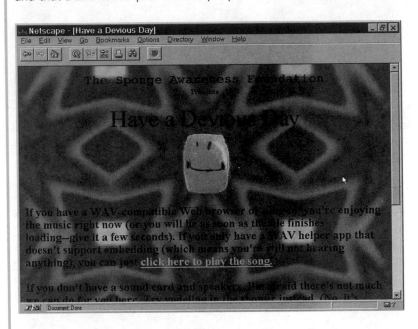

Listing 15.3. /saf/devious.htm.

```
<HTML>
<HEAD><TITLE>Have a Devious Day</TITLE></HEAD>
<BODY BACKGROUND="theland.jpg"
  BGCOLOR="red" TEXT="black" LINK="yellow" VLINK="silver">
<CENTER>
<FONT SIZE=6><TT><B>The Sponge Awareness Foundation</B></TT></FONT><BR>
<B>Presents</B><P>
<FONT SIZE=7>Have a Devious Day</FONT><BR>
<IMG SRC="devious.gif">

<EMBED SRC="devious.wav" WIDTH=2 HEIGHT=2>
<NOEMBED><BGSOUND="devious.wav"></NOEMBED>

</CENTER>
<FONT SIZE=5><B>
```

```
If you have a WAV-compatible Web browser or plug-in, you're enjoying the
music right now (or you will be as soon as the file finishes loading--give
it a few seconds). If you only have a WAV helper app that doesn't support
embedding (which means you're still not hearing anything), you can just
<A HREF="devious.wav">click here to play the song.</A><P>
If you don't have a sound card and speakers, I'm afraid there's not much
we can do for you here. Try yodeling in the shower instead.
(No, it's fun--really!)<P>
Oh, did we mention that this song, recorded in 1992, has never before been
publicly released? So you're pretty lucky to have this opportunity to hear
it, don't you think? We thought so.<P>
<CENTER>
<A HREF="saf3d.htm"><BR>
<IMG SRC="saf3d.gif" BORDER=0><BR>Click your heels three times, Dorothy...</A>
</CENTER>
</B></FONT>
</BODY>
</HTML>
```

The TV Table

Embedding video that is compatible with both the Netscape and Microsoft extensions to HTML is as simple as embedding sound or VRML files. On the /saf/sos.htm page pictured in Figure 15.10, I added nested table borders around the video window, so viewers could get that cozy and comfortable boob-tube feeling even before the video begins.

Writing the actual HTML to implement was just slightly easier than programming the clock on my VCR. (Okay, yeah, it was a lot easier. The real reason you can't buy books about VCR programming is that they can't find any authors who have actually figured it out.) As with the embedded VRML world, the EMBED, NOEMBED, IMG DYNSRC, and IMG SRC tags are all used together:

```
<EMBED SRC="sos.avi" WIDTH=320
  HEIGHT=200>
<NOEMBED>
<IMG DYNASRC="sos.avi" WIDTH=320
  HEIGHT=200 SRC="sponges.jpg">
</NOEMBED>
```

If you're using Netscape Navigator 2.0 (or higher) and an AVI plug-in is installed, it will play sos.avi using the EMBED tag (see Figure 15.10). If no AVI plug-in is installed, or if a non-Netscape browser is being used, the IMG tag comes into play. If Microsoft Internet Explorer 3.0 is being used, it sees the DYNASRC attribute and embeds the sos.avi video. Any other browser will just see the IMG attribute and display sponges.jpg instead (see Figure 15.11). Isn't standardization wonderful?

And the plot thickens: If a user of an aging browser sees those sponges just sitting there, but still wants to see the video, she or he can click on the link provided a little farther down the page to display the video in a separate window (see Figure 15.12). If this page were online instead of on a CD-ROM, those users would have to wait for the whole video to download before they could start viewing it.

Figure 15.10.
Make it look like
a TV, and
Americans will
watch anything.

Figure 15.11.
Browsers that
don't support
embedded video
(such as Explorer
2.0) will politely
display a still
image instead.

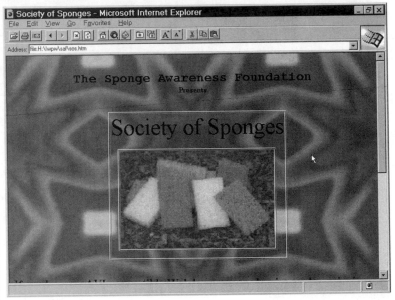

Listing 15.4 reveals the whole sos.htm document, just to prove there's nothing else fishy up my sleeve this time.

Figure 15.12.
Almost
everybody has
some sort of
helper app to
display video
clips, so you
should always
provide a
clickable link to
your media even
if you also
embed it.

Listing 15.4. /saf/sos.htm.

```
<HTML>
<HEAD><TITLE>Society of Sponges</TITLE></HEAD>
<BODY BACKGROUND="theland.jpg"
  BGCOLOR="red" TEXT="black" LINK="yellow" VLINK="silver">
<CENTER>
<FONT SIZE=6><TT><B>The Sponge Awareness Foundation</B></TT></FONT><BR>
<B>Presents</B><P>
<TABLE BORDER=20>
<TR><TD>
<FONT SIZE=7>Society of Sponges</FONT><BR>
<TABLE BORDER=15>
<TR><TD><EMBED SRC="sos.avi" WIDTH=320 HEIGHT=200>
<NOEMBED>
<IMG DYNASRC="sos.avi" WIDTH=320 HEIGHT=200 SRC="sponges.jpg">
</NOEMBED></TD></TR>
</TABLE>
</TD></TR></TABLE>
</CENTER>
<FONT SIZE=5><B>
If you have an AVI-compatible Web browser or plug-in, you're enjoying a
music video right now. If not, well, hey, what's the problem? Come on,
this is the '90s. Go to <A HREF="../programs.htm">the software page on
this CD-ROM</A> and install a video plug-in already. And while you're at
it, check out Photomorph 2, the program used to make the Society of Sponges
video. It's on the CD-ROM, too!<P>
Or, if you're using Microsoft Explorer 2.0 or some hokey helper app that
plays AVI videos in a window, I guess you could just <A HREF="sos.avi">click
here to play the video</A>.<P>
<CENTER>
<A HREF="saf3d.htm"><BR>
<IMG SRC="saf3d.gif" BORDER=0><BR>Enough of this. Take me home now.</A>
```

continues

Listing 15.4. continued

```
</CENTER>
</B></FONT>
</BODY>
</HTML>
```

Tip: If this were *really and truly* the high-bandwidth site of the far distant future, we could make a bigger table full of multiple copies of the video for that totally hip "TV store" look.

Such things are easy enough to code in HTML. Now if somebody would just run fiber optics to every home and business in the world already....

Onward and Upward!

The sample pages in this chapter obviously haven't even begun to exhaust the possibilities for enhancing this modern site. Here are some of the ways to add even more cutting-edge features to this site:

✦ Add an interactive multimedia animation like the ones discussed in Chapter 7, "Creating Interactive Animation with Shockwave and Friends."

✦ Use ActiveX controls or OCX-compatible plug-ins to link Windows programs directly into the Web page, as discussed in Chapter 11, "ActiveX and Object Linking and Embedding (OLE)."

✦ Insert Java applets as demonstrated in Chapter 12, "Finding and Using the Hottest Java Applets," and Chapter 14, "The Home Page of Your Dreams, Today!"

✦ Use JavaScript or Visual Basic to link parts of the page together, as suggested in Chapter 13, "Combining Multiple Media Formats."

If you ever outgrow all the options that this book has introduced, at that point, you're probably ready to hire (or become) a programmer, and start producing your own custom OC components, Java applets, or CGI scripts. The many prebuilt components and programs included on the *Web Page Wizardry* CD-ROM should give you an idea of the power and flexibility that you can gain from custom programming, but of course, the intricate art of programming itself is far beyond the scope of this book.

A no less ambitious way to add sophistication to a high-bandwidth site is to improve the production quality of the audiovisual media files you post there. However, this book would need many thousands more pages if it were to include a complete course on cinematography and interactive multimedia production!

What this book has given you is the chance to fully participate in the world of online, interactive media today. And those who are involved today will undoubtedly be a step ahead tomorrow, when professional-quality productions can be successfully served over the Internet (or the speedier parts of it, at least).

As the technical and economic barriers continue to come down, a 21st-century Renaissance of multisensory, interactive art is almost certain to follow. With the techniques and examples in this book, you should be ready to enjoy that Renaissance in style. Looks like it's going to be a great century!

Appendixes

part **VI**

appendix A

by Dick Oliver

HTML in a Nutshell

This book assumes that you are already familiar with basic Hypertext Markup Language (HTML), the language used to produce Web pages. But just in case you're new at it, this appendix gives you the basics you need to know to get started with HTML. Then you'll want to turn to the other chapters to discover the full range of tricks and techniques you can use to make your Web pages shine.

Create It

Say you've got a photo and a word processor file with some text that you want to put on the Web. Here's how to do it, fast. First, get your materials ready. Scan the photo, or take it to a graphics service bureau to be scanned. Use the Image ¦ Resample command in Paint Shop Pro (a shareware graphics program you'll find on the *Web Page Wizardry* CD-ROM) to change the size of the graphics file to around 200 pixels square, and save it in the GIF or JPEG format. Use JPEG for photos and larger images; use GIF for line art or logos.

Save the text in plain ASCII format with line breaks only at the end of each paragraph. You can use any word processor or text editor to mark up this text and make it into a Web page as explained in the following sections. Or you can use a dedicated Web page editing program, such as HTML Assistant, which you'll find on the CD-ROM in this book.

Mark It Up

To turn your plain text file into a Web page, you must add special formatting codes called *HTML tags*. This process is called marking up the text. HTML stands for *Hypertext Markup Language*.

Add the following lines to the beginning of your text file:

```
<HTML>
<HEAD>
<TITLE>My Very Special Page</TITLE>
</HEAD>
<BODY>
```

You may want to use a title different than "My Very Special Page." Though, you must admit it has a certain ring to it. The text you enter between the `<TITLE>` and `</TITLE>` tags doesn't appear on your Web page. It is the name given to the Netscape window when the page is loaded and the name is placed on someone's bookmark list when he or she saves the location of your page.

Now you can mark up your text, which should all go after the `<BODY>` tag shown in the preceding code. If you want a big heading at the top, put an `<H1>` tag at the beginning of the heading and an `</H1>` tag at the end of the heading, as in the following line:

```
<H1>Welcome to My Very Special Page</H1>
```

You can use `<H2>` and `</H2>` to make a slightly smaller heading or `<H3>` and `</H3>` to make an even smaller subheading. (You can go down to H6, but it's usually hard to tell H4, H5, and H6 apart.)

At the end of each paragraph, put a `<P>` tag. If you want some text to be italicized, put `<I>` in front of it and `</I>` after it. Similarly,

`<B>` and `</B>` make boldface text, as shown in the following example:

```
I'm so <I>very</I> sure that you'll love
  my page <B>very much</B>.<P>
I thank you <I>very</I> sincerely for
  stopping by <I>My Very Special Page
  </I>.<P>
```

You can place a horizontal rule (a line across the page) with the `<HR>` tag. To end a line (without inserting a blank line between paragraphs), use the `<BR>` tag. Like `<P>`, these tags *don't* need any corresponding `</HR>` or `</BR>` tags.

You can also indicate numbered or bulleted lists. Numbered lists are called ordered lists; they begin with the `<OL>` tag and end with `</OL>`. The browser automatically adds the numbers (1, 2, 3, and so on). Bulleted lists are called unordered lists; they begin with `<UL>` and end with `</UL>`. Each new item on the list starts with an `<LI>` tag, and you can put an optional `</LI>` tag at the end of each line if you want to. For example this:

```
<OL>
  <LI>The phone rings.
  <LI>Pick it up.
<LI>Say, "Paul's pachyderm packing. If it
  weighs a ton, we'll ship you one."
</OL>
```

would result in the following display:

1. The phone rings.
2. Pick it up.
3. Say, "Paul's pachyderm packing. If it weighs a ton, we'll ship you one."

At the end of the text, you must put the following lines to close the `<HTML>` and `<BODY>` tags you put at the beginning of the text:

```
</BODY>
</HTML>
```

That's really all you need to know to create a Web page. You can now save your document as plain text, and then load it in Netscape Navigator with File ¦ Open File. It's a page!

Adding Images

To add that photo, choose where you want to put it in relation to the text (probably near the beginning), and insert the following:

```
<IMG SRC="myphoto.gif" ALIGN="top">Here
  I am!<P>
```

If your graphics file has a different name than `myphoto.gif`, insert that name instead. You can also put any message you want instead of `Here I am!`, but keep it short because only the first line of text will be lined up with the top of the picture, and you can never be sure exactly how much space will be available for that line on the reader's screen.

Tip: Netscape Navigator 2.0 supports inclusion of GIF and JPEG images only. Microsoft Internet Explorer 3.0 also includes support for BMP and PNG images, and Netscape will probably support these formats in its next release. Other image formats can be viewed using external helper applications and plug-ins, but you should generally convert all images to GIF and JPEG for inclusion in the main body of a Web page.

To line up the caption with the bottom or middle of the photo instead of the top, enter `ALIGN="bottom"` or `ALIGN="middle"` instead of `ALIGN="top"`. If you say `ALIGN="left"`, the image will be placed on the left edge of the window, and the text will wrap around the right side of it. `ALIGN="right"` puts the image on the right side of the window with text wrapping around its left side.

You also can put a rectangular border around the image by including `BORDER="1"` for a one-pixel border; use higher numbers for thicker borders.

HTML gives you a way to send a special message to readers who don't see your graphics. You can give each image an `ALT=` attribute that displays the text you specify whenever the image itself can't be shown, or while users are waiting for the image to download.

Getting Hyper

The *hyper* in hypertext means you can hop and skip around the Web like a psychotic spider. Until you add a hyperlink or two to that page of yours, it's just a dead-end thread and not part of the Web at all. Adding a link is easy. In front of the text or image that you want to highlight as a link, put the following:

```
<A HREF="http://someplace.com/home.html">
```

Then put an `</A>` tag after the link, so the whole thing looks like this:

```
<A HREF="http://someplace.com/
  home.html">Click here to go someplace.
</A>
```

Of course, you can put any URL where `http://someplace.com/home.html` is in the preceding example. (In case you're wondering, the A stands for Anchor, which is another name for a link, and HREF stands for hypertext reference.)

Though there are many more things you can do to spice up your Web pages, the tags discussed so far in this brief tutorial are really all you need to make a large variety of Web pages.

Post It

Once you've got a page, you need to put it on a Web server (a computer permanently connected to the Internet and equipped to send out Web pages upon request). If you run your own Web server, this procedure is simply a matter of copying the file to the right directory, but most people use an Internet service provider's Web server to host their pages. Almost all service providers that offer Internet access also now offer space to place your own Web pages for little or no additional cost.

To upload a page to your Web site, you need to use the file transfer protocol (ftp). Though a specialized ftp program, such as `CuteFTP` (on the CD-ROM in this book), offers the most control for managing files, you can now use Netscape Navigator to upload your pages if you prefer. Follow these steps:

Note: The following procedure will not work if you are posting Web pages to CompuServe and some other online services that require you to use their proprietary software for posting files.

1. Enter the address of your Web directory in Netscape Navigator's Location box, as in the following example:

   `ftp://myname:mypassword@myisp.net/home/web/wherever/`

   Put your username and password for accessing the site instead of *myname* and *mypassword*, your Internet service provider's address instead of *myisp.net*, and the top-level directory where your Web pages reside instead of */home/web/wherever/*.

2. Drag the icons for the HTML and graphics files you want to upload from any Windows 95 file-management program (such as Windows Explorer) into the Netscape Navigator window.

3. A dialog box appears and asks you whether you want to upload the files. Click OK, and wait while the files are transferred.

4. Test your page by clicking on the HTML you just uploaded in the ftp directory listing (in the Netscape window). You're on the Web!

Some other Web browsers support similar ftp upload capabilities.

The Fancy Stuff

Table A.1 summarizes the most commonly used tags. As you can see, they are easy to learn and use.

Table A.1. The most common HTML tags.

Usage	Opening Tag	Closing Tag
Entire document	<HTML>	</HTML>
Document header	<HEAD>	</HEAD>
Title (within header)	<TITLE>	</TITLE>
Document body	<BODY>	</BODY>
Top-level heading	<H1>	</H1>
Second-level heading	<H2>	</H2>
Third-level heading	<H3>	</H3>
Italic text	<I>	</I>
Bold text	<B>	</B>
Monospaced text	<TT>	</TT>
New paragraph	<P>	(</P> is optional)
Line break (within a paragraph)	 	
Horizontal rule	<HR>	
Ordered (numbered) list	<OL>	</OL>
Unordered (bulleted) list	<UL>	</UL>
New line in list	<LI>	(</LI> is optional)
Image	<IMG>	
Anchor/link	<A>	</A>

The latest versions of most Web browsers also support a number of new and proposed extensions to HTML. Besides these tags, these extensions give you the ability to do these things:

+ Add background images, multicolored text, and other flashy stuff
+ Format complex information (both text and images) into tables
+ Display multiple documents at once in resizable frames
+ Map different parts of an image to different links
+ Automatically reload or change pages without user intervention
+ Include a wide variety of media types in your Web pages

Appendix B, "HTML Quick-Reference" is a compact summary of all the HTML tags currently supported by Netscape Navigator or Microsoft Internet Explorer. (These are by far the two most popular browser programs.)

You'll learn how to use many of the more advanced tags in the chapters throughout this book, but you may also want to refer to the online documentation at

```
http://home.netscape.com/
```

and

```
http://www.microsoft.com/
```

for details on exactly which tags each of
these companies' browsers can handle.

HTML Quick-Reference

This appendix is a reference to the HTML tags you can use in your documents. Unless otherwise noted, all of the tags listed here are supported by both Netscape Navigator 2.0 and Microsoft Explorer 3.0. Note that some other browsers do not support all the tags listed, and that most of the tags listed as (MS) are supported in the preliminary testing versions of Netscape 3.0.

There are also a few tags, most notably <OBJECT> and several new table tags, that were not completely finalized when this book went to print. Refer to the Netscape (http://home.netscape.com/) or Microsoft (http://www.microsoft.com/) Web sites for details on these and other late-breaking changes to the new HTML 3.0 standard.

HTML Tags

These tags are used to create a basic HTML page with text, headings, and lists. An (MS) beside the attribute indicates Microsoft.

appendix B

by Dick Oliver

Comments

`<!-- ... -->`   Creates a comment. Can also be used to hide JavaScript from browsers that do not support it.

Structure Tags

`<HTML>...</HTML>`   Encloses the entire HTML document.

`<HEAD>...</HEAD>`   Encloses the head of the HTML document.

`<BODY>...</BODY>`   Encloses the body (text and tags) of the HTML document.

Attributes:

`BACKGROUND="..."`	The name or URL of the image to tile on the page background.
`BGCOLOR="..."`	The color of the page background.
`TEXT="..."`	The color of the page's text.
`LINK="..."`	The color of unfollowed links.
`ALINK="..."`	The color of activated links.
`VLINK="..."`	The color of followed links.
`BGPROPERTIES="..."`(MS)	Properties of a background image. Currently allows only the value FIXED, which prevents the background image from scrolling.
`TOPMARGIN="..."`(MS)	Top margin of the page, in pixels.
`BOTTOMMARGIN="..."`(MS)	Bottom margin of the page, in pixels.

`<BASE>`   Indicates the full URL of the current document. This optional tag is used within `<HEAD>`.

Attributes:

`HREF="..."`	The full URL of this document.

`<ISINDEX>`   Indicates that this document is a gateway script that allows searches.

Attributes:

`PROMPT="..."`	The prompt for the search field.
`ACTION="..."`	Gateway program to which the search string should be passed.

<LINK>   Indicates a link between this document and some other document. Generally used only by HTML-generating tools. <LINK> represents a link from this entire document to another, as opposed to <A>, which can create multiple links in the document. Not commonly used.

Attributes:

`HREF="..."`	The URL of the document to call when the link is activated.
`NAME="..."`	If the document is to be considered an anchor, the name of that anchor.
`REL="..."`	The relationship between the linked-to document and the current document; for example, `"TOC"` or `"Glossary"`.
`REV="..."`	A reverse relationship between the current document and the linked-to document.
`URN="..."`	A Uniform Resource Number (URN), a unique identifier different from the URL in `HREF`.
`TITLE="..."`	The title of the linked-to document.
`METHODS="..."`	The method with which the document is to be retrieved; for example, FTP, Gopher, and so on.

<META>   Indicates meta-information about this document (information about the document itself); for example, keywords for search engines, special HTTP headers to be used for retrieving this document, expiration date, and so on. Meta-information is usually in a key/value pair form. Used in the document <HEAD>.

HTTP-EQUIV="..."	Creates a new HTTP header field with the same name as the attribute's value; for example, HTTP-EQUIV="Expires". The value of that header is specified by the CONTENT attribute.
NAME="..."	If meta data is usually in the form of key/value pairs, NAME indicates the key; for example, Author or ID.
CONTENT="..."	The content of the key/value pair (or of the HTTP header indicated by HTTP-EQUIV).

`<NEXTID>`	Indicates the "next" document to this one (as might be defined by a tool to manage HTML documents in series). `<NEXTID>` is considered obsolete.

Headings and Title

`<H1>...</H1>`	A first-level heading.
`<H2>...</H2>`	A second-level heading.
`<H3>...</H3>`	A third-level heading.
`<H4>...</H4>`	A fourth-level heading.
`<H5>...</H5>`	A fifth-level heading.
`<H6>...</H6>`	A sixth-level heading.
`<TITLE>...</TITLE>`	Indicates the title of the document. Used within `<HEAD>`.

All heading tags accept the following attribute:

Attributes:

ALIGN="..."	Possible values are CENTER, LEFT, and RIGHT.

Paragraphs and Regions

`<P>...</P>`	A plain paragraph. The closing tag (`</P>`) is optional.

Attributes:

ALIGN="..."	Align text to CENTER, LEFT, or RIGHT.

\<NEXTID>   Indicates the "next" document to this one (as might be defined by a tool to manage HTML documents in series). \<NEXTID> is considered obsolete.

\<DIV>...\</DIV>   A region of text to be formatted.

Attributes:

ALIGN="..."	Align text to CENTER, LEFT, or RIGHT.

Links

\<A>...\</A>   With the HREF attribute, creates a link to another document or anchor; with the NAME attribute, creates an anchor that can be linked to.

Attributes:

HREF="..."	The URL of the document to be called when the link is activated.
NAME="..."	The name of the anchor.
REL="..."	The relationship between the linked-to document and the current document; for example, "TOC" or "Glossary" (not commonly used).
REV="..."	A reverse relationship between the current document and the linked-to document (not commonly used).
URN="..."	A Uniform Resource Number (URN), a unique identifier different from the URL in HREF (not commonly used).
TITLE="..."	The title of the linked-to document (not commonly used).

`METHODS="..."`	The method with which the document is to be retrieved; for example, FTP, Gopher, and so on (not commonly used).	
`TARGET="..."`	The name of a frame that the linked document should appear in.	

Lists

`<OL>...</OL>`	An ordered (numbered) list.

Attributes:

`TYPE="..."`	The type of numerals to label the list. Possible values are A, a, I, i, 1.
`START="..."`	The value with which to start this list.

`<UL>...</UL>`	An unordered (bulleted) list.

Attributes:

`TYPE="..."`	The bullet dingbat to use to mark list items. Possible values are DISC, CIRCLE (or ROUND), and SQUARE.

`<MENU>...</MENU>`	A menu list of items.
`<DIR>...</DIR>`	A directory listing; items are generally smaller than 20 characters.
`<LI>`	A list item for use with `<OL>`, `<UL>`, `<MENU>`, or `<DIR>`.

Attributes:

`TYPE="..."`	The type of bullet or number to label this item with. Possible values are DISC, CIRCLE (or ROUND) SQUARE, A, a, I, i, 1.
`VALUE="..."`	The numeric value this list item should have (affects this item and all below it in `<OL>` lists).

`<DL>...</DL>`	A definition or glossary list.

Attributes:

COMPACT	The COMPACT attribute specifies a formatting that takes less whitespace to present.
<DT>	A definition term, as part of a definition list.
<DD>	The corresponding definition to a definition term, as part of a definition list.

Character Formatting

<EM>...</EM>	Emphasis (usually italic).
<STRONG>...</STRONG>	Stronger emphasis (usually bold).
<CODE>...</CODE>	Code sample (usually Courier).
<KBD>...</KBD>	Text to be typed (usually Courier).
<VAR>...</VAR>	A variable or placeholder for some other value.
<SAMP>...</SAMP>	Sample text (seldom used).
<DFN>...<DFN>	A definition of a term.
<CITE>...</CITE>	A citation.
<B>...</B>	Boldface text.
<I>...</I>	Italic text.
<TT>...</TT>	Typewriter (monospaced) font.
<PRE>...</PRE>	Preformatted text (exact line endings and spacing will be preserved—usually rendered in a monospaced font).
<BIG>...</BIG>	Text is slightly larger than normal.
<SMALL>...</SMALL>	Text is slightly smaller than normal.
_{...}	Subscript.
^{...}	Superscript.
<STRIKE>...</STRIKE>	Puts a strikethrough line in text.

Other Elements

`<HR>`   A horizontal rule line.

Attributes:

`SIZE="..."`	The thickness of the rule, in pixels.
`WIDTH="..."`	The width of the rule, in pixels or as a percentage of the document width.
`ALIGN="..."`	How the rule line will be aligned on the page. Possible values are `LEFT`, `RIGHT`, and `CENTER`.
`NOSHADE`	Causes the rule line to be drawn as a solid line instead of a transparent bevel.
`COLOR="..."` (MS)	Color of the horizontal rule.

`<BR>`   A line break.

Attributes:

`CLEAR="..."`	Causes the text to stop flowing around any images. Possible values are `RIGHT`, `LEFT`, and `ALL`.

`<NOBR>...</NOBR>`	Causes the enclosed text not to wrap at the edge of the page.
`<WBR>`	Wraps the text at this point only if necessary.
`<BLOCKQUOTE>... </BLOCKQUOTE>`	Used for long quotes or citations.
`<ADDRESS>...</ADDRESS>`	Used for signatures or general information about a document's author.
`<CENTER>...</CENTER>`	Centers text or images.
`<BLINK>...</BLINK>`	Causes the enclosed text to blink irritatingly.
`<FONT>...</FONT>`	Changes the size of the font for the enclosed text.

Attributes:

`SIZE="..."`	The size of the font, from 1 to 7. Default is 3. Can also be specified as a value relative to the current size; for example, +2.
`COLOR="..."`	Changes the color of the text.

FACE="..." (MS)	Name of font to use if it can be found on the user's system. Multiple font names can be separated by commas, and the first font on the list that can be found will be used.

<BASEFONT>	Sets the default size of the font for the current page.

Attributes:

SIZE="..."	The default size of the font, from 1 to 7. Default is 3.

Images, Sounds, and Embedded Media

<IMG>	Inserts an inline image into the document.

Attributes:

ISMAP	This image is a clickable image map.
SRC="..."	The URL of the image.
ALT="..."	A text string that will be displayed in browsers that cannot support images.
ALIGN="..."	Determines the alignment of the given image. If LEFT or RIGHT (N), the image is aligned to the left or right column, and all following text flows beside that image. All other values such as TOP, MIDDLE, BOTTOM, or the Netscape only TEXTTOP, ABSMIDDLE, BASELINE, ABSBOTTOM determine the vertical alignment of this image with other items in the same line.
VSPACE="..."	The space between the image and the text above or below it.
HSPACE="..."	The space between the image and the text to its left or right.
WIDTH="..."	The width, in pixels, of the image. If WIDTH is not the actual width, the image is scaled to fit.

HEIGHT="..."	The width, in pixels, of the image. If HEIGHT is not the actual height, the image is scaled to fit.
BORDER="..."	Draws a border of the specified value in pixels to be drawn around the image. In the case of images that are also links, BORDER changes the size of the default link border.
LOWSRC="..."	The path or URL of an image that will be loaded first, before the image specified in SRC. The value of LOWSRC is usually a smaller or lower resolution version of the actual image.
USEMAP="..."	The name of an image map specification for client-side image mapping. Used with <MAP> and <AREA>.
DYNSRC="..." (MS)	The address of a video clip or VRML world (dynamic source).
CONTROLS (MS)	Used with DYNSRC to display a set of playback controls for inline video.
LOOP="..." (MS)	The number of times a video clip will loop. (-1 or INFINITE means to loop indefinitely.)
START="..." (MS)	When a DYNSRC video clip should start playing. Valid options are FILEOPEN (play when page is displayed) or MOUSEOVER (play when mouse cursor passes over the video clip).

<BGSOUND> (MS)	Plays a sound file as soon as the page is displayed.

Attributes:

SRC="..."	The URL of the WAV, AU, or MIDI sound file to embed.
LOOP="..." (MS)	The number of times a video clip will loop. (-1 or INFINITE means to loop indefinitely.)

`<EMBED>` (N)	Embeds a file to be read or displayed by a Plug-In application.

> **Note:** In addition to the following standard attributes, you can specify applet-specific attributes to be interpreted by the plug-in that displays the embedded object.

Attributes:

`SRC="..."`	The URL of the file to embed.
`WIDTH="..."`	The width of the embedded object in pixels.
`HEIGHT="..."`	The height of the embedded object in pixels.
`ALIGN="..."`	Determines the alignment of the media window. Values are the same as for the `<IMG>` tag.
`VSPACE="..."`	The space between the media and the text above or below it.
`HSPACE="..."`	The space between the media and the text to its left or right.
`BORDER="..."`	Draws a border of the specified size in pixels to be drawn around the media.

`<NOEMBED>...</NOEMBED>` (N)	Alternate text or images to be shown to users who do not have a plug-in installed.
`<OBJECT>` (MS)	Inserts an embedded program, control, or other object. (This tag was under revision when this book was printed—see the note at the beginning of this appendix.)
`<MAP>...</MAP>`	A client-side image map, referenced by `<IMG USEMAP="...">`. Includes one or more `<AREA>` tags.
`<AREA>`	Defines a clickable link within a client-side image map.

Attributes:

`SHAPE="..."`	The shape of the clickable area. Currently, only RECT is supported.
`COORDS="..."`	The left, top, right, and bottom coordinates of the clickable region within an image.

	`HREF="..."`	The URL that should be loaded when the area is clicked.
	`NOHREF`	Indicates that no action should be taken when this area of the image is clicked.

Forms

`<FORM>...</FORM>`		Indicates an input form.

Attributes:

	`ACTION="..."`	The URL of the script to process this form input.
	`METHOD="..."`	How the form input will be sent to the gateway on the server side. Possible values are GET and POST.
	`ENCTYPE="..."`	Normally has the value applica-tion/x-www-form-urlencoded. For file uploads, use multipart/form-data.
	`NAME="..."`	A name by which JavaScript scripts can refer to the form.

`<INPUT>`	An input element for a form.

Attributes:

	`TYPE="..."`	The type for this input widget. Possible values are CHECKBOX, HIDDEN, RADIO, RESET, SUBMIT, TEXT, SEND FILE, or IMAGE.
	`NAME="..."`	The name of this item, as passed to the gateway script as part of a name/value pair.
	`VALUE="..."`	For a text or hidden widget, the default value; for a checkbox or radio button, the value to be submitted with the form; for Reset or Submit buttons, the label for the button itself.
	`SRC="..."`	The source file for an image.
	`CHECKED`	For checkboxes and radio buttons, indicates that the widget is checked.

SIZE="..."	The size, in characters, of a text widget.
MAXLENGTH="..."	The maximum number of characters that can be entered into a text widget.
ALIGN="..."	For images in forms, determines how the text and image will align (same as with the <IMG> tag).

<TEXTAREA>...</TEXTAREA> Indicates a multiline text entry form element. Default text can be included.

Attributes:

NAME="..."	The name to be passed to the gateway script as part of the name/value pair.
ROWS="..."	The number of rows this text area displays.
COLS="..."	The number of columns (characters) this text area displays.
WRAP="..." (N)	Control text wrapping. Possible values are OFF, VIRTUAL, and PHYSICAL.

<SELECT>...</SELECT> Creates a menu or scrolling list of possible items.

Attributes:

NAME="..."	The name that is passed to the gateway script as part of the name/value pair.
SIZE="..."	The number of elements to display. If SIZE is indicated, the selection becomes a scrolling list. If no SIZE is given, the selection is a pop-up menu.
MULTIPLE	Allows multiple selections from the list.

<OPTION> Indicates a possible item within a <SELECT> element.

SELECTED	With this attribute included, the <OPTION> will be selected by default in the list.
VALUE="..."	The value to submit if this <OPTION> is selected when the form is submitted.

Tables

Note: Several additional table tags from the HTML 3.0 specification will be supported by all major browsers when that specification is complete. These new tags are not included in the following list. Refer to the Netscape or Microsoft Web sites for more details on these powerful new tags.

<TABLE>...</TABLE>	Creates a table that can contain a caption (<CAP-TION>) and any number of rows (<TR>).

Attributes:

BORDER="..."	Indicates whether the table should be drawn with or without a border. In Netscape, BORDER can also have a value indicating the width of the border.
CELLSPACING="..."	The amount of space between the cells in the table.
CELLPADDING="..."	The amount of space between the edges of the cell and its contents.
WIDTH="..."	The width of the table on the page, in either exact pixel values or as a percentage of page width.
ALIGN="..." (MS)	Alignment (works like IMG ALIGN. Values are LEFT or RIGHT).
BACKGROUND="..." (MS)	Background image to tile within all cells in the table that do not contain their own BACKGROUND or BGCOLOR attribute.
BGCOLOR="..." (MS)	Background color of all cells in the table that do not contain their own BACKGROUND or BGCOLOR attribute.

`BORDERCOLOR="..." (MS)`	Border color (used with `BOR-DER="..."`).
`BORDERCOLORLIGHT="..." (MS)`	Color for light part of 3D-look borders (used with `BORDER="..."`).
`BORDERCOLORDARK="..." (MS)`	Color for dark part of 3D-look borders (used with `BORDER="..."`).
`VALIGN="..." (MS)`	Alignment of text within the table. Values are `TOP` and `BOTTOM`.

`<CAPTION>...</CAPTION>`   The caption for the table.

Attributes:

`ALIGN="..."`	The position of the caption. Possible values are `TOP` and `BOTTOM`.

`<TR>...</TR>`   Defines a table row, containing headings and data (`<TR>` and `<TH>` tags).

Attributes:

`ALIGN="..."`	The horizontal alignment of the contents of the cells within this row. Possible values are `LEFT`, `RIGHT`, and `CENTER`.
`VALIGN="..."`	The vertical alignment of the contents of the cells within this row. Possible values are `TOP`, `MIDDLE`, `BOTTOM`, and `BASELINE`.
`BACKGROUND="..."(MS)`	Background image to tile within all cells in the row that do not contain their own `BACKGROUND` or `BGCOLOR` attributes.
`BGCOLOR="..."(MS)`	Background color of all cells in the row that do not contain their own `BACKGROUND` or `BGCOLOR` attributes.
`BORDERCOLOR="..."(MS)`	Border color (used with `BOR-DER="..."`).
`BORDERCOLORLIGHT="..."(MS)`	Color for light part of 3D-look borders (used with `BORDER="..."`).
`BORDERCOLORDARK="..."(MS)`	Color for dark part of 3D-look borders (used with `BORDER="..."`).

`<TH>...</TH>`   Defines a table heading cell.

ALIGN="..."	The horizontal alignment of the contents of the cell. Possible values are LEFT, RIGHT, and CENTER.
VALIGN="..."	The vertical alignment of the contents of the cell. Possible values are TOP, MIDDLE, BOTTOM, and BASELINE.
ROWSPAN="..."	The number of rows this cell will span.
COLSPAN="..."	The number of columns this cell will span.
NOWRAP	Does not automatically wrap the contents of this cell.
WIDTH="..."	The width of this column of cells, in exact pixel values or as a percentage of the table width.
BACKGROUND="..." (MS)	Background image to tile within the cell.
BGCOLOR="..." (MS)	Background color of the cell.
BORDERCOLOR="..." (MS)	Border color (used with BORDER="...").
BORDERCOLORLIGHT="..." (MS)	Color for light part of 3D-look borders (used with BORDER="...").
BORDERCOLORDARK="..." (MS)	Color for dark part of 3D-look borders (used with BORDER="...").

\<TD\>...\</TD\>	Defines a table data cell.

Attributes:

ALIGN="..."	The horizontal alignment of the contents of the cell. Possible values are LEFT, RIGHT, and CENTER.
VALIGN="..."	The vertical alignment of the contents of the cell. Possible values are TOP, MIDDLE, BOTTOM, and BASELINE.
ROWSPAN="..."	The number of rows this cell will span.
COLSPAN="..."	The number of columns this cell will span.

NOWRAP	Does not automatically wrap the contents of this cell.
WIDTH="..."	The width of this column of cells, in exact pixel values or as a percentage of the table width.
BACKGROUND="..." (MS)	Background image to tile within the cell.
BGCOLOR="..." (MS)	Background color of the cell.
BORDERCOLOR="..." (MS)	Border color (used with BORDER="...").
BORDERCOLORLIGHT="..." (MS)	Color for light part of 3D-look borders (used with BORDER="...").
BORDERCOLORDARK="..." (MS)	Color for dark part of 3D-look borders (used with BORDER="...").

Frames

<FRAMESET>...</FRAMESET>	Divides the main window into a set of frames that can each display a separate document.

Attributes:

ROWS="..."	Splits the window or frameset vertically into a number of rows specified by a number (such as 7), a percentage of the total window width (such as 25%), or as an asterisk (*) indicating that a frame should take up all the remaining space or divide the space evenly between frames (if multiple * frames are specified).
COLS="..."	Works similar to ROWS, except that the window or frameset is split horizontally into columns.

<FRAME>	Defines a single frame within a <FRAMESET>.

Attributes:

SRC="..."	The URL of the document to be displayed in this frame.
NAME="..."	A name to be used for targeting this frame with the TARGET attribute in <A HREF> links.

`<MARGINWIDTH>`	The amount of space to leave to the left and right side of a document within a frame, in pixels.
`<MARGINHEIGHT>`	The amount of space to leave above and below a document within a frame, in pixels.
`SCROLLING="..."`	Determines whether a frame has scroll bars. Possible values are YES, NO, and AUTO.
`NORESIZE`	Prevents the user from resizing this frame (and possibly adjacent frames) with the mouse.
`FRAMEBORDER="..."` (MS)	Specifies whether to display a border for a frame. Options are YES and NO.
`FRAMESPACING="..."` (MS)	Space between frames, in pixels.
`</NOFRAME>...</NOFRAMES>`	Provides an alternative document body in `<FRAMESET>` documents for browsers that do not support frames (usually encloses `<BODY>...</BODY>`).

Scripting and Applets

`<APPLET>`	Inserts a self-running Java applet.

Attributes:

Note: In addition to the following standard attributes, you can specify applet-specific attributes to be interpreted by the Java applet itself.

`CLASS="..."`	The name of the applet.
`SRC="..."`	The URL of the directory where the compiled applet can be found (should end in a slash / as in `"http://mysite/myapplets/"`). Do not include the actual applet name, which is specified with the CLASS attribute.

ALIGN="..."		Indicates how the applet should be aligned with any text that follows it. Current values are TOP, MIDDLE, and BOTTOM.
WIDTH="..."		The width of the applet output area in pixels.
HEIGHT="..."		The height of the applet output area in pixels.

<SCRIPT>   An interpreted script program.

Attributes:

LANGUAGE="..."		Currently only JAVASCRIPT is supported by Netscape. Both JAVASCRIPT and VBSCRIPT are supported by Microsoft.
SRC="..."		Specifies the URL of a file that includes the script program.

Marquees

<MARQUEE>...</MARQUEE> (MS)   Displays text in a scrolling marquee.

Attributes:

WIDTH="..."		The width of the embedded object in pixels or percentage of window width.
HEIGHT="..."		The height of the embedded object in pixels or percentage of window height.
ALIGN="..."		Determines the alignment of the text *outside* the marquee. Values are TOP, MIDDLE, and BOTTOM.
BORDER="..."		Draws a border of the specified size in pixels to be drawn around the media.
BEHAVIOR="..."		How the text inside the marquee should behave. Options are SCROLL (continuous scrolling), SLIDE (slide text in and stop), and ALTERNATE (bounce back and forth).

`BGCOLOR="..."`		Background color for the marquee.
`DIRECTION="..."`		Direction for text to scroll (LEFT or RIGHT).
`VSPACE="..."`		Space above and below the marquee, in pixels.
`HSPACE="..."`		Space on each side of the marquee, in pixels.
`SCROLLAMOUNT="..."`		Number of pixels to move each time text in the marquee is redrawn.
`SCROLLDELAY="..."`		Number of milliseconds between each redraw of marquee text.
`LOOP="..."` (MS)		The number of times marquee will loop. (-1 or INFINITE means to loop indefinitely.)

Character Entities

Table B.1 contains the possible numeric and character entities for the ISO-Latin-1 (ISO8859-1) character set. Where possible, the character is shown.

Note: Not all browsers can display all characters, and some browsers may even display characters different from those that appear in the table. Newer browsers seem to have a better track record for handling character entities, but be sure to test your HTML files extensively with multiple browsers if you intend to use these entities.

Table B.1. ISO-Latin-1 character set.

Character	Numeric Entity	Character Entity (if any)	Description
	`&#00;`–`&#08;`		Unused
	`&#09;`		Horizontal tab
	`&#10;`		Line feed
	`&#11;`–`&#31;`		Unused
	`&#32;`		Space
!	`&#33;`		Exclamation mark
"	`&#34;`	`&quot;`	Quotation mark

Character	Numeric Entity	Character Entity (if any)	Description
#	&#35;		Number sign
$	&#36;		Dollar sign
%	&#37;		Percent sign
&	&#38;	&amp;	Ampersand
'	&#39;		Apostrophe
(	&#40;		Left parenthesis
)	&#41;		Right parenthesis
*	&#42;		Asterisk
+	&#43;		Plus sign
,	&#44;		Comma
-	&#45;		Hyphen
.	&#46;		Period (fullstop)
/	&#47;		Solidus (slash)
0–9	0–9		Digits 0–9
:	&#58;		Colon
;	&#59;		Semicolon
<	&#60;	&lt;	Less than
=	&#61;		Equals sign
>	&#62;	&gt;	Greater than
?	&#63;		Question mark
@	&#64;		Commercial at
A–Z	A–Z		Letters A–Z
[	&#91;		Left square bracket
\	&#92;		Reverse solidus (backslash)
]	&#93;		Right square bracket
^	&#94;		Caret
–	&#95;		Horizontal bar
`	&#96;		Grave accent
a–z	a–z		Letters a–z
{	&#123;		Left curly brace
		&#124		Vertical bar
}	&#125;		Right curly brace

continues

Table B.1. continued

Character	Numeric Entity	Character Entity (if any)	Description
~	&#126;		Tilde
	&#127;–		Unused
¡	&#161;		Inverted exclamation
¢	&#162;		Cent sign
£	&#163;		Pound sterling
¤	&#164;		General currency sign
¥	&#165;		Yen sign
¦	&#166;		Broken vertical bar
§	&#167;		Section sign
¨	&#168;		Umlaut (dieresis)
©	&#169;		Copyright
ª	&#170;		Feminine ordinal
‹	&#171;		Left angle quote, guillemet left
¬	&#172;		Not sign
-	&#173;		Soft hyphen
®	&#174;		Registered trademark
¯	&#175;		Macron accent
°	&#176;		Degree sign
±	&#177;		Plus or minus
2	&#178;		Superscript two
3	&#179;		Superscript three
´	&#180;		Acute accent
µ	&#181;		Micro sign
¶	&#182;		Paragraph sign
·	&#183;		Middle dot
¸	&#184;		Cedilla
1	&#185;		Superscript one
º	&#186;		Masculine ordinal
›	&#187;		Right angle quote, guillemet right
1/4	&#188;		Fraction one-fourth
1/2	&#189;		Fraction one-half

Character	Numeric Entity	Character Entity (if any)	Description
3/4	&#190;		Fraction three-fourths
¿	&#191;		Inverted question mark
À	&#192;	&Agrave;	Capital A, grave accent
Á	&#193;	&Aacute;	Capital A, acute accent
Â	&#194;	&Acirc;	Capital A, circumflex accent
Ã	&#195;	&Atilde;	Capital A, tilde
Ä	&#196;	&Auml;	Capital A, dieresis or umlaut mark
Å	&#197;	&Aring;	Capital A, ring
Æ	&#198;	&AElig;	Capital AE dipthong (ligature)
Ç	&#199;	&Ccedil;	Capital C, cedilla
È	&#200;	&Egrave;	Capital E, grave accent
É	&#201;	&Eacute;	Capital E, acute accent
Ê	&#202;	&Ecirc;	Capital E, circumflex accent
Ë	&#203;	&Euml;	Capital E, dieresis or umlaut mark
Ì	&#204;	&Igrave;	Capital I, grave accent
Í	&#205;	&Iacute;	Capital I, acute accent
Î	&#206;	&Icirc;	Capital I, circumflex accent
Ï	&#207;	&Iuml;	Capital I, dieresis or umlaut mark
Ð	&#208;	&ETH;	Capital Eth, Icelandic
Ñ	&#209;	&Ntilde;	Capital N, tilde
Ò	&#210;	&Ograve;	Capital O, grave accent

continues

Table B.1. continued

Character	Numeric Entity	Character Entity (if any)	Description
Ó	Ó	Ó	Capital O, acute accent
Ô	Ô	Ô	Capital O, circumflex accent
Õ	Õ	Õ	Capital O, tilde
Ö	Ö	Ö	Capital O, dieresis or umlaut mark
×	×		Multiply sign
Ø	Ø	Ø	Capital O, slash
Ù	Ù	Ù	Capital U, grave accent
Ú	Ú	Ú	Capital U, acute accent
Û	Û	Û	Capital U, circumflex accent
Ü	Ü	Ü	Capital U, dieresis or umlaut mark
Ý	Ý	Ý	Capital Y, acute accent
	Þ	Þ	Capital THORN, Icelandic
	ß	ß	Small sharp s, German (sz ligature)
à	à	à	Small a, grave accent
á	á	á	Small a, acute accent
â	â	â	Small a, circumflex accent
ã	ã	ã	Small a, tilde
ä	ä	&aauml;	Small a, dieresis or umlaut mark
å	å	å	Small a, ring
æ	æ	æ	Small ae dipthong (ligature)
ç	ç	ç	Small c, cedilla

Character	Numeric Entity	Character Entity (if any)	Description
è	&#232;	&egrave;	Small e, grave accent
é	&#233;	&eacute;	Small e, acute accent
ê	&#234;	&ecirc;	Small e, circumflex accent
ë	&#235;	&euml;	Small e, dieresis or umlaut mark
ì	&#236;	&igrave;	Small i, grave accent
í	&#237;	&iacute;	Small i, acute accent
î	&#238;	&icirc;	Small i, circumflex accent
ï	&#239;	&iuml;	Small i, dieresis or umlaut mark
ð	&#240;	&eth;	Small eth, Icelandic
ñ	&#241;	&ntilde;	Small n, tilde
ò	&#242;	&ograve;	Small o, grave accent
ó	&#243;	&oacute;	Small o, acute accent
ô	&#244;	&ocirc;	Small o, circumflex accent
õ	&#245;	&otilde;	Small o, tilde
ö	&#246;	&ouml;	Small o, dieresis or umlaut mark
÷	&#247;		Division sign
ø	&#248;	&oslash;	Small o, slash
ù	&#249;	&ugrave;	Small u, grave accent
ú	&#250;	&uacute;	Small u, acute accent
û	&#251;	&ucirc;	Small u, circumflex accent
ü	&#252;	&uuml;	Small u, dieresis or umlaut mark
ý	&#253;	&yacute;	Small y, acute accent
	&#254;	&thorn;	Small thorn, Icelandic
ÿ	&#255;	&yuml;	Small y, dieresis or umlaut mark

Online Resources and Cutting-Edge Web Sites

This appendix lists several Web sites mentioned in the various chapters in this book, as well as many others. The sites are categorized by media content or utility type. For example, you'll find sites for both audio players and audio clips; VRML renderers and virtual reality worlds; both Java applets and Java forums. Sites for business, entertainment, news and sports, ActiveX and OLE are also included—everything you need to add a Webmaster's touch to your Web pages. Happy surfing!

Note: You can access many of the sites listed here through live links on the *Web Page Wizardry* CD-ROM. (Open the hotlinks.htm document.)

appendix C

by Dick Oliver

Graphics Viewers

`http://www.jasc.com`

Paint Shop Pro

`http://www.corel.com/corelcmx/`

Corel's CMX Viewer plug-in

`http://www.adobe.com`

Adobe Acrobat

`http://www.twcorp.com`

Envoy plug-in

Graphics Sites

`http://netletter.com/`

Dick Oliver's Nonlinear Nonsense Netletter

`http://netletter.com/cameo/hotlist/hotlist.html`

Texture and Background Wonderland

`http://www.n-vision.com/panda/c/`

Clip Art

`http://fohnix.metronet.com/~kira/icongifs/`

kira's icon library

`http://www.cbil.vcu.edu:8080/gifs/bullet.html`

Buttons, Cubes & Bars

`http://www.vrl.com/Imaging/`

Imaging Machine

`http://fohnix.metronet.com/~kira/colors/`

256-color square

`http://www.netcreations.com/ramper/index.html`

Color Ramper

`http://www.artn.nwu.edu/`

(Art)^n

```
http://www.art.net/Welcome.html
```

Art on the Net

Audio Players

```
http://www.buddy.org/softlib.html
```

The Buddy Sound Editor Software Library

```
http://www.realaudio.com
```

RealAudio

```
http://www.xingtech.com
```

Streamworks Audio

```
http://www.vocaltec.com/iwave.htm
```

Iwave

```
http://www.dspg.com
```

TrueSpeech

```
http://www.prs.net/midi.html
```

MidiGate

Audio Sites

```
http://www.music.sony.com/Music/SoundClips/index.html
```

Sony Music Clips

```
http://www.iuma.com
```

Internet Underground Music Resource

```
http://www.audionet.com
```

AudioNet

```
http://www.rockweb.com
```

RockWeb

```
http://www.prs.net/midi.html
```

The Classical Music MIDI Archive

Video Players

http://quicktime.apple.com

QuickTime

http://www.VDOLive.com

VDOLive

http://www.xingtech.com

StreamWorks Video

Video Sites

http://www.sony.com/Music/VideoStuff/VideoClips/index.html

Music Video Clips

http://www.acm.uiuc.edu/rml/Mpeg/

Rob's Multimedia Lab

http://www.best.com/~johnp/film.html

MPEG Bizarre Film Festival

http://www.synapse.net/~ob/welcome.htm

Cartoon Animations

Interactive Media Players

http://www.macromedia.com/Tools/Shockwave/index.html

Macromedia's Shockwave Page

http://www.macromedia.com/Tools/Director/index.html

Background on Director "Movies"

http://www.excite.sfu.ca/NCompass/

NCompass OLE Plug-in

Shocked Sites

http://www.macromedia.com/Gallery/Movies/Shockwave/index.html

The Interactive Gallery

http://www.mcli.dist.maricopa.edu/director/shockwavelist.html

Shockwave List o' Sites

http://www.mcli.dist.maricopa.edu/director/faq/index.html

The Director FAQ

http://www.best.com/~harold/shambala.html

Shockwave Seed Site

http://www.mcli.dist.maricopa.edu/alan/nojava/

alan's NoJava

http://www.turntable.com:80/shockwave_plug/

Turntable's Needle Drop

http://www.toystory.com/toybox/shock.htm

Toy Story Game

http://www.dmc.missouri.edu/shockwave/plan.html

SPG Staff Blast

http://www.mdmi.com/nomis.htm

Nomis

http://www.dreamlight.com/dreamlt/gallery/verttice.htm

DreamLight Verttice

http://www.mackerel.com/bubble.html

Virtual Bubble Wrap

http://www.hyperstand.com/shockwave

New Media Magazine

VRML Renderers

http://www.chaco.com/vrscout/

VR Scout

http://www.cts.com/~template/WebSpace/monday.html

WebSpace

http://www.paperinc.com

WebFX Plug-in

http://www.intervista.com

WorldView Plug-in

http://www.ids-net.com

VRealm Plug-in

http://www.dimensionx.com

Liquid Reality Plug-in

Virtual Reality Sites

http://www.sdsc.edu/vrml/

The VRML Repository

http://vrml.wired.com/

The VRML Forum

http://www.oki.com/vrml/VRML_FAQ.html

VRML Frequently Asked Questions

http://www.vrml.org/vrml/

WorldView Alpha Test Page

http://vrml.wired.com/vrml.tech/

VRML*Tech: The Virtual Reality Modeling Language Technical Forum

http://www.newtype.com/NewType/vr/index.htm

Virtual Reality Center

http://qtvr.quicktime.apple.com

QuickTime VR Home Page

http://www.netproductions.com/balcony/default.html

The Balcony

http://www.paperinc.com/wrls.html

Paper Software's Cool List of VRML Worlds

`http://www.cybertown.com`

Cybertown Virtual Freeway

`http://www.neuro.sfc.keio.ac.jp/~aly/polygon/vrml/ika/`

Interactive Origami

`http://www.ocnus.com/models/mall.wrl`

VRML Mall

`http://www.tcp.ca/gsb/VRML/models/pc-win95sky.wrl`

Virtual PC

`http://www.hyperreal.com/~mpesce/circle.wrl`

Zero Circle

Java and JavaScript

`http://java.sun.com/`

Center of the Java Universe

`http://www.javasoft.com`

Java Home Page

`http://www.gamelan.com/`

Gamelan—Java Resource Registry

`http://home.mcom.com/comprod/products/navigator/version_2.0/script/index.html`

JavaScript

`http://www.hotwired.com/java`

HotWired's Java Page

`http://www.applets.com`

Java Applet Library

`http://www.phoenixat.com/~warreng/soup.html`

Soup's Up E-zine

`http://www.earthweb.com`

EarthWeb Java Development

Java Applets

http://www.cnet.com

Scrolling Text

http://www-elec.enst.fr/java/n/test.html

Three Dimensional Cube

http://www.virtual-inn.co.uk/orbital/beta/adSpace

Advertising Space

http://www.acl.lanl.gov/~rdaniel/classesJDK/PickTest2.html

TeleMed

http://storm.atmos.uiuc.edu/java

The Weather Visualizer

http://www.umich.edu/~dov/webPoker

WebPoker

http://home.netscape.com/comprod/products/navigator/version_2.0
/java_applets/Crossword/index.html

Crossword Puzzle

http://www.zorg.com

Zorg

http://www.dimensionx.com/chat/cafe.html

Café Chat

http://www.acm.uiuc.edu/webmonkeys/juggling

Learning to Juggle

http://www.sdsu.edu/~boyns/java/mc

Missile Commando

http://www.javasoft.com/JDK-prebeta1/applets/TicTacToe/example1.html

Tic-Tac-Toe

http://tech-www.informatik.uni-hamburg.de/dance/JDance.html

Learning to Dance

ActiveX and Object Linking and Embedding

http://www.microsoft.com/internet

Microsoft Internet

http://www.w3.org

W3 Standards

http://oberon.educ.sfu.ca/NCompass/home.html

NCompass Labs

http://www.busweb.com

Business@Web

http://www.microsoft.com

Microsoft

http://www.busweb.com/software/components/excel.html

Excel Control

http://142.232.132.45/ocx/default.htm

OCX Example

http://www.olebroker.com

OLE Broker

Multiple Media Formats and Scripting

http://www.cnn.com

CNN

http://www.realaudio.com

RealAudio

http://ESPNET.SportsZone.com

ESPNET SportsZone

http://www.browserwatch.com

Browserwatch

http://www.VDOLive.com

VDOLive

http://cool.infi.net

Cool Sites

http://www.projectcool.com

Project Cool

http://www.cybertown.com

Cybertown

http://www.marketcentral.com

Market Central

http://www.flinet.com/~rummy/javahtml/javasc1.html

JavaScript Source

http://home.netscape.com/comprod/products/navigator/version_2.0/script/index.html

Netscape JavaScript

http://adaweb.com/adaweb/influx/GroupZ/LOVE/love.html

Love

http://www.netscape.com/comprod/products/navigator/live3d/examples/fighter/
  fghtentr.html

Fighter

http://uttm.com/welcome2.html

UTTM

Internet Directories

http://www.yahoo.com/

Yahoo!

http://www.nosc.mil/planet_earth/everything.html

Planet Earth Home Page

http://gnn.com/wic/wics/index.html

GNN Select

`http://galaxy.einet.net/`

TradeWave Galaxy

`http://cool.infi.net/`

Cool Site of the Day

`http://www.ncsa.uiuc.edu/SDG/Software/Mosaic/MetaIndex.html`

Internet Resources Meta-Index

`http://www.eskimo.com/%7Eirving/web-voyeur/`

Web Voyeur (Live Camera Views)

`http://www.commerce.net/directories/products/isp/`

Internet Service Provider Directory

Internet Search Tools

`http://www.lycos.com/`

Lycos Search

`http://www.webcrawler.com/`

WebCrawler Searching

`http://www.cs.colorado.edu/wwww`

World Wide Web Worm

`http://web.nexor.co.uk/public/aliweb/search/doc/form.html`

ALIWEB Search

`http://cuiwww.unige.ch/w3catalog`

CUI W3 Catalog

`http://www.infoseek.com/`

InfoSeek

`http://pubweb.nexor.co.uk/public/archie/servers.html`

Nexor's Archie List

`http://www.scs.unr.edu/veronica.html`

Veronica Home Access Page

Software Archives

http://cwsapps.fibr.net/

Stroud's Consummate Winsock Apps List

http://www.teleport.com/~alano/coolhelp.html

Cool Helpers Page

http://wuarchive.wustl.edu/

The Washington University Software Archive

http://www.winsite.com/

WinSite

http://coyote.csusm.edu/cwis/winworld/winworld.html

The CSUSM Windows Shareware Archive

file://oak.oakland.edu/SimTel/

SimTel

ftp://mirrors.aol.com

AOL Mirrors

http://ftp.sunet.se/

SUNET FTP Archive

http://www.shareware.com

Shareware.com

News, Weather, and Sports

http://nytimesfax.com

TimesFax

http://cnn.com

CNN Interactive

http://www.nando.net/nt/

The Nando Times

http://www.realaudio.com/contentp/abc.html

ABC News Reports

http://www.sjmercury.com/

Mercury Center Subscriptions

http://www.pathfinder.com/

Time Warner's PathFinder

http://www.intellicast.com

NBC Intellicast Weather

http://iwin.nws.noaa.gov/

Interactive Weather Information Network

http://www-geology.ucdavis.edu/eqmandr.html

Earthquake Information

http://cirrus.sprl.umich.edu/wxnet/

WeatherNet

http://ESPNET.SportsZone.com

ESPNET SportsZone

http://www.igolf.com

iGolf

http://www.audionet.com/audio211.htm

AudioNet Sports

http://www.nba.com/Theater/index.html

NBA Theater

http://qtvr1.quicktime.apple.com/duke/duke.html

Duke Basketball

http://www.tns.lcs.mit.edu/cgi-bin/sports

World Wide Web of Sports

Entertainment

http://www.film.com

Film.com

`http://movieweb.com/movie.html`

Movieweb

`http://web3.starwave.com/showbiz`

Mr. Showbiz

`http://hollywood.com/`

Hollywood Online

`http://tvnet.com/`

TV Net®

`http://www.scifi.com`

Sci-Fi Channel: The Dominion

`http://www.netshop.net/Startrek/web/`

Star Trek

`http://www.whitehouse.gov/`

The White House

`http://www.comcentral.com/com-menu.htm`

Comedy Central

`http://moonmilk.volcano.org/`

Moonmilk (How'd they do that??)

`http://www.cs.curtin.edu.au/~squizz/cryptics.html`

Squizz's Cryptic Crosswords

`http://www.unitedmedia.com/comics`

The Comic Strip

`http://netboy.com`

NetBoy

Travel and Exploration

`http://www.exploratorium.edu/`

Exploratorium Home Page

http://www.si.edu/

Smithsonian Institution Home Page

http://www.gsfc.nasa.gov/

NASA Home Page

http://www-swiss.ai.mit.edu/webtravel/

Web Travel Review

http://www.franceway.com

Franceway

http://www.odci.gov/cia/publications/95fact/index.html

CIA World Factbook

http://www.csulb.edu/gc/

The Global Campus

Business

http://update.wsj.com

The Wall Street Journal

http://www.cbot.com

Chicago Board of Trade

http://www.cs.virginia.edu/~cd4v/graph/StockGraph.html

Stock Trace

http://www.ora.com/gnn/bus/ora/survey/index.html

Defining the Internet Opportunity

http://www.net101.com/reasons.html

20 Reasons to put your business on the Web

http://www2000.ogsm.vanderbilt.edu/intelligent.agent/index.html

The Challenges of Electronic Commerce

http://www.tig.com/cgi-bin/genobject/ibcindex

The Internet Business Center

What's on the CD-ROM

On the CD-ROM included with this book, you'll find a wealth of resources to add interactive excitement to your Web pages. Dozens of software programs, applets, helpers, and plug-ins will make you an Internet magician without putting a curse on your wallet. Over 100 Web pages give you real working examples of every trick in the book. And hundreds of hotlinks connect you to the latest developments and most spellbinding sites.

> **Note:** Everything on the *Web Page Wizardry* CD-ROM is detailed in the Web pages on the CD-ROM itself. Just open the home.htm document with your Web browser to begin exploring. (For best results, use Netscape Navigator 2.0 or greater, or Microsoft Internet Explorer version 3.0.)

Software

Web browsers use programs called *helper applications* (or just helper apps) to view the contents of graphics, multimedia, or other files that its own internal viewers can't handle. Netscape Navigator can also use specially designed programs called *plug-ins*, which allow a wide variety of data types to be integrated right into Web pages. The authors of this book have combed the Internet for the most essential helper apps and plug-ins and have included them all on this CD-ROM for you to install and enjoy.

Read the short descriptions below to decide which programs will be useful for you or browse through the list in the software.htm document on the CD-ROM. (You can also click on the Read This: link on the CD-ROM for installation instructions and other information from the program's authors.)

Then install each program you want to your hard drive and try running it. (Most helper apps can either be run by themselves or called automatically from a Web browser as needed. Other programs are standalone applications only; for example, CuteFTP is a file transfer program).

Please note that most of these programs are shareware, which means that you can try them for free (usually for up to 30 days) to see if they meet your needs. If they do, you must send a registration fee directly to the author of the program. See the online help and documentation for each program for more details and contact addresses.

To find the latest versions of the programs on this CD and to get the inside scoop on the hottest new Internet software, check out Stroud's Consummate Winsock Apps Page at

http://cswapps.fibr.net/

or

http://www.cwsapps.com/

This site is updated constantly with reviews and links to the best Windows Internet programs and graphics viewers. Most of the programs that you find on this CD-ROM are on this list, so you should check there for the latest and greatest in the fast-changing world of the Net.

Note: In addition to the programs listed here, the Java Developer's Kit and many Java applets are included on the CD-ROM.

(Macintosh software is also included on the CD-ROM and is listed later in this appendix.)

Recommended Programs

HTML Assistant is our favorite HTML editor. (But you should check out **HotDog**, too, and see which one suits you best.)

Macromedia Director Demo is an evaluation version of the leading multimedia authoring tool.

Paint Shop Pro is an incredible shareware graphics editor with all the bells and whistles (now supports transparent images, too).

Goldwave is a shareware sound editor, player, and recorder.

Arena Design VRML ED is a full-featured 3D modeling program with built-in VRML input and output.

DXF to VRML Converter converts AutoCAD DXF files and other 3D models into VRML format.

VideoAction ED is a nonlinear digital video editing and special effects program.

Live3D is a Netscape plug-in for viewing 3D and VRML Worlds.

CuteFTP is a dedicated File Transfer Protocol (FTP) program for uploading files to your Web site.

Other Windows Software

Shockwave—for Interactive Director Movies by Macromedia.

WIRL Virtual Reality—by VREAM.

Envoy Plug-In—by Tumbleweed Software.

Formula One/NET—by Visual Components.

ActiveX Control Plug-In—by NCompass.

WinZip—a Windows utility that supports ZIP, ARJ, TAR, g-zip, and other compressed formats.

W32s125—lets you run some 32-bit applications in Windows 3.1.

Tropic TCP/IP—a program that provides the TCP/IP protocol for the Windows 3.1 environment.

ACDSee—a fast graphics viewer.

MapEdit—a WYSIWYG editor for image map files.

MPEG2PLY—an MPEG viewer.

UltraEdit-32—a Windows disk-based text or HEX editor.

Acrobat reader—lets you view and navigate through PDF documents.

AAWIN—contains the Autodesk animation player drivers.

WPLANY—a sound player that supports most common formats.

CoolEdit—a sound editor, player, and recorder for MS Windows.

HotDog HTML—editor.

Hotspots WWW—imagemap editor for Windows.

WebForms—a utility to create HTML forms.

Internet Assistant—an HTML add-on to Word for Windows (non-32-bit at this point).

Web Watch—a utility for tracking changes to your Web site.

IPHONE (demo)—a utility that permits telephone-like conversations to occur over the Internet.

PowWow—a program that allows up to five people to chat, send and receive files, and browse the WWW together as a group.

WSIRC—a chat client for use with the IRC.

Macintosh Software

Shockwave—for Interactive Director Movies by Macromedia.

Envoy Plug-In—by Tumbleweed Software.

InternetConfig—a utility to permit easy Internet configuration among Mac Internet clients.

ObiWan—a general help system and database manager for Internet resources.

MacPPP—PPP—support for the Mac.

MacTCP—TCP—software.

HTML.edit 1.7.

HTML Editor 1.0—(WYSIWYG).

Web Map—tool for graphics imagemaps.

Web Weaver 2.5.2.

GlobalChat—IRC client.

Talk—a client for one-to-one "chat" sessions with other talk clients.

Adobe Acrobat reader.

Fast Player—QuickTime movie player.

GIF Converter.

Graphics converter.

Sparkle 2.4.5—MPEG movie viewer.

Fetch—FTP client.

Anarchie—FTP and Archie client.

Stuffit Expander—compression/archiving utility.

Sample Pages and Sites

All of the following sample pages are accessible from the `home.htm` document on the CD-ROM. These files are organized by chapter so that you can easily refer to the examples they represent, or simply browse through the CD.

"Visions and Changes" from Part I: The WOW! Factor: Gonzo Graphics Stunts

Chapter 1, "Bigger, Faster, Better Graphics"

`look/bfb.htm`	The Bigger, Faster, Better Page

Chapter 2, "Wild Type, Far-Out Layouts, and Cheap HTML Tricks"

`maple/syrup.htm`	Pure Vermont Maple Syrup
`look/looklook.htm`	LOOK: The Site of the 90's

Chapter 3, "Animation the Easy Way: Multi-Image GIFs"

`examples.htm`	Web Page Wizardry

"Actions and Incantations" from Part II: Five Million Channels: Multimedia Over the Net

Chapter 4, "Putting Multimedia on Your Web Pages"

`downeast/downeast.htm`   The DownEast Restaurant

Chapter 5, "Creating Online Audio"

`ski/chrdchim.wav`   A Short WAV Sound

Chapter 6, "Do-It-Yourself Digital Video"

`ski/ski.avi`   Skiing AVI Video

Chapter 7, "Creating Interactive Animation with Shockwave and Friends"

`shock/welcome.htm`   Shockwave Sample Pages
`hot/bigbro.htm`   Big Brother
`hot/chevy.htm`   Cartoon Chevy
`hot/walk.htm`   Walking Skeletons

"Worlds and Objects" from Part III: A World of Your Own: Virtual Reality

Chapter 8, "The World Wide Web Isn't Flat"

`vrml/dolphins.wrl`   Three Dolphins
`vrml/spanner.wrl`   A Spanner Wrench
`vrml/vrmlwiz.htm`   A Way Cool Animated 3D Demo

Chapter 9, "Building 3D Cyberspace"

`vrml/cube.wrl`   The Quintessential Cube
`vrml/conecube.wrl`   Transparent Cone and Colored Cube
`vrml/texture.wrl`   Simple Texture Mapping

Chapter 10, "Fancy Modeling Tricks"

"Brews and Mixtures" from Part IV: In the Driver's Seat: Interactive Programs

Chapter 11, "ActiveX and Object Linking and Embedding (OLE)"

All examples for this chapter are online. See `hotlinks.htm` *for links.*

Chapter 12, "Finding and Using the Hottest Java Applets"

Chapter 13, "Combining Multiple Media Formats"

Many examples for this chapter are online. See `hotlinks.htm` *for links.*

"Pages and Recipes" from Part V: Putting It All Together: Complete Sample Sites

Chapter 14, "The Home Page of Your Dreams, Today!"

Chapter 15, "The High-Bandwidth Site of the Future"

ndex

E

Earthquake Information (Web site), 375
EarthWeb Java Development (Web site), 369
echo effects (digital audio), 94
editing
　audio files, 91-92
　digital video, 112-118
　　creating final movie, 117-118
　　importing files, 114
　　special effects, 117
　　timelines, 114-115
　　transitions, 115-117
　　trimming clips, 115
　　Video Action ED screen, 113-114
<EM> tag, 343
<EMBED> tag, 76-77, 305, 347
　current status, 85
　forced downloads, 84-85
　non-Netscape browsers, 82-84
　troubleshooting, 78
　video parameters, 101
　VRML files, 223
embedding
　multimedia, 275-283
　　helper applications, 79-82
　OLE objects in Web pages, 239-240
　Shockwave movies, 125-126
　VRML in Web pages, 223
Emblaze Creator plug-in, 150
emissiveColor property, 194
ENCTYPE attribute (<FORM> tag), 348
entertainment Web sites, 375-376
Envoy plug-in, 364, 381
ESPNET SportsZone (Web site), 371, 375

event markers (Lingo), 138
events in JavaScript, 287
examining mode (VRML), 157
Excel Control (Web site), 371
Excel spreadsheets (OLE example), 243-244
exploration Web sites, 376-377
Exploratorium Home Page (Web site), 376
extensions (HTML), 335
extracting graphics from Web pages, 7

F

FACE attribute (<FONT> tag), 27-29, 345
fast display (image files), 15-21
Fast Player, 382
faux video (Shockwave), creating, 142-143
Fetch, 382
Fighter (Web site), 372
file formats
　digital audio, 88-90
　　compressing, 95
　　converting, 95-96
　　helper applications/plug-ins, 96-97
　　mixing, 93
　　saving, 94-95
　　trimming silence, 92-93
　　volume changes, 93
　video, 100-105
　　AVI, 100-101
　　MPEG, 103
　　QuickTime, 101-103
File Transfer Protocol (ftp), Archie searches, 8-9
fill lights, 110
Film.com (Web site), 375
flange effects (digital audio), 94
flat shading (3D objects), 186

fly mode (VRML), 160
flying (VRML), 157
<FONT> tag, 15, 344-345
　FACE attribute, 27-29
　size/color attributes, 27
fonts, Text window (Director), 131-132
FontStyle node (VRML), 220
forced downloads (<EMBED> tag), 84-85
<FORM> tag, 348
formatting, character formatting tags (HTML), 343
forms, HTML tags, 348-350
Formula Graphics plug-in, 150
Formula One/NET, 381
<FRAME> tag, 353-354
FRAMEBORDER attribute (<FRAME> tag), 354
frames, 45
　HTML tags, 353-354
　Java applets in, 262
　Shockwave movies, 129
<FRAMESET> tag, 353
FRAMESPACING attribute (<FRAME> tag), 354
Franceway (Web site), 377
ftp (File Transfer Protocol), Archie searches, 8-9

G

gallery window (Video Action ED), 114
Gamelan (Web site), locating Java applets, 270, 369
games, Duel (OLE example), 245
GIF Construction Set, 52-54, 297
GIF Converter, 382
GIF files
　animations, 51-52
　　26-image, 306-309
　　creating, 52-54

HTML Assistant, 380
HTML Editor 1.0, 381
HTML.edit 1.7, 381
HTTP-EQUIV attribute
  (<META> tag), 340
hypertext links
  adding to Web pages,
    333-334
  creating with Lingo, 139-140
  HTML tags, 341
  to multimedia, 73
  setting colors, 14-15
  to voice recordings, 298
  within VRML worlds,
    208-209
Hypertext Markup Lan-
  guage, *see* HTML

I

<I> tag, 332, 343
if statement (JavaScript), 287
if...then command
  (Lingo), 140
iGolf (Web site), 375
imagemaps, 45-48
  client-side, 47
  client/server, 47-48
  server-side, 45-47
Image menu commands
  (Paint Shop Pro),
  Resample, 331
images
  adding to Web pages, 333
  aligning text around, 333
  alternate text, 21
  background images, 14
    *extracting from Web
      pages, 7*
    Lingo example, 141-142
    *seamless background
      tiles, creating, 34-37*
    setting colors, 14-15
    as text, 30-32
    tiling, 315
    VRML, 219
  borders, 333

color depth, 16-17
compressing, 18-19
designing Web sites, 4-5
dithering, 17
extracting from Web
  pages, 7
GIF animations, 51-52
  creating, 52-54
  *creating via Photoshop
    layers, 56-57*
  looping, 60-61
  optimizing, 61-64
  palettes, 58-59
  transparency, 59
imagemaps, 45-48
  client-side, 47
  client/server, 47-48
  server-side, 45-47
interlaced GIFs, 18-19
locating, 6-11
  Archie, 8-9
  Veronica, 9-11
Paint Shop Pro, 12-14
  *saving transparent GIFs,
    13-14*
preparing for Web pages,
  331
progressive JPEGs, 19
resolution, 16-17
speeding up display, 15-21
text as, 30-33
translucent images, 38-40
viewers, Web sites for, 364
Web sites for, 364-365
WMF files, 314
Imaging Machine (Web
  site), 364
<IMG> tag, 20-21, 333,
345-346
  displaying multimedia, 71-72
importing
  multiframe animations for
    Shockwave movies, 135
  video files for editing, 114
  VRML objects, 173
Indeo R.32 codec, 107

Indeo Video Interactive
  codec, 107-108
IndexedFaceSet node
  (VRML), 210-212
InetOLE mailing list, 246
InfoSeek (Web site), 6, 373
ink effects (Shockwave
  movies), 136
<INPUT> tag, 348-349
installing
  Java applets, 262-263
  Shockwave, 121
intensity property
  directional light, 199
  point light, 198
interactive 3D applications
  (NCompass plug-in), 238
interactive 3D robotic arm
  demo (NCompass plug-in),
  235-236
The Interactive Gallery (Web
  site), 366
interactive games, Duel (OLE
  example), 245
interactive multimedia
  players, Web sites for, 366
Interactive Origami (Web
  site), 369
Interactive Weather
  Information Network (Web
  site), 375
interlaced GIFs, 18-19
Internet
  directories, 372-373
  search engines, 373
Internet Assistant, 381
The Internet Business Center
  (Web site), 377
Internet Explorer 3.0, OLE
  support, 241-242
Internet Resources Meta-
  Index (Web site), 373
Internet Service Provider
  Directory (Web site), 373
Internet Underground Music
  Resource (Web site), 365

X-Y-Z

Web Site Administrator's Survival Guide

— Jerry Ablan, et al

The World Wide Web Administrator's Survival Guide is a detailed, step-by-step book that guides the Web administrator through the process of selecting Web server software and hardware, installing and configuring a server, and administering the server on an ongoing basis. Includes a CD-ROM with servers and administrator tools. The book provides complete step-by-step guidelines for installing and configuring a Web server.

Price: $49.99 USA/$67.99 CDN   *User Level: Inter-Advanced*
ISBN: 1-57521-018-5   700 pages

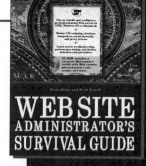

Web Publishing Unleashed

— Stanek, et al

Includes sections on how to organize and plan your information, design pages, and become familar with hypertext and hypermedia. Choose from a range of applications and technologies, including Java, SGML, VRML, and the newest HTML and Netscape extensions. The CD contains software, templates, and examples to help you become a successful Web publisher.

Price: $49.99 USA/$61.95 CDN   *User Level: Casual-Expert*
ISBN: 1-57521-051-7   1,000 pages

Web Site Construction Kit for Windows 95

— Christopher Brown and Scott Zimmerman

The Web Site Construction Kit for Windows 95 provides readers with everything you need to set up, develop, and maintain a Web site with Windows 95. It teaches the ins and outs of planning, installing, configuring, and administering a Windows 95–based Web site for an organization, and it includes detailed instructions on how to use the software on the CD to develop the Web site's content: HTML pages, CGI scripts, image maps, etc.

Price: $49.99 USA/$67.99 CDN   *User Level: Casual-Accomplished*
ISBN: 1-57521-072-X   500 pages

The Internet Business Guide, Second Edition

— Rosalind Resnick & Dave Taylor

Updated and revised, this guide will inform and educate anyone on how they can use the Internet to increase profits, reach a broader market, track down business leads, and access critical information. Updated to cover digital cash, Web cybermalls, secure Web servers, and setting up your business on the Web, *The Internet Business Guide* includes profiles of entrepreneurs' successes (and failures) on the Internet. Improve your business by using the Internet to market products and services, make contacts with colleagues, cut costs, and improve customer service.

Price: $25.00 USA/$39.99 CDN   *User Level: All Levels*
ISBN: 1-57521-004-5   470 pages

Teach Yourself Netscape Web Publishing in a Week

— Wes Tatters

Teach Yourself Netscape Web Publishing in a Week is the easiest way to learn how to produce attention-getting, well-designed Web pages using the features provided by Netscape Navigator. Intended for both the novice and the expert, this book provides a solid grounding in HTML and Web publishing principles, while providing special focus on the possibilities presented by the Netscape environment. Learn to design and create attention-grabbing Web pages for the Netscape environment while exploring new Netscape development features such as frames, plug-ins, Java applets, and JavaScript!

Price: $39.99 USA/ $47.95 CDN   *User Level: Beginner-Inter*
ISBN: 1-57521-068-1   *450 pages*

Teach Yourself CGI Programming with Perl in a Week

— Eric Herrmann

This book is a step-by-step tutorial of how to create, use, and maintain Common Gateway Interfaces (CGI). It describes effective ways of using CGI as an integral part of Web development. Adds interactivity and flexibility to the information that can be provided through your Web site. Includes Perl 4.0 and 5.0, CGI libraries, and other applications to create databases, dynamic interactivity, and other enticing page effects.

Price: $39.99 USA/$53.99 CDN   *User Level: Inter-Advanced*
ISBN: 1-57521-009-6   *500 pages*

Teach Yourself Java in 21 Days

— Laura Lemay and Charles Perkins

The complete tutorial guide to the most exciting technology to hit the Internet in years—Java! A detailed guide to developing applications with the hot new Java language from Sun Microsystems, *Teach Yourself Java in 21 Days* shows readers how to program using Java and develop applications (applets) using the Java language. With coverage of Java implementation in Netscape Navigator and Hot Java, along with the Java Development Kit, including the compiler and debugger for Java, *Teach Yourself Java* is a must-have!

Price: $39.99 USA/$53.99 CDN   *User Level: Inter-Advanced*
ISBN: 1-57521-030-4   *600 pages*

Presenting Java

— John December

Presenting Java gives you a first look at how Java is transforming static Web pages into living, interactive applications. Java opens up a world of possibilities previously unavailable on the Web. You'll find out how Java is being used to create animations, computer simulations, interactive games, teaching tools, spreadsheets, and a variety of other applications. Whether you're a new user, a project planner, or developer, *Presenting Java* provides an efficient, quick introduction to the basic concepts and technical details that make Java the hottest new Web technology of the year!

Price: $25.00 USA/$34.95 CDN   *User Level: All Levels*
ISBN: 1-57521-039-8   *207 pages*

Netscape 2 Unleashed

— Dick Oliver, et al.

This book provides a complete, detailed, and fully fleshed-out overview of the Netscape products. Through case studies and examples of how individuals, businesses, and institutions are using the Netscape products for Web development, *Netscape 2 Unleashed* gives a full description of the evolution of Netscape from its inception to today, and its cutting-edge developments with Netscape Gold, LiveWire, Netscape Navigator 2.0, Java and JavaScript, Macromedia, VRML, Plug-ins, Adobe Acrobat, HTML 3.0 and beyond, security and Intranet systems.

Price: $49.99 USA/$61.95 CDN   User Level: All Levels
ISBN: 1-57521-007-X   Pages: 800 pages

The Internet Unleashed 1996

— Barron, Ellsworth, Savetz, et al.

The Internet Unleashed 1996 is the complete reference to get new users up and running on the Internet while providing the consummate reference manual for the experienced user. *The Internet Unleashed 1996* provides the reader with an encyclopedia of information on how to take advantage of all the Net has to offer for business, education, research, and government. The companion CD-ROM contains over 100 tools and applications. The only book that includes the experience of over 40 of the world's top Internet experts, this new edition is updated with expanded coverage of Web publishing, Internet business, Internet multimedia and virtual reality, Internet security, Java, and more!

Price: $49.99 USA/$67.99 CDN   User Level: All Levels
ISBN: 1-57521-041-X   1,456 pages

The World Wide Web Unleashed 1996

— December and Randall

The World Wide Web Unleashed 1996 is designed to be the only book a reader will need to experience the wonders and resources of the Web. The companion CD-ROM contains over 100 tools and applications to make the most of your time on the Internet. Shows readers how to explore the Web's amazing world of electronic art museums, online magazines, virtual malls, and video music libraries, while giving readers complete coverage of Web page design, creation, and maintenance, plus coverage of new Web technologies such as Java, VRML, CGI, and multimedia!

Price: $49.99 USA/$67.99 CDN   User Level: All Levels
ISBN: 1-57521-040-1   1,440 pages

Teach Yourself Web Publishing with HTML in 14 Days, Premier Edition

— Laura Lemay

This book teaches everything about publishing on the Web. In addition to its exhaustive coverage of HTML, it also gives readers hands-on practice with more complicated subjects such as CGI, tables, forms, multimedia programming, testing, maintenance, and much more. CD-ROM is Mac- and PC-compatible and includes a variety of applications that help readers create Web pages using graphics and templates.

Price: $39.99 USA/$53.99 CDN   User Level: All Levels
ISBN: 1-57521-014-2   804 pages

Teach Yourself Web Publishing with HTML 3.0 in a Week, Second Edition

— Laura Lemay

Ideal for those people who are interested in the Internet and the World Wide Web—the Internet's hottest topic! This updated and revised edition teaches readers how to use HTML (Hypertext Markup Language) version 3.0 to create Web pages that can be viewed by nearly 30 million users. Explores the process of creating and maintaining Web presentations, including setting up tools and converters for verifying and testing pages. The new edition highlights the new features of HTML, such as tables and Netscape and Microsoft Explorer extensions. Provides the latest information on working with images, sound files, and video, and teaches advanced HTML techniques and tricks in a clear, step-by-step manner with many practical examples of HTML pages.

Price: $29.99 USA/$34.95 CDN   User Level: Beginner-Inter
ISBN: 1-57521-064-9   518 pages

Web Page Construction Kit (Software)

Create your own exciting World Wide Web pages with the software and expert guidance in this kit! Includes HTML Assistant Pro Lite, the acclaimed point-and-click Web page editor. Simply highlight text in HTML Assistant Pro Lite, and click the appropriate button to add headlines, graphics, special formatting, links, etc. No programming skills needed! Using your favorite Web browser, you can test your work quickly and easily without leaving the editor. A unique catalog feature allows you to keep track of interesting Web sites and easily add their HTML links to your pages. Assistant's user-defined toolkit also allows you to add new HTML formatting styles as they are defined. Includes the #1 best-selling Internet book, *Teach Yourself Web Publishing with HTML 3.0 in a Week, Second Edition,* and a library of professionally designed Web page templates, graphics, buttons, bullets, lines, and icons to rev up your new pages!

PC Computing magazine says, "If you're looking for the easiest route to Web publishing, HTML Assistant is your best choice."

Price: $20.00 US/$46.99 CAN   User Level: Beginner-Inter
ISBN: 1-57521-000-2   518 pages

HTML & CGI Unleashed

— John December & Marc Ginsburg

Targeted to professional developers who have a basic understanding of programming and need a detailed guide. Provides a complete, detailed reference to developing Web information systems. Covers the full range of languages—HTML, CGI, Perl C, editing and conversion programs, and more—and how to create commercial-grade Web Applications. Perfect for the developer who will be designing, creating, and maintaining a Web presence for a company or large institution.

Price: $49.99 USA/$53.99 CDN   User Level: Inter-Advanced
ISBN: 0-672-30745-6   830 pages

Web Site Construction Kit for Windows NT

— Christopher Brown and Scott Zimmerman

The Web Site Construction Kit for Windows NT has everything you need to set up, develop, and maintain a Web site with Windows NT—including the server on the CD-ROM! It teaches the ins and outs of planning, installing, configuring, and administering a Windows NT–based Web site for an organization, and it includes detailed instructions on how to use the software on the CD-ROM to develop the Web site's content—HTML pages, CGI scripts, imagemaps, and so forth.

Price: $49.99 USA/$67.99 CDN   User Level: All Levels
ISBN: 1-57521-047-9   430 pages

Add to Your Sams.net Library Today
with the Best Books for Internet Technologies

ISBN	Quantity	Description of Item	Unit Cost	Total Cost
1-57521-030-4		Teach Yourself Java in 21 Days	$39.99	
1-57521-049-5		Java Unleashed	$49.99	
1-57521-007-X		Netscape 2 Unleashed	$49.99	
1-57521-040-1		The World Wide Web Unleashed 1996	$49.99	
0-672-30745-6		HTML and CGI Unleashed	$39.99	
1-57521-051-7		Web Publishing Unleashed	$49.99	
1-57521-018-5		Web Site Administrator's Survival Guide	$49.99	
1-57521-009-6		Teach Yourself CGI Programming with Perl in a Week	$39.99	
1-57521-068-1		Teach Yourself Netscape 2 Web Publishing in a Week	$39.99	
1-57521-064-9		Teach Yourself Web Publishing with HTML in a Week, Second Edition	$29.99	
1-57521-005-3		Teach Yourself More Web Publishing with HTML in a Week	$29.99	
1-57521-014-2		Teach Yourself Web Publishing with HTML in 14 Days, Premier Edition	$39.99	
1-57521-072-X		Web Site Construction Kit for Windows 95	$49.99	
1-57521-047-9		Web Site Construction Kit for Windows NT	$49.99	
		Shipping and Handling: See information below.		
		TOTAL		

Shipping and Handling: $4.00 for the first book, and $1.75 for each additional book. If you need to have it NOW, we can ship product to you in 24 hours for an additional charge of approximately $18.00, and you will receive your item overnight or in two days. Overseas shipping and handling adds $2.00. Prices subject to change. Call between 9:00 a.m. and 5:00 p.m. EST for availability and pricing information on latest editions.

201 W. 103rd Street, Indianapolis, Indiana 46290

1-800-428-5331 — Orders   1-800-835-3202 — FAX   1-800-858-7674 — Customer Service

Book ISBN 1-57521-092-4

HTML in 10 seconds!*

▶ No kidding.
In the time it takes
for a good slurp of coffee, *HTML Transit* generated this Web page.

Say hello to the template.

HTML Transit takes a new approach to online publishing, using a high-speed production template. It's fast and easy. You can turn a 50-page word processing file into multiple, linked HTML pages—complete with graphics and tables—in less than 10 mouse clicks. From scratch.

Customize your template—formatting, backgrounds, navigation buttons, thumbnails—and save even more time. Now in just 4 clicks, you can crank out an entire library of custom Web pages with no manual authoring.

Take a free test drive.

Stop working so hard. Download an evaluation copy of *HTML Transit* from our Web site:

http://www.infoaccess.com

Your download code is **MCML46**. (It can save you money when you order *HTML Transit*.)

Buy HTML Transit risk free.

HTML Transit is just $495, and is backed by a 30-day satisfaction guarantee. To order, call us toll-free at **800-344-9737**.

InfoAccess, Inc.
(206) 747-3203
FAX: (206) 641-9367
Email: info@infoaccess.com

▶ **Automatic HTML from native word processor formats**
▶ **Creates HTML tables, tables of contents & indexes**
▶ **Graphics convert to GIF or JPEG, with thumbnails**
▶ **Template control over appearance and behavior**
▶ **For use with Microsoft® Windows®**

HTML Transit is a trademark of InfoAccess, Inc. Microsoft and Windows are registered trademarks of Microsoft Corporation.
*Single-page Microsoft Word document with graphics and tables, running on 75MHz Pentium. Conversion speed depends on document length, complexity and PC configuration.

Web Page Wizardry
Free Newsletter Registration Form

☐ Please register me and start my FREE subscription to Dick Oliver's newsletter of Internet design and advanced PC graphics. Please also send the free Cedar Software catalog and compendium.

☐ I'd also like to receive a short summary of what's new in online graphics and related topics about once a month via e-mail.

Name: _____

E-mail: _____

Address: _____

_____

Country: _____

Phone or Fax (optional): _____

Fax or mail this form to:

Dick Oliver, Cedar Software, RR 1 Box 4495, Wolcott, VT 05680 USA

Fax: 802-888-3009   **Voice phone: 802-888-5275**

Or send a request to:

the-zany-folks@netletter.com

Must See CD.

DIRECTOR

AUTHORWARE

FREEHAND

EXTREME 3D

xRES

SOUNDEDIT 16

FONTOGRAPHER

Annual Report
Vision
Tools
Source and Center
Gallery
Multimedia 101
Free Demo Software

Free.

See The Future Now On Macromedia's Free Showcase CD.

If you want to see the best and brightest in multimedia, graphic design and Internet publishing, this disc is a must. It's the latest Showcase CD from Macromedia.

On it, you'll get an insider's view of the new media industry. In it, you'll learn how Macromedia's powerful creative tools work—and you'll see brilliant creations from award-winning developers, artists, and designers. With it, you'll find the inspiration and information you need to power your ideas in this new digital world.

It's incredible. It's free. It even runs on both Mac and Windows. And if you're ready to see how amazing new media can be, it's the CD to see.

Free Showcase CD-ROM
GO
1-800-326-2128

http://www.macromedia.com/

MACROMEDIA®
Tools To Power Your Ideas™

DIRECTOR

AUTHORWARE

FREEHAND

EXTREME 3D

xRES

SOUNDEDIT 16

FONTOGRAPHER

Macromedia Electrifies The Web: 37 Million People Feel The Shockwave.

Introducing a powerful new multimedia tool that will jolt the entire World Wide Web. Shockwave™ for Director.®

Now interactive multimedia can play anywhere. Author once in Macromedia Director, and you can play your productions around the world. From a Power Mac™ in Manhattan to a Windows® 95 PC in Perth. And now on the Web thanks to Shockwave. In fact,

Netscape's 2.0 browser already gives you seamless viewing of Director movies within Web pages. So today the same Director that produces award-winning entertainment CDs and outstanding corporate presentations can also create high-impact multimedia Web sites— with Shockwave. To learn more about Macromedia Director, check out our Web site at http://www.macromedia.com/

While you're there, go ahead and download Shockwave FREE. Or call us at 1-800-326-2128 for a free Showcase CD-ROM.* Either way, get ready for a shocking development on the Web.

Download Shockwave Free • http://www.macromedia.com/ • **GO**

MACROMEDIA®

Tools To Power Your Ideas